BY JAMES ALEXANDER THOM

Follow the River

From Sea to Shining Sea

Long Knife

Panther in the Sky

The Children of First Man

The Red Heart

Sign-Talker

BY DARK RAIN

The Shawnee:

Kohkumthena's Grandchildren

WARRIOR WOMAN

A NOVEL

Based on the life of Nonhelema,
Shawnee Woman Chief

DARK RAIN
and
JAMES ALEXANDER THOM

BALLANTINE BOOKS • NEW YORK

A Ballantine Book
Published by The Random House Publishing Group

www.ballantinebooks.com

Library of Congress Cataloging-in-Publication Data is available upon request from the publisher.

ISBN 0-345-44554-6

Book design by Susan Turner

Manufactured in the United States of America

First Edition: December 2003

1   3   5   7   9   10   8   6   4   2

We were their ruination, in ways I fear
History will not forget, nor God forgive.

—Dr. Justin I. Case,
Memoirs & Reflections on the War in the West

Reincarnation

Long time ago it was, an Indian listened to a missionary.
He got sprinkled and became a Christian and learned
about heaven and hell. He was very good. He didn't drink
or smoke.

When he died, he went to the Happy Hunting Ground,
but they wouldn't let him in there because
he was a Christian.

So he went to heaven, but they wouldn't let him in
there because he was an Indian.

So he went down to hell, but they wouldn't let him in
there because he was too good.

There was no place for him dead, so he came back to
life as one of those heathen Indians who drink and smoke
and won't listen to missionaries.

—Variation on an old Indian folk story

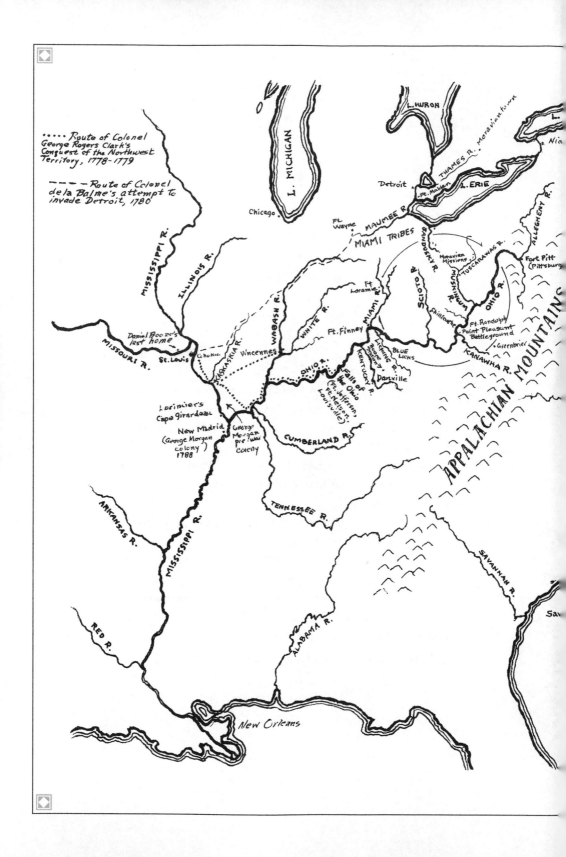

····· Route of Colonel
George Rogers Clark's
Conquest of the Northwest
Territory, 1778-1779

──── Route of Colonel
de la Balme's attempt to
invade Detroit, 1780

L. MICHIGAN

L. HURON

L. ERIE

Nia

THAMES R. Moravian town

Detroit
Ft. Malden

Chicago

Ft. Wayne   MAUMEE R.

MIAMI TRIBES

SANDUSKY R.

Moravian Missions

TUSCARAWAS R.

ALLEGHENY R.

Fort Pitt (Pittsburg

SCIOTO R.

MUSKINGUM R.

OHIO R.

Ft. Loramie

MIAMI R.

Chillicothe

Ft. Randolph
Point Pleasant
Battleground

Greenbrier

KANAWHA R.

WHITE R.

Ft. Finney

WABASH R.

Daniel Boone's
last home

MISSOURI R.

St. Louis   Cahokia

KASKASKIA R.

Vincennes

OHIO R.

Licking R.

Boone's
Station

Kentucky R.

BLUE
Licks

Falls of
the Ohio
(Ft. Jefferson,
Ft. Nelson,
Louisville)

Danville

APPALACHIAN MOUNTAINS

Lorimier's
Cape Girardeau

New Madrid
(George Morgan
colony)
1788

George
Morgan
pre-war
colony

CUMBERLAND R.

ARKANSAS R.

MISSISSIPPI R.

TENNESSEE R.

RED R.

ALABAMA R.

SAVANNAH R.

Sav

New Orleans

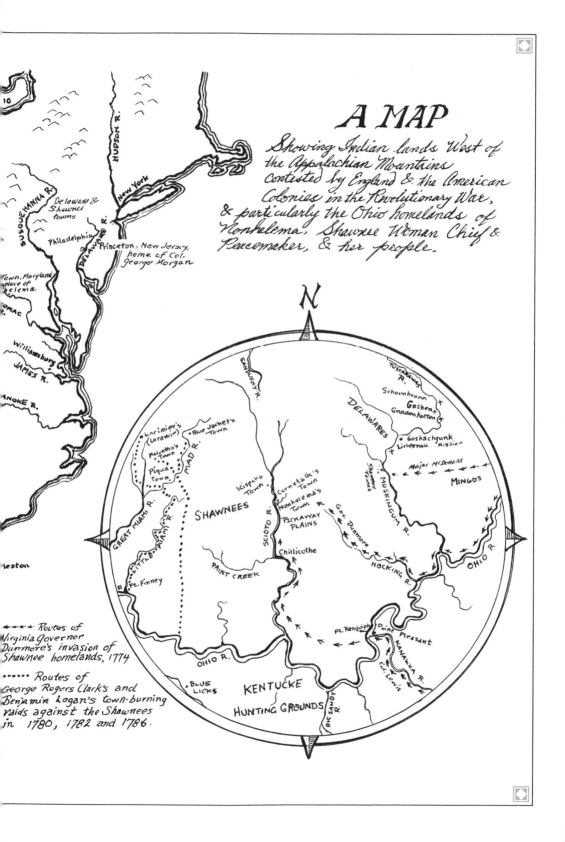

A MAP

Showing Indian lands West of the Appalachian Mountains contested by England & the American Colonies in the Revolutionary War, & particularly the Ohio homelands of Nonhelema, Shawnee Woman Chief & Peacemaker, & her people.

N

Routes of Virginia Governor Dunmore's invasion of Shawnee homelands, 1774

Routes of George Rogers Clark's and Benjamin Logan's town-burning raids against the Shawnees in 1780, 1782 and 1786.

HUDSON R.

New York

SUSQUEHANNA R.

Delaware & Shawnee towns

Philadelphia

DELAWARE R.

Princeton, New Jersey, home of Col. George Morgan

Town, Maryland, place of helema

OMAC

Williamsburg

JAMES R.

NOKE R.

eston

SANDUSKY R.

TUSCARAWAS R.

Schoenbrunn

Goshen

Gnadenhütten

DELAWARES

Goshachgunk

Lichtenau Mission

Shawnee Towns

MUSKINGUM R.

Major McDonald

MINGOS

Lorimier's (Loramie's)

Blue Jacket's Town

Moluntha's Town

MAD R.

Piqua Town

Kispoko Town

Cornstalk's Town

Nonhelema's Town

PICKAWAY PLAINS

Col. Dunmore

SHAWNEES

SCIOTO R.

GREAT MIAMI R.

LITTLE MIAMI R.

Chillicothe

PAINT CREEK

Ft. Finney

HOCKING R.

OHIO R.

Ft. Randolph

Point Pleasant

KANAWHA R.

Col. Lewis

OHIO R.

BLUE LICKS

KENTUCKE

HUNTING GROUNDS

BIG SANDY R.

10

This book is dedicated to Nonhelema, known as the Grenadier Squaw or Katy; and the Shawnee women, who have carried their People through good times and ordeals with their courage, strength, prayers, toil, dignity, sacrifices, and spiritual strength. They continue even now.

BOOK ONE

1774 – 1776

1

At this time of year, the first sunlight to come over the horizon shone through the one little window in the eastern wall of her house and illuminated the mirror on the western wall. Its reflection went back to the eastern wall, where it lit up two crosses that were her most cherished gifts.

One cross was a carved wooden crucifix hung on the log wall, with the suffering bleeding Jesus carved from cherry wood, Jesus with the long-muscled physique of a warrior, a body just like that of her first husband, who had died in one of the smallpox plagues brought by the whitemen. The crucifix had been a gift to her from Brother Schmick, a Moravian missionary whose family had been adopted by Chief Cornstalk, her brother.

The other gift glowing in the reflected sunlight, under the crucifix, was the pair of silver-trimmed pistols that the trader George Morgan had given to her when she was his guide and interpreter among the Shawnees, all along the Spaylaywesipe, or Ohio River, from Fort Pitt to as far as the Mississippi. In those years, she had lived with him and borne him a son whom she had named after him. The pistols were propped inside the open lid of their felt-lined case with their barrels crossed, and the sunlight on the red felt gave off a bloodred glow in that part of the dim room.

Another light, at the end of the room, was the cooking fire on the hearth, where her daughter, Fani, was boiling tea water and cooking griddle cakes. Fani was slender, pretty, and reticent; a widow already at less than twenty years of age. Fani had been born white. Nonhelema had adopted her when she was an orphaned child, carried in by a war party during the war between the English and French. She had no memory of being anything but Shawnee. She looked and thought Shawnee and was devoted to the people but especially so to her mother.

Many women were here from the other Shawnee towns to attend the Women's Council and vote on the war, and they had to be fed. Fani was dutifully preparing to feed many of them. The morning air outside Nonhelema's house was full of voices. In the sleeping loft upstairs, waking women were talking low. All night, the men's war drum had been like a heartbeat outside her town, in the camp of Pucsinwah, the principal war chief.

This morning before sunrise, Nonhelema had washed herself in the creek and had smoked a prayer pipe at the water's edge, blowing toward heaven the smoke carrying her prayer that she could persuade the women to vote for peace. Then she had come back to her house and made the same prayer to the God who was the father of Jesus.

The missionary Zeisberger had often scolded her that she should pray only to his God and quit praying to her people's Great Good Spirit Weshemonetoo, but this was too important to her people for her not to pray to their own god. Two Virginian armies were coming to attack this place where most of the Shawnee main towns lay within a day's walk of each other. The armies were coming by two routes, and when they joined together they would make one army of three or four thousand men. All the Shawnees and their allies together had been able to gather only about a thousand warriors.

Nonhelema and her brother Cornstalk believed it would be useless to fight such an army, and had been arguing so. They wanted to meet with the army leader, the governor of Virginia Colony, to plead for peace, to define boundaries. More than any of their people, Nonhelema and Cornstalk had traveled in the whiteman's cities in the East, and knew that whitemen were too numerous to count, and had horses and wagons and cannon and muskets without limit, and would always be able to send five or more armies if they lost one battle.

That was her argument, and it had been Cornstalk's argument also in the war council.

But Pucsinwah of the Kispoko warrior sept believed that if either half of the Virginia army could be ambushed and defeated before the halves could join together, the Virginians would flee with their tails between their legs and never dare come into the Kentucke or Ohio country again. Pucsinwah was a fiery talker and a greathearted chief who had never lost a battle, a man said to be impossible to kill, and he had convinced the Tribal Council that if the Shawnees begged for peace now, the Virginians would lose the respect and fear they had of the Shawnee nation, and then would never stop coming. Nonhelema remembered what he had said in council: "Their fear of us is a part of our strength. The other part of our strength is that the Master-of-Life knows we are right. *Weshe catweloo k'weshe lawehpah!* The Creator put us here, not the Long Knives! He knows we are right and will not let us be defeated in our own country!"

Upon those words the warriors had all howled, and when the hands were counted, those wanting to go and attack the Virginians had prevailed.

But now the war chief had to persuade the Women's Council to support the war. If the Women's Council said no, it would be useless to try to make a tribal war. The women had concerns that were beyond the understanding of the men, and the men had to heed the decision of Women's Council.

Nonhelema moved the mirror and set it up on the table in the middle of the room. She sat down, the sunlight on her face, and looked at herself in the mirror.

Nonhelema's name meant "not a man." She was taller and stronger than most men. British officers called her the Grenadier Squaw because her stature and bearing were like those of their giant grenadier soldiers, who marched at the right of the ranks.

The face in the mirror had always been one of her advantages. She knew that, of course, but she was not vain of it. Men had made fools of themselves upon being struck by the sight of her. But no man had been more foolish, or more often foolish, than she had been in response to their foolishness. They had given her as much as men, with their understanding, could give, and she had given back more. It had gained her and cost her equally.

George Morgan used to tell her that she was as handsome as beautiful, and as beautiful as handsome, and both within. That was a man who could make love with words.

Brother David Zeisberger had never said a word about her appearance, but she knew that, as a missionary, he saw trouble in it.

Old Colonel Croghan, at Fort Pitt, for all his power, doted and drooled and leered.

Women, even beautiful women, envied and resented her, unless they knew her well. Her daughter, who knew her best, was devoted to her, even though their beliefs were different on most important matters.

Nonhelema's face was built of strong planes, not coy curves, and her eyes were full of level, direct power. Her brother Cornstalk could humble men with a straight gaze, and she was almost his twin, though years older.

She herself had lived nearly fifty years, but no frailty showed in her face or body. One had to be this close to a mirror to see the white hairs in her black mane, or the tiny wrinkles around her mouth and the corners of her eyes. She had lived large, and that had sustained her. She had known as much joy as tribulation.

And in her spirit she saw two gods—her own and the Jesus God. And though they sometimes vied within her, and perhaps were just two names for the same one, together they gave her a greater soul than most people, who had only one god or another.

She folded back the flaps of a deerskin bag, took out a silver jar the size of a walnut, and pried off its lid. Inside was caked vermillion. She licked and dabbed the tip of her little finger and made a dot on her left cheekbone, then another on her right, and with another touch laid a line of red in the part of her hair. The red was the heart of Creator, Weshemonetoo, who had instructed Shawnee women to wear this heart-color so that he would recognize them as his People when the time came to die and there would be all that rush and confusion.

Now Nonhelema was ready, and it was time to call the women together for the council that would decide for war or peace.

Like her sisters the Shawnee women, who were strong and smart, she would listen to Pucsinwah's arguments for going to fight.

Unlike her Shawnee sisters, she knew in her heart, as Brother David Zeisberger had told her, that "The peacemakers are blessed, for the peacemakers will be called the children of God, Matthew five three eleven."

Now she was ready to persuade those people, whom she loved more than she loved her own life, to do what was for their own good: to make peace.

It was midday when the war chief came up the hill and made his formal request to speak to the great circle of women who sat on logs and blankets in the shade of the towering trees. The leaves were yellow and red, and some were already dropping off and tumbling through the air. The ground in the council circle was carpeted with their colors. This Council Hill and Burning Ground of Nonhelema's Town was the grandest place in the valley of the Scioto-sipe, a lookout from which the whole Pickaway Plains could be seen in every direction, flanked by wooded ridges so distant that they looked blue in the autumn haze. Any army that marched toward this place could be seen from here half a day before it arrived.

Nonhelema brought Pucsinwah into the center of the circle, where a fragrant fire of red cedar burned within a ring of stones. This chief of the Kispoko warrior sept was a tall man, and of a stature that made him seem still taller, but the crown of his head was level with her jaw. There was no man of greater courage and honor in the Shawnee nation and she admired him, even though he was here to speak as her adversary. Pucsinwah's wife, Methotase, A-Turtle-Laying-Her-Eggs-in-the-Sand, was already seated here in the circle. She was a beautiful Shawnee woman from their Creek community in the south. She was famous in her own right as a giver of extraordinary births. Six years before, a great, green shooting star had crossed the sky at the moment she gave birth to a son, who had been named Tecumseh, Panther-Crossing-the-Sky. Three years later, she had been the first woman ever known to have borne three boys at once, all three alive and healthy. Methotase was a wise and strong woman, and likely Pucksinwah himself did not know whether she would vote with her husband for war, or against him for peace. Her oldest son, Chiksika, was of warrior age and would be in battle beside his father if the women approved of the war plan.

Nonhelema knelt at the fire and with a burning stick she lit the ceremonial pipe, turned to the Four Winds, and exhaled the aromatic *kinnikinnick* smoke toward the earth and heaven. Then she passed the pipe to Pucsinwah, who repeated the process. Then the pipe was given to Methotase, who drew on it and handed it to the woman on her left, starting it on its way around the circle.

Nonhelema began her prayer: "Kijilamuhka-ong, He-Who-Creates-by-Thinking, Master-of-Life: This smoke comes to you bearing our prayers. We promise to speak true in this council. We ask you to see us doing right by your intentions, as we deliberate on the blood and the honor of your People of the Southwind. Have pity on us. Help us use all the wisdom that you gave us, for we know there is no matter more important than this one now before us. It will fall upon our children, and their children. As we begin, open our ears to the words of our esteemed *wapacoli oukimeh*, the war chief Pucsinwah who stands among us. When he has spoken out, he will retire away and wait for us to council. Each woman here who wishes will speak to all of us, for war or for peace. Listen to us, Kijilamuhka-ong, and give your blessing to the answer we will collect from our wise women."

And God of Jesus, likewise, she thought, remembering the missionary. "All my sisters," she said, "listen well now to the *wapicoli oukimeh*."

As much of Pucsinwah's greatness as a war chief lay in his good judgment as in his skill and courage. He was not reckless, and all his strategies minimized the risks to his warriors' lives. Nonhelema admired him as a man who defended his people but held their lives precious. Now Pucksinwah stood in the center of the circle of women and turned all the way around, with one hand outstretched as if to include all of them in a salute. Hundreds of women were gathered on this hill, and he had to speak in full voice to be heard by them all.

"Ketawpi, women of the council. Listen:

"You, the mothers and wives and sisters and daughters, it is you who carry the Southwind People from generation to generation. It is you who give birth to the people, and feed and heal them, and who bury them. You have put more into the lives of the warriors than the warriors themselves have done, and you dread most and suffer most the loss of their lives in battle. Knowing that, I come to you with grave respect and ask for your ears and your hearts. *Ketawpi:*

"War is the last thing to do, when there is nothing else that can be done. The Southwind People, and this land where Creator put us to live, are being attacked by an army of the Long Knives from Virginia. Their headman, called Governor Dunmore, leads them. He declares that he is coming to punish the Shawnee people. But the

Shawnee people have done nothing to his people. In truth, he wants to put us out of our hunting grounds. He pretends!"

The women were listening intently, but showed nothing yet in their faces. Pucsinwah looked now at Nonhelema, and said: "Your peace chief knows well that the Long Knives strike out at the innocent, pretending they have cause to do so. You remember not long ago when she was trying to help whitemen and was attacked for it? Remember that she and her brothers escorted the traders, Richard Butler and his comrades, to safety in Fort Pitt, to keep the Mingoes of Chief Tahgahyuteh from killing them? Remember, it was Nonhelema and her brothers Cornstalk, Nimwha, and Silverheels who saved those whitemen. But then they were attacked by militiamen who stabbed Silverheels in the chest! This strong and good woman Nonhelema fought them and carried her brother to safety, or he would be dead now.

"And you remember, before that, the reason why Tahgahyuteh was on the warpath? Remember that it was because whitemen tricked and massacred his family at Yellow Creek, even though Tahgahyuteh had always helped the whitemen!"

The women were murmuring now, glowering. They remembered that one of the murdered women, Tahgahyuteh's own pregnant sister, had been hung up, stripped, and cut open so that her unborn baby hung out of her corpse; the Mingo chief had found her that way.

"And you remember," Pucsinwah went on, "that Colonel McDonald from Fort Pitt crossed the Great River and burned our Wakatomica Town, along with the Mingo towns!

"And all the while, the Virginia men with measuring sticks and chains are drawing lines on our hunting grounds in Kentucke, dividing them up to sell to each other!"

Nonhelema kept watching the faces of the gathered women, to see how much they were being swayed by Pucsinwah's accounts. Many of them were nodding at every statement he made. Her own daughter, Fani, sat with jaw clenched and eyes cold. Her young husband had been found murdered and scalped in his hunting camp more than a year ago, and footprints around his body had been of whitemen's boots.

Pucsinwah went on: "Some of us are old enough to remember when the People of the Southwind lived far to the east. Our sister Nonhelema herself was born in Old Town, in a land they now call Maryland, that has all been divided and sold by whitemen. Now if she tried to go back to her birthplace, they would surely kill her for trespassing! Women of this council, those Virginia whitemen are now trying to make their lines on Kentucke, our hunting ground. They say it was sold to them by the Iroquois. But it was not land for the Iroquois to sell. It is *our* hunting ground!

"Listen! A Long Knife man you have heard of, called Washington. You remember him from the last war. He has been drawing lines on the ground at the mouth of the Kanawha-sipe, so he can sell that land in pieces. That is our hunting ground! How does a man who lives far to the east in Virginia come to believe he can sell our land? Because his home in the East used to belong to our ancestors, who were cheated and killed by his fathers! And so he believes he can do the same to us in Kentucke!

"Sisters, listen! We, the Shawnees, the People of the South-wind, stand on land that the Long Knives want to divide and sell for money. And although we have tried to be peaceful these last recent years, they blame us for everything that happens, and they bribe the other tribes to denounce us. Everywhere they see a place to drive a wedge between us and our old allies, they do it. They try to draw lines between our peoples just as they draw lines upon our land. They lie to our brothers the Delawares about us, and set them against us. We know that our sister Nonhelema has Delaware blood, and loves them. Many of our people live still with the Delawares, in the land of Penn. Many of us in our lifetimes came from there to live here, where there were fewer whitemen. Many of you women have relatives there. But the whitemen's agents are there among your relatives, telling them that you are the enemies of the Delawares. Why are they doing this?

"Sisters, they are doing this because they need a pretense to attack us and get our hunting grounds from us, to sell to each other for money. They have been doing that since they arrived, six generations ago.

"They will keep doing this, sisters, until we have no place left to fall back. That is why I ask you to approve of this attempt we make now: to stop their armies before they march into our home country. This is fine and rich land, and they want it. To get it, they will burn our towns, ravage our people, and make us give it to them if they can. That is their whole story since they came to this land from across the sea. They have defeated us and made us go to their treaty councils, and each time they take more land and say, *No more, we are satisfied, we will never bother you again as long as the sun shines and the grass grows,* but then they come on farther. I have put in my memory every word of those treaties and those promises, and if you want to listen, I will tell you how each was betrayed.

"Sisters, *kulesta*! This is our last chance to stop the Long Knife land stealers, our last chance to discourage them from plowing up the bones of our ancestors!

"While their army is still in two parts, before they join to march three thousand men to this place, I will catch them and thrash them, and prove to them that the People of the Southwind are not fools or cowards, as they think we are. If we do not now make them fear us, they will never stop coming and killing and cheating us. This land we live in is sacred with the blood and bones of our Ancient Ones, those who built the mound-hills we can see from this very place. The Long Knives from Virginia have no right to march here and threaten us. With full respect, I ask the mothers and sisters of the Southwind People to approve and help your warriors to turn the invaders back. I leave you now to the workings of your own wisdom, which men honor." He looked at Nonhelema. *"Megweshe, Coitcheleh,"* he concluded, calling her by the name that meant "Teacher-of-the-Life-Rules." "Now I withdraw to pray that you shall decide in support of fighting for the honor of our people, and for the land where the Master-of-Life put us to live."

Nonhelema said nothing. It was the custom to let a speaker reflect and add any thoughts he might have forgotten. He reached to her with both hands, and she took his hands in both of hers for a moment before he left.

"A-ho, *Wapicoli Oukimeh*," the women said as he went out of the circle and down the hill.

After he had gone, the women remained silent, deep in their thoughts. Whenever Nonhelema felt eyes upon her and looked over to meet the gaze, someone would just be glancing down. This was not good. It had been this way for about three years, since she had been going to listen to the missionaries. Nonhelema's mother lived at the mission town and had become so serene with the Jesus teachings that Nonhelema had gone there to visit and learn. She had left her young son, Morgan, there to learn reading and writing. She had come back and put the crucifix on her wall and had begun talking to some of these women about the Jesus story, hoping it would make the same rich feeling of pity rise in their hearts as it had in hers. But with that, some of the women had drawn a little off from her, as if to guard themselves.

She had continued with all her responsibilities as chief of her town and women's peace chief, and had always overseen the community's *Coitchelekwa* ceremonies and feasts. But it was a little different now. She sensed that some of her women trusted her a little less. Even before, some of them had resented, or envied, her close association with the whitemen, the officers and traders. Years ago it had been George Morgan. Then old Croghan had come slobbering over her, and although she had never been intimate with him, she had used his dotage to her advantage. More recently, she had been consorting with the commissary officer at Fort Pitt, Alexander McKee, a strong, handsome, yellow-haired half-breed with a spirit power around him, one that calmed animals and excited women. It had drawn Nonhelema in a way that complicated her life even more, because it was not the kind of attraction that the missionary would condone. She tried hard to be the kind of good Praying Indian that Brother David Zeisberger insisted she be, but between her traditional ceremonial responsibilities to her "heathen" people, as Zeisberger called them, and her natural inclination to give good men their due, she was usually out of favor with the missionary and waiting for his forgiveness.

But whether in or out of favor with the missionary, she was constant in her belief that peacemaking was her role. She was women's peace chief; her Mekoche sept was the Shawnees' peace and healing division; and Jesus had said plainly that the peacemakers are true children of God.

Besides that, she had seen too much bloodshed in her long years.

And in general, it wasn't in her nature to hate whitemen; she had been raised by her parents and grandparents to like and trust whitemen, and she enjoyed very much the company of the good ones.

Her grandfather Paxinosa had been a good friend of William Penn, known to the Indians as Brother Onas, whom Paxinosa had said was as good and honest as the very best of the Indians. Nonhelema was aware of all the murderous and deceitful whitemen's deeds that the war chief had just related, but she still believed that there were good and honorable whitemen who would be fair with her people if good agreement could be made. She believed that if the Shawnees would meet the whitemen and talk peace instead of attacking them, a good and fair agreement could be made. Even when the whiteman mob had surrounded her and her brothers and tried to kill them, she had known that not all whitemen were like that mob. In fact, one of the better ones, Colonel Croghan, had come out and fired his pistol to drive the mob away. Just as there were good Indian men and bad ones, there were some good whitemen. Surely, the governor of the Virginians must be the best of the Virginians, and therefore honorable. And if indeed, as they said, he was leading the army himself, this would be an opportunity to make terms with the one most honorable Virginian.

She hoped to have a chance to make that point. It was time now to begin.

"Our eldest may speak first," she said, and looked at a tiny humpbacked woman, silver-haired, brown as jerky, her eyes invisibly recessed in wrinkles. This was a cousin of Nonhelema's own mother, and she used the name Anne, which had been given to her when she was a mission Indian. Recently, she had quit the mission because rum and whiskey were forbidden there, and Anne was more compelled by liquid spirits than by the Jesus spirit.

"I shall speak sitting here," the old woman stated in a voice that seemed too big and strong for the little creature, "because it would take me longer to get up than to say what I have to say." The women laughed. The old woman raised a knobby, crooked hand toward Nonhelema and said, "We are fortunate to be Shawnee women. I tell you why: Our men ask us, and we tell them. The women of the whitemen cannot speak in council. They do not own their homes. It does not matter what a white woman believes, for the men do not let them say anything, or vote. I do not want men like that in our country. They would give our men bad notions. So I say: Go catch them and kill them on the other side of the river, before they come and say anything! That is all I have to say now, but watch out; I might have something else to say later."

"A-ho!" many of the women cried, laughing. This war council was the most serious of business, but the women were pleased to laugh while they might.

"Wait!" Anne's voice rose again. "I forgot to say this: It is another good reason not to make a peace treaty with the Long Knives. Our war chief did not mention it. I know this from the other wars: If you do not agree with what the white soldier officers say, they hold you hostage until you do. They call you their 'guest.' One of my husbands went to a treaty and I never saw him again. He was their 'guest' so long, he died of their hospitality. Remember that if you think of talking peace with them. That is all. But watch out; I might say more if I think of something . . . Wait, I thought of something: They try to make you drunk at a treaty so you will be easy to fool. That's the only reason *I* would go!"

Again the whole circle erupted in laughter, and the old woman sat smiling at herself.

"That is all," she said. "But watch out. I—"

"You might think of something else later!" a voice called in back, and they all laughed and hooted.

As it died down, Nonhelema spoke in a clear voice that everyone could hear, despite the strong breeze rustling the yellow leaves overhead. "Our chiefs and warriors waiting down there for our answer on their life or death will be annoyed that we are having too good a time up here."

"No," cried that voice from the rear again. "They will know that our elder has spoken!" The laughter was halfhearted this time.

"You keep speaking up, Blue Goose," Nonhelema said. "While you are in such voice, what have you to say about the *wapicoli oukimeh*'s words?"

Blue Goose, a bony-faced, sinewy woman with a single queue of hair long enough to sit on, rose up. Her expression made it clear she was no longer in a joking mood. She said: "Pucsinwah spoke truth. The whites want us dead so they can take our lands. But also they come to attack us because most of their soldier pay is in looting or in the pleasure of raping our daughters. We all know this from the earlier wars. I believe with Pucsinwah: We should kill them before they can cross the river."

"A-ho!" many women murmured as she sat down.

Then a quavery voice came from the other side of the circle: "No! We cannot condone more killing in battle! Already our village is nearly all women, because our warriors were killed. We have too few fighters to send to a battle!" The speaker was High Swallow, a young woman whose husband had been brought back severely wounded after going to help the Mingoes avenge the massacre of Tahgahyuteh's family. She was trying to feed her family and heal her husband so that he might someday be able to hunt again. All the families in her village shared with her, but there were few hunters.

"*Ketawpi!*" an old, harsh voice called. The women looked toward a stout old woman struggling to her feet. Once up, she passed her gaze over the whole circle and said, "In your hearts you know Pucsinwah speaks the truth. I am old. I have seen our people shoved from place to place for generations. This time the Long Knives come, it is no different from the other times they came. They promise sweet harmony, but give us the smoke of our burning homes, the stink of corpses, the weeping of bruised and shamed women they have raped. *Ketawpi!* We will all die someday anyway. Will we watch ourselves be duped and disgraced just to stay alive a little longer? *Ketawpi, meh shemas:*

"I would rather risk dying now in a fight to make them go back where they came from! Go talk peace again? We might as well walk out to the edge of our villages with our daughters and make them lie down at the soldiers' feet and then walk to the river and drown ourselves. Listen, my sisters. I am old and tired. I am equally tired of war and of peace treaties; the results of both are the same, except we die with honor if we die fighting them! So let us make this a true war, the last one we have to fight, the one our grandchildren's grandchildren will tell of in stories: the war that stopped the whitemen and saved the Shawnee people and their land! I say we support Pucsinwah and his thousand warriors in every way! I will sharpen their tomahawks myself!"

Instead of sitting back down, she crossed her arms and glowered all around. The muttering and murmuring of the women rose to an intensity that sounded like a growl. After a while, Nonhelema said, "Thank you for your words, *meh shemah*. They were well said. You may sit now and someone else may speak."

"One cannot fight sitting down," the old woman said. "Another may speak while I am standing."

Nonhelema wanted someone else to get up and make a good argument for pursuing peace, but this threat of the oncoming army had arisen so quickly that she had not learned how many of the women felt about it.

Her eyes met those of a woman whom she thought she knew well enough, and she called out, "Straight Head? What do you think? You had a white husband, and you have much experience trading with whitemen, and friendships with some of them. Do you think we should listen to the Long Knives about peace?"

Straight Head was never eager to speak. She was a strong, quiet, comely woman, related to the Shawnee mixed-blood wife of the trader Lorimier, and had a baby boy by a French Canadian interpreter from Detroit named Pierre Drouillard. Straight Head gracefully rose from her place on the ground near the front, her face full of thoughts, and began in a voice so soft it was barely audible.

"Yes, Coitcheleh Oukimakwa, I am used to whitemen. I do not hate whitemen. Some of them are good, and many are interesting. My own husband, Pierre, was interesting. And he was good to me, when he was sober. Lorimier, too, is a good friend of our people. He has his trading store among us and helps in every way we need."

Her voice grew stronger as she let her passions flow. "But these are Frenchmen that I speak of. They come to be with us and they become part of us. They don't try to take our land, or change the way we are." She paused, frowning now.

"Those *Shemanese*, the Long Knives, though, they are not like the French. They hate and disdain the Indian people because we are in their way. We have been here forever, but they had a king across the eastern ocean who got rid of them because they were too troublesome, and that king told them he was giving them all the land of our people. And they believed him, that king who sent them away! And they seemed to believe that he could do that, and that has been their excuse ever since they came.

"Now," Straight Head said, looking up into the wind-stirred leaves of the great trees overhead as if searching for the decisive part of her reply; then she turned all the way around, looking at all the hundreds of women sitting as colorful as flowers in the sun-dappled circle. "Now our beloved chief Nonhelema hopes that I will tell you that whitemen can be talked to and will open their ears and be reasonable. I must answer from my true belief, from what I have seen and learned:

"Yes, we could go and talk peace with them, and maybe get some good from it—if they were Frenchmen. But they are not Frenchmen, they are Virginians. They don't want to live in peace among us. They want us to be dead and out of their way, or so far toward the going-down sun that they never see us. Listen: My husband was an interpreter, not a killing soldier. He believed in different people talking to each other, not in fighting. But he said, '*Talking does no good if the other one will not listen.*' The Long Knives do not want to listen or to be among us. And so all we can do is try to keep them back as far away from us as they want us to be from them. I pray that our warriors will stop the Long Knives on the other side of the river and discourage them from ever coming closer. That is all." She looked once at Nonhelema with a wistful expression, knowing that she had disappointed her, and sat down. For moments, the only sounds were the wind in the trees, a woman's cough, the brief cry of a baby somewhere in the great circle of women, a cry stopped at once by a nipple.

Into that quiet came a lilting, small voice, almost like a bird's call, a voice familiar to the Mekoches of Nonhelema's Town. It was Qui-eteh, gatherer of medicine plants for the shaman, and his helper in the seasonal ceremonies. She was asking to speak, and Nonhelema summoned her to the center. She came forward, wending her way gracefully among the sitting women. She was a mature woman with two grandchildren, but she was as small and delicate as a girl.

As Qui-eteh came, Nonhelema spoke from deep in her chest, to be heard by all: "You have been speaking your hearts. Of anger, and vengeance, and fear. And of what the Long Knives are in your imaginings. Now we must ask about our own ability to fight. What is our health? What of our food? What of medicine? Qui-eteh, I hope you will speak on such things, which men never think about when they are whipping themselves into the war spirit."

"I can speak of that. And other truths." Qui-eteh faced out, and tried so hard to be heard that her voice almost shrieked. She had to stop often to fill her lungs. "I will begin. First, there is this: We are much fewer than their race. They have more and better weapons. They get guns and powder and lead from their government, as much as they need. We do not. Fighting is not equal, as it was in the old times, when warriors fought at arm's length with the strength of their bodies. Many of our beloved men will fall if we agree to go to war. That will cause great grief among us all. None of our families will be spared sorrow. In deciding, we have a responsibility to Creator. Or if you are one of our Christian Indians, to *their* god.

"When I am confused as to what I should do, like now, I remember our oldest teachings, the guidance our ancestors left us. They said our first duty was to Creator, to respect and protect life of all kinds; then our duties are to ourselves, our families, our tribe, to Turtle Island, the graves of our ancestors, to Mother Earth. Only then are we to reach out further, toward others. We are to be hospitable to strangers, to be generous to them and share all the blessings Creator has given us in such bounty, expecting that if we are ever in need, they will return generosity.

"My sisters, we have done all those things. We have done them over and over and over. But I believe the laws we live by are strange to those aliens, the Long Knives. Some of the words they speak, words that they say came from their god, sound like the ways we were taught, but they don't *live* as if they ever heard their own god.

"I have thought and prayed about this, what I am about to say. I have used my prayer tobacco, my pipe from my ancient ancestors. I have fasted and prayed for a vision to tell me. I believe the ancestors spoke to me in the wind, and they said:

"There is a different Creator for the whitemen. Their Creator is young and petulant. He teaches them behavior that creates death and destruction. He promises them things that he has no right to give them, because they are what *our* Creator gave to *us*. He tells them that it is all right to kill and to take what they want since he let them find Turtle Island, and we should be pushed out of the way. Their god has not taught them to respect anything but him, and also that stuff in their pockets they call *money*. You will remember, our clothes had no pockets."

Qui-eteh had to pause and ask a water girl to bring her a drink from the exertion of talking so loudly and long. She drank from the gourd twice, her face still full of concentration, then went on.

"Their god has not taught them of the long-times. Their sense of the world is short, only days and moons. They do not see ahead to the lives and needs of their grandchildren's grandchildren; they see only their wants of today. So they come and they kill and they take, and they waste. They must be an inferior kind, to be that way. We must accept that Creator allowed them to be, but we must stop them wiping us out by their ways.

"The voices of the ancestors said to me: It is our duty to see that all goes on in the way Creator set it going in the beginning when he rolled the Sacred Hoop along. It rolls in balance. If it stops, it falls over and the Sacred power revolves no more. We should pray for the spirit of those white aliens who have no understanding. It might be that we should teach them about the long balance, if they will listen. But they are not good listeners. They are tellers! They send us Black Coats to tell us what we must believe and Red Coats to tell us what we must do."

Nonhelema remembered teaching her own daughter about the balance of the rolling. She glanced and saw Fani smiling at her. But she knew that Qui-eteh's argument was going more to Fani's liking than to her own.

"I, Qui-eteh, have sons who will probably be killed by Red Coats in battle. I have daughters whose hearts will break. I have grandchildren who will die at the hands of those strange people of that strange god. My husband and I may die at their hand. Surely our homes will be destroyed, as they destroyed all the Shawnee houses at Wakatomica not two moons since. And surely our crops will be trampled and burned. If we survive, we will start again, for Creator has taught us the cycle of returning.

"But since they do not listen, we must try to preserve what we have left of Creator's gifts. That is what the Old Voices in the wind told me: that we must hold those wretched beings back off our sacred land.

"Creator needs the Southwind People to be stronger of heart, closer together in purpose, than at any time since he put us here. If we do not hold those people away from here, they will break the Sacred Hoop that has been turning here since the beginning. I heard this in the wind when I asked for wisdom. They said that one side of the balance is life and the other is death. If there is to remain balance, there must be sacrifice for it. I am ready for that. Though it crushes my heart, I know we must go and fight." Tears shone in her eyes. The women knew that Qui-eteh was one of those who heard the truth most clearly. They realized the warpath was opening up, and they probably would have to take it. Some women were beginning to weep for the pain and sorrow that must lie ahead down that path.

Qui-eteh went on: "Now I am to tell you of our people's condition for war. These are the matters our women know of, and the men have to learn from us, to know whether we are able to make and bear a war:

"Our people are healthy now. We have not had much sickness. Our crops are good this season, but we must finish the harvest and hide it before the soldiers come.

"There will be little meat, if our men have to go to war instead of to the hunting camps. You know the whitemen want to keep us from crossing the river to hunt in Kentucke, which is our best hunting ground. They say it is theirs now. Already they shoot our hunters they see there. This is the Hunter's Moon and our men would be bringing game by now, but they have to gather here in case of war. So our warriors might have to go to war with cow meat in their stomachs, and cow meat has no spirit power.

"Even so, our warriors are strong right now. My gatherer helpers have put by plenty of the medicines, of most kinds. They have helped me preserve and store the medicines in all the towns, in case some are burned. Also, Change-of-Feathers, as head shaman and medicine man for our entire nation, has asked us village healers to collect medicines and wound dressings to take to the battlefield, and that we have done, all that a packhorse can carry.

"Most of you are skillful with the bow. Some of us women have guns and can fight if our villages come under attack while the warriors are gone. Most of our old men could fight, too. Only a few are too sick or feeble. My sisters in the medicine society tell me the same is true in their communities. Also, this has been a healthy year for horses.

"*Meh shemas,* this is the strongest we have been in years. If we are ever to stand before the Long Knives and keep them out of our lands, this is when we could with the least suffering and least loss of lives."

Qui-eteh's report was not coming to the conclusion that Nonhelema had hoped it would. War instead of peace, and the sacrifice of her own wealth in cattle, as well? If no one else rose soon to argue for peace, she herself would have to do it.

Qui-eteh continued. "Now I should tell you of our young women's conditions. Right now only two of our women are pregnant. That is very uncommon, and may not last. If there is war, those two are barely along and might safely choose to abort rather than bear orphans. Knowing this council would take place, I discussed these things with the two young women and they understand what they could lose.

"I am a healer. I stand for peace and life. If we choose war, I shall go to the battlefield to help our warriors. I am ready for that. If we rely on whitemen's promises and paper treaties, I believe our people will cease to be. O-ho!"

A loud and busy murmur arose as the beloved little medicine woman prepared to yield the center of the circle. Nonhelema was alarmed that even this most kindly woman had nothing favorable to say about whites. Almost every family here had some white blood that had entered in recent generations—through adoption of captives, like Fani, or through early marriages to whites, or children of women raped by soldiers. In this crowd sat women with blue eyes, auburn hair, freckles. But inside, they were Shawnees, and their white blood was never mentioned. It was an argument for tolerance that had to stay unsaid.

Qui-eteh's argument had been too strong and practical in favor of fighting, and the whole crowd of women seemed to be stirring toward an accord. Nonhelema feared that her own peacemaker argument, based on the Bible, would be resented and rejected because of the women's frame of mind; perhaps its proper time had passed and would never come back around. She tried to think of some other way to argue for peace now, but she had been building her own speech so much on the missionary precepts that her mind seemed empty of alternatives.

And now she saw that Pucsinwah's own wife had risen to speak. The war chief's wife was so loved and admired throughout the whole nation that if she spoke her husband's argument, it would sway the whole council to demand a war vote this soon.

Methotase gave Nonhelema an unreadable glance and stood beside her to speak.

"*Meh shemas!* Listen to me! I live in a house where the war spirit is always strong, and there is the confidence that comes of being right. *Weshe catweloo k'weshe lawehpah,* my husband and son always repeat. We are stronger because we are right. This they believe, never doubting. And I, too, believe that being right makes us stronger.

"But does it make us strong enough? For a long time, I thought, yes, the Master-of-Life would not let us be defeated if we were right. And we are right. This land is made of the flesh and the bone dust of our ancestors." She stooped and poked her fingers into the trampled dirt beside the fire pit and held up a pinch of it. "In this dirt is the essence of our ancient ancestors, we have been here so long! The Long Knives have no sense of the holiness that has gone into this earth, first by Creator's making of it, then by our countless generations living on it and being buried in it. I am as angry at Long Knives as my husband and my son are. But listen:

"Two nights ago in a dream, I saw my husband all covered with his own blood and making the yellow leaves red with it as he died in my son's arms." She stopped, choking, her hand on her bosom, face contorted and suddenly gleaming with tears. The women gasped and moaned. Nonhelema herself saw the whole image as clearly as if it had been her own dream. She reached toward the stricken woman, as if to ease her down, but Methotase shook her head and blurted, "I have not finished . . . " She fought to brace herself and get her voice back.

"No!" she said. "I do not want him killed on a battlefield! It is true, he has never lost a battle. But if he dies, could our warriors keep fighting the Long Knives and win? I don't want to give my husband up to a whiteman's bullet! If I had not had that dream I could stand here and say, *Yes, war!* But now I say, *No! No war!* I am too selfish. I go against my husband's wishes. I want him to be alive as his sons grow up, so they can see in him the kind of man they should be. I beg you, *meh shemas,* send peace, not permission for war, to my husband!"

Nonhelema stood, shaken, feeling hollow, but beginning to hope that this powerful vision and plea by Methotase could turn the vote. Few could argue with dreams.

Methotase was wiping her cheeks with both palms and moving back to her seating place when Blue Goose called out: "Sister! Let me ask: Did you tell your husband of that dream?"

Methotase, blinking, swallowing, said, "All one day I tried not to. But then I told him."

"And," Blue Goose said, "it did not scare *him* from asking us for battle, did it?"

"No, *meh shemah,* it did not."

"Therefore, sisters," Blue Goose cried in her strongest voice, "that dream tells us that we must vote for battle! If the *wapicoli oukimeh* was seen dying in a dream, it will happen! We cannot change what has been dreamed by making a vote otherwise! It is to be! And did anyone dream that the battle was lost? Eh? Anyone?"

Here Nonhelema could have said she had. But that would have been a lie. She had had no such dream. Even if Pucsinwah were killed, the battle still might not be lost.

Then there followed long arguments about the ways the dream should be considered, and soon the dream had been absorbed into all the other considerations, both emotional and practical, until, as always in long councils, nothing new was being said, and everything was being repeated, and only the interpretation or emphasis varied. Girls with water pails and drinking gourds weaved among the women as the discussion resounded in the glade, sometimes in shouts, sometimes in sobs, sometimes in laughter. The central fire was fed with red cedar, and its aromatic smoke mixed in the slanting sunbeams with smoke from the women's personal smoking pipes, and if, as they believed, words and prayers were carried to the Great Good Spirit by smoke, much would reach Weshemonetoo this day. Nonhelema once found herself musing that Creator was getting so much smoke from this war council that he might think it was the gunsmoke of a battle already being fought, not just debated.

It was going too strongly in favor of the war vote, though. Much as she dreaded to do it, she was going to have to bring in the one new perspective, and hope that she could do it so eloquently that these women would consider it with open hearts and open minds. She was smoking her own white clay tavern pipe with its curved, long stem, and she took one last draw then blew it toward heaven with a prayer that the right words, the words for peace, would come down through her. One's head could shape arguments all day, but strong truths had to come down and through the speaker. She had always had faith in that, and always, words had come down that were better than anything she had known to say, and by that means she had won as many of her debates as Pucsinwah had his battles.

Just now, a hard little widow from the Kispoko sept was winding down from a spittle-spraying harangue about the cruelty, deviousness, greed, and godlessness of all the whitemen who had ever crawled to the shore of this land out of their sea of slime, and it was so excessive that Nonhelema could see even some of the war advocates frowning at the ranting woman, and she thought: *Now.*

It was as if Jesus had called down to her and said, *Now.*

When the little woman wiped the froth off her mouth and sat down, Nonhelema straightened to her full height and drew the back of her hand across her forehead, then raised it and pointed toward the west where the afternoon sun was declining, mottling the tree limbs with golden flecks of light. That gesture drew the attention of the wearying, restless crowd, and the circle of Shawnee women went almost completely silent.

"Sisters! I have heard the very music of your hearts. I know each of you has spoken your true belief. What is in your heart is true to you, but there might be a fuller truth beyond your own knowledge. Only a fool would claim to know everything.

"Our Kispoko sister who just spoke is a widow because into her husband's life came some whitemen who were the evil monsters she described. There are *some* whitemen like that; you have seen some, and I have seen some. But it is not true that they are all like that. When you speak that way, you are just like the murderers of Logan's family, those who say, *All Indians are vermin without souls—kill them all!* Sisters, it is never true to say one thing about any race or nation of people! Listen:

"We said here today that our ancestors of this land are speaking through us. You remember, don't you, that our Ancient Ones taught us to seek peace if we can. And they taught us to welcome newcomers. If we are here really listening to the voices of our ancestors, then we should be hearing them cry for peace.

"White people are like us—human souls, some good, some bad. They love, they marry. They cherish their children. They need food and shelter and a place to be. There are so many of them over the mountains in the East that they run out of ground to grow food and build lodges. They are like us. They love their Creator, whom they call God, and his son, Jesus Christ."

She was on delicate ground, mentioning the whites' religion. Only Nonhelema's family and a few friends among the Shawnees had ever converted to Christianity. Her mother had become a mission Indian called Elizabeth, taking in with her one of her daughters, who was now called Christiana, and no one in the village ever saw them anymore unless the missionary gave special permission for them to enter his compound where they lived.

In the council circle, Nonhelema had seen some faces harden when she mentioned the whiteman's God. It was risky. But she remembered the missionaries' admonition to trust Jesus, and she trusted Jesus to open their ears and soften their hearts, as he had hers. "They have the love of God who sacrificed his own son, Jesus," she said in her most passionate voice, "so they would not perish from their sins and go to hell, but could go to heaven instead and be with him. The missionaries came to our country and made their peace towns over on the Muskingumsipe, to share that with us! They know that God loves us, too, only we did not know about his son, Jesus. We have been proud and stiff-necked, and refuse to acknowledge our sins. Our ignorance and our sins make God very sad and hurt his heart. We are guilty of making God cry." The notion of God crying touched her powerfully; it was a notion that she had not heard from the missionaries, but it had come to her now to say it, and she was sure it would move them. But the Shawnee women around her were only glancing aside to each other, raising their eyebrows, puckering their mouths. It had been a mistake, perhaps, to try to make them feel sorry for God. Maybe it would be better to make them feel sorry for the missionaries.

"The Black Coats sacrifice much comfort to leave their fine homes far away in their own homelands, and live in a place that is hard for them, in order to share their knowledge of the way to heaven. They love us even when we are cruel or drunk or foolish and fail to understand.

"You know it is one of our twelve rules of living to share what we have with newcomers—especially newcomers who come to bring us their greatest gift: the gift of eternal life, the knowledge that God sacrificed his son for all of us, that we can go to heaven. We had not known the way. We were doomed and did not know it. It is only the bad people who God says shall really die. Once we believe in Jesus and are baptized, we are no longer bad people, but saved!"

With the most fervid sincerity she was trying to tell her women the sweet, sad story as the Moravians had told it to her over and over, in their mission house over by the Muskingumsipe, the missionaries with their white faces and shy smiles and shining eyes, the holiness exuding from them so strongly that one could feel it. And they served incredibly delicious sweet pastry cakes, and tea with cow-milk cream, as they told the Indian women about the loving Jesus. It was their way to enchant the women, and then—through them—draw in their husbands. Nonhelema had not yet been formally converted or baptized, because she had not quite achieved the piety or humility that Brother David Zeisberger demanded of her. But she was confident that her efforts as a peacemaker would before long make her a child of God in Jesus' eyes, and eventually even in Brother David's. She believed she would be received within a year or so. It was her faith in this that inspired her to keep talking this way to these women until their ears and hearts might open to the message of peace.

"It was God who sent those pure-hearted missionaries to our land," she went on. "It is his intention that we welcome all his children to come live here. They will share with us, as we did with the whitemen when they first came in their boats. We must not hate them. I am ashamed that we have not always been kind to them, and we have earned some of their disrespect and distrust. They try to make good treaties with us, but there are so many of them wandering about that not all of them know just what those agreements are, and so they act on their own, just like our own renegades. They *want* to be our friends. They are trying to come to an agreement that is good for everyone and will last from now on, for all our grandchildren and theirs.

"True, we were here before them. But many of the whites now have been here on Turtle Island long enough that the land now contains the bones of their ancestors, as it does ours. Truly, they love this land, as we do. They know we must share it."

At those words, several women snorted and muttered—a very rude act when someone was speaking in council. She tried to ignore that. Jesus would not want her to become angry while pleading for peace. She closed her eyes and envisioned him as he looked on the wall in her house in the sunglow, his muscular warrior body whose strength he had never used in violence against anyone, never, and of his sweet face cast down in pain and sadness because of the cruelty of sinners and mockers. These women who had snorted at her words, they were mockers, like those who had tormented him. Nonhelema loved these women, they were her people, but they were like the ignorant sinners who had mocked the suffering bleeding Jesus.

"My family and our sept," she said, "have the duty to be sure all roads to peace have been tried before we turn to war. We have paths still open. We can still speak to our white brethren sensibly and with kindness. If we sue for peace, they will listen. But if we go to war and kill some of them, and then lose the battle, we will lose forever their goodwill and forbearance.

"You, my sisters, who have never lived anywhere but here in the Middle Ground, have no understanding of the size of their cities. I have been there and seen them. The numbers of their people and their armies are like an anthill, always more ready to swarm and take the places of any who fall. All their soldiers have better guns than ours—even cannon, guns that shoot a ball as big as a gourd and can shatter a tree! One shot from a cannon burns more powder than one of our hunters has all year to hunt with!

"In the city of Philadelphia, they make *barrels* of gunpowder every day! The whites have so many people, they can replace every fallen soldier with two. No, with ten! But there have never been many Shawnees—not since the sicknesses started coming. Each one of our men lost will cause a hardship on his whole village, not just his family. We have no men to spare.

"Now, *meh shemas,* I ask you to confess that the whitemen have brought many good things to us. They brought horses to Turtle Island, here where everybody always walked before. They brought cattle that give milk and butter and cheese. You like those things. You come to my house and borrow some. They brought pigs, which are like fat bear, but can be raised so they are available at any time. We have been using their wonderful metal needles and awls, and knives and pots and pans. And glassware. And the mirrors that we love.

"Who remembers how hard it was to kill game for food and skins before they brought us guns and steel traps? And look at you, half of you are wearing calico clothing of cloth, so colorful, so much more comfortable than deerskin, so much easier to prepare and sew. They have brought things that have made our lives more pleasant, easier. Are not the glass beads brighter, and less trouble, than the quills we color and use with such labor?"

She watched their faces as she talked, and grew a bit hopeful. If Jesus had not made them open their ears, the trade goods had. That was a way the whitemen had already won them more than they would care to admit, a way so familiar they seldom gave it a thought. And they had seen hardly any of the finest whitemen things. They had not been to the cities, as she had, to hear violins or trombones, or ridden in carriages between rows of tall houses made of brick, or seen harbors full of giant ships with their poles and ropes high as forest trees, ships bringing spices and coffee and tea, and fine scissors, folding fans, the cloth called lace that one could see through, window glass that one could see through but rain could not penetrate . . .

If they could see all that, how they would want it! And the whitemen could teach them the wonder of writing and reading, which skills set Nonhelema apart a little even from her own beloved women. She was teaching her daughter to read; the missionaries had taught her son, Morgan, how to read; she herself could teach some of her own women to read, if there was peace, and books could be had. But if war started, all that her people would get from the whitemen would be smoke and fire and lead and death.

"*Meh shemas!* There is only good in choosing peace instead of war against the whitemen! War will shut us away from good things! It will separate us from our friends the Delawares, who want to be at peace. It will stir the Iroquois against us, who have left us undisturbed for generations. *Ketawpi!* I have heard some of you say all whitemen are demons, but not all of any people are of a kind! Most of any people are good! Most whitemen are of good and generous spirit and are humble under their God! Sisters, think of the sunlight of peace, not the smoke-clouds of war. Permit me then, your peace chief, to go down and tell our war chief that we are still on a path of peace, and want to go talk to the governor of Virginia. I believe that when the governor understands the truth, he will turn his army back, and we can live in peace."

Nonhelema had spoken truth. She had told them things they wanted to ignore. She had been a good Christian and told them of the suffering Jesus. She had spoken as a peacemaker, a child of God. She had also warned them of the desolation and loss they would bring upon themselves by striking instead of talking. She had done her best. She stood, silent and tall, in that moment they allowed for a speaker to add anything she had forgotten. She knew her Shawnee women were the true life-givers; that they treasured and nurtured life. In her heart, she had always abhorred strife and bloodletting, even before the Moravians came to tell the Indians about their peaceful Jesus. She looked about at the great circle of women, her Indian women with the traits of whitemen showing here and there, and even some who looked like black people because the Shawnees had harbored runaway slaves and sheltered them and adopted them. All that, to her, was the true nature of these women: the embrace of the hungry and needy, the tolerance of newcomers. She stood looking them over, hoping she had said it well enough, and that their true nature, not the words of the war chief, would influence them, make them vote for peace.

The quiet after the sound of her plangent voice was beginning to ring. Such a crowd of stubborn, passionate, bighearted, opinionated Shawnee women could not bear silence very long.

A square-faced, keen-eyed woman who had been sitting behind Methotase got up and stood with her fists on her hipbones, glaring at Nonhelema. She was Nonhelema's own sister-in-law Red Leaf, the wife of Nonhelema's half brother the Walker. The Walker was set against appeasing the Long Knives, and it was clear that his wife's resolve was as firm as his.

"Nonhelema! I am so tired of listening to you make this excuse and that excuse for your beloved whites! Let me remind our sisters that it is not three thousand missionaries marching here, it is soldiers with guns in their hands, and greed and violence in their hearts, and the lust for rape standing stiff in their breeches!

"*Share*, you say? How can you tell us whitemen want to share? All that once was ours in the East as far as the sea is now theirs, and if we try to go back there to visit the graves of our mothers, they will kill us for stepping on their farms! They are evil and full of hate. There is no truth in them. They have been deceiving and murdering our people since their first boat touched the shore. They are crowded in the East because they increase like maggots with no thought of how they will feed their offspring. Instead of food they grow tobacco, which used to be our praying herb, but they grow it for money. We know tobacco ruins the ground if you keep planting it in a place. They didn't listen when we told them that, and now they have ruined the ground they took from us before, and now want to come and take this, too! Wherever they go, everything falls and dies. They leave no tree standing, the medicine plants they pluck from the ground and sell for money, the game flees, our ancestors' graves are plundered and plowed over, the creeks and lakes are muddy with their excrement and that of their swine. Even the grass dies under their hooves and the hills dissolve in the rain! I, too, have been to visit in their great cities, and I had to pinch my nose shut and run back out!

"Even those good things you say they bring us, they cost us far too much. They do not trade even worth for the furs we take them; they get us drunk to cheat us so they can turn the difference into money. And have you ever talked to a whiteman who did not try to find out where the Shawnees dig their silver? What do you mean, *share*? They do not share, they only take! They share only their rum and whiskey, their diseased *passah-tihs*, and take advantage of us women, our bodies and our trades.

"You, Nonhelema, you have done nothing but help them since you were a young girl. Even before you moved to this Middle Ground, you helped those Moravian Black Coats follow your family into our country. They bewitched your family elders and they are bewitching you! You say they brave the discomforts to come and share with us? Ha! Our poor Delaware brothers in their mission sweat and bend their backs like slaves to feed and shelter those lazy Black Coats! I have seen Brother Zeisberger's fine rooms where he sits high and tells us we should always writhe in shame because we hurt God's son! What? We never heard of God's son, and never saw him!" Red Leaf was a powerful scold, and some said that was why her husband always wanted to be away at war. And Nonhelema could sense that she was stirring the women's fear and anger again.

"We have heard about your suffering bleeding Jesus until we are sick!" Red Leaf cried. "You have lost the good sense Creator gave women, and you have traded your intelligence for baubles and romance from those greedy, scheming, lustful people! Their officers and agents give you shiny gifts and things to make your life easy, things you show off to us! You have your slave, Caesar, who does your hard work and tends your cows and horses! You live in another world, Nonhelema! One day you are a Shawnee chief, the next you are a simpering Christian begging for a Black Coat's blessing, and then you are a paramour of whoever is in command at Fort Pitt, or the newest Indian agent. A merchant made you pregnant and left you with a boy child to raise without a father!"

This was disgraceful behavior in council, to attack someone personally, and Nonhelema clenched her teeth and waited for the women to shout down Red Leaf for the insulting language. But no one shouted at Red Leaf; she was doing all the shouting.

"You set a terrible example for our young women. They see powerful whitemen swarm around you, giving you trinkets, and they want to be beautiful and favored like you. They don't realize how much you give away that is sacred to us, for such flattery and shiny things that tarnish. The whitemen make you feel important as their spokesman among us. But nothing you have ever presented to us has ever been honored by your precious whitemen, nor will today's pleas for peace, either!

"Nonhelema, you are growing white! Even your smoking pipe is white! Look at it, *meh shemas*—a white tavern pipe, in our council!" Red Leaf's voice rasped with contempt. Dozens of women in the crowd unobtrusively slipped their own white tavern pipes out of sight, as Nonhelema noticed in her stinging chagrin. How badly this had gone! God seemed to be doing nothing to help his peacemaker here.

But Red Leaf was not through. She cried, "I can no longer respect your pleas for peace. You do not see those dirty, dishonorable people as they are. You blind yourself with this Jesus story, and think a dead man can save our living children.

"I have tried to be your good friend and sister, a good Shawnee woman. I do not want to be a white woman. I do like the beautiful cloth we can buy, and my iron pots, my looking glass. But I do not like their sickness of spirit that is so contagious and fatal to us. I do not like their strange idea that I must 'obey' my husband. My husband is a good man, but I have much more sense than he has. I would be foolish to obey him, as your missionaries and generals say a woman must do, just because he is the man, even if a man is a fool. If we lived like your whitemen, our women could not even have a council like this to decide our fate and the fates of our grandchildren!

"Listen, *Coitcheleh*! Listen, *meh shemas*:

"If we vote to go to war, as I feel we must, I expect us to see no more of my sister Nonhelema, for I believe she will go to the mission, to cower among the Praying Indians. Or to Fort Pitt, to be flattered by the generals and the traders. But not I! I say, Why live, if I cannot be a Shawnee woman, with freedom and a voice? I do not want my children to live in cities, or to be drunk, or to worship a mean-spirited god!"

Suddenly then, Red Leaf's voice rose almost to a scream: "I will live as my grandparents' grandparents lived! I speak for myself and my family, and almost every Shawnee woman I know! We want to help chase those Long Knives back across the mountains as far as we can make them run!"

She shut her eyes and gave forth the ululation of grief and exultation, her voice as shrill in her throat as an eagle's, her tongue vibrating.

And then all those women, who had begun to let the long drone of talk lull them, were instantly in a sweat with their hair standing on end. In the next breath, a score of women were trilling, and in the next, hundreds. Nonhelema's heart fell.

The trill had done it. She knew that peacemaking had lost in the Council of Women.

In truth, anyone within three miles of the Council Hill of Nonhelema's Town would have known it. The cry filled the air.

It was dusk when Nonhelema walked down the hill and through her town. She crossed the bottomland of the creek and entered Pucsinwah's smoky warrior camp. A runner went ahead of her into the heart of the camp. Warriors stood up beside their fires and watched her, confusion on their faces. She walked erect and grim into the stomp ground in the middle of the camp, where a war post had already been put up and painted blood red. There beside the pole stood Pucsinwah and Cornstalk, war chief and peace chief together, and they looked bewildered. In Cornstalk's handsome face there showed a tentative hint of hopefulness. But Pucsinwah was obviously as angry as he was confused to see the woman peace chief come down from council instead of a messenger from the war faction. He said: "Did the women not decide?"

"We did, *Oukimeh*."

"But, to sue for peace?"

"To go and strike the army. You heard their cry."

Both Pucsinwah and Cornstalk now looked even more bewildered. "But you are their peace chief . . ."

"It is the men's choice and the women's choice to go to war," she said. "What the councils want, it is the duty of their chiefs to lead them that way. I shall lead the warriors of my town."

Cornstalk took a quick, deep breath, and said, "And therefore I shall lead the rest of the Mekoches."

A murmur of astonishment went among all those standing around close enough to hear. At last, Pucsinwah said softly, "I did not think you would fight the whitemen."

"Neither did the women think so," she replied. "But even women can be wrong sometimes, eh?"

She had gotten at least that satisfaction out of her defeat in council. She had shown them that they didn't know her true heart as well as they thought they did. They had thought she would run away and join her whitemen friends.

"I am their *Coitcheleh*," she said. "I know the teachings better than they know them: that I belong to my Shawnee people, and that as their chief I lead them to do what they say must be done. I fear for us what will happen, but the women support war. And so it will be."

She looked at Pucsinwah and saw him covered with his own blood and dying in his son's arms. At that moment, she saw in his eyes that he knew his wife had told the women of her dream.

What a costly sacrifice to the women's anger this great man will be, she thought.

And in a battle against the whitemen's guns, I might be just such a sacrifice myself.

But this is what my people feel they must have.

2

AT THE MOUTH OF THE KANAWHA RIVER
OCTOBER 10, 1774

A soldier could not be brave when he felt this miserable.

Private Justin Isaac Case, of the Botetourt County Militia regiment, hurt from the bones out, having slept on the cold ground. His bowels were loose and seething, and it seemed to him that he had spent too much of his life this way, out in the wilderness, on campaigns against Frenchmen and Indians, almost twenty years since his first one. He had first gone to war as a drummer boy at the age of fourteen, had barely escaped with his life, and had been scared into a permanent case of abject, white-livered poltroonery. Yet here he was in Indian country again. It wasn't quite daybreak yet, and he hadn't slept more than an hour, lying awake—scared—half the night, then standing sentry watch the other half of the night, hearing things.

Now, when he might have slept a little more from sheer fatigue, his bladder and burbling gut and aching bones had harangued him to get up, go squat at the sinks, then hunker near a cook fire with tea, shivering. The October chill penetrated through his linsey-woolsey hunting frock with its fringed mantle, and through the shirt beneath it that stank with the old sweats of a 160-mile march through steep mountains and river-bottom thickets.

And to compound his misery, he was still scared, even with a thousand other militiamen and their officers around him. Most of them still lay in their blankets; a few, like him, were up and gazing blearily into smoky fires. In his veteran opinion, there could be no time when a rational man might be really braced in his soul for an Indian attack. But the time when one was absolutely least ready was this trembly, achy, hungry, miserable, bleak time after a sleepless night of dread.

It was the time when the savages preferred to attack.

Let it not be today, Private Case prayed silently. *If ever, let it be after I get a good sleep, if I ever do. If ever, let it be when my bowels aren't in flux.*

He sipped tea gingerly over the blistering hot edge of his tin cup and pondered his role in peace and war. A teacher and quilldriver as well as a farmer, he fancied himself just too intelligent to be a good fighting man. Anyone given to rational thought could see only folly going into combat. Once in battle, the only logic was that by killing someone, in violation of the major commandment, you might keep him from killing you. But you also provoke God's retribution by doing it.

Also, as a teacher, he was too imaginative. Any horror he met in warfare he suffered twice, having already endured it in dreadful imaginings. The crown of his head had many times felt the cruel edge of the scalping knife, though in reality it had not happened. So far.

And yet, whenever there was a call-up of militia, somehow he was caught in it. His relatives and community deemed him something of a hero because of his prior services, and so he never knew a seemly way to evade duty. His reputation as a shit-breeches had not reached home; his comrades in arms never told on him, as it had happened to many of them, too. It was one of those secrets, like their rape of Indian girls, knowledge of which would have stained their glory at home. Such carnal plunder was a primary motive for many of the Indian-fighting volunteers; Justin Case despised them for that. In truth, unlike such soldiers, he found all desire squelched, rather than stimulated, by the nearness of violence and danger. He doubted that he could have a fright and a cockstand in the same day.

He found himself now looking across the fire at a somber and disturbing face. The man was a subject of wonder and whispers in the army, called "Indian Tom" Ingles. He had been captured and raised from boyhood by Shawnees during the last war. His mother had escaped and made her way home to Virginia. By the time Tom Ingles was found and ransomed after the war, he was so much Indian that his family could scarcely keep him in Virginia. Now he was gazing over the river, a long, longing look in his eyes. Perhaps he was pining to be among the Indians instead of these militiamen. Private Case shuddered and looked back into the fire. The Ingles man, so close by, made him think more about Indians than he wanted to.

He was down to the sweet dregs of tea now, where the chunks of brown sugar had scarcely dissolved, when he noticed a stir in the camp and looked about. Many of the men were now getting up, rolling their blankets, yawning, coughing, venting their night gases as loudly as they could, heading to the latrines or to the cook fires with their cups in hand. Mist over the wide confluence of the rivers was glowing silvery gold with the first rays of sunrise that shone down the valley of the Kanawha and lit the far shore of the Ohio River; several huge herons rose through the mist on slow wingbeats; songbirds were twittering along the riverbanks to greet the day; lowing came from the army's beef herd; and the shady woods were loud with the scoldings of squirrels and crows. In the camp, wood smoke from the many fires hung low and dense, irritating his eyelids. It seemed a peaceful and beautiful morning, but heads were turning, shouts rising.

When he saw one of Captain Arbuckle's scrawny half-breed Catawba scouts running through camp toward the officers' tents, his heart skipped. Even before the regimental commanders came hurrying to Colonel Andrew Lewis's tent, Justin's dread was running over at the brim.

The colonels were able veterans, usually inspiring calm by their rugged self-confidence. But as they listened to the scout, they looked like chicks in the shadow of a hawk. They were all squawking at once and flapping their arms. Captain Arbuckle, Justin's own company commander, was barking at the scout.

In quiet haste, Colonel Lewis sent his brother, Colonel Charlie Lewis, and the other regimental commander, Colonel Jim Fleming, to assemble their troops under arms, without packs, just ammunition and water canteens. Justin knew what that meant: The enemy was nearby.

Although he had started his military life as a drummer boy, he hated the sound of drums. That maddening noise, the rattle of the snare drums calling the troops to arms, made him grind his molars in chagrin and dread as he gathered his gun, powder horn, and bullet bag and hurried to formation. His company milled and formed. Its commander, Captain Arbuckle, a rugged Scot in his early thirties, was one of those handsome, able, fearless men who inspired bravery in men who could be emboldened. But he made timid men like Justin feel so inadequate that they almost hated him for it. Arbuckle was a successful citizen of the gentry at home, and had been a commissioner and a justice of the peace in Botetourt County. But as a life-long hunter, trapper, and surveyor, he was more at home in the wilderness. Having been one of the first whitemen to trek the old buffalo trail down to the mouth of the Kanawha, he had been the guide and main scout for Colonel Lewis's army in this campaign.

Now, to the background racket of drums and shouts, he bellowed to his company the facts they needed to know.

"Boys, hear this:

"The big chief Cornstalk thought he'd snake down and surprise us this fine mornin'. Our scout found the Indian camp three miles up there, five acres o' braves packed nose to tail. Aiming to catch us in bed. But 'e won't, eh? Listen, now: Two regiments will march out to push 'em back so they can't corral us down here on the point. Colonel Field will hold the rest in reserve, including this company, sorry to say. But we might get a chance to fight. Mind all your weapons, not just your guns. Savages in the woods fight close. Your hatchet and knife are like to save your hide. Swear to me, gents: Y'll not let them pass!"

The men shouted in fierce agreement, but Justin was almost sick with dismay. The Indians were at most three miles—not fifty miles on the other side of the Ohio! And the army wasn't up to half strength yet. It was waiting here for Colonel Christian's regiment coming down the Kanawha to catch up, with plans then to join Governor Dunmore's two thousand troops who were marching down the Ohio. The whole great Virginia army would then parade to the Shawnee towns to frighten them into submission. But now . . .

As usual, he thought, *our officers underestimate the savages. As if they would be fools enough to wait for us to reach full strength!* This whole damned wilderness was full of Indian hunters, scouts, and runners, and they always knew where every part of the army was. A thousand men with five hundred packhorses and a hundred beef cattle was too big to hide. These colonels had fought Chief Cornstalk before, and should have remembered how alert and smart he was. Had they imagined he was just going to hang back and let the army march right into his people's towns?

Because he was so scared, Justin was angry at the stupidity of the officers who had put his life into such danger. Fear gave him lucidity, and his fearful imagination magnified every dire possibility into a tragic certainty. If a horde of Indians was this close to this unprepared and understrength army, the end of it was sure to be a massacre. He had seen exactly that when he served under General Braddock as a drummer boy twenty years before. Braddock, too, had underestimated the savages, and that had been the end of him and his whole overweening army. Justin stood here in rank keeping a tight sphincter and watching the advance regiments march upslope toward the woods, toward certain disaster, drums rattling.

Damn, damn, damn! he thought.

These two forward regiments, Colonel Fleming's and that of Colonel Charlie Lewis, the commander's brother, were ill-trained militia troops in drab linsey frocks but their drums were thrilling and terrible. Captain Arbuckle used his minutes in reserve to tell his sixty militiamen what they needed to know about the strategy of this coming battle.

"They must be kept back or chased off. This point o' land is a trap, two rivers flanking us. The farther we push, the thinner their line. Indians don't hold a line long anyhoo, once ye hit 'em solid. This shouldna take much o' the morn, boys. Now stand ready."

Soon it was time for the reserves to move, and they started up the gradual slope through the colorful autumn woods, leaving the smoky camp, the supplies, cattle, and packhorses behind under a guard company. Justin was once again doing the unthinkable: marching his cringing flesh toward lethal peril.

Footfalls crushed autumn leaves and fallen acorns. Men breathed shallow breaths, some wheezing with congested lungs. Gun butts clunked and clacked against sidearms. Drums chattered near and far along the front, which now stretched nearly a mile, from the Ohio almost to the Kanawha. Would all this ominous murmuring and chattering of the army's advance discourage the Indians and chase them away? It could happen; Indians often reassessed their chances and backed off to fight under better circumstances. But Justin had little hope of that. This morning his dread was total.

He was in the second rank of Captain Arbuckle's company. He was glad to have men in front of him. The troops were trained to deliver gunfire from the front rank, which then would kneel to reload while the second rank delivered its fire over them. Justin had studied war enough to know that such fire was effective on an open field, but it would scarcely work in these thick woods, where the ranks were uneven, weaving and swerving around huge trees and clambering over rotting downwood, broken ground, boulders, thickets, fern, and brush.

Captain Arbuckle strode along at the right of his company, sword drawn, his tricorn hat brim and his strong chin jutting forward like the symbol of his bold Scottish determination. The officers, like the troops, wore coarsely woven hunting frocks, but theirs were cleaner, almost white, their only sign of rank being their swords and the wide, crimson sashes around their waists. The Indians, of course, knew rank when they saw it, and the officers would attract the first musket balls and arrows as carrion attracts flies. It was not good to be anywhere near an officer, but here was Justin trudging along not eight or ten feet from the conspicuous Captain Matthew Arbuckle, and even closer to the captain were two of his brothers, John and William. The Arbuckle family might well be seriously reduced in these next few minutes, Justin imagined.

Oh, what folly, he thought: *stamping straight along like walking targets toward the savages, who know the art of invisibility!* In his quaking heart he cursed John Murray, earl of Dunmore, the Virginia governor who had mobilized this invasion of an Indian domain, which should have been none of his concern.

It was an axiom that Justin Case the teacher had arrived at—but seldom stated aloud—that most of the trouble in the world came from the top down and was suffered by those below—children, savages, workingmen, foot soldiers. Damn governors, he thought. Damn generals! Damn kings! Damn it all!

He was dry in the mouth and short of breath. This advance into the rough was terrifying. Soldiers who had expected to rampage through unsuspecting villages of squaws and elders and children, for rapine and trophies, were instead up against the exact opposite: The warriors who were usually away from their towns hunting at this time of year were instead congregated here to attack this army, if the scout's report was true.

Justin peered ahead among the dark tree trunks and scrub, sometimes squinting against a ray of sunrise penetrating the yellow and scarlet foliage, now and then catching a glimpse of the river down on his right. Sometimes he glanced at the captain, or along the uneven lines of ragged, rumpled, stubble-jawed militiamen slogging and stumbling forward in their dirty homespun, some bareheaded, most wearing droopy-brimmed felt hats, handkerchiefs, or shapeless, hand-sewn caps of cloth or varmint skins. All probably were scared, despite their long guns, their tomahawks and knives and pistols, despite all the boasting and threatening they had done all along the march. The scout had dampened their bravado with his account of a warrior swarm. Weathered faces were wan with fear, the pallor making every visage a plain, round target in the woods.

But they would be brave, damn them, when it came to it. Because they were marching with their countrymen, to whom they had bragged and boasted, with whom they would live out the rest of their lives and reputations. They hardly dared be cowards.

The rattling, droning bustle of the moving army was suddenly overpowered by a thunder of gunshots, immediately accompanied by that hair-raising trill of the war cry from countless throats ringing through the woods upslope. Justin was nearly unmanned by fright. A cascade of shivers ran from his scalp to his hips and he nearly stumbled as his feet resisted taking another step toward danger. He had to clench himself to keep from unloading his bowels.

The drummer had stopped his sticks in astonishment. The whole company seemed to have hesitated, breathless, to listen to the hellish uproar, which sounded very close although there was not yet a sight of anything except billowing smoke. Now the gunfire was a steady roar, near and far, the war trills sounded fanatical, and now voices were bellowing and bawling closer by: frantic commands, screams of rage and pain. Stray musket balls whiffled through the fall foliage. Captain Arbuckle and the other reserve company commanders along the line were looking to each other as if for a hint of what orders they should give: wait, or advance?

Before they could give either command, the woods in front of them seemed to rush into motion. Hundreds of figures were coming down through the woods running at full tilt, some falling.

They were not Indians, as Justin had feared at first, but soldiers in mad retreat, some stumbling, a few pausing to shoot back at the demons behind them, some helping others limp along. As far as Justin could see in either direction through the woods, they were fleeing rearward. It was, apparently, the whole army. His heart quaked. He wanted to turn and run with them, because if the regiments were in such flight, the Indians would in a moment be here on their heels.

A Botetourt County Militia ensign, hatless, eyes bugged with fear and mouth twisted, his frock bloody, came running straight toward Captain Arbuckle, sobbing, "Colonel Fleming's hit! Most every officer's hit! It's hopeless."

With one quick grab of his left hand, Arbuckle seized the pitiful young officer by the shoulder of his coat, stopped him, and spun him about. "Damn ye, milkliver! Turn to your duty, or I'll run this blade up y'r tail!" He thrust him forward. But the youth ducked out of reach and scampered on toward the rear after the other panicked troops. The woods upslope were swarming with motion, gunsmoke billowed through slanting sunbeams, and the nerve-jangling war cries were loud and close. Every fiber of Justin's being yearned to flee, and like that aggregate impulse that wheels a flock of birds as one, he felt the whole company around him on the verge as well.

Except the captain. Arbuckle was a force in himself. He yelled into the drummer's ear, drew a pistol from his sash, and, pointing it and his sword toward the enemy ahead, yelled something to his company and charged with his teeth bared. Perhaps other company commanders of the reserve regiment were doing the same, perhaps not. Gunsmoke was already beginning to hang in the breathless woods and veil everything in the distance, and Justin was too scared to look around. Captain Arbuckle's force of spirit began to draw his soldiers like a magnet, and they surged forward. "Oh God," Justin groaned. "I can't!" But he tried. He gathered himself to charge and started forward. He stumbled on a root and pitched forward onto all fours, fingers painfully crunched between his gun and the ground. At that moment a thundering volley of gunshots roared over him, so close he could feel their percussion in the air. Then the dreadful ululation of the war cry rose to a mad pitch. He felt an arrow nick his ear in its hissing passage, drops of warm blood from somewhere spattered on the backs of his hands, and a man from the front rank fell backward upon him.

Others right and left were grunting, reeling, falling.

Justin shoved the fallen man off himself and was ready to rise when more gunfire cracked and boomed, almost in his face, it seemed, and he decided to stay down.

The gunfire was deafening; shouts and screams mingled with the piercing war whoops. Everything was moving above and around him. The air he gasped was thick with the familiar sulfurous odor of gunpowder. He could not decide whether to flee or play dead, and so he remained as if paralyzed, on hands and knees, not yet willing to look up for fear of what he would see. He was afraid that the actual first sight of painted demon warriors would unnerve him totally, as it had done twenty years before, as it did each night in nightmares. As he shifted his weight off his mashed fingers, he became aware with misery and self-loathing that he had voided into his breeches.

Peering from under his hat brim left and right, he saw chaos. Several militiamen close by were fallen or falling. Some stood, shooting back. Some were turning to run. An arrow went into a man's mouth. Justin had glimpses of crimson that was not blood; it was the sash around Colonel Fleming's waist. The colonel's face was a chalk-white grimace. He was being dragged back from the battle line by a lieutenant and the flag boy, and Captain Arbuckle had stopped to help them.

Already the smoke was so dense that Justin could see only a few yards, but that was enough to show him that the ranks were breaking and falling back. Muzzle flashes flared yellow in the low-lying banks of smoke; chips of bark and leaf flew everywhere in the sunbeams as musket balls whistled and whacked through the woods. Wounded men were crawling and calling to God and to their comrades, but the gunfire and war whoops were so overpowering that the tormented ones seemed to be moving their mouths soundlessly. Justin was terrified of getting up or moving because he didn't want to rise to where the bullets and arrows swarmed. But at last enough sense came to him that he knew he couldn't stay here. Any moment the warriors would charge through here in pursuit of the retreating troops. He dreaded everything. But most of all he dreaded the thought of being caught alive by them.

Like a crawdad, he began scrambling backward and sideways after the retreating troops, never quite turning his back on the Indian line. He had his thumb over the cock of his flintlock, ready to shoot any warrior who might come right at him, but he wasn't intending to shoot just any Indian he saw. They were mad enough as it was, and it seemed foolhardy to draw vengeance upon himself. He was, in the midst of battle, trying to be neutral. He knew that was ridiculous, but he was a craven with soiled breeches, intent only upon staying alive and unhurt, too intelligent for delusions of personal heroism or glory. It would have suited him to have a living wall of soldier flesh between himself and those savages. Maybe that was why he had never condescended to become a casual comrade of any militiaman. He would have acquiesced to let any one of them die to save him, but it wasn't in him to return the favor.

This, then, was Private Justin Case of the Botetourt County, Virginia, Militia on October 10, 1774, determined not to die of wounds or heart failure, if he could possibly get through this day. But it was still early morning, and this whole thousand-man army already appeared to be in a plight as dire as the one General Braddock had been in nearly twenty years ago. And this time there was nowhere to retreat, as there had been in those Pennsylvania woods. At the army's back today were two converging rivers. Camp Point Pleasant, as the bivouac had been named, was a trap.

Justin knew these damned men. Many of them were hunters and veterans, and they were tough, proud, and stupid. They would rally somewhere, he was afraid, and feed their courage on their hatred of Indians, and would probably keep a battle going as long as they could—a battle from which he could not hide.

He slithered over the roots of a giant oak and down behind it, abrading himself painfully in his haste. Glancing about, he saw the men of his company taking cover in a ragged line and reloading their long guns. Now they would fight like hunters and marksmen, not like the orderly walking targets their officers expected them to be.

Musket balls were still splattering the vegetation everywhere, often thudding into flesh. The troops lay low behind logs, roots, and rocks, squinting into the stinking gunsmoke for targets: a moving silhouette, a figure darting between trees, an archer rising to send an arrow. But those targets were rare in the dense smoke as yet; the Indians were almost invisible. The best thing to shoot at was a place where a muzzle blast had just flared. Mostly that was what the men were shooting at, in the hope of hitting a warrior who had just fired.

But the Indians were shooting at muzzle blasts, too, and soldiers all along the line were being hit before they could duck and reload. Justin wanted no part of that lethal repartee of lead. Instead, he was trying to increase his distance from the combat without being too conspicuous. No one had any attention to spare for him, anyway.

Ordinarily, junior officers ranged behind the troops to stop—or if necessary, shoot—deserters. But he saw no officers; this battle line had become not a rank but an array of desperate and cunning individuals, without visible leadership, each practicing the killing art as effectively as he knew how. To most of them, it meant killing the way they were used to killing: as hunters of large game.

It was just as well that Colonel Fleming was out of action, Justin thought; if not, he would be waving his glorious sword and ordering everyone to charge and drive out the red devils, and soon everyone would have been dead. Instead the men were fighting as the Indians usually fought.

On the other hand, the Indians were not fighting as they usually fought. Instead of darting away before the army's first advance, instead of falling back and then drawing the troops into ambush pockets, trying to flank the companies, these Indians seemed to have held a well-disciplined defensive line, and delivered as much fire as they could, and then counterattacked. Even in his panting state of fear, Justin was aware of that curiosity; it was not exactly as he had feared or expected.

He was aware, too, of certain voices he had been hearing through the din: loud, rich, clarion voices, like bugles in battle. One was a man's voice, strong, full of command. The other—he was not sure what it was; it might have been a wolf howling. Or the voice of a boy or woman. Or even a spirit song of some strange sort. It might even have been some ringing in his own head, some echoing tone produced by the percussive gunfire in his ears, or by the constant frightful ululation of the war whoops. In his frantic mind, unwilling to face the awful reality of battle, that eerie but beautiful cry was beginning to anchor his attention, haunting him, puzzling him. Maybe it was the voice of a guardian angel, or maybe it was the siren song of military glory itself. Or perhaps Justin was just imagining it.

Suddenly now those voices grew louder, more thrilling. The chorus of war cries surged to a vibrant intensity. Justin, who still had not fired a single shot, tensed with panic and raised his head enough to see something besides roots. He went cold. Everything in front of him was coming at him in a rush.

The Indians, hundreds of them, had broken from cover and were making a charge. Justin knew that no creature is faster or more reckless than an Indian hunter-warrior rushing to the kill. Now here they were, coming by hundreds.

His most cunning inventions of self-preservation would not help him now. There was nothing for it but craven, headlong flight, or trying to kill whoever tried to kill him. Even those measures would at best preserve him only until another lethal moment.

His reluctant hand cocked the flintlock, and he rose to kneel. At that moment he was deafened by a muzzle blast, and his cheek and hand were burned by its sparks. An oncoming warrior lurched in mid-stride but hurtled on by his momentum and collided with the oak tree. Justin had not a moment even to glance aside at the outcome of that, because there now loomed before him a savage warrior, a nightmare of sinew and bared teeth, face painted black on one side, crimson on the other, bounding forward at pantherlike speed with a cocked arm aiming some sort of club, his crazed eyes right on Justin. There was no time to shoulder and aim; by good chance Justin was pointing his long gun where he was looking, and when he reflexively jerked the trigger his ball hit the warrior with enough force to slow him. He came reeling through the gunsmoke sideways, on tiptoe, hands upstretched as if in some graceful dance. The warrior landed against Case hard enough to wrench every tendon in his body and bowled him over backward in the leaves. Justin fought desperately to get the lean young Indian off him before realizing that he was dead. The body was musky with bear oil, and its leaking blood ran warm all over his hands.

By now most of the gunfire was farther up on the right. The din close by was now all voices, blows, and scufflings.

As Justin shuddered and whimpered and struggled under the carcass, he knew he was in the midst of a hand-to-hand, face-to-face, screaming, cursing brawl. Feet shuffled in the leaves, men grunted and slammed at each other with anything they had in their hands, knives and tomahawk blades flashed and slashed. There was no time for him to consider the remarkable fact that he had at last killed an Indian warrior, or to exult in it. He certainly was not emboldened by it. If a dying Indian could hit him that hard and painfully, he wanted nothing to do with any live one.

His one crucial purpose now was to find a place to hide until the battle moved elsewhere.

So he quit struggling, made himself as small and still as possible, and hoped he was well enough hidden under the Indian he had killed.

Covered with leaves, blood, shit, and inert flesh, he lay and whimpered and waited, trying not to think of all the names there were for him: *coward, poltroon, dastard, craven* . . .

Unfortunately, he was an educated man, a teacher, and he knew all the words for what he was.

It seemed a miracle: By late morning, Justin still had not been discovered. The battle had swept back and forth over this stretch of ground two or three times: charges by the Indians, countercharges by the Virginians, periods of crossfire between the two lines, and outbreaks of hand-to-hand fighting where forays ran into each other. At one point, as the Indians were retreating, they picked up their dead and wounded, including the one Justin had been hiding under. But, knowing it was their custom to retrieve their fallen, he had by that time crawled out from under the corpse while the battle was elsewhere, had retrieved and reloaded his long gun, and kept slithering and scooting downslope toward the bank of the Kanawha.

There, he hoped, he might somehow hide in the shore brush or wade to some safe place in the shallows. The river was low this season, and the fighting was up in the woods; if nothing else, he could bury himself in the mud and be invisible until this carnage was over.

He had passed corpses and moaning wounded, whites and Indians both. He saw a Virginian who sat on the ground groaning with his face in his hands and his whole head matted with blood from a hole where his scalp had been removed. Justin felt pity for him but crept on past in order not to be delayed in his escape. Fortunately for Justin, the man was blinded by his own blood and, surely, his agony, too.

Smoke mingled with fog and hung low in the dense, still air through the early part of the morning, keeping outlines vague, which helped him move unseen. Once he came upon a gut-shot, supine young warrior, evidently in a patient mortal struggle against pain, his eyes wide open toward leaves overhead, his mouth open, emitting raspy breaths. The youth saw Justin and made a summoning gesture with one blood-covered hand. Justin could have put him out of his suffering with a quiet tomahawk stroke, which might have been what the lad wanted; or he might have wanted to lure him within reach to kill him with his last bit of strength. But Justin wouldn't go near him; he was busy getting away.

The battle din had never entirely subsided. Gun blasts, shouts, howls continued in the near and far distance, and, above all the other voices, he could still hear that one remarkable male voice that he presumed to be a war chief, and now and then that haunting woman-like voice, which was closer every time he heard it. In his fear-deranged state of mind, the approach of that spiritlike wail chilled and haunted him.

He had not yet reached the riverbank when he saw Indians retreating upslope toward him. He was behind their line, and the battle was returning.

Heart pounding, he looked for anyplace to hide. A giant, half-rotted tree trunk lay across a dry rill, mere inches of space under it, the dip full of drifted yellow maple leaves. He scrambled down as far as he could squeeze in under the mossy black log, gasping, and reached out to scoop leaves in over himself.

Now he was in a blind, unable to see the dangers that he could hear sweeping back upon him. His only hope was invisibility, and he hoped he had created it well enough.

Maybe he had. The battle was soon all around his burrow. The warriors were being beaten back by yet another assault of the army's right wing, his own regiment. Now and then he heard Captain Arbuckle's strong voice haranguing them. Justin trembled and tried to shrink into the ground. The Indians were retreating through this very place. For a few minutes, some unseen warrior was using this same rotting log as cover, almost upon him. Justin could hear him panting, could hear the slide of his ramrod, could hear him get off a shot, could hear him shout a quick word in his language to someone nearby, could hear the clicking and sliding sounds as the panting warrior reloaded once more, then the rustle of leaves as he fled.

After another interminably long period of uproar all around him, Justin became aware of words in his own language, spoken in gasping, exhausted, rasping tones. Men braver than he. One voice sounded like that of a townsman he knew, a man named Blakey. But he couldn't be sure.

"Claude, I'm shot!" somebody cried.

"If that big bastard'd stand still, I'd—"

"Watch out, Jones!"

Then a deafening fusillade.

"What the hell's a woman—"

"Ghaaahhh! Oh oh oh oh oh! Oh help . . ."

And that mysterious voice, not far off. He was sure now that it was a woman's voice. He breathed the smell of leaf mold and cowered there, still invisible. He felt the soft jolt of what might have been a ball hitting the punky log under which he lay. It was still too lethal out there for a thinking man who valued his life. *But thank God,* he thought, *nobody knows about this. About me.*

Then in his exhaustion, burrowed in leaves, he lost all sense of time and progression; the battle was not a process with an outcome, but merely a noise storm, perhaps an eternal one; he would be here forever like a grub under a log. But it didn't matter.

He came out of that, not like waking from sleep, but by consciously realizing that he had been in such a state. The thunderous shooting and shrieking and howling continued, and he tried to reassemble his faculties, to make out what he could of the sway of battle, in order to plan how to get out, to survive, just to do something, anything . . .

He heard and felt footfalls; there was much running nearby again. But now dominating everything in his reawakening awareness was that thrilling female voice, or spirit call, or whatever it was. And it was very close by.

He had to see what it was. He raised his head and brushed away leaves, pushing his long gun out in front of him, his eyes seeking the source of what his ears were hearing.

Just ahead of him seethed a panorama of desperate activity: painted, blood-smeared warriors leaping and darting, falling, dragging wounded warriors to cover, yelling and yipping, kneeling to shoot their muskets or bows.

And in their forefront, in plain sight by the root bole of his own sheltering log, towered an Indian woman, tall, lithe, and muscular as a man but shown by nakedness to be a woman. She wore only warpaint, blood smears, and a loincloth, a tomahawk in one hand, pistol in the other, her long hair bound back by a leather wrap. She was crying to the warriors in that hair-raising voice, calling encouragement or commands, as if she was a chief herself.

Shivers cascaded from Justin's temples down his ribs; he had never seen anything so terrible, or so beautiful. All the mayhem of the battlefield momentarily faded and she shone in the center and her voice dominated all the uproar. Bullets were chewing the woods all around her, as if every militiaman downslope behind him were shooting at her but couldn't hit her. Her eyes were blazing; her teeth flashed white. She was splendid, too fantastic to be real.

He heard someone running up through the leaves behind him, close to his log. The woman warrior, apparently seeing that person, cocked her right arm and threw her tomahawk with great force. It whiffed right over Justin and struck something; the next thing he saw was a militiaman pitching past and falling sideways in the leaves, the tomahawk blade embedded in his gullet.

This man, gushing blood and gaping like a fish, was Blakey, a man of Justin's own unit. With a sudden reflex, Justin shifted on his elbows and raised his musket to shoot the woman who had thrown the hatchet, in fear that she had seen him and would kill him next.

But she had turned and was sprinting away. He saw brown buttocks, the tail of her loincloth, her long, muscular legs, her moccasins, saw her vanish beyond the end of the log. He rose to shoot over it, and there she was, ten yards away. She had stopped to help a warrior—a painted savage who looked like a Negro instead of an Indian—carry another wounded Indian out of danger.

And now, rushing down toward Justin was a warrior who had just seen him, one with a lance, his painted face exultant and brutal. Justin swung his weapon around and fired. Through the billow of smoke he saw the attacker tumble.

"Ye got 'im, Case! Yihee! Good!" someone yelled.

Soldiers were rushing up now, charging the retreating Indians. Justin was again amid troops of his own unit. He couldn't turn and run now. He knelt and drew his ramrod to begin reloading. A voice said, "Case! Thought th' heathens had got you!"

"No! I . . ."

They had no idea! They thought he had been fighting all this time! If they'd had any thoughts of him at all, that's what they'd thought! His mind was swimming, swooping. His disgrace was hidden.

"On, boys! We got 'em runnin'!" the captain was yelling.

A woman warrior! he thought, and then he could think of nothing else. *A savage woman, braver than I am?* He remembered that he had been hearing her voice since the beginning of the battle. For hours, a woman had been fighting with the kind of celerity and boldness she had just shown here?

Suddenly, his admiration for her courage lifted his soul to a height he had never felt, not through drums and fifes, or even the bagpipes of Braddock's Highlanders. Not through oratory, not through the study of philosophers. Until he had seen that savage woman with her whole life blazing in her face, he had not sensed the real height and breadth of life. With the white teeth of her screaming mouth, she had eaten his cowardice, and he had stood up in the presence of death to do combat. She had done more for him than anyone or anything ever had done.

With his musket reloaded, he slid the ramrod home under the

musket, gave a yell, and charged with his comrades up the slope after the fleeing Indians.

By midday the troops looked like chimneysweeps, clothes and skin besmudged by gunpowder and muzzle soot, stained by blood and tears. Many of their officers were dead, including Charles Lewis, the commanding officer's brother. Colonel Fleming had been out of the battle with severe chest and arm wounds since the first fire, and his Botetourt regiment mostly presumed that, if they survived this day, they would have the duty of burying him.

Private Justin Case was amazed to find himself still alive this long after his emergence from the cocoon of cowardice. He had stayed on the line with Captain Arbuckle's company through several fierce counterassaults by the Shawnees, still not feeling anything like bravery, but not running to hide as before. He had fired countless rounds at the swift figures and reloaded, lying on his left side while musket balls hummed and sizzled over and around him. Once, in his panic, he had left his ramrod in the gun barrel and fired it into a warrior's guts. It had not taken long to find another ramrod. The woods were littered with the guns and equipment of the fallen.

He had wood splinters in his right cheek, from a twig shattered by a close musket ball; the blood all over that side of his face had dried and, when he had a rare moment to think of it, he remembered the warrior with half his face painted red. He imagined that he must look like that now. He knew that if he survived this day, he would eventually have to reconcile in his soul that disgraceful poltroonery of the morning, but at least his comrades in arms would never know of it; his bloody face was now his badge of combat, not the dried shit in his breeches.

There seemed to be no hope anymore of forcing the Indians back. They now occupied a rise of ground extending nearly from the Ohio to the Kanawha, and the army was too depleted and fatigued to take it by frontal assault. These Indians were too determined, and apparently they were uncommonly well organized and led. Justin had heard Captain Arbuckle say that he was sure that Chief Cornstalk was their leader. "That," he said. "That's his voice." It was the powerful male voice that Justin had been hearing all day above the din of battle.

And still, now and then, he kept hearing the plangent voice of that wondrous woman warrior he had seen. In the midst of this seemingly endless battle, her image flashed in his mind whenever he heard the voice.

In the afternoon Captain Arbuckle led his company through the mud and brush along the Kanawha River bank, under the shelter of its bluff, moving upstream. They moved in single file, Indian-like, keeping under cover as much as possible, keeping an eye up toward the bluff for any sign of Indian scouts.

Justin was near the head of the column. Captain Arbuckle's broad shoulders were always in sight ahead; just behind him was his brother William. None of the Arbuckle brothers had been hit during the long storm of musket balls and arrows, though about a third of the company had been wounded, and several killed. Two other badly reduced companies followed Arbuckle's. One was that of Captain John Stuart, a close friend of Arbuckle's, a fellow gentryman.

Justin was glad to be out of the thunderous peril of that battleground for a while; it seemed he had been there forever. But his nerves still jangled with anxiety and his heart beat fast, because he was advancing into a new and different danger. His ears were ringing from the constant concussion of guns, his eyes burned and watered, his throat and nose were irritated and dense with the hellish smell of gunpowder smoke, and he ached in every part of his body. The wood splinters in the side of his face still felt like wasp stings. Above and to the left, the gunfire and howling kept on and on—from the sound of it, still deadlocked.

This sortie was Captain Arbuckle's idea, a desperate measure to break that deadlock and put the Indians in disarray. It was Arbuckle's idea because he, of all the officers, was the army's primary hunter and scout and knew the ground. And of course he was daring enough to carry it out himself.

A few hundred yards up this riverbank was the mouth of a creek. The gully through which that creek flowed provided a hidden approach, Arbuckle believed, around behind the left flank of the Indians' battle line. The bluff of the creekbank should dominate the Indians' flank, if these companies could get upon it without being discovered.

The captain had explained all this in his usual terse way before the detachment started up the river: The Indians, he felt, were sustaining their attack on sheer spirit and good leadership; Indians seldom had many good guns, or adequate ammunition, and these must be at the breaking point by now, their lines stretched thin along a mile front. A sudden burst of fire from behind might discourage them at last, Arbuckle said—especially if they mistook this body for Colonel Christian's regiment, which was expected to arrive down the Kanawha at any time.

It was a fine idea. Colonel Andrew Lewis, the commandant, trying to sustain his own morale despite the death of his brother, had leapt to it as a hope for victory. The one great drawback of the plan was the extreme risk to the attacking companies. If they were seen too soon by the Indians, they could be caught in the low ground, beyond any hope of rescue, enveloped, and quickly wiped out.

For that matter, Private Justin Case, the thinking soldier, thought, *what the captain left unsaid is that even if we* do *surprise them completely, they could nevertheless surround and massacre us anyway. It's the most likely thing they will do!*

Damn, damn, damn! God, why did you put me under command of such a brave and warlike Scot!

Now, as they approached the mouth of Crooked Creek, Justin was almost as scared as he had been before the battle began.

Captain Arbuckle seemed able to see things that were invisible to most of his soldiers. As they moved up the ravine of Crooked Creek, he gave a hand signal to stop the column, and summoned up a sharpshooter with a rifle. He pointed out an Indian sentry high on the creek bluff ahead, and had to point him out again, but the sharpshooter could not even see him. So Arbuckle took the man's rifle and fired it. Justin saw the warrior only when he toppled and slid a little way down the slope.

Justin was terrified that the rifle shot would give away their approach, but there was still so much shooting on the battle line that it probably had not even been noticed. The captain led his column on a few hundred paces more, then stopped them again. He pointed to a young brave, not much more than a boy, coming down the leaf-covered slope bearing two wooden pails with rope bails.

The creek at this point probably was the water source for the warriors on the line. It was almost certain that the youth would see the soldiers while he was down here filling the pails.

The captain turned and signaled for his followers to drop down. Then he vanished into the brush.

A moment later he reappeared, bloody sword in hand, and summoned the column forward. Justin saw blood in the creek water before he stepped over the boy's body, which lay beheaded on the bank. One pail, and the head, lay swaying in the current of the bloody water.

John Arbuckle joked into Justin's ear: "Matthew scalps 'em a mite close, eh?"

The captain left the creekbed and began climbing up the wooded slope to the left. Crouching at the top and glancing about, he gestured the command for everyone to come up, to come quickly. Justin wished he could hide. But there was no safe place, and he was surrounded by his fellows. And he wanted never again to know that shame of cowardice he had felt this morning. The bluff was beautiful at close hand: ferns curling in the carpet of fallen leaves, and above, the great yellow-red canopy of foliage, leaves drifting down. Would he ever see the woodland beauty again?

One falling maple leaf in his view suddenly disintegrated into yellow specks, a reminder that there were as many bullets in the air as falling leaves. The steady thunder of gunfire, which had been muffled a little, grew terribly loud as he climbed out of the creek gully and onto the promontory.

At the top it was just as Captain Arbuckle had foreseen: There to the west lay the left flank of the Indians' battle line, in plain sight, as far as could be seen through the woods and battle smoke.

Arbuckle gave the troops no time to enjoy the dominating view. He made them form a front of three ranks on the rise and began firing an enfilade into the flank of the exposed Indian line. The first rank fired a volley, then knelt to reload, and the second fired over them, then the third.

The effect was devastating. Realizing they were caught between two fires when several of their warriors were wounded by the volleys from behind them, the Indians scurried from their hiding places and began a withdrawal, pausing behind trees to return fire. A roar of cheers came from the troops below who had been deadlocked for so long, and their drummers began sounding; there would be a charge now from below.

"One volley more, lads!" Captain Arbuckle bellowed, "then reload and stand ready to charge!" The troops cheered and leveled their pieces onto the retreating Indians; here at last was a chance of actually gaining the field after a day of frustration and loss. Justin had reloaded, and awaited the order to fire.

Some of the Indians were returning fire as they retreated. "I want Cornstalk's scalp," he heard the captain say to someone. "I'll give it to Colonel Lewis for the loss of 'is brother!"

The three ranks raked the Indian lines again, reloaded, then followed Captain Arbuckle as he sprinted down the slope among the trees with his bloody sword held high and a pistol in his left hand. Everyone yelled as they tore down the slope with reckless jarring strides, leaping over logs and roots and Indian corpses, all this through a languid sifting-down of beautiful maple leaves like a golden snow. Gunfire had slackened here but was still heavy in the distance along the line toward the Ohio. There was more shouting, it seemed, even than before, as the troops below charged up and the Indians expressed their confusion and spread the warning down the line. Off somewhere to the north, that deep voice kept sounding, the one he believed to be Cornstalk's, and Captain Arbuckle was running recklessly ahead, toward it, as if he might have forgotten everything else except the prospect of getting Cornstalk's scalp for the colonel. Justin followed him close.

And then he almost ran into him when the captain stopped abruptly at the edge of a stony outcrop and pointed his pistol down.

Justin expected death to happen right under his nose again. He stepped up beside the captain with his flintlock cocked, aimed down where the captain's pistol was pointed, and went stock-still at the sight.

Down behind the outcrop were two Indians. One was a garishly painted warrior, head shaved except for a scalplock braid at his crown, blood pouring from his mouth, the front of his deerhide tunic covered with crimson, a big man very badly wounded. He was slumped, half standing, held up by the other Indian, whose hands were under his arms, lifting. The Indian who was trying to haul him off the battlefield after the retreating warriors was sinewy and bare above the waist, with a full head of long, dark hair. Justin's heart, pounding from the excitement of battle and the pursuit down the slope, almost stopped when he saw who it was.

She was looking up, right into the muzzle of Captain Arbuckle's pistol, her face a grimace, lips stretched back to reveal those straight, white teeth, that incredible blaze in her eyes.

It was the woman he had seen in the battle below, the woman of the rich, wild voice. Under the tawny skin of her shoulders as she held up the wounded warrior, her straining muscles were like ropes, and the veins stood vivid in her neck. She looked from Captain Arbuckle's pistol into his face, standing utterly still. She glanced at Justin, whose gun was also aimed at her, and then back to Arbuckle. Both had their fingers on the triggers of their cocked weapons. Justin was frozen, unable to fire, but he expected the captain to shoot. He remembered the captain's vengeful fury over Colonel Lewis's death, and he expected the man to show no mercy. He expected to hear the pistol now.

The captain raised it a little to aim between her eyes. It was in his left hand and his sword was in his right. She must have been expecting to die then, but she didn't flinch. Strangely, though, her stare was not defiant, either.

"Officer soldier . . . You going to kill me and my brother? Do it, but God will damn you. Because Jesus calls for mercy . . . You see we are helpless."

It was plain English! *Jesus,* she had said! Mercy. And *God will damn you.*

For a long moment, nobody moved. Then Captain Arbuckle uncocked his pistol and aimed it skyward, away from her. Justin looked at the captain and saw something in his face that he knew he would never understand. In the distance, some of the retreating warriors taunted the soldiers, calling them "sonabitches" and "men in skirts."

The captain said, pointing with his sword at the half-conscious warrior, "Is this Cornstalk?"

"No. Cornstalk is far over there. You hear him."

They could hear him in the distance, that great voice.

Other soldiers had gathered around Captain Arbuckle and Justin, and they appeared eager to kill these two Indians.

"Take him away, lady," Arbuckle said. "God be wi' ye."

She backed away, hauling the wounded warrior, her eyes blazing at Arbuckle. "You will be remembered, soldier!" she called back.

"Let them go!" the captain snapped at his men. Then: "Come on, boys!" He waved his sword toward the fading Indian line. "We've won the day! Cornstalk's yonder! I want 'im!"

The thunder of battle was over. Now the forest was full of the screams and groans, and pleading and weeping of wounded men.

Under virtually every tree along the battle line there lay a scalped corpse or a militiaman too badly hurt to walk. Some had died sitting up with their backs resting against the roots of the great trees. Some lay half-covered by the beautiful red-and-yellow maple leaves that had been falling upon them all day. The dull gray and butternut of their clothing was spattered and soaked in blood hardly brighter than the fallen leaves. Justin, sickened and weakened, stood transfixed for a moment at the sight of an oak with a broad patch of its bark shot away, the pale sapwood beneath spattered with gore.

He could see dead and wounded militiamen everywhere he looked, but saw no sign of an Indian warrior anywhere. They had taken their dead and injured as they withdrew from the battlefield, just as he had seen the warrior woman doing. They never left them to be mutilated.

The captains, Arbuckle and Stuart, called their surviving men in around them. Arbuckle had to speak above the din of the suffering to make his order heard. "We've heavy work to do while there's light! Any ye find still breathing, carry them down to the surgeon. We'll need horses and litters for some. If a man can tell you how to carry 'im, he knows where he is hurt, so listen to 'im! Let's get it done, now. We'll fetch the dead down later."

The surgeon looked stricken. An overweight, florid man of middle age, he was working in torn flesh, blood draining off his elbows, cutting bullets out and stuffing lint gauze in, but he kept looking around at the groaning, writhing wretches who lay everywhere in the glade that was serving as hospital, shaking his head and muttering. And the troops kept bringing more down from the woods. Some limped between two soldiers; some were simply carried in like babies on the arms of strong men. Many were dead by the time they were carried in. Some died while the surgeon was cutting or splinting them.

"Drag that poor fellow over there," the surgeon said to Justin. "He's gone."

Justin himself was thoroughly sopping with blood by now. His count of wounded was well over a hundred, though the number was never precise because some died and some were moved and some were brought in while he was helping the surgeon do this or that.

Justin had taken it upon himself to stay and assist the surgeon because there were plenty of others to bring the casualties in, but few sensible enough or suited by heart for this sort of butchery upon the living.

Two rows of corpses had been laid out at the edge of the glade:

Two dozen commissioned officers, a full half of them, were in one row, and nearly fifty enlisted militiamen in the other.

Justin worked as in a trance. He fetched kettles of water, and jugs of whiskey for painkilling; he cut dressings from bolts of linen; he thumbed down squirting arteries and twitching meat while the surgeon seared them with the cauterizing iron; he held struggling men down while the surgeon put their gray guts back into their ripped bellies, or probed for bullets in their necks and jaws. He cut away blood-soaked frocks and shirts to help the surgeon find where the balls and blades had gone, while the wounded screamed or gurgled right in his ear. Colonel Lewis's body servant, a brawny black slave, helped restrain some wounded while they were being cut. Justin vaguely remembered that he had seen a Negro dressed as a warrior on the battlefield. Now and then the surgeon would look at Justin and say, "That was just the right thing to do. Good work, Case."

As they worked through the dusk, and into the night by torch and lantern light, numbed by the suffering, gasping with exhaustion, Justin gradually became the specialist in extracting arrows, except those whose points were embedded deep in the flesh or organs. One dared not try to pull an arrow back out unless it simply couldn't be passed on through. The easy ones were those that had entered one side of an arm or leg and protruded out the other; he would cut off the arrow shaft ahead of the fletching, give the soldier a gill of rum, and, while he was downing it, grasp the arrow by its tip with his swaddled right hand and suddenly draw the rest of the shaft through, then pack the wound with gunpowder.

One man from Captain Arbuckle's company had an arrow that had entered his open mouth, sliced his tongue, passed through his jaw muscle, locking his mouth wide open, and stopped with its point just beneath the skin under his left ear. Justin had seen it happen. The man had been drooling blood since morning. The surgeon at the moment was busy trying to keep an officer from bleeding to death, so Justin chose to get the arrow out himself. He cut the arrow shaft off close to the soldier's lips, the man groaning and gurgling blood. Then he sliced open the swelling under the ear, found the flint point with his fingers, and, with all his strength, pushed it with one hand and pulled it with the other as the soldier convulsed and rasped and spewed blood. When the arrow was out, the jaw unlocked and the wretch at last was able to close his mouth, which he did with much groaning and whimpering.

"Very neat indeed!" the doctor's voice said in Justin's ear. He had come close and watched the extraction. "Tent the wounds with lint, and then come help me with this gent over here . . ."

They were still working, tracking back and forth through a mud made of earth and blood, when day broke. They were glad to have light to work by again, though in the harsh light the trampled place looked like an abattoir, and Justin and the surgeon had been alleviating their aching fatigue with whiskey, and were stumbling, less steady of hand. Justin heard a bugle and drumroll, but didn't leave for muster because the surgeon said he couldn't spare him. "Truly, Case," he said, "I couldn't have gotten through the night without you. You're a natural physician, know it or not."

"No, I'd never thought . . ."

"When this campaign's over, come back to Rockbridge with me, and we'll get you a proper medical education. I do mean that."

During the night, someone had carried in the body of the militiaman Blakey from Arbuckle's company, the same man Justin had seen struck in the gullet by the woman warrior's thrown tomahawk. The tomahawk was no longer in the wound. It had been removed by someone, perhaps as a trophy, or even for reuse as a weapon during the battle back and forth over that ground.

But Blakey's bloody corpse evoked in Justin's memory that awful and memorable moment when he had at last raised himself from his abject cowardice and begun to fight like a soldier. The image of that mighty and agile woman returned to him in his exhaustion, in the half-stupor that all this carnage and exhaustion had put him into, and he remembered now that strange and remarkable heartening that he had taken from the sight of her courage in battle.

Justin Case had come through the longest and most horrible day of his life, and he had been so thoroughly transformed by it that he could scarcely remember how it had felt to be the person he was yesterday at this hour. Something had come into him from that woman, and he was the better for it. The Private Justin Case of yesterday would not have faced combat all day, or worked all night amid death and bloody agony; that previous self would have gone to hide and hate himself.

That woman. Beautiful and terrible. As he had never expected to see any woman. She, whoever she was, had changed him forever.

Through their efforts he and the surgeon had saved many lives and limbs. But they had failed to save many others. Some men they had repaired in such awful desperation had died anyway; others were still dying now, and in others there would be infections and crippling, and in the days to come there would have to be amputations of gangrenous arms and legs, and there would be raging fevers that would leave some of those veterans tetched in the head forever. Justin had seen old veterans like those all his life; some, no older than he, survivors of the Braddock massacre, were but dotty old shamblers back home in Virginia. Others had prospered as revered veterans, severe, hawk-faced, intimidating old silver-maned bombastics who had built legends around themselves upon the basis of a day's, an hour's, or even a minute's combat somewhere, by never letting anyone forget it.

After what he had gone through and done in the last circuit of the sun, Justin Case himself might go home and become a legend. Already the surgeon had sown in him the notion of becoming a prestigious physician someday, and he might carry around himself an aura of having battled the Indians in this horrific and famous frontier conflict. And what was more—of having saved scores of lives. There would even be old crippled soldiers in the community who could attest to it.

If, that is, he or any of this battered, stunned, and limping army ever should get home. Colonel Lewis's arrogant force had strutted down the Kanawha expecting to whip and subdue all the savages of the whole Middle Ground. From the looks of it, they had barely escaped the kind of fate that pompous General Braddock had suffered two decades earlier, up by the forks of the Ohio. Who had expected the Indians to catch Lord Dunmore's Virginian army divided like this, or to fight so bravely, so fiercely?

And who could say with confidence that the terrible war chief Cornstalk was even done with them yet? The Indians had withdrawn yesterday after being outflanked, true. But they certainly had not been routed, and had quite obviously not suffered losses to compare with this army's: seventy-five dead at least, half the officers killed, and perhaps 150 wounded. This army had been humbled by the savages, and it now sat here, far from home, in the heart of Indian country, licking its wounds and mourning its dead, only now digging the fortifications it should have used yesterday.

The Indians might come back today to finish the annihilation. It would be a good time for them to do that, before Lord Dunmore's two thousand reinforcements arrived down the Ohio.

The hardest and most extraordinary day of Private Justin Case's life might yet prove to be his last.

Maybe he would die today and never get back to Virginia. Anyway, he wasn't as afraid of dying as he had been yesterday morning. But now, somehow, he felt that he had more to live for, and he prayed that Cornstalk would not come back.

3

Here the women came, out along the beaten trail, their faces twisted with anxiety and shame and grief, and Nonhelema rode toward them, looking down on their faces, one by one, remembering what each of them had said as they clamored for war in the great, fierce council circle less than one moon since.

Nonhelema sat straight in the saddle and did not let them see in her face the pain and anger she felt. They could see the dried blood on her bandages, and on the clothes of her brother Silverheels who rode beside her, barely supporting himself with both hands clenched on the pommel of his saddle. They could see the grim fury in the face of Cornstalk, who rode on the other side of Silverheels, his own tunic bloodstained up to the shoulders.

She had no impulse to gloat. The women could see how wrong they had been to encourage the attack. They could recognize the horse of the war chief Pucsinwah, its saddle empty, being led by his son Chiksika, himself grimacing from bad wounds. The war chief, by custom, had been buried near the battleground where he had fallen,

as he had fallen in the dream. And there were many other horses returning without their riders, and some of the warriors who had been
their owners did not even have graves; their bodies had been thrown
in the rivers to keep the Long Knives from scalping or mutilating
them as the battlefront surged to and fro all day.

Nonhelema dreaded most seeing Methotase, who had dreamed
the fatal dream and who had begged the women to ask for peace
instead of war. Methotase, and all the other women, already knew
that the battle of the Kanawha had failed. Runners had already
brought that news back to the Shawnee towns. The new widows waiting beside the trail now had already grayed their faces with ashes and
raked their arms bloody with fingernails, filled their hair with dirt
and chaff, and started their year's mourning time in which they
would not bathe or change clothes, nor speak to anyone outside their
homes.

For every dead warrior left in the ground or the rivers at the
Kanawha, there came ten wounded warriors home in this dismal procession. Some were able to walk, if they could rest now and then beside the trail. Some could ride, if supported by a fellow horseman
alongside. Some lay unconscious on makeshift pole litters suspended
between horses. Two had bled to death during the terrible three-day
retreat, and their bodies were being brought home for burial. Qui-
eteh, the little medicine woman who had gone to the battleground
with the warriors, had stopped their bleeding with hematite stones,
had eased their pain with willow bark, had cleansed their wounds
with goldenseal. She had made teas for fevers and poultices for
wounds from roots and barks she carried in bags, so many kinds and
in such quantities that she had carried them on a packhorse. She and
old Change-of-Feathers, the principal shaman, had saved many lives
after the battle, even extracting musket balls from lungs and brains.
But more than a hundred warriors here in this procession were too
badly hurt to fight or hunt for a long time ahead.

And after the battle, many of the Shawnees' Mingo and Wyandot allies, who had clamored for the attack, had split off from the
Shawnees and departed in shame, leaving Cornstalk with only a few
hundred warriors, almost out of powder and ball. And the bigger part
of the Virginians' army was still coming down the Ohio, led by their
governor, while Colonel Lewis's troops, hurt but not destroyed, were
building a fort at the battleground and would probably join up with
the governor's army to come against the Shawnee towns here.

Cornstalk and Nonhelema took no joy from having been right. The consequences were too severe. He had sent word ahead that a Great Council would be held as soon as the warriors got home. Even the wounded would be brought into the council circle to hear Cornstalk explain the disaster they had brought upon themselves.

Nonhelema, so weary that her bones ached, kept her head up. So when her eyes fell upon Blue Goose, she seemed to be looking down her nose at her, with disdain.

It was not good to look like that at the women. For Blue Goose, though she had cried for war, was one of the women who had lost a son in battle. Nonhelema herself, with the help of her black man, Caesar, had dragged the mortally wounded son of Blue Goose off the battlefield.

Nonhelema thought, *I would not want to be Blue Goose—a woman who chose to send her own son off to die for no purpose.*

Cornstalk, the peace chief, could be harder to face than war itself. He was especially fearsome in the eyes of those who were wrong when he was right, and he was usually right.

Now he had been right in a most crucial matter, and his moral stature, even more than his physical stature, made him a giant in the center of the great Council House.

Cornstalk was still wearing his war shirt, whose sleeves were dark with the blood of whitemen he had killed in the battle, and of the wounded warriors he had carried out of danger on that battlefield. His eyes were too terrible to look at, and the people looked down or away when his gaze swept over them.

The ceremony of the prayer pipe was done by his uncle Moluntha, known as the king of the Mekoches, a revered old warrior-turned-peacemaker, bony and white-maned.

While the smoke still drifted, Moluntha sat down at Cornstalk's right. To their left sat Nonhelema, equally handsome and severe, a blood-darkened linen bandage on one arm, a scabbed, bruised cheekbone where a musket ball had barely missed her eye.

Cornstalk stood silent in the drifting smoke, his noble and haggard face lit from above by daylight through the smoke vent in the roof of the Council House.

This Council House was the biggest building in the Shawnee nation, more than a hundred paces long, with benches along log walls, and upright posts made of straight tree trunks supporting the ridge-pole high in the cobwebbed shadows above the cedarwood council fire. The hundreds of people in the building were shoulder to shoulder, knee to back. Around the center sat many other chiefs and headmen, many of them still in dusty, torn, and bloody war clothes: Black Hoof, Blue Jacket, Red Pole. And Black Snake, having been elected by the warriors to be the war chief after Pucsinwah was killed. Directly behind them were the chieftains Nimwha and the Walker, Captain Johnny, and lung-shot Silverheels, four brothers of Cornstalk and Nonhelema. Also near the center there sat or reclined the warriors who had been wounded in the battle, those not too severely hurt to attend.

It was toward the wounded ones that Cornstalk now directed his first words:

"You brave men. You fought better than anyone I ever saw.

"My heart is on the ground with sadness, because I must tell you that your pain and blood were wasted. Your bravery and strength did not stop the Long Knives; they are even closer now, and we are weakened. We have more widows and orphans. Our lead and powder are gone.

"Just a few days ago, remember, my brave sister Nonhelema and I asked the people to let us go and talk peacefully to the governor of Virginia. To tell him that he came wrongly accusing us of being his enemy, and to send him away. I believe that we could have done that. But your people said, *Go and attack them!*

"Now the Long Knives are close by, in full strength. And now we cannot tell them we are not their enemy, because we killed many of their officers and men. Now they come as victors, and they will tell us what we must do."

He let them think on that, then he said: "Or do you still want war? You, who said it was right to attack them: Is it not still right to attack them? Should it not be even more right to attack them, now that they are at our doors? Tell us that we should fight the invaders now, and we will do it again. With bows and clubs and spears, we will attack their guns. Now that they are full of vengeance for their dead, and now that they are close enough to catch our children and drown them in the creek, and catch our daughters and rape them on the ground, should we not fight them even more rightly, and with more fury? Now do your brave people want more war? Let them direct us so, and we will do it. It is for warriors to do what the people want. Tell us.

"But if you have no stomach to lose a war right here where you live, then tell us that, and we will go out on the field and meet that Virginia governor, and smoke with him, and hear his demands.

"My sister Nonhelema and my uncle Moluntha, and I, Hokoleskwa, we will go out and talk to them, as we wished to do before under better circumstances." He stared around at them for another long time, and Nonhelema could see in their shamed faces that they were not going to vote for war this time.

Cornstalk went on: "I tell you this: The Long Knives, Virginia and the other whiteman councils, will soon be fighting a war with the king of England. The British and the Long Knives will put us in between them, as the French and English did before.

"If we the People of the Southwind are to survive another of their wars, we had better be neutral. But if you want to fight again, you may do it without me. Take this and use it!" And with a motion that made them start and gasp, he drew his tomahawk from the sash about his waist, raised it high overhead, and flung it to stick in the ground at his feet.

Nonhelema looked up at his profile, and the expression she saw was of such contempt and grief that her throat swelled.

Here was a man who could be warlike in his demand for peace.

And when the vote was taken, all agreed to send out the peace emissaries. Even those, like some of her own brothers, who hated and distrusted the Long Knives like poisonous snakes, were ready to plead for mercy.

The scouts said that the army was still coming in two parts. It had not joined into one.

The part of the army the Shawnees had fought was coming up from the south, along the Scioto-sipe.

The governor's bigger part of the army had come up the Hockingsipe, from the southeast. The Shawnee towns, therefore, were being approached by two forces. Crops were being taken in as fast as the people could work, and the women and children were being readied to flee to the northwest, taking the harvest with them. Now all the people were very anxious to go and make talks.

At last the governor's bigger part of the army stopped and made a great, sprawling war camp a few miles up Scippo Creek to the east of the Shawnee towns. The runners came in and said that messengers were coming from the governor's camp, holding up a white flag. One of the messengers was a speaker of many tongues, a friend of the Indian agent McKee at Pittsburgh.

"Ah," Nonhelema said. "I expect Girty is the one. *Wehsah!* That is good! Girty never lies to Indians."

When they came in, one of them was Simon Girty. The other man was a big bodyguard for Girty. Only Girty spoke the Shawnee tongue. He gave Nonhelema greetings from Alexander McKee, and then told her and the other chiefs what the governor wished to happen:

If the Shawnee chiefs and their allies would come to the governor's camp, they could make a truce, and the governor would not come on and attack unless they refused.

Cornstalk said, "Should we believe that? The governor has stopped and asked for our attention, but we see the other part of the army coming up the Scioto-sipe, they whom we fought, and they are not stopping."

Girty, a dark, hard, weathered little man with a badly scarred forehead, said, "The governor is going across to stop Colonel Lewis from coming on. Lewis wants to destroy all your people because you killed his brother in the battle. He doesn't want to be stopped, but if you will agree to come to truce, the governor will stop him."

Nonhelema could see that Girty was guarding his words. "There is more," she said. "What?"

"Since you asked, then: They do not agree with each other on some matters. The governor is for the English king. Colonel Lewis is for the colonials. The governor does not want the colonials to claim a victory over you. But he does mean to have peace along the river between Indians and Virginians. As I see it, you have these choices: You go talk truce or you're destroyed."

"Girty," said Cornstalk, "we did not bother the whites. It was the Mingoes, in vengeance for the massacre of Chief Logan's family." Logan was the name by which most whitemen knew Tahgahyuteh.

"I know that. And the governor wants you to bring Logan to the truce talk. It is said he lives near you now."

"Tahgahyuteh is not Shawnee. We cannot tell him what to do. You go invite him. We will encourage him. But he is very bitter and might not go. You speak his tongue well. Go and try. He was always a good friend of the whitemen before; maybe he will forgive and go. Or maybe the betrayal seems too great. But tell your Governor Dunmore that the headmen of the Shawnees will come to his camp and listen to him, and reply. Tell him to stop his other army. Or it will be too late to talk of peace ever again."

"Girty," Nonhelema said, "you and Colonel McKee always tell us the truth. I ask you: Can we trust this governor?"

Girty looked down, then looked up. "As matters stand, what does it matter? You have little choice."

"Then tell me this: What weaknesses has he?"

"Pride and vanity. He's a lord, over in his own country."

"Pride and vanity. Eh-heh. *Megweshe!* Those are good weaknesses. We can use those."

Private Case had seen land sharks at work back in Virginia often enough to know what was going on here.

The young lieutenant named Clark, leader of the company of scouts for Governor Lord Dunmore's army, handed his spyglass to Captain Arbuckle and pointed to a forested hill about two miles to the north; it was a rounded prominence higher than any of the other hills in this broad, beautiful lowland through which the Scioto River flowed south to the Ohio. Vast fields were burgeoning with tall corn and beans. Indian women and children were everywhere, pulling the ears of maize.

Clark, like his friend Arbuckle, was a Virginian and a surveyor, and his covetous appreciation of this rich Shawnee countryside practically glowed on his face. As Arbuckle peered through the glass, Clark said: "Grand, isn't it? What a place for a city!"

"Aye, 'tis indeed."

Justin watched the two officers with envy. He had never seen two men more alike. George Rogers Clark was younger than Matthew Arbuckle, but at the age of about twenty or twenty-one had all the confidence and gravity of a mature gentryman. In physique, he was erect and muscular, trim in the waist, deep-chested. His face had that same raptor look as Arbuckle's and the tawny complexion of an outdoorsman, rendered more striking by his thick, sun-bleached red hair, which he wore pulled back in a queue.

A fourth member of this small scouting party was an uncouth contrast to the two handsome officers: stocky, olive-complexioned, square-faced, with an ugly scar from his hairline to his eyebrows. Or perhaps it would have been more accurate to say *eyebrow*, as they met, uninterrupted, above his nose. This surly scout and interpreter, Girty by name, seemed, like an iron ingot, to give off no warmth or light. He seemed to have a cold, dense center.

Nonetheless, he was a significant presence. Clark was attentive and respectful to him, for Girty knew and understood Indians. He had lived years of his young life as a captive of the Seneca tribe, was fluent in several tribal tongues, and knew all the Indian trails and towns between the Great Lakes and the Ohio River. A man like Simon Girty could be of more value to a scout company than its commander himself.

"This chain of hills," Clark said with a sweep of his arm, "they keep lookouts and signalers up there. They can pass a warning all the way up here from the Ohio in an hour, smoke by day, or fire by night. They always know where we are."

"They do," said Arbuckle. "They watched us all the way down from Greenbrier to the point, and Dunmore all the way down from Pitt. That's how they knew when to strike us, before we merged. And they damned near got us, George."

After burying his dead and building a small fort to house his hundred badly wounded, Colonel Andrew Lewis had crossed the Ohio and marched in a vengeful fury up into this Scioto valley, meaning to annihilate the Shawnees completely, to avenge his brother and the other dead. He had presumed that it would be easy once his troops were combined with Governor Lord Dunmore's.

But Dunmore had ordered him to stop here, just short of the Shawnee towns, telling him that the Shawnee chiefs had sued for peace. Lewis, infuriated by that order, had tried to disobey it. The governor had found it necessary to draw his sword on Lewis and repeat the order before Lewis backed down. There existed now a bitter distrust between the governor and his officer. Lewis had settled down, sullen, in a temporary camp, while Lord Dunmore negotiated peace with the chiefs at his own headquarters camp a short distance to the east. Those talks were in progress now.

Captain Arbuckle was still studying the distant hill through the telescope. Lieutenant Clark turned and said, "Mr. Girty, kindly step up here and tell us what y'know of this place."

Girty said, "That there's the squaw chief's town y're lookin' at, Cap'n." The mention of her brought Justin to full attention, and he stared, wishing he had the spyglass. Girty went on, pointing: "Right there on the hilltop, the clearing, that's the Burning Ground. Burn prisoners there. Council House, Great House, her big house, most of the lodges are all over on the far side of the hill. Cornstalk's Town is farther on, t'other side of the creek. They're both Mekoche faction of the Shawnee. Strong bent for peace.

"Next big town's farther north," he went on, "other side of the Scioto. Them's Kispokos. Main war chief always comes from the Kispokos. Rumor is, he was killed in your battle. Pucsinwah was his name."

"What's that name mean in their tongue?" Clark asked.

Girty squinted and thought. "Something-Falling-Hard," he said. "Striking down. Like a club on a head."

Arbuckle snorted. "Good to know we killed a war chief. If I knew who fired that shot, I'd give him a medal. But I thought Cornstalk was their chief. He was a proper demon on the battlefield."

"Here it is about that, Cap'n: That family's peacemakers. They're Mekoche, like I said. Medicine men. Ceremonials and all. But more than that: Back east, their grandfather was a good friend of Penn. And the missionaries, them Moravians, got their hooks in 'em. That Cornstalk family, they're Christian."

"Like hell! If they're Christians, I'm a Hindoo! You're tuggin' my tail, Mr. Girty!"

The scout shrugged. He wasn't going to argue with a captain, obviously.

Justin was just as astonished: The naked fighting woman he had seen twice that day surely could not ever have knelt to Jesus Christ!

But then he remembered her words: *Jesus calls for mercy.*

"So tell me this," Captain Arbuckle demanded. "If they're the blessed meek, peacekeepers as ye claim, how come it is they led that fight against us at the point, howlin' like all the dogs of hell?"

Clark answered: "They say they tried to council for peace but their nation voted for war. So they do what their council says. And when their war chief fell, they led."

"What good's being a chief," Arbuckle said, "if you can't tell your people what to do?"

Lieutenant Clark chuckled. "Different, isn't it? A white chief, Dunmore, won't let us go punish the Shawnees, even though all the men want to."

The expression on Arbuckle's face showed that this was a really sore point with him. Clark went on: "But now that we've marched right up to their doors, some of them who wanted a fight are seeing it Cornstalk's way. Isn't it odd how bein' right can become wrong so quick? Good lesson to keep in mind."

Arbuckle handed Clark's spyglass back to him and glowered up the creek in the direction of the governor's treaty camp. "I can see why the savages might want peace now. What I don't see is why His Lordly Flatulence the governor wants treaties, just when we could give 'em such a larrupin' that they'd get out of our way for good! I don't see the sense in acting weak when you're strongest. When d'ye think we'll ever get this much advantage over 'em again?"

"Likely never," Clark said. "Listen well, Matthew. Ye'll never make sense of what the governor does unless ye keep the king in mind."

"What do you mean, the king?"

"His Lordship serves the interest of King George. As we all suspect by now, that's not the same as the interests of the Virginia Colony."

Justin, as a teacher in Virginia and as a scrivener in the regiment, had for years tried to keep abreast of the growing rift between England and the colonies, about the purposes of the new Continental Congress, the Committees of Safety and Correspondence, even the looming possibility of a war between the colonies and the mother country. All this had loomed dark in his thoughts, as he was sure it must in the thoughts of many learned men. The power of the king of England, though he was thousands of miles away across the broad Atlantic, was almost palpable even here on the frontier. Serving here under Dunmore, one could feel it.

"One thing you may be sure of," Clark said, glancing sideways at Arbuckle and lowering his voice. "If there comes a conflict between Virginia and King George, His Majesty will sure have an advantage in any treaty he makes with the Indians. D'ye catch my drift?"

"I do." Arbuckle gazed off toward the high ground of the Shawnee town for a while, and nodded. "Colonel Lewis was about to walk right over the governor to get at those towns. It was as if the governor were as much our enemy as the savages. I guess the colonel's got a notion of things to come."

Clark nodded, but said, "When y' speak this way, mind who y're talking to. For the time being, this is still the governor's militia we're in." He shook his head. "I hate to think how ugly and suspect we'll all look to each other when the break's made."

Girty stood, gazing up at the distant village, seeming not to listen, and Justin wondered what such a man, living on both sides of the frontier, might make of such matters. Whether he would even assume a loyalty, unless it might be to choose between Indian and white.

Clark continued, "Now, Matthew, something you'd do well to remember, as ye serve in this part of the country: I know y've fought Cornstalk before, and ye fought him again just days ago. But if ye can get over that, do. He and that sister chief of his are like t' be the best allies you'll ever have out here. Indeed, maybe the only ones. Most of the Shawnee people, and their chiefs, don't want peace with us under the terms they are getting. The only reason they're talking peace with the governor is because he's here in their dooryard with three thousand soldiers. So I advise you, friend, to make use o' those two, whatever way may present itself."

Arbuckle gazed over the rich valley, then said, "Odd that they should feel so different from the rest of their people. Do we owe that much to the missionaries?"

Clark shook his head. "That's not all of it. I think it's this: Cornstalk and his family have been more in our cities than their people have. As interpreters and couriers, on trade, diplomacy. They have a notion of what they're up against. They've seen how many white people there are. How much wealth we have. They've seen ships, cannon, forts, big buildings. The way we can make things and move things. Why, just the sight of one smithy at his forge and anvil is enough to give an Indian something to think about for a long spell. Now, Cornstalk and his family have been most every place, New York to New Orleans. They know what we have and they don't. They know, too, that only we make guns and powder.

"That is to say," Clark concluded, "they see the handwriting on the wall. Mind you, the missionaries have helped. But a look at our strength, I reckon, has done the most to show 'em their fate. That's why I expect they'll persuade many chiefs to talk peace. They know just damned near everyone, and enjoy prestige everywhere. We'd be fools not to use 'em."

Private Case saw that Captain Arbuckle was pondering it. Maybe Arbuckle was remembering the moment when he had chosen not to kill the Indian woman and her wounded brother. Justin himself had relived that moment over and over in his memory and his emotions.

Arbuckle said, "Damned if I know, George, how ye've got to know friendly Indians from the rest. They're all one to me."

Clark looked down, toed the earth with his boot, bent and picked up a flint spear point from the grass, ran his thumb along the edge, then flipped the piece over and over in his palm, thoughtfully. "I got to know them when I stayed with Tahgahyuteh the Mingo. Back before the late trouble started."

"Tahgahyuteh's Chief Logan, right? I can't tell one damned Indian name from another. Damned barbarians all of 'em, I say."

Clark chuckled. "Aye. That's what my English ancestors said about your Scottish ancestors, Matthew. *Barbarians all of 'em.*" Smiling at his own joke, Clark slipped the missile point into his shot bag and raised his head for another longing look over the fertile valley. "Aye! What a site for a city!"

When they went to sue for peace, the Shawnee chiefs did not crawl or cringe. Colonel Lewis had not defeated them at the Kanawha; they had just run out of powder and lead before they could defeat him.

The chiefs rode into Lord Dunmore's army camp so tall and proud and elegant that they looked like victors, not supplicants. They were on their best horses with their fanciest saddles and trappings, silver flashing: silver headbands and armbands, brooches pinned to their yokes and mantles, silver earbobs and nose rings, silver pendants even in their horses' bridles. The men's scalps had been plucked, leaving only their braided scalplocks, decorated with silver chains, feathers, bear claws, beads, or deer-hair crests; even their eyebrows had been plucked. Some of them had painted vermillion over their jaws, or over one side of the face.

The camp consisted of hundreds of small, peaked tents in countless rows, a pall of smoke, a crude breastwork of logs and brush.

Governor Dunmore had lined up two long ranks of his Red Coats inside the fortification, facing each other, making a lane up through which the chiefs rode, between upright bayonets, toward the commander's beautiful white marquee tent with its pennants and banners. At the end of that stoic gauntlet stood a white-wigged man waiting for them, resplendent in crimson coat and golden braid and frogging, sword at his hip, boots to his thighs. Even with his huge epaulets, his shoulders were substantially narrower than his beam, and his pearly silk waistcoat was filled with such a protuberance that

Captain Johnny leaned to Nonhelema and joked, "We should have brought Long Tits for the governor." Long Tits was a midwife.

As they rode close enough to see his face clearly, Nonhelema thought, *Yes, Girty said it well. This man is all pride and vanity.*

Girty, looking awkward and scruffy in a red uniform coat, stood with some trim young officers near a field table in the shade of the marquee. Dunmore said something to him, and he came out to meet the chiefs. They reined in.

"Eh, Girty. *Wahsi mahmo.* Greetings," Cornstalk said in Shawnee. "You will be the translator?"

Girty chuckled. "You talk better English than me. But I will be here as a witness to what-all's said." He looked back along the line of chiefs and chieftains, nodding at several of them as his eyes met theirs. Girty often trod delicate ground. Most Indians who knew him trusted him. Still, he was a part of the army, though not of an appearance or nature to inspire much respect among other officers. He preferred to be among Indians. Sometimes he forsook human company altogether and disappeared for months into the forests.

"His Lordship is waiting." Girty smirked. He had pronounced it *Lardship,* which made Nonhelema smile. She and the other chiefs swung out of their saddles and got down, giving their reins to the retinue of warriors who had ridden in with them. They walked in a slow and stately manner the last few yards toward the haughty body who stood awaiting them. The late-fall breeze was brisk and blew their feathers, fringes, and locks. Most of the foliage was off the trees beyond the camp clearing, but late leaves were still letting go and tumbling aslant down the wind, yellow against the gray tracery of the woods. The governor's flushed, fleshy visage appeared to be rouged on the cheeks. Though he was watching the approach of the whole procession, he seemed to have his eyes mostly upon Nonhelema. She was used to that, but this whiteman's expression was not the usual male attention. This was the kind of annoyance, or consternation, she saw now and then in the expressions of self-important whitemen who believed that anything of consequence was the province of men and should not be attended by women.

This governor would have to learn something here today.

The negotiations began with the ceremonial pipe, and the governor went through the motions, which were explained to him, step by step, by Girty. The pipe was a tomahawk pipe: a blade, with a tobacco bowl in the blunt end of the head. He tried to veil his disgust in taking the stem from their lips to his, but they all noticed.

"Damn this idiocy," he muttered to his officers. "Smoke, painted faces, nose rings . . . and what has that freak done to his ears!" He was speaking of Nonhelema's brother Nimwha, whose earlobes were a native masterpiece: slit around the edge, stretched, wound with silver wire, making the lobes into great, glittering loops that hung nearly to his shoulders. A gold watch ticked in each loop.

Nonhelema chose that moment to begin educating the lord governor. In perfectly articulated English, she said: "Excellency, your wig is beautiful, and the rouge upon your cheeks is most becoming. You see, I, too, wear it. May I compliment you upon your beauty!"

His eyes, below their puffy lids, widened. And then his lips began opening and closing, reminding her of a fish.

Cornstalk said, in equally precise English, "This pipe, Your Excellency, we have smoked as testimony to our sincerity here. Our words go to heaven on the smoke. Now I, Hokoleskwa, present the pipe to you as a gift. Whenever you look upon it from now on, it will remind you of the sacredness of the promises we shall make each other here today." Now the governor's face was as red as his coat.

"In the name of our Lord Jesus," Nonhelema added, "amen."

From that beginning, Lord Dunmore could only try to redeem himself from his embarrassment and rise to the level of his visitors.

Tahgahyuteh, the Mingo chief, had refused to come to the truce talks—even though it was his warriors, avenging his family's deaths, that had given the governor his excuse to invade the Ohio. Girty and a small party had traveled to his village and come back with a written statement from him. It was read aloud to the assembled chiefs and officers by John Gibson, who had written it down from Girty's translation. Gibson was known to the Indians as Horsehead because of his equine appearance, but he had a strong clear voice, so much like Tahgahyuteh's own that by not looking at the homely Gibson, Nonhelema could imagine she was hearing the great Mingo himself. The words rang out, quickly transfixing everyone who could hear them:

"I would appeal to any whiteman to say if he entered Logan's cabin and I gave him not meat, if ever he came cold or naked and I gave him not clothing. During the course of the last long and bloody war, Logan remained idle in his tent, an advocate for peace. Nay, such was my love for the whites that those of my own country pointed at me as I passed and said, 'Logan is the friend of the whiteman.' I had even thought of living with you."

Nonhelema, her throat feeling swollen, nodded and glanced at her brother Cornstalk. Just like their great friend Tahgahyuteh, they had often been mocked and chided by their own beloved people for trusting and befriending the whitemen.

Gibson read on, citing in Logan's words the unprovoked murder of his closest family. "They murdered all the relatives of Logan, not sparing even the women and children. There runs not a drop of my blood in the veins of any living creature!

"This called on me for revenge. I have killed many, I have fully glutted my vengeance.

"Now, for my country, I rejoice at the beams of peace, but do not harbor the thought that mine is the joy of fear. Logan never felt fear . . ."

Gibson himself was hoarse with emotion as he concluded: "Who is there to mourn for Logan? *Not one!*"

"A-ho!" exclaimed Cornstalk. Then he raised his eyes to Lord Dunmore. "Excellency, now you see by this what trouble comes when lawless whitemen come into our country. They molest or murder our people, and they are never punished for it, or even made to withdraw. Even Indians who were your friends are provoked to seek vengeance and drive you away.

"You yourself have ordered the white people not to cross the mountains and come here, but they come anyway. And surveyors come down the river, with their measuring chains and their guns, to divide up our hunting grounds. Your officer Washington, whom we know from the war before, has words in the papers in the East, offering to sell pieces of our hunting ground in the valley of the Kanawha. There where we just fought the other part of your army, only a few days since. Right there"—he pointed to a tall red-haired lieutenant—"is a surveyor who was in the Kanawha bottomlands not long ago. His name is Clark, I remember; Tahgahyuteh befriended him, even though he should not have been making lines in our country—by your own laws! How can your Virginia people be doing that? How can you think it will not cause trouble? You have seen how much trouble!"

Nonhelema looked at the young officer, recognizing him. He was the kind of young man any woman would notice and remember. He had taken advantage of Logan's hospitality and had dallied with one of the young Mingo girls. And Nonhelema, though perhaps twice the age of Clark then, had been a little jealous of the Mingo girl. That rueful memory passed quickly through her mind and she watched the governor for his reaction to Cornstalk's words.

"My son," Dunmore said. Even though he was younger than Cornstalk, he used a term that implied Indians were children and the English officials their fathers, with the right to tell them what to do. "My son, we are in agreement that when my people and your people cross into each other's country, some of them are likely to clash. My government is far away and cannot control what those do who come here. Your Great Father the king of England is even farther away, and he must speak to you through me."

Nonhelema expected her brother to retort, as she had heard him do before, that he had no Great Father who was English, not even one who was king. But Cornstalk was trying not to provoke the governor, who was so close here with his huge army, and he didn't make that usual retort.

Lord Dunmore, blinking and pursing his lips gravely, went on: "Much of the trouble occurs when some, Virginians or Indians, do not understand where the boundaries are. The boundaries have to be so plain that there is no dispute over where they are. They must be like a large river. Like the Ohio River."

Cornstalk's eyes flashed, but he kept his voice calm. "The mountains are as visible as the river. And your law said your people should not come to this side of the mountains, but they come, and they keep coming. Their boats are always coming down the river, full of surveyors, and hunters, and people with cattle and plows. Fort Pitt, up the river, is like a place where the beaver dam has broken, and the white people pour through that place like water, into our country!"

"My son," the governor said with a scowl, "there are two truths you do not understand. By the Virginia charter, many generations ago, the king of England gave the colony all the land as far as the land runs, to the western sea." He pointed vaguely westward. "More lately, the Iroquois sold to our government the land below the Ohio River, what you call Kaintucke, which falls within those charter boundaries. And so you see, Kaintucke belongs to Virginia, by authorities both old and recent. In fact, even this land where we sit now is within the Old Dominion charter. But since we need a boundary everyone can see, that boundary must be the Ohio River. Is that not plain enough for you?"

Nonhelema could see that Cornstalk was struggling so hard with anger that he wouldn't talk yet. And as Girty translated for the rest of the Shawnee chiefs, including the warlike ones, she could feel the stirring of their fury begin to fill the space around her. And so she took it upon herself to say what she knew they were thinking, in as polite a way as she could express it.

"Excellency, with the respect due to you as the king's man here, our people protest that the old king in England could not give the colony land that was not his to give, land where he had never even put his foot. In the same way, more lately, the Iroquois could not sell your colony our hunting grounds. It was not theirs, either, nor was it *ever* theirs." When the governor's eyes came to settle on her face, they were so full of indignation that she felt it prudent to try to disarm him with the kind of smile that usually moved the stiffness out of whitemen's collars and into their breeches.

But this man was not disarmed. He stared at her as if she were some vermin that had bothered him. Then he snapped his fingers at Girty and commanded: "Don't translate what this woman said!" Then, with a delicate, disdainful movement of his head, he turned back to Cornstalk and said, "Chief, will you kindly have this woman refrain from interrupting in men's affairs?"

Cornstalk cleared his throat. "She is my sister, and she is my equal as a chief of our people. She was beside me in trying to keep our people from attacking Colonel Lewis. You know her village has three times more Shawnees than my own. If Your Excellency will not listen to her, none of our other headmen will have anything to say, as we all shall leave now."

All the soldiers in earshot heard that, or felt the tone of it, and there evolved a rustling, hushing noise, the sound of shifting, of tensing. Nonhelema saw all the chiefs bracing themselves, aware of their helpless situation, surrounded by thousands of soldiers who hated Indians. She knew them all and doubted that anyone was afraid, but they were bracing themselves to die here, if it came to that.

Governor Dunmore apparently perceived that Cornstalk was not bluffing, and he said earnestly, "Please. We shall continue to talk together. We must do so."

The tension was eased—for the moment.

It was done. The army would leave the Shawnee people unharmed and return to Virginia. The last pipe was being smoked and the Virginia governor was smug and cheerful and acting as if the Indians were his friends.

But Nonhelema and her brothers could not look each other in the eyes, nor into the eyes of the other chiefs, and she thought she might choke on the smoke of the calumet.

It would be hard to talk with the People about this. Peace had been bought, but the price had been total humiliation of Shawnees. Every point of negotiation had gone in the governor's favor. It would all become official next year at a grand peace council at Fort Pitt—which Governor Dunmore wanted to rename Fort Dunmore—but the Shawnees had been forced to give away so much that many of their leaders probably would refuse to go and make it final. Nonhelema could almost feel the wall of difference sliding between her family's peacemakers and the other leaders. She and Cornstalk would have to exert themselves all winter and spring and give up the rest of their prestige to persuade the chiefs to go to that council next year. Those chiefs were sullen, not feigning an amiability toward the fat, pink governor.

"Look at them," Cornstalk hissed into her ear. "They blame *us* for this outcome! It was *their* insistence on war that rendered us so weak in this council!"

"Brother," she murmured in reply, hoping to soothe him, "remember: *Weshe catweloo k'weshe lawehpah.* It still means the same. Peace is right: You and I are strong, because we stayed true to peace."

But it was hard for her to believe in her own words. The Shawnees had had to agree to yield their hunting rights in Kentucke, for the governor had decreed that the Spaylaywesipe, the Ohio, would be the boundary between Virginia and the Indians.

The Shawnees would have to return all their white captives, even the adopted ones, to Fort Pitt at the beginning of the Great Council there.

The Shawnees would not be allowed to attack boats going down the river.

The Shawnees would have to abide by trading rules that would be dictated to them at Fort Dunmore.

And four hostages would be taken from their beloved family to Virginia and held as surety that the Shawnee leaders would come to the fort and abide by the conditions decreed here by the governor. Some other warriors had volunteered to go in their place, warriors who believed that they could escape on their way to Williamsburg, or after they got there. But that would not do. It all had to be done in good faith, for the Shawnees were honorable even if the whitemen were not. Besides, the governor did not want hostages who were ordinary men. He had to have hostages of political importance—hostages who could be used for leverage in bargaining. This governor was very shrewd. He used every advantage he had. When Nonhelema looked at him now, after these days of negotiations, she remembered what she had thought before the negotiations began, and how wrong she had been. She had presumed that the governor of Virginia, like a chief of a tribe, must surely be the best and most honorable Virginian. That had not proved to be true. Instead he was devious and ruthless.

And she had presumed that his weaknesses—the pride and vanity Girty had mentioned—could be used against him in the negotiations. He had indeed shown himself to be proud and vain, but he had proved himself too cunning to give anything in return for flattery. Being a lord, apparently, he was so accustomed to flattery that he took it as his due and could not be disarmed by it.

And even her femininity, which almost always disarmed men, had not affected the governor. Indeed, he had resented her very presence in the bargaining, and had reddened and quivered every time she had presented any strong point of reason. Many thoughts ran through her head about this strange type of Virginia man. Perhaps his odd responses were because he was one of the Scottish type of Englishmen, whom she had observed to be hard and quirky.

Though he was wrong, the governor had prevailed in every regard. Being right had not helped the Shawnee people at all. The Long Knives had done wrong from the beginning but had won everything. They had killed Tahgahyuteh's innocent family; they had burned Mingo and Shawnee towns; they had come making false accusations against the Shawnees and had invaded their country; they had made demands they had no right to make; they had claimed the Shawnees' hunting grounds; now they were kidnapping four Shawnee chieftains to coerce the tribe to go to a treaty council they would prefer to avoid.

Already she felt heavy with dread. She thought of the unpleasant tasks she and Cornstalk would have in the coming winter: keeping up the peace talks among the infuriated bands, dispelling the bad lies the whites were telling the Delawares about the Shawnees, and, especially, trying to persuade Shawnee families everywhere that they must give up all the white captives they had taken in and adopted. The Long Knives had no idea, it seemed, that adopted captives were no longer white people. That they were Shawnee sons and daughters, brothers and sisters, wives and husbands, and wanted to remain so. Of the scores of adopted whites she knew in the Shawnee nation, none would want to leave their tribal families. Almost all had been adopted to replace family members lost to whitemen's bullets, diseases, and drunkenness, and were as much embraced in the families' affection as the lost ones they had replaced. *And how,* Nonhelema wondered with an ache and a chill, *how can I ask them to yield up what I myself could not: Would I give my daughter, Fani, up to the Long Knives?*

She thought of the girl, who had been Shawnee so long that she had no real memory of her white family. Fani was tall, dark, and pretty; she was a devoted daughter, totally accepted by the girls of the tribe as a friend and a sister. She was so much a Shawnee that she would not listen to the missionaries with their strange Jesus story, and made it plain that she disliked her mother's fascination with it. Fani was Indian, through and through. But even with her long dark hair and native dress, she might be recognized up close as a white girl. For that reason, she had been kept away from Governor Dunmore's camp. At treaty councils like this, where the exchange of prisoners invariably became an issue, Fani had to be kept out of sight, and out of the attention of the white officials. It was only at times like these that Fani was not at Nonhelema's side.

The Shawnee families never mentioned, or even considered, the white origins of their adopted kin. Through the ceremonies, their whiteness was washed away and became invisible. Few Shawnees were mean enough or petty enough to bring up their alien birth. It just was not done.

But if Nonhelema, in trying to meet the demands of the governor and his Indian commissioners, went about in the coming months pleading or demanding that Shawnee families must cast out their white-blooded members and send them away to Fort Pitt, any one of those families might politely inquire: "And you, Nonhelema; will you be giving your daughter, Fani, to the Long Knives?"

She had had to ponder that before, at various times when demands for prisoner exchanges were in the air. One solution she had thought of was that she might enter Fani into the mission school of Brother Zeisberger, where she would become a Christian and learn to read. She had thought that this might suffice to keep Fani from being surrendered to the whites. She had sent her son, Morgan, there, even though he was her birth son and thus not subject to repatriation.

But Fani was a Shawnee in heart and spirit and disliked and distrusted the missionaries, so that would not work.

Being a peacemaker was not easy. Everything in Indian life had become delicate and complicated since the whitemen came. Even though she liked the whitemen and found them interesting, and advocated them to her own people, she had to admit to herself sometimes that they were a difficult nuisance, and sometimes she yearned for the early times, before they had come here.

She looked at the round, pink, arrogant face of the governor of Virginia. Then she shut her eyes and envisioned the long, squarish, sad-eyed face of Brother David Zeisberger, and she recited in her mind: *Blessed are the peacemakers for they shall be called the children of God, Matthew five three eleven.*

When Brother David approves me and christens me in the river, she thought, *then I will know the answers to all these questions, and it will not be so hard then.*

WITH GOV^R DUNMORE
CAMP CHARLOTTE
PICKAWAY PLAINS N OF OHIO RV^R
NOVEMBER 1774

Honored Parents,

Your dutiful son conveys herewith his fond hopes that you & family are in robust health & good spirits.

I myself continue very well despite the rigours of a long campaign with Col Andrew Lewis deep into ye Indian country. Here Govr Dunmore has attained success above expectations in quelling the late Indian uprising. I trust you know the recent hostilities were provoked latterly by frontier ruffians who massacred the entire family of a friendly Mingo Indian chief called Logan, who forthwith avenged his family, ten lives to one and then put down the hatchet but by then the Govr had his excuse to invade here. Whatever the policy of the State of Virginia regarding the natives, there are lawless scoundrels ranging these borderlands, and there shall never be an end to such troubles, I fear.

There is animosity between Col° Lewis and Gov' Dunmore; the policy of ye Crown is suspicious, the Gov' having dissolved the Virg° Assembly three times for revolutionary sentiments.

This is a country rich and fertile beyond my powers to describe justly—broad bottomlands full of Indian corn and prolific gardens. Timber trees are enormous attesting to ye fertile soil & yielding great quantity of mast, & so much walnuts & hickory nuts as could make the diet of a small citizenry if all other crops & game failed. The rivers abound in fish some catfish the size of hogs. The Shawanoe Indian women excell^t gardeners, vast acreage in corn, squash & beans, which they put by in diverse ways for winter. The men are resourceful hunters esp^ly this season of year—deer, buffalo, bear—th° being at war with us precluded their hunting expeditions this fall, which they will doubtless regret as winter sets in.

As to the campaign, Col° Andrew Lewis was attacked on ye morning of the 10th ult. by a confederation of tribes mostly Shawanoe. Struck us at ye mouth of the Kanawha where we had arrived the day before & had not yet built fortifications. The Ind^s shrewdly attacked Col° Lewis before the joining of our force with that of ye Gov', & the chiefs led with sagacity & order worthy of a General. Heavy toll, Col° Chas Lewis fell mortally wounded. At end of day our soldiers held the field the Ind^s apparently having not enough powder & ball to continue, withdrew. By the Grace of Our Lord I safely passed through that heated encounter.

Of remarkable interest, a section of the Indian front was commanded by a woman chief, known to be a sister of ye famed Corn Stalk, a woman of formidable stature strength and ferocity. I saw her in battle and if I might play with words was "Amazed by an Amazon." Her Ind^s fought with uncommon tenacity, as I believe to prevent our army from penetrating to the heart of their country. On the offensive, warriors usually don't risque so much but fight coy and retreat before their foes' advantage—not for want of bravery, rather for frugality with lives. Th° some of our officers scoff, I prefer the Ind Mode of covert battle, winning objectives with less effusion of blood. Their losses were slighter than ours in ye engagement.

The surgeon of the Regiment being overwhelmed by casualties, I assisted him considerably in the wake of battle, to his approbation, and he

*offered to apprentice me were I to accompany him back to Rockbridge Co.
I shall have to weigh such an oppt' with much deliberation, being rather
older than a novice usually is, and such skills as I may have learned
from you, Father, in doctoring our farm beasts might not truly designate
me a likely physician, th° many of these militiamen bear great resem-
blance to asses, oxen & geese. After this campaign my course is problem-
atick. Imminence of War between ye King and Colonies will largely
decide it. LIBERTY is the fomenting word so oft proclaimed by our officers, and croaked after them like crow calls by many of these ring-tailed
roarers in the ranks, who like the sound of it because they detest any
sort of restraint upon themselves; I doubt they imagine what else it
might mean.*

*While ye treatie was in session at this place, I went with a scouting
party into the Plain of the Scioto valley; here is Chillicawthee, capitol
of the Shawanoes.*

*There stand nearby many ancient earthworks, great monuments of
earth in perfect symmetry, and one huge circular earthen dike. Parallel
levees may have defined a broad road; ye Indians say their ancestors built
it all as sacred temples &c, the road was their earthly counterpart of ye
Milky Way, which they call the Shining Path, to the afterworld. Most of
our officers contend that white men must have been here in times long
gone, as savages could not have laid out and built anything so monu-
mental & perfect. Great mystery.*

*The village of Aforesaid female Chief is larger even than that of her
brother CornStalk. Her house was pointed out, not a hut but a large
well made log dwelling of two storeys. She has wealth in domestic livestock and household goods, owing to her activities in trade at Ft Pitt,
and to her association with traders there & Morgan a partner in one of
the Philadelphia establishments. It is something of an odd notion to our
militia to think of a savage as "wealthy" and having seen her fighting
naked on ye battleground we were bemused by her elegant dress at treatie,
a glorious mixture of finest Indian decoration and such finery as a Belle
Lady of Virg^a might wear, even to silk, lace and a plumed tricorne.*

*Her town occupies a grand elevation east of Scioto R and contains
the Burning Ground where upon certain prisoners are executed at ye
stake. The women of that tribe express most cruel vengeance, their fathers, sons, & husbands being slain in such proportion, the females in a
village far outnumber adult males. Thus the women claim the privilege
to dispose of enemy prisoners. Most often they spare them the stake, and*

adopt them, to replace their lost kin, and the proportion of adopted captives is very large among ye Indians. 'Tis rumored that the Shawanoe Queen's own daughter is an adopted captive, but not having seen her I cannot attest.

Father & Mother, I quaked at the sight of that barbaric Burning Ground, but was reminded by the scout that we are most of us lately from England, where burning at ye stake, decapitation, and drawing & quartering were publick spectacle, and so perhaps we should not judge too piously.

In treatie council at this place the Shawanoe were a grave, dignified & handsome retinue, in particular their chief Corn Stalk & his aforesaid sister; both standing no little over six ft in stature and extremely handsome of visage & physique. These Shawanoes have a manner of constraining their infants on a carry-board that affects their later posture to become erect as soldiers. In fact the Queen herself is called "the Grenadier Squaw" by ye officers at Pitt, for her height & bearing. Her name is Non He Le Ma. Our interpreter said the name means "Not A Man." These persons are of the Mekoche division of the Shawanoes and are strongly favorable to peaceful resolutions of ye differences with Virg*, expecting better protection of the Safety of their people than by War. Their family have long been influenced by a peaceful sect of Protestant missionaries called Moravians. Tho the Shawanoes have much associated with Frenchmen formerly, they seem not to have taken to Catholick blandishments.

The treatie here is preliminary to one larger and more formal to be convened at Ft Pitt next year, when other tribes also will negotiate over boundaries, trade regulations, neutrality, &c &c, and the return of all captive white people now among them. It is a clever policy of our treatie makers to hold hostages to ensure compliance with promises made; Lord Dunmore now takes several of their beloved chieftains to Williamsburg with him, among them sons & brothers of Corn Stalk himself; they shall be returned at Ft Pitt in the future council. 'Tis deeply affecting to see these savages prepare for a long separation, demonstrating great tenderness, lamenting as if they might never meet their kin again. The Gov* departs presently, to be accompanied perhaps as far as Pittsburgh by Corn Stalk & his sister, who are familiars there.

I shall send this letter by the part of the army that leaves now.

It must seem to you that I have devoted a disproportionate part of this letter to telling of this woman, while saying little about so large an *event as the battle. That, Dear Parents, is because I imagined she would seem an interesting wonder to you, as she is to me, whereas particulars of ye campaign will be published before long, for all to read.*

When you may expect to see me, and I you, depends upon decisions that shall be made providing for the defense of this western country.

I remain always y^r *most dutiful and affectionate son—*

JUSTIN

4

The Shawnee people knew that at Tapistewamigi-sipe, Where-the-Rivers-Meet, there is a strong spirit force, and people like to live there. In such places, events flow together, as do the waters down from the hills, and so those are important places. The Delawares called this Menach-sink, the Flowing-Together Place.

Nonhelema, astride her elegant saddle at the head of the column of chiefs coming here for the peace treaty, looked down from the bluff of the Allegheny-sipe and breathed deep with admiration of the place. From the town beyond the fort a mile away came the clanking of smiths' hammers.

As long as the oldest ones could remember, there had been villages at this place where the two rivers, the swift Allegheny from the north and the deep Monongahela from the south, flowed together to become the great river—called Spaylaywesipe by the Shawnees, La Belle Rivière by the French, the Ohio by the English.

In the Ancient Times, many of the True People had lived here in great numbers, trading for goods brought up and down the river by other tribes. Long ago those people had died away, and their bones and their tools and pots were washed out of their earthen mounds by floods. Later, people found them there, and wondered about the old True People.

There had always been trading here, at this beautiful confluence of the rivers among the steep hills. The French had come long ago and traded with the Indians. Then the English had come and fought with the French. Many soldiers had died in those battles, and eventually the English had won the place. Then the Englishmen from Pennsylvania and Virginia had conflicts over the control of this place. There had been several forts here.

The newest fort had been called Fort Pitt, until the Virginians of Governor Dunmore took it over, and now it was called Fort Dunmore. It was built within earthen ramparts as tall as two man-heights, with brick and wooden walls even higher. A moat, fed by water from the Allegheny River, separated the fort from the town. To go into the fort, it was necessary to cross a drawbridge. Cannon on the high walls of the fort dominated both rivers. And so, now the power of cannon was added to the power of the old spirits of the place, and it was a more powerful place even than it had been before, but in a different way.

From the high distant bluffs and cliffs above the confluence, one could look down and see the five-sided star shape of the fort and the buildings and broad parade ground inside. From whatever way one came by land, that shape was the first sight, looking down on it.

Coming to the fort in a boat or canoe, as Nonhelema had done often, one first saw the fort as if it were a low bluff on the lowland, with roofs and a flag on a pole above the mist and shimmer of the broad river, and with steep hills behind it—the stone cliffs of the Monongahela to the south, the wooded steep bluffs of the Allegheny to the north.

The whitemen knew of the power of the place, but they saw it through different eyes. Once, in the house of Colonel Croghan, Nonhelema had seen a large map of the confluence, drawn with much detail. A map was a strange marvel, viewing a place as God, or an eagle, must see it—from straight above. On the map were lines showing the packhorse trails coming down from the mountains, and the star shape of the fort on the point of land between the converging rivers, and the sandbar island in the Monongahela where buckwheat grew, and the other island off the Allegheny shore where Killbuck's

Delaware village stood, and narrow lines going off in all directions—the Indian trails from here to the distant places where they lived.

Seeing this place as lines on a soldier's map had revealed to her how the whiteman saw its power.

The wedge of land between the converging rivers was like an arrowhead, pointing westward down the Ohio, as if to tell whitemen: *Go that way, down the Ohio into those rich lands, where only a few Indian tribes stand in your way. Put behind you the crowded East, with its laws that limit you, with its surveyed land occupied by selfish people with whom you must compete for everything. Go that way, into the Great Middle Ground, where lies rich land beyond measure, where game animals for meat and hides abound, and furbearers swarm. There is no end to the trees you need to build your houses and boats and wagons. It is all there for the taking; go and be first to claim it. The Indians can't stop you. As they never have before. Look how far we have advanced through land that once was theirs. Soldiers and treaties will help smooth your way. The Indians grow weak, and they will die or take flight before you. Go that way. I am the power behind you, pointing you downriver to the West. Hurry on!*

That was what she had understood when she had seen this place on a soldier's map. The map was like a drawing of the whitemen's long intentions.

Nonhelema herself knew too well about the pushing westward of the whitemen. In her lifetime, her people had been pushed over past these mountains and westward into the Ohio country. And last year, even in that far place downriver, a Virginian army had come and fought and forced them to sue for peace. Indians who thought they could stop whitemen by fighting them back were fools. It would do no good; it would lead only to violent death for the whole Shawnee people. That was why she always would speak for peace, no matter how much provoked. She and Cornstalk had worked and cajoled the whole winter and spring to coax their people to come to Pittsburgh and negotiate for peace.

Below the bluff, near the north shore, lay the island of Killbuck's Delaware town: woods, houses, *wegiwas*, lodges, gardens, cornfields. It was not easy to live so close to a big whiteman's town. Killbuck worked hard always to keep his people, and any others who would listen to him, neutral between the warring white nations. Killbuck favored the peace-seeking Mekoche and Chillicothe Shawnee over the factions that wanted to fight whitemen. Nonhelema knew her people would be welcome on his island. It would be the safest place for them to stay while here for the treaty talks.

The wind, cooled by blowing over the river, ruffled the treetops below. Her hair whipped around her face; fringes, feathers, and her horse's mane blew in the wind. Everything was in motion, and the Wind Spirit whispered and whistled. Wind Spirit told her that this was an important time in a powerful place. Much of what was to happen here would happen because of her own beliefs and her efforts. A chief could never rest or stop listening or watching. The people always had to be brought along or given the Spirit and the means to do what was needed.

She was going to a gathering of several hundred Indians, many of them her friends. Some of the important whitemen who would be there were also her friends. One of the whitemen who would be there, Colonel Morgan, was an old love, for whom she still had warmth and respect. Another was a new love, McKee. But her greater love was for her people.

Some of the white officials had specifically asked for her presence at the talks because they esteemed her judgment and her influence. All that was good. Also it was good that the men of her family who had gone to Williamsburg as hostages had been brought here, and would be returned. She anticipated their faces and their embraces, and the interesting stories they would have to tell about their confinement in Williamsburg. That, too, would be good.

The best of the good things that lay ahead was that she was coming to this powerful place as a peacemaker. As a child of God.

Surely the missionary Zeisberger would be pleased with her.

"*Tapistewamigi-sipe,*" she said, turning to look at Cornstalk beside her in the bright slanting sunlight of the afternoon. "Here is where we bring together all that flows from elsewhere."

He leaned in his saddle and put a hand on her hand. She saw in his eyes that he understood what she meant. But it was plain that he did not know what would come of it, either. There was determination in his eyes, but not hope.

Most of Pittsburgh's motley population arose from its summer torpor and thronged the dirt streets to watch the last of the Indians come across in canoes from Killbuck's Island. This haughty and stately procession debarked at the north edge of town and turned toward the massive fort. For more than two weeks the chiefs and tribal leaders— four hundred of them—had been arriving for the Grand Council convened by the Virginia government. The Iroquois League and more than a dozen other nations were already present. Now came Shawnees, Ottawas, a few Munseys and Wyandots. This arrival was the core of the western resistance tribes: They were the last to arrive. Now the peace talks could begin. Guyasuta would speak for the Iroquois, White Eyes for the Delawares, and Cornstalk for the Shawnees.

At the head of these latecomers strode Cornstalk. The townspeople gaped at the profusion of glittering jewelry these savages wore. There were enduring rumors that the Shawnees had their own silver mines; it appeared to be true. This crude town had never before seen so much silver on such seemingly casual display.

The display, however, was not as casual as it looked. The women and men had worked on their regalia for weeks, and the result was such an array of colors and variety of fur, feathers, paint, skins, jewelry, and fabric that the drab onlookers were awed.

In the manner of wild birds, the men were even showier than the women. Some wore on their heads owl tails spread full, draped at the sides in lush brown mink skins; others wore the red tail feathers of the hawk in the same manner. Headdresses with red-and-yellow feathers, fixed to pivot and tremble with every breeze or movement, gave the appearance that fire was dancing around the wearers' heads. The ears of some of the Shawnee and Delaware men had been cut and stretched and wrapped in silver wire, or had adornments attached so that they drooped onto their shoulders. Most of the men had plucked out their eyebrows, imparting a startled look to their handsome faces. Almost naked in the September heat, some had painted their faces and bodies, mostly red, some black or blue. Many warriors were shaved bald except for queued scalplocks, adorned with feathers, beads, silver cones, even arrows. They wore nose rings with baubles and pendants down to their lips. Gorgets and necklaces of silver glittered on their bare chests, or necklaces of bear claws, bird bones, fawn hooves, squirrel skulls—any animal part that could be beaded or tied to a thong. Moccasins were decorated intricately with beads, quills, and paint in patterns that rivaled the finest European embroidery.

Some wore bright calico fabric shirts with ribbons or scalplocks sewn to breast or sleeve. Animal heads and dressed skins were worn as headgear, and one chief wore a shimmering cape made entirely of pigeon wing feathers. All in this procession, including the women, came with the look in their eye of proud warriors, confident of their place, and considering everywhere their place.

The women were keenly proud of the impression they made in this grand entrance. Their thick, glossy, hip-length hair swayed as they walked; they walked so as to accentuate the motion. They wore decorated leggings and moccasins that showed below their skirts. Many of the women wore skirts of dark blue stroud, decorated with intricately woven and stitched silk ribbon of scarlet and white, sometimes with a touch of black. They had simulated the plaids and tweeds of British fabrics in such ribbon work. To their colorful calico blouses they had added ruffles, and covered the yokes with silver brooches. Some of the women had so many silver brooches, they pinned them in rows down their sleeves and around their shirttails and skirt hems. Their arms were ringed with many silver bracelets. All of them, their children as well, wore earrings. Most of the women wore several earrings in each ear, having so many to flaunt.

These woodland women were not merely handsome women, but also the best formed and most attractive of the nations, and they did not doubt it. Some were so aware of their splendor that they could not keep from smiling, their straight teeth white against dusky skin.

These were the elite of the tribal people. Living so far away from the whites, they were still healthy and vigorous. The traders here knew them as fine hunters and trappers, shrewd and independent in dealing. They had not been weakened by alcohol or disfigured by the pox, as the nearer tribes had been. The townspeople of Pittsburgh were used to the dissolute, half-tame Indians who hung around the fort and trading establishments, but these were free, self-contained, and proud, and in such numbers they were as intimidating as they were glorious to behold.

Returning to this familiar town, Nonhelema had to get used to the smells again: the putrid tanneries, the searing smell of charcoal pits. The dirt lanes between houses stank of trodden garbage and chamber pot waste, and the white people stank with their summer sweat. Few of them ever bathed.

Every morning she, like most of her Shawnee women, went to the water, cleaning themselves, scrubbing their teeth and gums, rubbing their bodies with mint and other herbs. By her own experience, she knew that most whitemen were aroused by the musky but fresh scents of Indian women, by their tawny, bear-oiled skin, and by their natural boldness and good humor. The Shawnee women were clean and wholesome, but just bawdy and flirtatious enough to titillate whitemen. Whitemen could laugh with Shawnee women, and be frank about their desires without giving offense. They just had to learn not to try to force themselves upon them, because these women worked hard and were as strong as most men, and had been taught a *painful* way to discourage a man who was too aggressive. Sometimes a man who had been discouraged that way was unable to walk for a while.

Amid these colorful woodland Indians were a few of a noticeably different cast. Though dressed and decorated like the others, they had, on close look, the features and complexions of white people. Some had blue eyes and blond hair. A few were children.

These were white-blooded people who had been living their lives among the tribes, captives originally, most of them adopted into native families. They had been brought to be turned over to the commissioners, who would return them to their white communities, whether they wanted to go back or not. Most did not. In their hearts, they were now Shawnees, or Delawares, or Wyandots, or Mingoes. But this was one of the primary demands made last fall in the negotiations with Governor Dunmore. And it was the condition under which Virginia would release the members of Cornstalk's family who had been held hostage in Williamsburg since the previous fall. As Nonhelema walked through Pittsburgh's malodorous population, she anticipated the reunion with her brothers and nephews. But it was hard for her to look into the eyes of these repatriated wretches whose lives were about to be turned upside down. On the long trip from the Shawnee towns to Pittsburgh, several had tried to run away. One boy, slipping away from a night camp, had not been found.

Not present among the captives was Nonhelema's adopted white daughter, Fani. Though she always accompanied her mother everywhere, she was now remaining at home, where the commissioners would not see her. Fani did not remember anything about her white family, so she couldn't have been returned to them anyway. And among whites, the young woman could never have lived as well as she lived with Nonhelema, or be as much loved and cherished.

In the Shawnee queen's entourage there was, however, one non-Indian member of her household.

Though dressed and painted like a warrior, Caesar was a mulatto, a runaway slave who had come to the Shawnees and been raised in Nonhelema's family. Because he was a Negro and worked—tending livestock, cutting firewood, repairing things—whites classified him as her slave. She knew that in whiteman's language a slave was an owned person. She did not think of Caesar as someone she owned, but *slave* was the word they used—Croghan, McKee, Morgan, Zeisberger, all of them—and she didn't argue with them. Caesar was contented in Nonhelema's household; he was a warrior, had fought at the battle at the Kanawha, had a Shawnee wife and an infant, and did not want to go back to the whiteman's world, where he really would be a slave. Therefore, he had been uneasy about going to the prisoner exchange at Fort Pitt, where he might be presumed a captive and seized from her. But Caesar was an able interpreter and a gunsmith, and he would be needed, and so she had brought him to Pittsburgh. "Do not dread," she had told him. "We will say, *Caesar is my slave, and you cannot take from me what I own.* So if we use their word, they will not offend me by trying to take you from me."

They had laughed together at that, and Caesar had come along more willingly.

Girty, in his red officer's coat, came out and met them and led them into the fort.

They crossed a bridge over the moat and walked through a gate with sentries looking down on them, passed between log buildings, and emerged in the open space of the parade ground. In the center, smoke rose from an iron brazier.

In front of the flagpole stood a rank of soldiers in red uniforms, their chests crisscrossed with white belts. These were neat, straight soldiers, all alike, not the ragged militiamen of the sort that had fought in the battle at the Kanawha. At an officer's shout, a drummer with wooden sticks made a long rattling sound, and stopped. At further commands, the rank of soldiers raised their muskets to their shoulders, aimed them over the roofs, and fired all at once, making thunder and a cloud of smoke. Nonhelema was impressed, as always, by the officer's ability to make all thirteen soldiers do their movements at the same time. It was as if the officer was the one mind, and the rest were fingers of his hand. She wondered if they all relieved themselves at one command. It would have been an amusing thought—except she knew what soldiers could do when they all did what they were told and fired their weapons at once. She remembered the soldiers at the battleground who had suddenly appeared out of the creek in a straight line and sent such a storm of lead into the Indians, hitting Silverheels and wounding so many others that they had to retreat. She remembered the officer who had not shot her when he could have. She remembered that she had spoken to him of Jesus' mercy, and he had let her carry Silverheels to safety. She had thought often of that day, and believed that Jesus had saved her life that day for the purpose of being a peacemaker.

Cornstalk walked forward, carrying a string of white wampum beads to the officer. The officer extended his right hand. Girty, standing beside him, said, "Captain Neville, sir, left hand's for receiving, right for giving."

"Oh yes." The captain extended his other hand, palm up, and Cornstalk laid the strand across it.

"Brother," he said in English, "this string of sacred white beads means that my Shawnee people come here with goodwill, to speak of the way to peace with your country. Thank you for greeting us with your drum and your guns. When I last heard the sound of your drums and guns, it was at the battle by the Kanawha River. May our peoples never face each other with guns and war drums again after we talk here. Now let us smoke together. Creator will see our smoke and he will know that all our words here in the coming days will be true." He drew from his sash a brass tomahawk with a pipe bowl in the head, its handle a hollow stem. He pinched tobacco from a pouch and tamped it into the little bowl. Girty reached into the brazier with tongs and brought out an ember, from which the pipe was lit.

All was solemn and still. Blowing smoke from his mouth, Cornstalk turned the stem to the four directions, pointed it at the ground, then at the sky. "Weshemonetoo, who creates by thought: Listen to us when we talk. We will see ourselves at peace as we talk, and you will see us at peace as you hear us, and what you see becomes what is." He handed the pipe to the officer. "You smoke. On the day when all your commissioners and all our headmen have finished talking here, we all should see the future alike, and Creator will see it the same, and peace will be possible. When we have all smoked, I will give you this pipe to keep. It will always remind you of the truth we speak together here in the days to come, so that there never again will be any falseness."

Outside the moat of the great fort, on the breezy point, was spread an encampment of four hundred Indians. The fort's agents and the government commissioners had laid out nicely all the accommodations to make a large number of Indians feel welcome and comfortable, while subtly keeping them in a controlled circumstance for the peace of mind of the townspeople of Pittsburgh, as well as the fort's small, nervous military garrison.

The arrangement was meant to keep the Indians confined without making them feel confined. A wide, smooth, grassy meadowland lay between the fort and the river, usually serving as a hay field for the fort's livestock, and it made a spacious, handsome campground. An orchard of apple and peach trees gave shade, and some of the fruit was ripe. Along the edge of the river bluff ran the fort's outermost palisade. The Indians' encampment was thus inside the palisade but outside the fort's moat and walls. The only access to the meadow was a narrow bridge, easily covered by musket, rifle, or cannon from three of the fort's five bastions.

Along much of the riverside palisade, the commissioners had erected pole awning frames, roofing some with canvas, others with brush, to give the Indians shelter from wind, sun, or rain. These were within range of gunners as well, and open to observation from the fort's parapet.

It was, of course, hoped that none of these security measures would be needed, that the treaty talks would be peaceable and productive. The agents and commissioners knew how to provide good food, drink, gifts, and protocol to keep Indians mollified even if something in the proceedings should make them resentful.

Usually something did.

Cornstalk and Nonhelema sat at a small fire and smoked with their brother Silverheels. Instead of sitting opposite each other around the fire, they sat almost shoulder to shoulder, so their backs were toward the wall and they could all keep their eyes on the parapets of the fort, in case the soldiers up there might decide to shoot someone in the back. All three had been conspicuous in the battle at the Kanawha the previous year, and had killed and wounded soldiers. It was possible some of the sentries on the high parapets over there might have been in that battle, and it was not unusual for chiefs and warriors to be assassinated at peace councils by soldiers who could not forget battle incidents.

Silverheels was as tall as his brother but a slender and graceful man. He had not yet recovered all his strength after the wound he had taken in the chest at the Kanawha. There was still a sound in his lungs when he breathed, and if he inhaled while turning his head to the right, the pain in the left side of his chest made him jump. The musket ball was somewhere in his chest still. He could only vaguely remember being saved on the battlefield by his sister, and he was talking about it now.

"I remember seeing soldiers standing above on a rock with their guns ready to kill us. But somehow you persuaded them not to shoot."

She had never told him about that, in all the time she had spent doctoring him after his wound. Now she said, "I spoke to them in their tongue and reminded them of the mercy of Jesus. Brother, you are alive because of Jesus."

He thought for a while, then said smiling: "I did not see a Jesus at the battle. Maybe he was hiding behind you, then, as you helped me."

Nonhelema nodded, and said, "Then that is why I could not see him, either. But he was there. That is why we are alive, brother."

"Meh shema," Silverheels said, "sister, you are such a fool about that Jesus! You should go to the Jesus town when we leave here and have them sprinkle you, and give you one of those strange names. Mother and sister would be so happy then." He was teasing her. Their mother and a younger sister had lived for years in the Moravian mission called Gnaddenhutten as Elizabeth and Christiana, names Silverheels had never been able to pronounce.

Nonhelema answered, "Perhaps I am ready to do that now. I have had some dreams. The bleeding suffering Jesus, he tells me those words: *Blessed are the peacemakers. They shall be called the children of God.* I believe he intends me to be a peacemaker, as war keeps coming toward us. In our own nation we Mekoches are the peacemakers. Jesus knows that is so, and he would use us for that. Consider your brother Hokoleskwa." She pointed with her chin at Cornstalk. "Even he—so bloody in his youth that generals tremble at his name—he, too, is now a peacemaker! Both of you should go to the mission, too. We will all go there together. When we go home from this council, and have Nimwha and the Wolf back with us, we must take them to see *nigeah* Elizabeth and *shemah* Christiana and show them that all our kin are released from captivity. Then all of us should be christened. We will all be peacemakers. *Nigeah* and *NiShema* would so like that! And our father's spirit would be pleased also. He liked the missionaries so much."

Silverheels shook his head and chuckled, which made him cough, and he squinted in pain. Then he said, "I am uneasy about that Jesus town. If I went there, the old Zeisberger would unman me, make me be like the Delawares he has there. No longer do they have their guns. Nor their balls, neither the lead ones nor the other kind. They carry a hoe, not a gun. And to me they all seem like many male wives of the old Zeisberger—growing food for him, listening to his orders, obeying him." He made the *no* sign with a sweep of his hand, and said, "I do not want to wear a skirt and be called by one of those strange names from his Black Book. I am Silverheels. I have always been Silverheels. I am a man."

Silverheels was his name because when he was born there was no word in the Shawnee tongue for "spurs." A Shawnee infant was named for something remarkable noticed within ten days of its birth. The elder relative who was to find a name for him had seen, on the fourth day, a pair of spurs worn by a Red Coat officer who was in their village. The elder had never seen spurs before, so it was remarkable enough a sight to become his name. Though he had never worn spurs, and probably never would, Silverheels was his name, and he was proud of it, and he would never have a name like Jeremiah, or Abraham, or Noah.

It seemed to Nonhelema that all was right, as good as it could be. She felt that true peace could begin here, in this place.

She closed her eyes and took slow breaths, and she could feel that this was the good center of everything, the place from which peace would move outward, like ripples on water when one raindrop falls upon it.

It felt as if this round arbor with tables, chairs, a keg, and a council fire in the center, here at the sacred and powerful old place, Tapistewamigi-sipe, which the Delaware called Menach-sink, Where-the-Rivers-Meet, had filled with strength and wisdom. Her own heartbeat felt like a drum.

And when she opened her eyes, it looked the way it felt. The vast sky above was untroubled by any clouds, the broad rivers glittered, the arbor was round like the wheel of life where the Sacred power moves, her feet in soft moccasins were on grassy earth. Good people around, with good intentions. *Och-quo-tee, noolech-tonee-peh, wawha-eeakee, weshe-t'heekee, skota,* she prayed in pictures: clear sky, smooth water, sacred circle, well-meaning people, fire.

In the circle of shade, she saw the faces of most of the strongest and wisest people she knew, both Indian people and white people. For these people, she had every kind of respect and affection that her heart knew how to bestow. They had influence in every part of the country. If they became one in heart at this place and carried their goodwill back to their own places, there would be peace. She and Cornstalk had done everything they had known how to do to get them to come here and take up the spirit of peace. In her own heart, she believed that this was the best thing she would ever be able to do. She had seen too much war and blood, pain and revenge, too much dark distrust and fear. Peace must be made, she had come to believe, or there would be nothing worth living for. To fight was thrilling, yes, and to feel the glory that made one's breath scream out, yes, but she understood the long pain, the healing or the failing to heal, and the remorse, and the bad dreams, the people frightened and fleeing from enemies, the mourning for those lost. War glory was too brief, like a moment of *soos*, the man–woman thrill, which also had its glory but then long consequences.

The outburst of war joy was a false kind of joy, and the suffering that followed was far too heavy.

But peace was a joy that lasted long and could be savored bit by bit. In peace, one could wake to beauty and sacredness, and savor the calm of it, and listen to the laughter of children, and give silent thanks for all the good things Creator had made, from morning to night, through the seasons. To make peace was the best thing one could want to do, and she recited to herself still again, as she looked around at the men and women in this circle passing the pipe and displaying the great peace belt of wampum, with its thirteen star shapes, one for each of the colonies: "Blessed are the peacemakers. For they shall be called children of God."

And so she felt that she was sitting here with the children of God.

Her own forebear Paxinosa with William Penn the Quaker and Tamanend the Delaware had given much of their lives for this purpose: a land without war, a land without the fear of war. When Paxinosa died, that had been the best thing he could remember before crossing over: that he had helped great men try to bring peace.

The great men here in this circle, now smoking from the shared pipe for peace, had all been warriors. Behind their faces, surely, were memories of brutal acts—some of which, at least, were their own. Hardly anyone here had not spilled blood or cut open the flesh of enemies. She herself had done so. Few of the women in the council had done so on a battlefield as she had, but most of them had, in vengeful fury, whipped or burned the enemy prisoners their husbands and brothers dragged back from war.

That was the greatest aspect of this: to make peace seekers out of warriors. People who had never fought, who had never looked into an enemy's eyes and struck him dead, such people could think and talk of peace and it meant little.

But to make killers sit together and desire peace, and forswear further killing—that was a great and noble work. Jesus would surely say that was a greater thing to do.

Her eye passed along, looking at the faces of the killers who now sought peace.

First there was her own brother Cornstalk. She could remember scolding him, long ago, when he came home from raids in Virginia carrying scalps of children and women, as well as men's, back in the years when the French were at war with the English, and the Shawnees had taken the Frenchmen's side. After that scolding, Cornstalk had killed no more children. Instead, he had brought her alive a little girl daughter of some Virginians he had killed. That little girl was now her beloved Fani.

Red Pole, Pluggy, Black Hoof, Black Fish, Blue Jacket, Hard Man, White Eyes, Killbuck, Buckangahelas, Big Cat, Montour, Captain Pipe, Chief Crane of the Wyandots, Guyasuta the Seneca, sitting in this great circle: They all were killers. They all had slain white people.

But she knew that they were not killers for love of killing. They had killed while trying to protect their people, and their croplands and hunting grounds, and had become involved in the whiteman's wars, or they had killed to avenge the deaths of their own people. Now there was pressure from every direction to stop making war. The Iroquois nations in the northeast had been persuaded by their Indian agent, the great Sir Johnson, to come here and help quiet the anger of southwest tribes who were being crowded by Virginians. The missionaries had been trying to disarm and settle the Delawares, among whom they had influence. The whiteman's governments were always sending out emissaries carrying pleas for peace.

Now, Nonhelema hoped, the desire for peace was so widespread and strong that it might actually be achieved.

Among the whitemen at the tables in the center of the circle stood three whose lives were most interwoven with hers—with her personal fortunes, with her hopes for her people, and with her woman's heart. Morgan the trader, Croghan the Indian agent, and McKee,

Croghan's deputy. Each was a man with understanding of the Indian heart; each had some power to make the peace work; and, although they all were very different from one another, each was the kind of man who could turn a woman's heart over.

It had been more than a decade since she traveled the breadth of her homeland with George Morgan, serving as his guide and interpreter as he tried to build trading colonies from the mountains to the Mississippi's shores. He had traded for years in the Shawnee communities, was honest and generous, and was a gentleman of great charm and politeness. He was a man of much learning, but with no ear for Indian tongues, and had needed her to translate every word for him in all those eventful years. Thus she had become his escort and his consort and had borne him a son, whom she had named Morgan in his honor.

George Morgan had a white wife and children back in Princeton, New Jersey. He was married to a daughter of one of his business partners, but like most Indian traders who stayed in the Indian settlements for months at a time, he had enhanced his connections in the Shawnee towns through his Indian marriage to Nonhelema. She, in turn, had prospered by her intimate association with the successful trader, and had become wealthy. Even since their pathways had parted, she and her family sustained their respect and affection for the trader. He had been given the esteemed name *Tamanend*, "the Affable One," by the Delawares, and was called Wapeymachikthe by the Shawnees, which meant "White Deer." Handsome of face, his balding forehead making him look more intelligent with the passing years, he was stubborn when he thought he was right, which was most of the time. His ancestors were from Wales, as he was proud to claim, and over the course of their years together she had been entranced by legends he told her of that old part of England. He had told those tales so vividly that she could imagine ancient kings as she watched the firelight flicker on the ceiling above their bed. She could remember even now those images. He had told her about a Christian prince of Wales, who had come to this land hundreds of years ago and made colonies, but had been killed by the Indians. When they were lovers, her heart and mind had soared high and far, and she still cherished in memory the wonder of those times, and looked tenderly at him across this place of peacemaking.

As she sat here in the circle of shade with the breeze off the river moving everything—the grass, the smoke, the flag, the feathers, the ribbons, the plume of Morgan's three-cornered hat—his eyes wandered to meet hers now and then, and they both would nod and smile. There would be time, while she was here, to talk with him again, perhaps to drink with him. She would tell him about the growing-up of his son Morgan, who was every year a better hunter, not warrior age yet, but as tall as George Morgan himself. The boy had been raised and trained by his uncles as a Shawnee man, but had also spent some time at the mission, learning to read and write.

These were good things that both Indians and whites should share. They made her heart warm and calm, helped her believe that the peace would work. The Indians and the good, intelligent whitemen like Morgan would be able to live close to each other and share their knowledge and their beliefs. Morgan had learned much from Indians that even the wisest whitemen did not know, and he had taught her about matters the Indians had never imagined. Someday her Shawnee people would get to see that the whitemen were not all like the aggressive, murderous renegades who infested the frontier bringing death and drunkenness to the Indians. Those who had come to know Wapeymachikthe understood that most of the conflicts had been with the worst of the whitemen, and that there were better ones.

Also there among the commissioners of peace was old red-haired Colonel George Croghan, a *mithochquie lenni*, a lusty, robust man, the Indian agent at this fort. He was an uncle of George Morgan. So many white men were named George, perhaps because three kings of England had been Georges in the last hundred years.

Croghan was a favorite of many Indians, for he treated them as warm friends and always managed to get for them whatever goods they desired; he was free with liquor, and was a brave old soldier.

In an incident here, a few years before, when a mob of Indian haters had attacked her and her brothers and stabbed Silverheels, all three might have perished if Colonel Croghan had not fired his one pistol into the air and threatened to discharge the other into the first man who touched the Shawnees.

Often since then Croghan had given Nonhelema hints—subtle when he was sober, not so subtle when he was drunk—that he would welcome a reward from her for the rescue, and she knew what the reward was that he had in mind. Instead, she had managed so far to show her gratitude through kindness, friendship, and respect. That sort of gratitude could be sustained much longer.

Nonhelema knew something that most of her people did not: that George Morgan disliked Croghan, and dealt through him only because he had to. Morgan thought Croghan dealt deceitfully with Indians. But Croghan was a close friend with one of the older partners of Morgan's trading company, so Morgan was stuck with him. In the past ten years, Croghan had made bold dealings that had nearly ruined the company. The Indian trade was a complicated and delicate business, far from the supervising partners at Philadelphia, and Croghan was involved in a web of Pennsylvania land speculators whose machinations bewildered Morgan. Nonhelema knew of these complications and these doubts, and she could only hope that peace would smooth it all out.

Croghan, too, met Nonhelema's eyes from time to time as he surveyed this circle of Indians. When she saw him looking at her from the center of the council ground, she nodded and smiled at him, very slightly. It did no harm to keep a powerful man interested. There might come a time when she could use his infatuation in behalf of her people, or for her hopes of peace.

Her glance fell most often upon Alexander McKee, however. It was not only because he was such a pleasure to behold, but also because she believed that her life and McKee's were like the place Menach-sink, flowing together sacredly after coming long distances. They both had known it at once the first time they saw each other here three years before.

She had known of McKee long before she first saw him. When Indians spoke of him, there was warmth and wonder in their voices and their faces. Some said that he must be one of the ancestors, returned in the mask of a half-breed whiteman. Deer would come to him, it was said. He was not a solemn man but was as wise as an elder, and every answer he had favored the Indians, in long-seeing ways. He was of a large clan of trading McKees; his mother had been the Shawnee wife of one named Thomas McKee. Nonhelema had loved his reputation even before she saw him. And then she had seen him, and he had seen her.

His hair was so light a yellow that it looked like those powdered wigs the elegant whitemen wore to hide their dirt-colored hair. His face was bold but serene, his complexion like copper.

Instantly, he had become the whiteman of her most intense affections. It was so good to be close enough again to look at him. And sometime while they were here for all this peacemaking, there would be times for being much closer.

These preliminaries were long and slow, because of the large numbers of Indians present. The passing of the pipe, the long greeting speeches, and the tedious translations of English into various tongues could not be hurried. Nonhelema herself understood all the languages. Her Negro man, Caesar, stood out there among the commissioners, alongside Girty, patiently helping them understand some of the Indians' responses. She herself stood up now and then to explain what someone was trying to say. It all required much patience and concentration. Now and then she looked over and watched the Delaware chief Buckangahelas as he tried with all his might to follow the speeches. Buckangahelas was a scar-faced man who had stretched his earlobes until they reached his shoulders. In his concentration, he often put an earlobe into the corner of his mouth and sucked on it.

Most of the white officers and commissioners were like Morgan, unable or unwilling to learn any Indian languages.

There were Indian men like that, too, who would not even try to learn the whiteman's tongue, because it was too strange, or because they disliked and distrusted whitemen so much that they did not want their untruthful language to enter and corrupt their spirits.

Translation was tedious. The shade moved as voices droned on.

Nonhelema was eager for the part of the proceedings when her kinfolk would be brought out and returned from captivity, and she was eager for the debate over the terms of the peace, and for the agreements to be reached. But first there was all this formality, which was good, because it confirmed that these whiteman commissioners respected the chiefs gathered before them. There would be the traditional giving of gifts, which would be generous. There would be the giving up of the Indians' captives. This would be just the first of many days. It might last until the days grew shorter and the leaves began to turn red.

Nonhelema was not the only woman sitting in the council. She was not even the only woman chief. In every tribal delegation sat a few women who were village chiefs, national peace chiefs, or clan mothers. Among the Delawares sat the formidable Montour women of the Susquehanna, women of famous ferocity and stubbornness. Most of them were matronly at least, or elderly. Whitemen who were not experienced in counciling with Indians usually made the mistake of trying to exclude women from such business, but had to learn quickly that they would not be excluded, that tribal business was as much women's business as men's. As if embarrassed by the indignity of having to hear women speak and vote on important issues, the whitemen usually omitted mention of the women in their reports and their documents. When women marked a treaty, it was hardly ever acknowledged that any signatory was female. The whitemen did not want their women to know that Indian women had authority. When Nonhelema stood up to say something, the whitemen would usually look at Cornstalk, the man sitting nearest to her, as if they expected him to verify what she was saying or tell her to shut up.

I am glad I am not a white woman, she thought. *What poor creatures! They might as well be slaves!*

Stiff-necked Shawnee chiefs like Hard Man and Red Pole and Blue Jacket had come reluctantly, giving evidence of their desire for peace even though they had some things to say that the peace commissioners would not like to hear.

Hard Man now stood in the afternoon sunlight haranguing the whitemen, but he meant for all the Indians to understand his feelings as well. Nonhelema hoped he would not be too severe.

"Brothers! The whites tell us of their enlightened understanding, and the wisdom they have from heaven, at the same time they cheat us to their hearts' content! For we are as fools in their eyes, and they say among themselves, 'The Indians know nothing! The Indians understand nothing!'" There arose a murmur of agreement from the other chiefs.

As that was translated to them, the commissioners tried to keep their displeasure off their faces.

Hard Man went on: "Listen, brothers! If they have all that understanding from heaven, why are they always set one against the other among themselves? Why does not heaven tell them whether this sacred place, Menach-sink, is in Pennsylvania or in Virginia, so that they would not have to fight each other over that question? If they have all that understanding from heaven, why must the king's soldiers in Boston and New England be shooting at the colonists, and the colonists shooting at the king's soldiers? Maybe it is true that we Indians understand nothing. We do not understand why a governor of Virginia moves an army into the valley of this great river, far out of

Virginia, far into Shawnee land, to punish a Mingo chief, who merely avenged the murders of his family by white criminals who should never have been there at all."

The chiefs muttered agreement. That was how most of them had seen the events from Tahgahyuteh's tragedy and the invasion by Dunmore, and most of them resented the humiliation of having to come to this council at the summons of the Americans.

"Brothers of Virginia, and of your Congress, Listen:

"As it was your desire that we should restore the prisoners we had among us from previous wars with you, we have spent the greatest part of the last winter in getting them together, and have not had time to think of anything else.

"Brothers, surely you do not understand how difficult it has been. Our towns are spread far apart. Our chiefs of the different towns do not all agree with each other. All the people of our towns may choose what they wish to do in their lives. The chiefs cannot force them to do what they feel is bad. The chiefs and the council all must talk and decide what to do. Even then, the council must persuade the people that it would be a good thing.

"Brothers of Virginia, you told us to send all your flesh and blood. All that we could find we have brought, but some have run away. Some of those we have since collected. This is our part that we promised to do. We have done our best at it. We brought them here to give to you, but many of them will be hard for you to keep. Some told us they will run away from you, so you must not blame us if they do. Some told us they would kill themselves if they had to go back, and you must not blame us if they do.

"Brothers of Virginia, some of the people you call our captives we did not capture. They were your slaves, and when they ran away we took them into our families as our brothers and sisters, and they do not want to go back and be slaves again. Some of them are husbands or wives to our own people. We will not bring their children to you because they were born with Shawnee blood. When you demand we bring you such a Negro mother of our children, then you force us to divide families, just as the slave owners were always free to do to them.

"Listen, brothers of this commission, if you think it should be no trouble for us to return everyone you want: There is an old woman who used to be a slave. You may get her if you carry her on your back, for she will not walk to you.

"Listen brothers! In our nation, a chief does not have a right to make our people give up what they wish to keep. A chief can only try to persuade them that giving up what is dear to them would please the whitemen. They would rather please their families, by keeping them together, than please whitemen, who have never done anything to please the Shawnees, but rather have only tormented us. Think of these things, brothers. We try to do what you demand. But the white-man often demands too much. I am Hard Man. I am one of the Mekoche Shawnees who want peace with you. But there can be no true peace unless you try to understand us. I will have more to say later on other matters, but I will sit now."

All this was hard for Nonhelema to listen to, because it was making the commissioners' faces harden. It was not making anyone feel peaceful. But she had known, even while persuading Hard Man to come here, that he would say such things, because he had warned her that he would say only what was true.

Hard Man turned to sit down, but instead straightened up.

"Brothers, there is one more thing I would say." He raised his hand and gestured toward a wooden keg that stood on a rack beside the commissioners' table.

"You have set the keg here in our sight. You know that our people are awaiting the moment when you open that. The keg reminds me to speak of some whites who are always tormenting us. They are the rum sellers and the whiskey sellers."

Here he let his face twist into a leering half-smile. "See them coming into our towns with their rum! See them offering it to us with persuasive kindness! Hear them cry, 'Drink! Drink!' And when we have drunk, and act like the crazed, behold these good whites, these men of a benevolent race, who get their wisdom from heaven, stand-ing by, laughing among themselves, and saying, 'Oh, what fools! What great fools the Shawnees are!' But who made them fools? Who are the cause of their madness?"

Now Hard Man turned to face George Morgan, and extended a hand toward him, waited for the interpreter to finish, then said: "Brother Wapeymachikthe, thank you for being generous with what is in that keg. I wish it were fresh water from a spring, but I fear it is not water. I wish I could forbid you to open the keg, but I cannot. My own peers here are already slobbering for it. But I will say this:

"As long ago as my grandfathers, they came home from treaty

councils like this one, with their chins down, lamenting, 'We got drunk. We made promises and can't remember what they were.'

"Wapeymachikthe, listen. Before we get drunk, remember, these are the only promises we came to make: To return prisoners. Not to attack boats on the Ohio-sipe. To abide by the trade regulations. To stop hunting in our old hunting grounds south of the Ohio. That is an evil and unfair thing your governor made our chiefs agree to, and I believe Cornstalk was wrong to promise that; he was a little drunk then. But we will obey it, because it is a promise that was made.

"Those are the promises your governor compelled us to make, after the battle at the Kanawha, when his army came close to our homes and threatened our women and children. Now remember what your governor promised to *us*: that whites would not hunt on *our* side of the Ohio River!

"Brother, they have been breaking that promise ever since it was made. They keep coming over, and they kill not just the deer, but some of our hunters, as well. Brother Wapeymachikthe, brothers of Virginia, brothers of Congress: Remember—before we get drunk— what those promises were. Make your rough and lawless men stay on the other side of the river, or there cannot be any peace to follow this council! I have spoken what I had to say. Now I shall sit down and listen to another!"

After Hard Man's strong words, the commissioners whispered for a while, and then announced that they needed to talk among themselves about the things he had said. They said that they should adjourn for the rest of the afternoon, and would resume the next morning.

Cornstalk, who had meant to get up and say some words that would soften the criticisms they had just heard, was annoyed that he would not have that opportunity, but knew better than to argue. Most of the Indians were already rising, chatting happily about the things Hard Man had said so well, and were drifting toward the liquor keg. No matter that he had spoken so scornfully about the subject of whiskey, he had spoken truly when he said they were almost slobbering for it.

Cornstalk stared sharply at Hard Man for a moment. Then he shook his head and grinned. "Good, my brother. I had meant to say those things but more gently and sweetly. I think it was better they heard you say it so well. Shall you and I be foolish Indians and go to the keg before the rest of the foolish Indians drink it empty?" He turned then to Nonhelema. "Sister, did he speak well for our cause of peace?"

She shrugged. "What is to be negotiated, if they think we have no grievances? It was a good start for the days to come."

Cornstalk, Hard Man, Silverheels, Red Pole, and Black Wolf all gathered up their robes, surrounding Nonhelema. In the presence of strangers or enemies, Shawnee men accompanied their women as bodyguards.

A flush-faced old George Croghan came limping over. With outstretched hands indicating all of them, but looking at Nonhelema, he said, "May I beg your favor? I invite you and your entourage to dinner with me and the commissioners." He was nearly breathless as he spoke. While he was dressed as a proper gentleman with knee breeches and waistcoat, one could tell by his rosy cheeks and sun-bleached, graying red hair that he was a man who had lived most of his life outdoors. Most of his life he had been a trader among the western Indians. He had the sense to address the male chiefs, but they had noticed for years that he could not keep his eyes off Nonhelema. Many whitemen were similarly afflicted. Croghan went on: "It would be our pleasure if you would join us. We have taken the liberty of providing some entertainment afterward. We know your family's love of violin music, and our fort fifer plays elegant music as well. All your family are invited who would like to come."

Nonhelema turned toward Silverheels and read his eyes as they glittered in brotherly amusement. All of them were used to the effects she had on strangers, especially the whitemen. With the slightest nod he let her know he thought it would be good to accept the invitation, then gave her a teasing roll of the eyes and smirk.

She turned to Croghan. "Colonel, you know that we owe you even our lives and would deny you nothing. What could we love better than such music and the pleasure of your company? Will it be at your house? Yes? We know the way. We will go to Killbuck's first, and refresh ourselves. Then we will come." With that, Nonhelema turned, holding her cape closer to her body, and walked away between Cornstalk and Silverheels.

"It would have been better," Cornstalk mused as they walked down toward the river, "if the whiteman had never come here in their boats. But would it have been this interesting?"

"For some reason, Weshemonetoo directed their boats this way," Nonhelema said. "We must make of it the best we can."

She anticipated an evening with the sweet excitement that music put in her heart. She wondered if McKee would be there, too. Surely he would be.

The large dining room in Colonel Croghan's house was hot, being so full of people and candles. Nonhelema fluttered a fan made of a hawk's tail feathers. The officers, in their fancy woolen coats and waistcoats, were wilting quickly, and their faces shone with running sweat. Candles burned in the wall sconces and along the tables; far too many candles, she thought.

She wished her daughter could have been here to see all the glittering crockery and the silverware. But Fani would be suffering here. She was miserable in hot, close places. If she had been here, she would have been over by one of the room's two open windows, with her head sticking out. Or she would be outside, sitting under a tree.

The dinner would have been perfect fare for midwinter. It was a heavy feast of great variety. There was roast pork on a bed of noodles and vegetables, covered with a raisin and mustard sauce. Huge portions of beef lay on platters, in moats of brown gravy with silver slivers of sweet braised onions. Nonhelema was fascinated with the colorful kinds of garden vegetables that had been introduced by the white people: passionately colored vegetables like the beet and the carrot and red radish. The sauces were intense with herbs and seasonings that the Shawnees had not had until the traders brought them and their seeds. Nonhelema often took seeds and shoots of the foreign herbs back to village women, who had learned to raise and use them in their native dishes.

She loved dill sauces. When she bit into the tiny seeds, she relished their sharp and pleasant flavor. Cornstalk watched her rapturous expressions; then he would lean to her and say, "Are you pretending, to make Colonel Croghan proud of his cook? There are too many flavors all thrown on the meat. My mouth is confused." But Cornstalk also smiled as he watched her eat with such great appreciation. She was heavy with the responsibilities of peacemaking, and it was good to see her childish delight in these foods.

Occasionally something would arrive from the kitchen that made Cornstalk and Silverheels look at one another until they saw the officers eat some. They then would try it cautiously themselves. Nonhelema watched with sly amusement as her brothers put dabs of food in their mouths and made faces. She saw Silverheels mouth something until he thought no one was watching. He put an empty spoon in his mouth and when he set it down on the table it was full. She covered her mouth to hide her mirth, and just then saw Alexander McKee watching what Silverheels had done. She and McKee looked at each other with their hands over their mouths, quaking with mirth.

Croghan's servants had been serving wine steadily, and it was different from whiskey in its effect on her. It was making her think everything was amusing. When she felt sweat trickle down her spine and between her nates, she had a notion of announcing across the table to McKee that her behind was getting moist. She had better sense than to do that, but the notion of it made her feel even more giddy.

Directly across the table from her sat a white woman, the "fort wife" of one of the officers. Some of the officers had real wives back east but would take up with camp followers or whores and elevate them to demimondaine roles while stationed here. The pretty red-haired girl was giggling wildly at something that was being whispered into her ear by Colonel Croghan. Her pale bosom, almost spilling out of her bodice, was flushed and mottled, as was her face, from the heat and drink. Now Croghan raised an eyebrow and darted a look at Nonhelema even while trifling with the poor lass, and Nonhelema realized that the old fool imagined he was making her jealous. So she threw him a sham frown and wagged a forefinger at him, which made him look very smug. She looked over at McKee, who was nodding at her with a barely perceptible smile; he had been watching. Then she felt her brother Cornstalk leaning close, so she eased toward him and he said in her ear, his voice a soft rumble, *"Mithochquie wanni thotah."* Lusty drunkard.

She nodded, chuckling. Cornstalk put his hand on her wrist and said, "But his lust is just for you, not for *Wapey Ullene.*" That meant "White Breasts."

"Ie nie," she replied. "That's right."

"I remember," Cornstalk went on, "the last time we were visited by our friend Colonel Croghan, I came out of my lodge early in the morning. I saw the colonel standing by a tree. He was trying to make water on it. He didn't know I was nearby. He was making pain noises in his throat."

"Ah-heh?"

"Yes. I think one might find his old *passah-tih* to be truly rotten by now."

She gave Cornstalk a sidelong smile and said, "If my brother means that as advice, thank you. But there was no danger."

He grunted and nodded and started to lean back in his chair, but she took his wrist now and leaned to him, smiling. "Listen, brother. If you should happen to see Captain McKee pissing by a tree, please tell me how he does."

Nonhelema had no self-control when sweets were put before her. In her people's natural diet, very little was sweet, besides fruits and berries and maple sugar. Here at Colonel Croghan's, the dessert chef had created mountains of cakes, flaky ones and crumbly ones, some slathered with icing, some filled with fruit jams and ground nutmeats and honey, and custards in shells, dusted with nutmeg, cinnamon, and clove, wonderful flavors brought from the other side of the world. By the time the room was cleared of its dining furniture to make room for musicians and dancing, she was almost wheezing and her middle felt as tight as a drumhead. She pulled her little clay pipe from her bag, filled the bowl with *kinnikinnick*, and picked up a candle to light it. Then she went to the back door of the house, following others. Outdoors under the stars, waiting for her turn in the outbuilding, the sweat on her face and in her clothes chilled her to shivering. The noises issuing from behind the plank door of the privy hinted that everyone else had been near bursting. She looked up at the stars that shone among the trees, those clean, cold points of light that were said to be the souls of all the warriors from the beginning of time; she saw the bright path of stardust the whitemen called the Milky Way, but the Shawnees knew was the road to the otherside world, and as she looked at all the unreachable splendor she was hearing the spewing, the wet crepitations, the tricklings, the grunts, the ploppings, the proud fart-buglings of wealthy whitemen who believed that everything they did must be done powerfully. They seemed to have not a shred of the strict farting etiquette that her Shawnees exercised.

She blew a stream of smoke, looking skyward.

Or were those stars not the souls of warriors, but the candles of saints? Was this a glimpse of the heaven of peacemakers, the heaven that the missionary Zeisberger told of, the heaven one could reach only by renouncing everything but the suffering bleeding Jesus?

Zeisberger. There was the other whiteman in her life making her turn her back on the ways of her ancestors.

Traders who brought you things you never knew you needed.

Soldiers who came into your country and forced you to make promises.

Whiskey sellers who brought visions and miseries in jugs.

And missionaries who told you that your god was no good.

But, the little outbuilding reminded her, always you were a person, whatever color or god you had, a person who lived by putting something in the hole at one end of your body and expelling it out from the hole at the other end. It smelled so delicious as it came in. And it stank so badly when it went out.

But, she thought as she went into the little black room, *one's own does not stink quite like that of the others.*

She puffed vigorously and breathed her pipe smoke to mask the smells of those who had gone before.

The benches were moved to line the walls. A few chairs were lined up near the musicians, next to the fireplace, and on a table sat a small cask of whiskey. The musicians began with several lively tunes using fife and drum. Then came a fiddle player who stomped his foot to make his rhythm. Soon many of them were patting their hands and feet as the spirits became more carefree. That was inspired by the happy music, but also by the free-flowing whiskey that the officers and commissioners kept pouring into the Indians' cups, tending especially to the ladies.

After a few jigs and reels, Croghan could not keep his own Irish feet still and asked Nonhelema to dance with him. When she stood, he was tall but she was taller. Off they went around the room, skipping and stomping to the beat of the tune. Her moccasins were soft on the floor, while his hard-soled shoes clattered. Both of them laughed like children. Whenever she caught a glimpse of Alexander McKee, he was watching her.

Soon there were four couples out swirling and stomping and then two more couples, and the floor became full of sweating dancers. She saw McKee sweep past with a comely young Mohawk woman. Several of the men standing by decided to dance even though they had run out of women.

Other dancers changed partners and danced until they were dripping sweat and nearly out of breath. Croghan kept her to himself. She could smell his desire, and she imagined even the stink of his diseased loins. But there was good purpose to be served by keeping such an influential old dear in rut. She kept her eyes dancing with mischief and teasing, and laughed bawdily at his leering remarks, even though she could hardly hear them amid the music and thundering feet. She saw that Croghan admired her jewelry, it seemed he was watching it as much as he watched her. It was mostly silver. She wore brooches on her deep red blouse, and her arms were full of bracelets. On her upper arm she even wore wide silver circlets like the warriors. Her ears were pierced along the row of the outside rim, allowing her to wear more than a dozen small and dangling earrings, all tastefully arranged, with an ear cuff in the middle of the rim with dangles of its own. Contrasting to all her silver were her several long pearl necklaces. One was of gunmetal blue-and-pink-colored pearls, while others were strangely shaped white pearls. The most unusual piece she wore was a necklace that had a strange rounded arrowhead shape ornament made of pure white mother-of-pearl, beautifully smooth.

Nonhelema finally had to insist that Croghan let her rest, that she just could not keep up with him. It was calculated flattery, and it got her free of him.

Now, at last, she was with Alexander McKee, the one man she had been following with her eyes as well as her yearning all day and into the night.

He held her hand high, then bowed low, then touched her waist and guided her as they pranced and turned through the exertions of the dance. Now she did not feel bloated discomfort anymore. She felt as light as laughter, as if she were dancing on violin notes, not the floor. At arm's length with their hands touching, she would see him smiling at her with direct gaze and plain delight, his blue eyes glinting with specks of candlelight, then he would be close with an arm around her waist, and the other people and the walls of the room whirling by beyond his jaunty profile. And through his arm she could feel the warm power that she believed to be the invisible tie between them, that oneness that she had been able to feel even when looking at him across the wide council ground this morning, but now with even greater pull because they were hand to hand, hip to hip. His small, straight teeth—not rotten like those of most whitemen his age—were in contrast to the ruddy brown of his weathered face. And she could study in one moment the whole pretty shape of his lips, and the indentations in his cheeks that reminded her of a mischievous boy even though he was a mature man of strength, accomplishments, and good reputation. It was a marvel how many fine things Creator could put together in the making of one man. Had she been able to imagine one to be made just to her pleasure, even then she would not have had the cleverness to wish for some of the attributes that Creator had assembled in this one. She had given heart and body to men who had been irresistible and admirable in their own ways, and she still carried within herself a gratitude for what they had shared with her, even those who had become disappointments. But she could not remember ever having felt an acceptance as complete as this. It passed through her mind that Weshemonetoo, or perhaps Jesus, was rewarding her with this excellent lover at last because she had turned to being a peacemaker.

When the music stopped, McKee's final flourish was a quick, arching embrace that for a moment pressed the length of their bodies together, surprising her, and before she even thought, she flexed her loins against his. He looked at the ceiling and blew a breath through pursed lips as he released her. They had not been able to talk together through the whole day or evening, not even during the dancing, but she doubted they could have been more eloquent toward each other with any words. There would be much to say about this treaty, about the needs and wishes of the Indians, the demands of the commissioners, in the many long days to come. This, tonight, had been their greeting after a long absence.

The musicians were bowing, dancers clapping and laughing, the roomful of crowded people reasserting itself around her, her feet in their moccasins felt the boards of the floor, Cornstalk was looking at her from a far bench, and Croghan was shouldering through the guests, coming over but getting detained by guests once and again. Commissioners and officers were at the liquor cask, smoking their pipes; one commissioner was going on loudly above the drone of male voices. Nonhelema fanned her face with the hawk-tail fan that had been hanging from her wrist. And Alexander McKee was still holding her other hand in his, looking into her eyes, nodding and chuckling, his eyes looking as if they would brim over if he let them.

"Aye, glory!" he breathed. "I have missed ye, m'lady! Y'd be surprised how frequently you're in my thoughts. And what those thoughts are, I might add."

"I, too. I lean toward the east all day, because east is where you live."

"I do pray the business will allow us time soon for some ease, in your exclusive company. This very night wouldn't be too soon for me. Eh?"

"Nor for me, but too soon for my family. I am escorted by brothers who are grave and seemly men. Let us sit and smoke before we leave. I have a question for you."

They found a bench near an open window and the air was a relief. Both were sweating through their clothes. She sat down and McKee went to the keg, where slender clay tavern pipes stood in a rack. She filled her little pipe. Colonel Croghan was still engaged in some guffawing conversation with the trader Richard Butler in the middle of the room. Butler had been married to one of her sisters, but abandoned her. Once Nonhelema had saved his life. And Croghan had saved hers. It seemed odd to sit here in Croghan's house now and think of such connections and such events, once so crucial, now mere memories. Peace was the crucial matter now.

Cornstalk had stood up by his bench on the other side of the room and was stooped down to hear a commissioner who was talking to him.

"Now, my dear, a stirrup cup." McKee returned and gave her a glass of whiskey and touched his to it, holding both his glass and pipe in one hand. "To what are we drinking? Health? Love?"

"To peace."

"Aye, if you're my piece, I'll drink to that!"

She shook her head, but with a smile, and sipped. "Dear friend, I want to know when the government will bring our brothers and restore them to us. Governor Dunmore said he would keep them to assure that we would come. Now we are here."

McKee lifted an iron sconce from the wall, and held it while she lit her pipe from its guttering flame. She could tell that he was reluctant to answer.

"The commissioners," he said, "don't think the chiefs tried hard enough to bring all your captives back. They are, um, thinking to keep your chiefs—and perhaps more—from the other tribes here, until more of the named captives are brought in."

"No! That could not be done this year! That was not his promise, that governor! He said he would hold them only until we came here. We promised to bring the captives we could bring, and we have done so. The commissioners are changing his promise!"

"Aye. It seems."

"How can we make peace if they are in bad faith? They must bring our brothers to us!"

"Look, my dear." McKee tilted his head toward the conversation on the far side of the room. "I'm sure your brother is stating the case to the gentleman commissioner. There's time yet to say it all. Hard Man made them think today. Oop! Here comes our red-faced host. And here comes Silverheels. I fear I'm about to lose the moment, alas." He chuckled. "Keep me in your heart till the next one."

Nonhelema and her entourage were being escorted to the council grounds camp by four soldiers assigned to protect them from lawless night people of the Pittsburgh streets, or from the sort of harm that had befallen them here three years before. One soldier carried a punched-tin candle lantern to light their way past the long, dark warehouses. They were talking softly but angrily among themselves about the commissioner's treachery. Suddenly Cornstalk raised his hand and exclaimed: "*Ketawpi!* Listen!"

They could hear it—wails, trills, shouts, drifting up from the campground in the meadow below Fort Pitt. All too familiar, the mayhem of many Indians gone wild on liquor. A gunshot banged and echoed.

"*Motchee!*" Nonhelema cried. "The devils have got them all drunk! They'll be hurting each other! Hurry!"

At the gate to the enclosure, soldier sentries were laughing and yelling taunts into the tumult. "Hey, Chief Boozy! Who gave ye permission to puke on army land? Ha he heee!" The sentries were having a good time, but were edgy; they had fixed bayonets and were staying just outside the compound. When Nonhelema, Cornstalk, and the other chiefs came running up behind them with their soldier escort, and the sentries turned and saw the tall, formidable Indians next to them, their eyes went round and they almost fled their post.

Inside was a firelit scene that looked like the place Brother Zeisberger and his preachers were always describing, the hell where unsaved souls went to burn forever. A bonfire was roaring in the center of the council circle, sending up a tower of smoke and sparks, casting a glow over the whole scene, and dozens of smaller campfires flickered throughout the grounds, lighting the faces and figures of staggering people, half-conscious ones crawling, many more slumped around their fires, grinning, heads bobbing. Little groups of sober ones huddled fearfully together for safety, looking about for help or guidance. Throughout the garish, smoky scene, men were lurching, waving their arms, hooting at each other, some striking out at each other with weapons or bare hands. Overlooking the whole debauch were soldiers up on the high walls of the fort, needling, hooting, pointing, uttering simulated Indian war cries.

Nonhelema's heart ached at this spectacle, and old hatred of the whiskey sellers flared inside her.

But she knew that, while this was happening here, the powerful whitemen and officers had been plying their chiefly guests in their homes with whiskey and wine, including her brothers and herself, who, fortunately, usually were more restrained. *We're not free of the shame of this,* she thought.

But there was no good in thinking now about guilt or shame. Now this pitiful recklessness needed to be brought under control before many people hurt themselves or each other or grew too sick to engage in the treaty. She and her brothers knew they must now go in, find the chiefs, help them get sober, help them get their people under control.

The condition of the Indians would be pitiful when the talks resumed. They would be dull-witted, without dignity, remorseful, and thirsty for more liquor. All that would be to the advantage of the treaty commissioners, and the commissioners knew it.

"Come," Cornstalk said. "This will require all we can do the rest of the night."

"You're going in there?" the soldier in charge of their escort stammered, no doubt afraid of the consequences to himself if any harm came to his charges, or, worse, if these chiefs wanted to take the bodyguards in there with them.

Nonhelema spoke right into his tremulous face. "We are going in. You go to the fort and find Simon Girty. Tell him we need him."

Cornstalk was already striding into the midst of it. "First," he yelled over his shoulder in that mighty voice, "we will break the kegs."

Neither the council grounds nor the Indians were in condition to resume the talks the next day. And when the council resumed on the following day, Nonhelema was not able to feel that same sense of its possibilities and sacred purpose as she had felt in the beginning.

The Virginia commissioners and those of the Continental Congress made their statements, explaining that the king of England

and his subjects here in America were having a quarrel, and that the thirteen colonies, represented by the shapes on the great wampum belt, had joined together to face the king with one voice. Their voice was called Congress. The king had not listened to the voice of Congress, they said, and soldiers of the king had fought with militiamen of Massachusetts Colony. A soldier named George Washington—who once had fought against the French at this very place—had been appointed to command all the soldiers of Congress. Some of the older chiefs leaned to each other and laughed. They remembered that the French had defeated Washington easily.

"Brothers," intoned one of the commissioners, a grim man named Wilson, speaking for Congress—"the thirteen colonies are now together as one great and strong man, and we came here to ask all the Indian nations to lie neutral and keep out of the dispute between Congress and the king. We need no assistance from you in our fight. We do want your friendship, but ask that you shall not go on the warpath for us, nor for the king. The British are already trying to get the Indians on their side, and we know that they have already invited some of your peoples to war councils. We implore you not to listen to them; they are bad birds flying over and calling you to help them do the wrong thing."

Nonhelema was happy to hear these words calling for peace. But most of the chiefs were stolid and showing no response. They always heard these words at treaties, but had learned that there usually was something behind them that they would not like.

Throughout most of the day, the Delaware chiefs spoke long about their desire for that kind of neutrality and peace, and their most ardent peacemaker, Chief White Eyes, used all his oratorical powers to make sure the commissioners should depend upon him and his people for steadfast friendship. He made it clear that his Delaware people would withdraw from the influence of the Iroquois if it would strengthen their ties to the Americans. The Iroquois delegates, sitting under another part of the arbor, said nothing in response to that, but their eyes were steely as they watched him. For many generations, Delawares in proximity to the Iroquois tribes had taken a submissive role, to the degree that the Iroquois called them "Petticoat People" and overrode most of their concerns in council matters. The Iroquois League's great friend William Johnson, superintendent of Indian affairs for the North, was very loyal to the king and very generous to his Iroquois tribes, and had made old treaties and boundary arrangements long ago that ignored the rights and territorial claims of the Delawares and other Algonquian tribes. One of those land deals was the basis upon which Virginia claimed it had obtained title to Kentucke lands south of the Ohio River, which was actually the Shawnees' hunting ground.

In declaring his friendship now to the Americans, as he had to their predecessors the colonists, White Eyes went so far as to dispute Iroquois territorial claims. These peace talks were already worrying old wounds, creating tension between the Iroquois League and the congressional commissioners. Nonhelema tried to keep looking for peace and harmony, but every day there were tensions rising anew over every issue.

Trying perhaps too hard to prove his dedication to the commissioners, White Eyes now made a statement that caused Cornstalk to stiffen with anger.

"Our friends the Shawnees," White Eyes said, "perhaps should have tried harder to make this a good peace. Surely they could have brought more of their captives than they did. Surely they could have brought more of their own tribal chiefs to this council. Cornstalk and his family are good peacemakers themselves, but there are many important Shawnee leaders who did not come here."

Indian manners forbade anyone in a council to interrupt another speaker. But when White Eyes concluded, Cornstalk was on his feet at once, looking even taller and haughtier than usual.

"Brothers, listen! Hard Man already told you how hard we tried to bring in all our captives. He explained it all to you. I tell you now that my Shawnee people will keep trying into the next year to find them and bring them. I brought as many as I could, in good faith, expecting you to honor your promise and return my brothers to us, which you have not done yet. My friend and brother White Eyes does not have any of his family in your custody, as we Shawnees have. Therefore he speaks too hard about what the Shawnees do.

"Now let me say something about why some of our chiefs do not want to come here and talk peace with you. It is our hunting ground in Kentucke, which he spoke of:

"All of you commissioners keep saying that Virginia possesses that land, but it is ours! We never sold it or gave it to Virginia, nor even said you could come in there. The Iroquois say they ceded it to you, but it was never theirs. That is the truth as I and all other Shawnee chiefs and people know it to be. Your Governor Dunmore, when he invaded our country and made us agree to terms, he pretended Kentucke was his, and it mattered not what we told him about that. You heard White Eyes himself say just now that the Iroquois had no claim to Kentucke to cede to Virginia. And so he himself knows why so many Shawnees are too angry to come here and listen to you.

"My tribe and family are very close to the Delawares. Delaware blood flows in my family's veins, through our grandfather. My mother and sister are Christians who live with the Praying Delawares in the mission town. My sister Nonhelema, here beside me, has used much of her time since Governor Dunmore's treaty trying to persuade our people to come here for this, as have I and my brothers. My other kin put themselves in your custody for almost a year to assure this peace!" He stood, breathing hard, eyes glittering, as those words were translated for all.

Then he said: "Brothers, listen: White Eyes is a great peace chief, and a man of honor, and you may count on him. So is his friend Killbuck, who sits beside him. But brothers, they are no more so than I. And I tell you this: If you want all the Shawnee chiefs to come and listen to you speak for peace, all you have to do is withdraw your white people from our hunting grounds in Kentucke, where they have no right to be, and where they are killing all the game that my Shawnee women and children need to live. They are also violent people who shoot our hunters when they see them, as if our hunters were game themselves. We did not invite them there. We tell them to go home. My Shawnee chiefs are angry. It is in your power to make my people lay down the war hatchet. All you have to do is make your people leave our hunting lands and go back to Virginia. But you are not doing that. You have land offices here, and you keep selling our hunting grounds, and sending boats down into our country.

"I, Hokoleskwa, Mekoche chief of the Shawnee nation, promised Governor Dunmore that I would never raise the hatchet against Virginians anymore, and I shall not. I shall send home to my other chiefs your words of peace that you *say* here. But you should understand, brothers, that if your Long Knives keep filling up our hunting lands and taking the food from our mouths, my chiefs will not be able to believe your peace talk. You might not like to hear my words as much as White Eyes' words. But the words you don't like to hear are often the truest words. By saying them, I serve you as well as White Eyes.

"Brothers, that is what I have to say. Now I think my sister, who is a chief and peace woman of the Mekoche Shawnees, has something to say. I know that women do not speak in whiteman's councils. She is a true friend of your cause for peace. You will do well to listen to her with all your ears."

She stood and stepped forward from the shade into the sunlight. She turned left and right to pass her gaze over all the Indians in the circle, then faced the commissioners. Alexander McKee nodded when her eyes momentarily met his.

"Brothers," she began. She had chosen to speak to them in English so that none of her meaning would be changed by the interpreters. "All that my brother Cornstalk just told you is true. You must think hard about what you are doing.

"We Shawnee people are sorry you have to go to war with the king. It is sad that you cannot have the king come and stand close to you in this circle and speak with him of peace, until he understands what is in your hearts. Then no blood would have to be shed. Your king is of your own blood. War is bad enough when your enemy is a stranger. It is worse when you must kill your own relatives. We are sorry for you." She let them think about that for a while, watching their faces closely. She could see that it was a very serious matter to them. Two of them had shut their eyes.

"And so, brothers, you from Virginia and you from Congress: You ought to know that what you do in Kentucke is setting our Shawnee people brother against brother, like that. Some in our nation resent us because we made peace with Governor Dunmore last year. They will resent us more when we go back to them and say they must give up more of those people you call captives.

"Let me explain why we don't call them captives.

"We brought them home from raids and wars, that is true. They have been adopted into our families to replace our people who were killed by Long Knives, who invaded our hunting ground.

"When they are taken into a family, it is with a ceremony. The Great Good Spirit makes that person become the person that family had lost. The affection of that family then is the same affection it had for the lost person, as if they were born in the same family. And so it is not easy to persuade families to give up their adopted brothers or children. No chief can make a family do that. You commissioners need to understand that Virginia, or Congress, cannot just give an order and make the Shawnee people do it. To try that will only anger the Shawnees, who are already angry at you for invading. Brothers, that is not the way of peace."

Two of the commissioners were leaning forward, seeming very interested in this Indian view of captives. She had known they had no notion of it before Hard Man explained it, and thought they needed to understand it, so she was repeating it. But one of the Virginia commissioners, whose name she knew to be Walker, raised a finger and pointed at her.

"Madame," he said, "that is all very touching, I suppose, but I would like your answer to a question that's on my mind." She narrowed her eyes at him, annoyed that he had spoken before she was finished. "You profess to be a great peacemaker," he continued, "and you say that your brothers are also. Yet there are men in this fort who saw you on the battleground at Point Pleasant last year, men who with their own eyes saw you killing their comrades. You stand there now, a woman, a woman said to be a peace chief, part of a mission family, and you have in your belt a tomahawk and a knife. They say you even had pistols in your belt that had to be taken from you before you entered this council.

"Madame, it is astonishing, a woman warrior witnessed on a battlefield, professing to be a peace chief, and bristling with weaponry. I have never seen a white woman so armed to the teeth. Explain that to me, if you will."

She clenched her molars and controlled her breath, then replied, "Brother, it is because no white women are chiefs." All around the circle, laughter arose from the Indians.

She continued: "We already explained to Governor Dunmore about that battle. My brothers and I had counseled our people not to go to war with the governor when he invaded us, but to talk to him and ask him to leave our country. In our council, more voted for fighting him than for talking. And since it was the will of our nation, we went to fight. The principal war chief, Pucsinwah, was killed in that battle. And so we led the warriors. Then, after the battle, it was our duty to talk peace with the governor, because there was no will to fight after that. Your question is answered, brother."

Walker was leaning forward with one hand on a knee and his head tilted, as if he had been impatiently waiting for her to finish. "So you *are* a warrior woman. Aren't you? And I suppose that you, yourself, have gone out raiding and brought home some of those very captives that you say you 'adopted.' Is that so?" He glanced around at the other commissioners, looking smug about his ability to challenge her position.

"No, brother Walker, that is not so. I do not go raiding. A woman goes to war only to protect her people. When the governor invaded our country on the north side of the Ohio River, I had to lead my own warriors. Only then did I go to battle. Brother, the chief of a town has too much to do at home to go raiding.

"And that is the other thing I wish to tell you, if you are through interrupting me. We the chiefs who have come here have much to do, back in our own country. It is soon time for our harvest ceremony and our sharing feast, which must be done at the right time, and require many days of preparation. Therefore, I hope that our visit here, that you have made us come to, will not be prolonged too much by arguments about the weapons I wear. I told you I am here for peace, and it hurts this council if you refuse to believe it. Also, this council was delayed for a whole day because your foolish agents got our foolish people very, very drunk. Even after Hard Man shamed your whiskey sellers for that.

"You commissioners made your speeches about peace when we first got here. Now we want you to listen to us, and think about what we say, instead of disputing it, because we need to go home and attend to our people." The commissioner was not pleased, judging by the way he was leaning back and looking along his nose at her. She looked all about the circle again and saw Alexander McKee biting a smile.

"Brothers, we are happy to be hearing about your desire for peace. But you must act in good faith, as we have done, and let us go home in time. My family intends to stop at the mission of the Praying Delawares on the Muskingum as we go home. Here is why. On our way here, we went there and spoke to our old mother and our sister, who are Christians. We told them good news. That on our return we would bring our mother her sons who have been so long gone from her, in your custody. We promised her that because she has been lonely for them and afraid she might not live long enough to see them again. We promised her that, because we believed your promise that you would return them to us. Therefore, you see, we want our brethren returned to us, and soon, so that we can go back home and assure our Shawnee people of your peacefulness, and get our people ready for the harvest and for the winter. Brothers, I have spoken. Thank you for the attention of your ears and your hearts."

One of the Virginia commissioners had large, sleepy-looking, wide-set eyes, a head that looked almost as wide as his shoulders, and a tiny, thin-lipped mouth. From time to time as the treaty talks went on, Nonhelema would feel a chill on the side of her face, and would turn to find that man's strange eyes fixed upon her. He was emanating the most intense hatred she had ever felt.

The man was Andrew Lewis. He had been in command of the army in the battle on the Kanawha-sipe. The Indians had killed his brother in the first moments of the battle. Later he had marched his army up to the very edge of the Shawnee towns, ready to take revenge by killing all the Shawnees and burning all the towns, when Governor Dunmore had made him stop, at the point of his sword.

Nonhelema had never seen Andrew Lewis before coming here to Fort Pitt. In the battle he had not been near the fighting, but back in the command post in the army camp. And Governor Dunmore had not let him attend the talks when the truce was made.

Cornstalk knew Lewis by sight, though, because they had fought each other years before, in the earlier wars, and the general's hatred of Cornstalk was as hard and cold as steel. When, in these peace talks here at Fort Pitt, Cornstalk professed himself the most ardent of the Shawnee peace chiefs, Andrew Lewis would snort. It had become necessary to move the delegations into and out of the council circle, and around the other events in Pittsburgh, so that Lewis was never within arm's length of any Indians who had fought at Kanawha. To Nonhelema, it seemed foolish that a man so full of implacable hatred had been put on a commission for peacemaking. When she had spoken of that to Alexander McKee, he had replied, "Some of the others just conceal it better. Thomas and John Walker of the Virginians are almost as bad. The Congress commissioners, Wilson and Morris, are fair. The Virginians . . ." He shook his head. "Never turn your back to them, any of you." Raising his eyebrows, he added, "My fond advice."

In the course of the negotiations, she had noticed something curious about the men who sat at the commissioners' tables with writing quills. They wrote rapidly all day, filling sheets of paper with marks as the Indians and the commissioners made their speeches, but when she or any other of the Indian women chiefs got up to talk, the scribblers rested their quills.

Nonhelema herself could read and write, of course, but she couldn't understand how anyone with a quill could make letters fast enough to write down all the things that were said in the long speeches. One day a strong gust of wind carried a scrivener's pages off his table, and everyone scrambled to retrieve them. Nonhelema grabbed up two sheets. In a glance, she saw lines of marks that were not any letters or words she had ever seen before, and that troubled her with the suspicion that they were only pretending to write. When she gave the papers back to the commissioners, she said, "This is not writing. Why not?"

With laughter, they explained that it was something called shorthand writing, a trick of scriveners to write many times faster. Later they would rewrite it in regular letters that any readers could understand.

It seemed a wonderful kind of writing knowledge. But it frightened her that the whitemen had so many tricks and skills that her people didn't know.

The end of the negotiations neared, and the Indians needed to return to their homes soon for the harvests and their thanksgiving celebrations, and to take the news of the talks home to the rest of their people.

Cornstalk had given up, as futile, his protest that Kentucke had not been sold or yielded by the Shawnee people; the Virginians were just not going to admit that they didn't own it, and the Iroquois were not going to admit that they had had no right to cede it to the whitemen. And so that was dropped, and the arguments went on about captives.

The days were cooler now, and Nonhelema sat with a blanket around her shoulders. The Virginia commissioner named Thomas Walker got up to speak.

"To assure that the Shawnees will bring in next year every captive who lives among them, I propose that Virginia shall keep until that time the chieftains who have been in our custody. I hope that would move them to—"

Suddenly, Cornstalk was on his feet, and in his battlefield voice he bellowed, "All my people stand up!"

Then he pointed at the startled commissioners and said: "You men listen! You will return our brothers to us now, or there will not be *any* Shawnees come to your council next year! If we do not see our brothers released to us today, the only Shawnees you ever see will be those who come to drive your squatters from our hunting lands of Kentucke!

"Listen! These Shawnees you see standing with me have tried to induce the Shawnee nation to be at peace with you. Many of our people are mad at us for trying. They say you are not worthy and you are not to be trusted. I begin to think they are right!" Nonhelema quailed at such strong words, which threatened to undo all her efforts for peace, but she, too, was appalled by the Virginians' stubbornness and their duplicity. It seemed that McKee had given good advice not to turn one's back upon them. She looked at Andrew Lewis and saw such hatred in his face that she feared he might leap up with his sword.

"We are ready," Cornstalk said, "to walk away from here without marking your peace paper. Give us our young men. Now! I have spoken."

Within an hour, the hostages had been brought down from the fort, embraced their relatives and friends, and sat down with them to hear the rest of the council. Cornstalk at last had won something from the whitemen.

She dreamed that she was asleep in the woods and a buck deer was walking slowly toward her, coming close to sniff her face. When its leafy-smelling breath and damp muzzle touched her face, it awakened her in her dream and she saw its long-lashed big eyes and its antlers above her like a tree.

When it woke her in the dream, it also woke her from her dream, and she was being nuzzled by a buck deer standing by the bed, its antlers looming over her. When it saw her eyes open it started back, hooves clattering and scraping on the wooden floor. Nonhelema started up also, heart hammering, waking up from a dream of waking up from a dream with a buck deer . . .

Then McKee laughed behind her and she remembered. She fell back on the pillow, rolling her eyes, breathing fast through her mouth, patting herself on her bare chest with her palm, matching the heartbeat. She turned her head and saw him with his head propped up on one hand, softly laughing at her. She heard the deer's hooves going out the door.

"You," she said. "Man with a deer in his house!"

"You," McKee replied. "You are indeed a dear in my house. A dear *saa sa ketwi k'wehwa.*" Naked woman. He grasped the edge of the bedding, a linen sheet and wool blanket, and flipped it down to reveal her and himself.

"Saa sa ketwi h'lenni," she exclaimed. "Naked man, cover me! It is

cold!" She was not young anymore and wasn't comfortable being seen in this bright morning light by the man she wanted to keep desiring her.

"I'll cover you," he laughed, crawling upon her copper-skinned nakedness with his own, all hard-muscled and covered with blond body hair. She started laughing, feeling his rigidity prodding her. This was a rare man who did not become all solemn and forceful like a rutting animal just because his *passah-tih* was up; he was jolly, and playful in his passion, playful not just with their bodies but also with words. The morning sunlight was shining into the room, onto the lower part of the bed, dust specks were whirling, and his long blond hair, which he had unbraided from its queue last night when they started mating, was tangled and mussed, wild and funny looking. It was good to laugh after all the ill will and disappointment of the treaty with those commissioners, who were arrogant, untrustworthy men, always changing their statements and promises. The joy she had with Alexander McKee had kept her spirits from getting too low. She liked this laughing with him, but now her desire was overtaking mirth, and she felt her passion again rising into a craving that caused a quick and involuntary clenching of her lower belly and moist opening; she was laughing no more when she took him inside her and the long rising pleasure began and she saw only bright mist behind her eyelids, while the inside of her body had its own vision of that part of him that was inside her and was reaching closer and closer to her heart. Then she hung on to him with all her strength.

She had never drunk breakfast tea with a man and a buck deer. The deer stood beside McKee and waited for him to sprinkle a pinch of salt on the tabletop. Then it would lick it and move its jaws and tongue, savoring it, while McKee held his teacup with one hand and massaged above its ears with the fingertips of the other. It was not the first deer that had adopted McKee. It was his third. It had come to him as a yearling four years ago, he said, and had followed him wherever he could reasonably let it do so. The two previous ones had been killed—one shot by a drunken hunter who could not resist it when it came walking down a Pittsburgh street, the other mauled by a pack of cur dogs that caught it in a deep snowbank. McKee had told her about it, leaving in her mind a picture of bloody snow.

Nonhelema and McKee were trying not to be melancholic now. She was full of tenderness and did not want to leave. But the treaty council was over. She had hard travel ahead, going home to her village by way of the missionaries' town where her mother and sister lived. Still tingling and sensitive in the loins from their excesses, she tried to keep Brother David Zeisberger out of her mind. By the mission's strict rules, all this joy had been a horrible sin, for McKee was not her husband. If Brother Zeisberger knew of this, he would try to shame her into a black chasm of guilt from which only Jesus could lift her—and that only when Zeisberger thought she had writhed in shame long enough to suit him. She had been condemned so often by Brother Zeisberger that she knew how he would dole out *his* Jesus' forgiveness. She had sinned by drinking, more than once. She had sinned by conducting the heathen ceremonies of her ancestors for the people of her village, which she had to do as their chief. She had sinned terribly by killing Long Knife soldiers in the battle at Kanawha-sipe. And now this. She did not understand how love could be a sin, love like this. Maybe a street whore copulating with strangers for coins or rum would be a sin, for that would be ugly. But this was wholehearted and every moment of it generous and good-spirited and full of beauty. And she respected McKee for his stature among men, white or Indian. The deer that came to him were proofs of a different kind of goodness, a thing of animal magic very rare among any people, especially rare among people with whiteman blood. She wondered what a comparison there might be between Zeisberger and his Jesus magic, which he really did have, and McKee and his animal magic. That would be something to think about on the long ride to the Praying Town by the Muskingumsipe.

At least this had happened far away from the mission and from the gossips of her town, so the missionary might never know of it— good as he was at learning everything everybody did. Zeisberger looked so hard for sins to shame the Indians with that he seldom missed one. Maybe he had God's own eye, she thought sometimes.

She knew very well that she was a challenge to the Zeisberger. She was so bad that it would be one of his best triumphs if he saved her. She wanted to be one of God's children and be in Jesus' Name Book, but she thought the Zeisberger wanted to make her small and unimportant. In that, he was a whiteman; a woman should not be a chief or anything.

Sometimes she had come very close to lowering herself to the humility he demanded of a convert. But then something always happened. He would insult her with his pious scorn for Indian women. Or she would have to go do the traditional ceremonies of her Shawnee people, who were not Christians and had no desire to be. Or, being so close to conversion, she would let some temptation turn her away just in time. Usually that was whiskey.

One of McKee's Negro servants brought in breakfast from the kitchen house, a platter of a savory mincemeat made from the flesh of ducks' necks, currants, diced apple, and spices, which McKee declared was his favorite breakfast, and hoecakes fresh from the griddle with fruit preserves. They ate hungrily after their passionate exertions, looking at each other with wistful, knowing eyes, listening for the hoof steps of the horse that McKee's aide would bring for her ride to the fort.

She dreaded going to the mission, guilty of sins with McKee.

But there would be some joy in going there. She had done her best at God's work as a peacemaker. She had made the commissioners understand some things they had never tried to understand before.

But the best pleasure of going there would be that her mother would get to see that Nimwha and the Wolf were alive and safe, returned to their people from captivity. That reunion would bring relief and joy to the old woman.

The pet buck came through the door, sniffing the table for salt again, and McKee sprinkled out a pinch for him to lick. Nonhelema reached across the table and took both of McKee's hands in hers, and looked deep into his eyes.

"Do you know," she began in a soft voice, looking not at his face but at the embrace of their hands, "that when the Master-of-Life gave the four-leggeds and the two-leggeds their rules to live by, this was what the deer was told: 'You will help the People by being food for them to eat and hides for their clothing, and, further, you will lead them to the medicine plants they need when they are sick.' One more thing, very important: Among the four-leggeds, only the deer can see through the disguises of Motcheemonetoo, the Evil Spirit. Therefore it is that the deer is able to warn you of evil. That comforts me."

He sat very quiet for a while, not looking at her or at their hands or the buck deer, but vaguely at some point on the table. As if talking to himself, he said, "Mhm. That might explain some of my luck . . ." Then he looked into her eyes. "May I say one thing before you go? Concerning the Americans you're trying so hard to please. Mmm . . . well, may the deer watch over you, as well."

She was thinking of that warning as she rode down the wagon road from McKee's plantation toward the fort, escorted by two armed men who worked the place for him. She thought of the warning, and of the pleasures that she could still feel inside. The wind coming off the river was chilly; the trees on the distant bluffs across the river were turning red and yellow. The men rode behind her, talking in such low voices that she couldn't hear their words with the wind in her face. Judging by their tone and their occasional laughter, she could imagine that she was the subject of their talk. She would have been happy not to have an escort, but an Indian riding alone in these parts, especially an Indian woman, would be in danger of unpleasant encounters.

A lone rider appeared in a turn of the road ahead, coming up the road. It was a woman, riding sidesaddle, not astride, at a pretty canter on a very respectable gray mount with black legs. As she approached, Nonhelema recognized her as someone she had seen before in Pittsburgh, a striking young woman from one of the trading families, Indian blood evident in her face and coloring, but decked out in a white woman's riding habit with billowing skirts and a dainty tricorn hat. The men behind Nonhelema had fallen silent at the approach of the oncoming rider.

Nonhelema nodded to her, but the young woman gave back only a haughty look, no greeting, as she passed. Nonhelema heard one of the men say, "G'day, Miss Atkins."

Atkins. Yes. A trader name, Nonhelema remembered.

Nonhelema was a good distance around the curve when she wondered why the young woman would be going up that road, which led only to McKee's plantation and a few hovels.

The two men riding behind her were talking low again, snickering and snorting.

—— ◇ ——

STATUTES FOR THE BELIEVING INDIANS
Written by Brother Zeisberger in August 1772

1. *Whoever wishes to live here must worship God, our Creator and Savior, as the one and only God and must look for everything good, to Him alone.*

2. *Nobody can live with us, who intends to go to heathen feasts and dances held at other places.*

3. *Nobody who wishes to bring rum here to get drunk, or to make others drunk, or who runs after rum at other places.*

4. *Nobody who keeps a whore or attempts to seduce the wives of others.*

5. *Nobody who deserts his wife, nor a wife who runs away from her husband.*

6. *No son or daughter who, after thorough admonition, wantonly disobeys parents.*

7. *No thief, nor any person who is in the habit of stealing.*

8. *Nobody who abuses or strikes his neighbor.*

9. *Nobody who employs objects of heathen superstition in hunting or in curing diseases, or gives them to others.*

10. *We will keep the Sunday holy, and will not hunt or work on Sunday, except out of love of neighbor, or from dire necessity.*

11. *Whoever tells stories about other's preparing poison, hunting people at night, and practicing witchcraft, must prove this before the committee, and he of whom such things are proved shall not live with us. If, however, the accuser has been found lying, we will regard him as a tool of the Devil.*

Additional rules (added) November, 1776

12. *No one can live here who wants to be treated medically according to the heathen methods.*

13. *No one can live here who thinks of going to war, or even to take part in war party.*

14. *No one who wants to live here should paint themselves, nor hang wampum, silver, or anything on himself.*

Other Amendments:

- *A man shall have but one wife . . . A woman shall have but one husband, be obedient to him, care for her children, and be cleanly in all things.*
- *No one shall contract debts with traders, or receive goods to sell for traders . . .*
- *Whoever goes hunting, or on a journey, shall inform the minister or stewards.*

- *Young persons shall not marry without consent of their parents and the minister.*
- *Whenever the stewards or helpers appoint a time to . . . work for the public good, we will assist and do as we are bid.*
- *Whenever corn is needed to entertain strangers, or sugar for love-feast, we will contribute from our stores.*
- *We will not go to war, and will not buy anything of warriors taken in war.*

5

BEAVER RIVER VALLEY
AUTUMN 1775

The Great Trail along the ridges and between the forks of the Beaver River was glorious with the colors of turning leaves and the blue haze of autumn light on the distant hills. But Nonhelema's view was darkened by her resentments against the whitemen she was trying to serve. As the Shawnees rode westward, her anger at the commissioners in Fort Pitt was gradually transferred toward the missionary she soon would have to confront. She began fuming to anyone who would listen that the pious missionary Zeisberger was a Nanabusho, or maybe even Motcheemonetoo in disguise. "He is like the commissioners and pretends women know nothing. You will see," she said. "He will ignore me because you and the other men are there. But when I go to visit Mother alone, he wrings information from me as if I were a wet rag!"

She complained until finally Cornstalk said, "Sister, please! My ears are tired! You make this missionary too important to yourself. If you dislike him so much, turn away. You don't have to live there. Our mother and sister have chosen to do so, but you are still free to ignore him. But it seems to me that you want to criticize him and serve his god at the same time."

"Yes, I will respect his manner of worshiping. But I will also offer prayer tobacco that Creator opens his eyes and heart so he will not be so mean-spirited. I think he has confused and misled our mother, who is too sweet to see evil in anyone."

Nimwha, who had been listening, turned in his saddle. "*Misled*, you say? She seems to be happy. She is healthy. She lives in a sturdy house that protects her from harsh weather. She has a daughter and nieces and friends all around her there, who love and honor her. She doesn't have to work very hard anymore. If she can have such comforts just by taking the blame for killing the bleeding suffering Jesus, what more could you want for her, *meh shemah?*" He laughed mockingly. He thought all his women relatives were foolish about the missionary.

But Nonhelema was not to be mocked about this. "I want her to be free. I do not want my mother to have to ask to come see us. I do not want to have to ask permission to go see my mother, and be denied because I drank, or failed in a tribal marriage, or had to kill soldiers. That is none of the missionary's business what I do. His list of rules is as long as a river! I resent that he treats all of us as if we were stupid children. That is no orphanage he is running, it is his own little kingdom, and he acts like he is the Creator of it all, with everyone else just his servants. Does he hunt or provide them food or clothing? No! Does he protect the people there? No! He has everyone else doing the work he is supposed to be doing. He sits and criticizes everyone and judges them. He tells them what is good and what is not. Well, many things were good until he came to live here, and we all got along fine."

Her brothers rolled their eyes, smiling, nodded and shook their heads, as if they didn't know whether they should say yes or no.

She went on: "I do not think he loves his 'brown children' as he professes. You listen to his words. He only loves us because his bleeding suffering Jesus tells him he must. He is forced to love us. I do not need that kind of love!"

"Eh-heh!" Nimwha exclaimed, pointing his thumb back over his shoulder. "You get the kind of love you want, sister! We know that! Ha, ha!"

She shook her head and rode in silence for a while, seething about the whitemen and the complications they had brought to this land, the evils, the sickness, the troubles. But they were too many and too strong to fight anymore. It was necessary to figure out how to accommodate them peacefully, or be destroyed. She thought back on the soldiers and commissioners and traders at Fort Pitt, and remembered the drunkenness.

"Two good things about the missionaries," she said at last, "they don't shoot you, nor do they bring you whiskey. I will admit that."

"I am glad to hear that your heart is warming," Nimwha exclaimed. "I was worried that you would jump off your horse at Gnaddenhutten Town and hit Brother Zeisberger with a tomahawk!"

They guided the horses carefully down a steep, rocky bluff toward the fording place at the forks of the Beaver River. They had to concentrate here, and didn't talk much. Then they rode on through the bottomland thickets where big yellow-brown leaves were dropping off the pale limbs of sycamore trees, covering the ground and floating on the surface of the river. They hoped to reach Painted Post, the trail-marker place where a debarked tree was painted with symbols of the places where the trails went from there. Tomorrow morning they would take the trail that split off southwestward from the Great Trail and led to the Moravian missionaries' towns on the Muskingumsipe.

After a while, Cornstalk started talking in a slow and thoughtful tone. "The whiskey and the bullets," he said, "are just some of their tools. The writing quills and the kettles and fire strikers, and all the treaty gifts—those all are tools, too. They are tools they use for getting the land away from us. Like getting our hunting grounds, and getting us out of them—those were tools they used for that, with the Iroquois to help them.

"You saw, there are many kinds of trade at Pittsburgh. But the main business of all the important men there, and all the way back into Virginia, is the business of getting more land. Every big man—even our old friend Croghan, even the soldier Washington they made their war chief, even their governors and their commissioners—they all are in one business: getting the country and selling it for money.

"And then when they have it, and make us leave it, then they will bring in their other tools, the axes and the shovels and the plows.

"Here is the worst thing they brought from across the ocean, sisters, brothers: not the guns, or the diseases, or the whiskey, or the confusion made by their Black Coat missionaries. No, the worst thing they brought is the belief that Creator's land can be divided up and bought and sold, and turned into money.

"That is the worst thing. It will kill all us Indians, no matter what we do."

They smelled wood smoke, then just a little farther on they saw the brightness of the clearing, and a young man ran out of a garden and sprinted ahead of them, calling, "Brother Abraham! Cornstalk comes! Get Sister Elizabeth! Her children are back from Pittsburgh!"

Soon most of the Indian residents of the Moravian compound had run out to greet the returning Shawnees and were helping with their bundles and offering them fresh water. All these were plain, drab Indians. They were allowed to wear no ornamentation or bright clothing.

Brother Zeisberger—tall, long-faced, with small, sad eyes—came deliberately toward the group where Cornstalk, Nonhelema, and the other family members were standing. Singling out the newly released hostages, Zeisberger stretched one hand to Nimwha and the other to the Wolf and said, "I see God has blessed thee and brought thee safe back to your worried mother. Praise to God!" His German accent made his words hard to understand. "We will prepare a small love-feast to celebrate the safe return. Come now, let's go to thy mother so she can rejoice at what the protecting hand of our Lord has done in providing your safe return." He guided the Wolf and Nimwha toward a small herb patch in back of the house reserved strictly for housing the old widows. She had already been notified, and was hastily washing dirt from her hands in a bucket. Thin, still erect at her great age, she wore wool gaiters and a deerskin tunic without sleeves, revealing wrinkled brown arms with gnarled hands and swollen elbows. Her long hair, graying but still dark, was tied back and hung far down her back. Elizabeth saw them coming and gave a small cry of thanks to Jesus for saving her sons, as she ambled as quickly as her arthritic knees would allow her on the broken ground to come and embrace them, one and then the others. Her coppery face shone with relief and joy, all the lines in her face upturned, the evidence of a lifetime of smiling. She gazed deep into their eyes and pinched their arms and cheeks, checking them for the soundness of their health. "Oh, my sons! Tell me, they were good to you?"

Nimwha glanced at the Wolf and chuckled. "Not much room to

move in, but it was warm. We were not lonely, for there were many rodents in there visiting us. Williamsburg has so many rats the people could feed themselves if they ate them." He laughed at her surprised expression.

"The rats might have been better than what they did feed us," said the Wolf. "All their cooking seemed waterlogged, like something lying in the bottom of a canoe a long time."

"We saw people," Nimwha said. "Often they walked us into town so people could look at us. Soldiers came and talked, and people of their governments. Always in town we heard children crying and quarreling."

"They are not a happy people, I believe," the Wolf said. "It is good to be among our own people and hear laughter. *Nigeah,* we have been gone for a long time, and thought you would have sweet treats for us to celebrate. We're famished for some of your spice cakes." Elizabeth pretended to be flustered at the request. They all laughed together and she led them by the hand to the mission's spare but clean dining room, where she sat them down on chairs whose bottoms and backs she had caned herself, as she pointed out with pride. "I will bring you berry cakes and tea, to keep you alive until we all eat together this evening."

Cornstalk and Nonhelema were already in deep conversation with Brother Zeisberger, telling him the news from the peace talks at Fort Pitt. Cornstalk was saying, with a deep frown: "Brother Zeisberger, they keep saying they are for peace, but they do not tell the truth about purchasing the hunting lands from us. So how can we believe they are telling the truth to us about anything? I do not believe they will leave us alone, even if we stand neutral in their war."

Zeisberger spoke earnestly, sitting forward with his elbows on his knees. "But will the *Shawnees* be neutral, Cornstalk? Will they stop killing? It is the young warriors who are at fault, going down to Kentucke and on the Ohio and killing settlers. Killing breaks the heart of our Savior. There can never be any peace until they stop killing."

Nonhelema's simmering annoyance boiled over. Glaring at the missionary, she said, "You never tire of blaming everything on the Indians, do you? As if those whites were not coming where they do not belong. Yes, killing is bad. But why then don't you help convince the whites to stop killing Indians, to stay where they belong, instead of always finding fault with us, your 'beloved brown brethren'? Sometimes I think you preach to the wrong people. You should be teaching your own kind about your suffering bleeding Jesus, and how distressed he becomes when *they* come killing *our* people. For generations they have moved in on us. We have given up everything they wanted. We have moved back and back to get away from where they want to live! Why could they not stay where Creator put them in this world? Brother David, I am trying to be a peacemaker. As you taught us, I want to be a child of God. I have angered many of my own beloved people by trying to do what you said. But how can the Shawnee people be at peace alone? Both sides have to be at peace or there is no peace. Do you ever tell *them* to stop killing?"

Her eyes were flashing at the missionary, her body taut and straight, daring him to respond.

He acknowledged her presence only by glancing disdainfully at the silver brooches on her shirt and jewelry, then, assuming a patient, saintly look, turned to Cornstalk.

There had been times in the past when Brother Zeisberger had almost persuaded her to follow him in obedience. But then he would lose her. Normally, she was respectful and calm. This outburst stemmed from having so recently listened to the American commissioners tell her what bad children her people were.

"Tell me, Brother Zeisberger," she said loudly, leaning close to his ear. "Do you and the peace commissioners all go to the same school to learn how to scold Indians? We just heard those commissioners say the same things you say!"

She kept staring so hard at his profile that he surely must have felt it. He was a highly esteemed and beloved holy man, loved by the Delawares, even by her own mother and sisters, famous for his piety and his peacemaking efforts. No doubt it was true, as he preached, that Jesus favored peacemakers. But she suspected that he was frantic for peace mostly because he had rendered his own Indians helpless by pacifying them. He was forever begging all his Indians for information about what their clans and tribes were doing. He had asked her and Cornstalk to come and report on the peace talks. But now when she came to tell him some real truth about them, he had brushed her aside, not looking at her, speaking only to her brothers. This Zeisberger had no manners, acting as if only her brothers had intelligence or value. Nonhelema fumed. This was another way he and those haughty Virginia commissioners were just alike, so she stared at him with all her concentration to make him look at her.

Reaching forward to Cornstalk and touching his arm tenderly,

Zeisberger said, "I am sorry your sister seems upset today. She cannot understand that I was told by our gracious Lord to come and save only my precious lost brown brethren, to share with you Christ's blood and love. I fear we have much to pray for in her case. Come along now, all of you. The sisters should have the repast ready for your refreshment. You can tell me more after we eat."

With that Zeisberger got up and guided Cornstalk and the others toward the tables, leaving Nonhelema to follow or not, dismissing her.

She had long observed the way Brother Zeisberger used the women of his flock. He hated having to speak with these Indian women, especially those not under his total jurisdiction, like herself. Shawnee women bowed to no one, not even their husbands. And yet the women were more open to spiritual teachings than their husbands were, and would come to listen, come for the cakes and teas and gossip, and he would begin to preach, and undermine their pride. He would find out what they were ashamed of, and drive his Jesus pity into those weak places, make them even more ashamed, and then hold out the promise that Jesus would forgive them. Zeisberger had a magic for breaking the Indians' hearts and making them weep and beg for forgiveness for their heathen ways. Once he had humbled a woman, he could convince her that in her ignorance she had sinned against his precious suffering bleeding Jesus. Sometimes he would let them worry a while, once he knew he had them hooked and aware of their sinful and lost state. He let them wallow in despair and fear for their souls, until he thought they had been punished enough for their past arrogance. Only then would he pronounce them saved and begin offering his ceremonies of salvation to them. Nonhelema had seen him humble one haughty woman after another that way, then lift her soul to glory. Once he had a woman so enveloped in the fold, it was easier to go to work converting her husband. The mission needed men. Zeisberger taught them trades, and gave them authority if they could earn it. Few men had ever had such control over their wives as they had in the mission, and they came to like it. It was the white-man's way.

Now they entered the room where several of the Indian converts were gathering, speaking with Nimwha and the Wolf and their mother. The long smooth wooden table was spread with remainders of the mission's earlier meal of beef and fresh-cooked late vegetables from the compound's gardens. On the sideboard were many cakes and sweet treats. Pots of coffee stood ready to be sweetened and seasoned just before they were poured. The aromas were tantalizing. Elizabeth and her sons were surrounded by relatives and other residents listening to their adventure as hostages.

"Oh God bless you!" Zeisberger said, as he went up to them. "You know that in your ordeal, you were instruments of the Lord for peace. We have all worried for your safety but trusted the Lord to protect you. As usual, the Lord was in charge and you were well taken care of. Now we rejoice at your return. Let us give the women a few minutes to finish putting out the food and we will all eat our evening meal together and you can tell us of your experiences. And please," he said, turning to Cornstalk, "you, Brother Cornstalk, can tell us more details of the peace talks." Again he was ignoring Nonhelema.

At the evening meal, Brother Zeisberger announced to his flock that the next day was going to be a love-feast day, and that he had asked assistant Johann Jungman to preach the morning service. Nonhelema had not heard the shy Johann speak to the congregation before. She hoped he might not speak as long as Zeisberger usually did.

The women cleaned up the tables and floor. The people were beginning to show signs that it was time to say good night. Their days began very early. Most of the travelers from Fort Pitt were trail-weary and went off early to sleep, husbands and wives together, all other men and women in separate buildings. It was one of the primary mission rules. Nonhelema went to the house of the elder widows, where her mother lived, so they could talk later.

Brother Zeisberger kept Cornstalk, Nimwha, and the Wolf with him in the dining hall to quiz them more about details of the peace council and the long captivity in Williamsburg.

Nonhelema and her mother talked softly and tenderly in the dark.

Nonhelema was nursing her resentment of Zeisberger's rudeness toward her. But she was used to it. And she knew that once her brothers were not available, he would have attention to give her again. He depended upon her for news of the Shawnee communities. Often he sent messengers and pleaded for her to come and tell him what was going on. He always pretended it was because her mother was worried. When she came, her mother would explain fearfully that Brother Zeisberger was concerned some of the activities of the Indians would cause the Americans to come attack the compound. Old Elizabeth pleaded that as long as Zeisberger had some tidbits of information to feed the Americans, he felt the compound would be spared and considered friendly. "Please keep him informed," her mother would say, "of what the other Indians and the Shawnees are doing and planning."

"*Nigeah*," Nonhelema murmured to her mother, "I know Zeisberger forbids his people to participate in war, or even defend themselves with firearms. He talks always of being peaceful and neutral. But he isn't neutral if he is giving information to an army. It disturbs me, thinking what an army could do with the information. Zeisberger is like a spy. Someday blood will be on his hands because of what he tells the army! That is not good peacemaking, *nigeah*. It bothers me."

"*Nitanetha*," the old woman whispered, reaching to stroke her hand. "Daughter, there is something in the Bible that explains it. It says God authorizes the kings, and the kings are to protect God's people. That way God's people never have to kill. The armies are paid to do this job. This is not for common people to do. Or warriors, like your father once was. It is for armies to do. So his hands would not be bloody." It sounded so simple the way she expressed it, and it seemed to satisfy Elizabeth. But, Nonhelema thought: *Would a loving God create a kind of people—soldiers—who would be destined for hell?* She decided not to argue that awful idea with her mother.

Elizabeth was very kind and simple in her thoughts. Kindness and love motivated her, and she accepted simple answers. Nonhelema did not want to distress her with her questions. Maybe sometime she could challenge Zeisberger to explain what God meant by that.

Nonhelema knew Zeisberger was using all of them, but now she felt especially ill used by him. *Next time he needs information,* she vowed to herself, *he will have to get it from someone else. I will no longer spy on my own people. I won't help armies come and kill my people. I will work trying to help each side be honorable, so no one will have to die.*

She thought of war, of soldiers and warriors. They were the same. But warriors were not condemned to go to hell. There had been no such thing as hell until the missionaries came here talking about it. Warriors learned to fight and kill to protect the lives and the honor of their people. Even if there really was a hell, they shouldn't be sent there for that.

Once Nonhelema had been married to a Shawnee warrior of the finest kind—strong, brave, and honorable, and a joy to look at. The whitemen had killed him, but not in combat. He had died of *mamk'thiwah*, their disease called smallpox. An officer during Pontiac's uprising had given infected blankets to Indians at Fort Pitt, and the sickness had spread through the country, killing the people all winter. Her family being friends with important whites, she had been inoculated with matter from a sick cow, a scratch on her thigh, so she had not caught the smallpox.

Sometimes she still missed her warrior husband. But in the way of her people, she never said or thought his name. Mentioning the dead might cause them to turn around on their spirit path and delay their journey. And one could not cry after the burial day for fear the dead would think the survivor too grief-stricken and come back and take the widow with him on the spirit journey. She had done well. She had not wept. She had been silent. But she was still lonely for that handsome and kind warrior. He had been her equal, and their love was very deep. She sometimes, even now, could feel the way his touch felt. But she didn't think or speak his name. He was still traveling on his long spirit journey, on that bright path of stardust, and would keep traveling until his bones in the earth were also dust. It was bad to call one back from that journey. It was better to stay closer to the ones still alive. She often lamented that she and her mother lived so far apart. Elizabeth was healthy, but she was very old, about eighty summers, and it saddened Nonhelema that she was a prisoner here in the mission in her last years, instead of living free among Shawnee women.

"*Nigeah,* I wish you would come home with me and Cornstalk to our villages. My home is a fine two-story log house as good as this one. We can take good care of you there."

Elizabeth's voice came through in the dark, "*Nitanetha,* thank you. But I would rather have you come live safe near me in this holy place."

"Ha! Whenever I think of doing that, the Zeisberger treats me as if I were invisible. Or tries to use me as a gossip or a spy!"

Elizabeth shook with silent laughter. "Daughter, you must not be so hard on Brother David. You were the one being disrespectful with your flash of a temper. He is being respectful according to the customs he was raised with. Of course he respects you. He just believes that our women need to be more humble and let our men speak for us. That lets our men feel respected. It all works out nicely. Don't be so quick to be offended, daughter. You know Brother David listens to everything you tell him and writes it down for the armies so they can protect us. They know, thanks to you and your help, that we are a neutral village, and will only help them, and are no threat. I am safe here. And our Lord will protect us; he has many times." Elizabeth's voice was fading with long pauses. She was growing drowsy as she talked. For a while her breathing was long and easy. Then she jerked and began talking again. "There was always danger out there. I don't know if it will ever be simple or safe. I can only trust in the Lord Jesus. Either it will be safe or not. If it is, and I live, good. If it is not safe and I die, I will join my Lord. There really is little to worry about. It really doesn't matter . . ." After another pause, she murmured, "To think! A sermon by poor, shy Brother Jungman! I hope he can get his words out!" She chuckled, and then she was snoring.

Nonhelema held her mother's bony hand, and listened to owls out in the woods.

Everyone was up early. The women prepared a large breakfast and, after a prayer of thanks, all ate heartily and the tables were cleared.

Zeisberger called everyone to services. He announced the order of the speakers for the day. First, his assistant Brother Daniel would read the Scripture and speak to them. Daniel read from a book called Chronicles and spoke to them about being "stiff-necked." He also spoke about God's wrath when people worship other gods instead of him, and said God punishes even their land for their sins. He did not speak long, but it was thought provoking. Nonhelema wondered if this could be why the Indians' land was no longer behaving as they had been taught by their ancestors that it would.

One of the converted Delaware brethren led them in several songs. Then a broad-faced whiteman in a black coat rose and went to the front of the assemblage.

Brother Johann Jungman stood near the main table and looked down for a minute as if gathering his courage to speak. His manner was painfully shy. He then raised his head and began to sweep the room with his gaze. He began speaking quietly.

"Oh brothers and sisters! This is a day I have lived for! I am at last ready to tell you a story. This is the story of how I came to know of my wretched, my sinful, my condemned state!" He looked heavenward, eyes blinking.

"Before then, I never thought I was an evil man. I revered my parents, I loved my wife and treated her gently. I was generous.

"Yet I was lost! Utterly, totally lost! If I had chanced to die during that time, all of those things would have meant nothing, because my name was not written in blood in the Book of Life, by the sacrificial Lamb of God, who was God's son, Jesus.

"Brethren, I did not know then that it is impossible for man to be good enough to be allowed into heaven. There are too many flaws and sins in our nature. You know that sometimes our thoughts are evil, though we control our actions.

"We are judged on our hearts and what is in our hearts, on what we think as well as what we do. No man can live and not have evil thoughts at some time. When we are not able to control ourselves, those terrible thoughts become actions that hurt others!"

Brother Jungman paused, his eyes on the rafters and his pink hands gripping each other so hard his knuckles were white. He breathed deeply and blinked. Tears were starting to shine. A few women murmured in sympathy.

"I had been told that God is like a heavenly father," Brother Johann said, "but I had not given that much thought. Once I did something foolish that embarrassed my mother, and made her weep. I loved my mother, and so I vowed to never embarrass her again by doing bad things.

"Then I lost my temper and hurt someone else. I was sorry, but it was impossible to take back the hurt. There were people who had hurt me, and I wished ill things to happen to them. Then I realized that I did not control myself very well. So I tried very hard for years to be good. It was no use. I was flawed.

"Then I heard Brother David speak, and he made me understand this: Since God made us, he knew that we would not be able to control ourselves no matter how hard we tried. Like any good parent, he wants to help us, and provide for us only the best things. But when he looks down on us, we have so many evil, sinful things we do that it breaks his heart."

"Amen! Amen!" some of the senior converts exclaimed.

"Besides the many ways that we sin," Brother Johann went on, "the Devil, the one in charge of hell, is always enticing us to be bad . . . because then he gets our soul, and we will spend time without end in hell with hot flames and torture. For thousands of years, people have been breaking God's heart. God shed tears and his heart was breaking like a parent who helplessly watches his child die!"

"Ahh!" Nonhelema sighed. It was as she had said in the Women's Council: *God shedding tears! I was right to say that!*

Several of the Indians moaned at that sad image.

Brother Johann went on: "I had a dream, and I saw this happen: One day God's heavenly son, Jesus, could stand his father's tears no longer. He said, 'Send me, Father. Let me go tell them of your love. Let me help them save themselves. I cannot stand to see your grief. Please, Father. I love these children of yours who live down below. I will go save them.' God said, 'No, my son, they are so wicked they will kill you if you go. I know that they will. You do not need to do this.' Jesus smiled and said, 'I know, Father, but they can only take my earthly life. I will come back then and show them your power. I can show them they do not have to die and be condemned to burn in hell forever. I will make miracles to prove that I am telling the truth.' God said, 'No! They do not deserve you. I would rather just wipe them out, or just give them to the Devil right now.' 'No, Father,' said Jesus, 'I really love them. I know I can do this for you and for them. Please, let me give them the gift of salvation. Let me save their souls. They seem to want to try, but they are flawed. Father, I will die for them. It will be good to have them here in heaven with us. Once they accept my words in their heart, they will be purified and healed of all their flaws and sins. They will be bathed in my blood if I have to die, and my blood will wash them clean as new snow. I will keep a book, and I will call it the Book of Life. Once one of them accepts my gift of salvation and gives me his heart, I will write his name in my Book of Life with my blood. Father, you have been keeping a ledger with their sins listed. In my book, once I write their name in it, all their sins will be erased. It will be as if it never happened. Father, give me your blessings to go and help the sinful ones on earth.'

"God wept. 'My son, if you must do this thing, you must. Let me send you to a comfortable home so your stay on earth will not be one of poverty or pain.' But Jesus replied to him, 'No! They will never accept me if I go as a wealthy man or a king. I must be one of them, born humbly. If I am to understand them, I must live just as they do, even with hunger, cold, pain. I must work with them, eat with them, be friends with them.' "

Brother Johann's story was enchanting his listeners, touching their hearts to their tender centers. They had never heard it told like this, with God and his son talking. He went on: "Jesus told his father how his death would make the people understand. That he would find great men and teach them to go everywhere and teach others. 'They will witness that although they killed me, I came back to life, and they talked with me, touched me, ate with me again. Then they will understand, and they will believe and be saved! The men I choose as teachers will travel all over the world, Father. They will teach the people that they are personally guilty of my murder, that I would not have had to come and suffer and die if they had given their heart to you. Now all people who ever believe will be guilty of my murder but I will forgive them if they will believe in me, and I will wash them in my blood and they will become clean and pure and white. I will write their name in my Book of Life; I will forgive and forget all their past sins. While I am in the netherworld of death, I will fight the Devil. I will go to and break the gates to hell and bring back those who want to be saved, and I will take the evil powers from the Devil! Father, the people will sing your praises for loving them so much that you are willing to sacrifice me, your only begotten son, and make me suffer pain for their sake. Their voices will fill the earth singing your praises and with their gratefulness. All of heaven will rejoice!' "

Brother Johann continued for hours, telling them all about how it was worked out between God and Jesus, how the angels were brought in to help Jesus carry out his plans. He spoke of Jesus being born poor. He told the Indians of Jesus' life, the messages of love and forgiveness that Jesus always spoke, how he was betrayed by one of his favorite beloved teachers whom he had sought out and instructed to carry on the good message after his death. Johann told of the betrayal and the crucifixion, tears streaming down his cheeks, his soft face quavering as he struggled to speak through the images in his heart—the nails through his hands, spear in his side, crown of thorns. He explained that the missionaries are some of those whom Jesus called to be teachers of his story. That God and Jesus knew there were Indians in the world long before they were discovered by Europeans. He explained that the Moravian brethren had been singled out to come and teach the Indians about their sinful ways, point out how each of them was responsible for murdering the most love-filled man who ever walked this earth.

"Amen!" The converted Indians and native helpers were by now crying out whenever Johann paused for breath.

Johann told them over and over that there was nothing they could do to make themselves worthy of living in heaven with God. The only thing they could do was give up their heathen life they were leading now and give their lives and hearts to Jesus, so he could write their name in his Book of Life. They had to give up their sinning now that they knew they were doing wrong. Jesus could not forgive them if they did not change after being told how sinful they were.

That was how he would know to write their name in his book: He would see whether or not they had given up their heathen practices. No more heathen sacrifices or ceremonies. They caused God grief. No more worshiping false gods and idols. "Our God is a jealous God and does not want people to worship anyone but him," he exhorted. They had to live as Jesus had, simple, honest, caring, loving, no more talking with spirits, no drinking, no whoring or copulating like wild animals, but must marry within the fellowship of the mission by one of God's missionaries, for only believers and church members were acceptable spouses. There could be no lies, no killing under any circumstances. They had to submit to God's will for their lives, and be totally obedient to their teachers. Everyone must work hard for their daily bread. Laziness was a great sin. They must not expect to go into the woods for food, but must labor, garden and raise the animals they used for meat, not go out on wild hunts to the woods as before like wild people. They must wear clothes and hide their nakedness as it offended God to see them that way.

Brother Johann went on and on for many hours in his kindly manner. Telling them how to be saved, why they needed to be saved, what they were being saved from: He told them of God's love and Jesus' suffering and bleeding on the cross all because they were wicked and sinful. It was impressive, that long list of pronouncements that God had given.

"God cannot bless you as long as you keep sinning. And you can't help but sin, because it is your nature. Your land will not be healed unless you are forgiven. These strange illnesses, the fevers and pox and others, they will not be cured until you give your heart to Jesus and are healed! The land, the waters, the animals—all will be returned to you once you stop your sinning and give your heart to Jesus! You are being punished for your sins and the sins of your parents and all those before you. If you do not turn now and save yourself, you will send this punishment on to your children."

Nonhelema straightened in her seat. This was one of the distressing things that she had often inquired of Zeisberger. "Why has Creator forsaken us? We still hold our ceremonies as our ancestors taught us. Before you came, when we prayed and made our ceremonies, they were accepted and our people were blessed. Now Creator does not hear our pleas for pity." He had merely responded that the Indians were heathens, and bad and full of sin, and needed to surrender their proud hearts and repent and stop their killing. It had not been a satisfactory answer just to tell her that her people were bad, when Nonhelema felt many whites were worse. But now she was beginning to understand. Once they had been told of what they were doing by Jesus' teachers sent specially to them, they were no longer dealing directly with God. He had closed his ears to their prayers; he no longer smelled their tobacco offerings. They could be blessed now only by accepting this salvation that God's son Jesus had to offer. It had to be done through the missionaries. These missionaries were essential to the salvation of the wretched savages.

It seemed too easy for Nonhelema, so she continued to listen to poor Brother Johann's wonderful way of telling the sad story of Jesus. Why had Ziesberger not been kinder to her? she wondered.

She had known a long time that she probably needed Jesus' salvation. But she was a chief. She had to continue holding the ceremonies for her people who chose the ways of their ancestors. That was the Shawnee way. No matter what her heart said or did, neither she nor any chief could stop participating in or leading the ceremonies. Indians never argued about how others worshiped Creator, and they never forced their ways on others. All of that was personal and decided between Creator and each person. All their national ceremonies were to thank Creator and to remind the people that Creator, not they, was in charge of the world.

"You must stop your sinning," Brother Johann continued. "I can see that many of you are sorry for your past sins, but that is not enough. God will not accept your prayers. He will not accept anything now but Jesus showing his father your name in his Book of Life, with no sins written after your name. You must give your heart to Jesus. It is the least you can give him for all the suffering he had to endure for your sake hanging on that cross. This Lamb without blemish or blame took your humiliation and pain and the death you purchased with your sins! He died so you could live forever in glory with him in heaven at the right hand of God our father." Brother Johann's voice cracked as he pleaded, "He was nailed through his hands and feet and left hanging in the hot sun for hours as his life ebbed away slowly! He was pierced through his side with a spear by the soldiers, and given bitter vinegar to drink. He was tormented by vile people. They cast lots for his clothes. They laughed at him as he suffered. They pushed a crown of thorns onto the tender flesh of his head! His earthly mother watched, brokenhearted, powerless, weeping at the foot of his cross, helpless as he died." Brother Johann had to wipe his own sincere tears from his eyes as he continued.

Nonhelema had noticed before, during Brother Zeisberger's endless lectures, that much of the Jesus story was hard to believe until a listener had become weary, with an aching head and a sore behind from the hard wooden benches. Sometimes, only tedious repetition made it believable.

Now Brother Johann was so emotional that one might have believed he had grown up with Jesus. Or, at least, they were great friends. Everyone was weeping in the room. Now he came to the best part, the one he had been leading up to all day. The part he had dedicated his life to: It was time to save someone.

"Who will come forward and give Jesus their heart today? Who will stop their sinning and fill their heart with God's love? Who wants *all their sins* forgiven today—not just the ones others know about, but the ones you know about and have kept hidden deep in your wicked heart; the ones God knows about, too? Who wants to be washed in the blood of God's Lamb, our forgiving loving Lord Jesus, who suffered only because of you and your terrible sins? Who wants to be purged of wickedness? Who will have their name written in the Lamb's Book of Life? The book of those with life eternal?"

With that he caught Nonhelema in his glance for the briefest moment. He scanned through the others to concentrate on those most affected by his telling. "Give him *your* heart! Have your sins forgiven! Who will be brave enough to admit you cannot save yourself from being condemned to hell? Who does not want to burn in the fiery pits of hell? Who wants everlasting life?

"Please I beseech you, give your heart now! All the brethren love you. We don't want to see you go to hell. Come! Come now! Don't wait," he said, pleading. "Jesus died in agony just to save . . . you," he ended in an emotion-filled whisper. He was cooing to them now, as if they would be breaking his heart as well as Jesus', as if he knew deep down they wanted to come but just needed coaxing. "Will you refuse his sweet salvation knowing what it cost him?" Johann asked. "Do you *want* to burn in the eternal flames of hell?"

Shawnees knew of eternal flames. They carried with them a fire to Jesus. Then he said, "Now, of course, you will have to give up your old ways and live here with us. You must labor with humility for the sake of the brethren. Only when we are sure that you are truly ours in Jesus, and not deceiving us or yourself, only then can you be baptized and named into Christendom." He gave her a sweet pious smile.

"But, brother," she protested, "I have to go to my town. I have hundreds of people and I am their headwoman. I've been gone so long already, making peace with the Long Knives as you wanted me to do!"

Zeisberger frowned, and made a scornful puffing noise with his lips. "Nonhelema! Where is your sincerity gone so quickly? Nothing in your old existence can be put ahead of your commitment to Jesus!"

Elizabeth leaned forward and asked when Nonhelema could be baptized. After a long pause, Zeisberger looked at Nonhelema and said, "We must see how you behave for a while. We must be sure you do not change your mind the first time the traders offer you a bottle of liquor or try to get you abed in exchange for a pretty bauble. And how can I watch you if you aren't here?"

She felt heat rising in her face, and braced herself to be respectful and calm as she explained. "My people want news of the peace talks. Then we have harvest, and our thanksgiving, and the sharing! It is the most joyous of our ceremonies."

"But it is a *heathen* ceremony, madame. Just what you have given up for Jesus! The gift of salvation is *all* you should be thinking of! Brother Johann is a kindly man, but perhaps his sermon was a bit soft, and you are not taking this seriously enough. I have known you a long time, Nonhelema. You have been filled with great sin for many years. You yourself confessed many sins when you came forward, did you not?"

She had thought that if she accepted Jesus, the missionary would forgive her old ways. Maybe not. Perhaps she really did not deserve this salvation. She had thought that if her name was in the Jesus Book of Life, then peace, health, and prosperity would come through her to her own people, even if they remained faithful to their ancestors' own religion. She had been elated, full of hope, until Zeisberger said these things.

I must not hate this great missionary, she thought. *He brought salvation to us.* She hung her proud head and said, "I will try to be worthy of Jesus' blood, but I cannot stay. I will come back for the love-feast of Jesus' birth. I pray I might be baptized on that great day. Meantime I will try to show you I can live without sinning."

that never needed to be fed but never went out. It was something their most ancient ancestors had carried with them on their migrations for hundreds of hundreds of years. Fire was a spirit and alive, sacred and life-giving. They knew about offending the Fire Spirit when it was treated with disrespect and when it went out of control. They had seen houses set afire by enemies and flames roaring with power. Nonhelema had read of the burnings of cities, in which hundreds of people had perished, and she looked up into the dry wooden rafters and roofing of this big building.

And she could remember the agony of prisoners as they had burned at the stake, in the old days in her town.

Brother Johann had brought many of the visitors to tears. All the women here had lost a son or a daughter or brother before their time. To think of losing one on purpose, for the sake of saving bad people who did not care, moved them to the depths of their souls.

And these listeners knew that their Indian people were in terrible health and there was much sorrow on the land that had never been here before. It was as though the whites had brought this "hell" with them in the boats so many years ago. And as they spread through Turtle Island, so did this hell, with all its plagues and mean spirit. If all this was true, the Book of Life might be the answer they had all been praying for in their own ceremonies.

"Every one of you is guilty of murdering Jesus," he pleaded, wringing his hands, tears shining on his saintly face. "Only Jesus can forgive you for his horrid death! Let us pray with you as Jesus fills you with the Holy Spirit and your old evil is washed away. Jesus is waiting, patiently *waiting . . . just for you,*" he said, his voice again becoming softer and kinder with each word until the last few words were more like a whisper and he wept and waited. "Oh, beloved brown brethren, give your heart this minute to our Lord and be saved! Do not perish when salvation is here at hand," he implored. "All you have to do is reach out. Believe in our Lord's promises and what his sacrifice can do for you. Step forward and save your soul!" Brother Johann was sincerely distressed as he finished his plea. "I am only a messenger. I can tell you of salvation! I can warn you what follows if you refuse! But only Jesus can save you if you will let him."

Nonhelema's heart was shaken by the pleas of this sweet man. His words had made her see the reasons he had given as Zeisberger never had. It seemed that Brother Johann had been talking forever, but she didn't want him to stop. He bowed his head, again glancing around the room to see who was most affected.

"Oh Jesus! We have touched many hearts this day! Help them, Jesus! Bring home to them the weight of their terrible sins! Convict them in their hearts! Break those who are stiff-necked! Make them bow at your precious, bleeding, nail-scarred feet, oh Lord, that they might have this everlasting life! Speak to their hearts, Lord! Brothers, sisters, pray harder! I can feel the Holy Spirit is here! He is working, softening hearts. He is convicting many hearts of their wickedness. He is standing here waiting to heal them and bless them. Pray with me, brethren! Strengthen the Spirit as he works on these wicked sin-filled hearts and casts out the evil demons that have tormented their lives! Oh Lord Jesus, save these people, these children, these brown brethren that you have sent us into this wilderness to preach to. Lord clean out their ears, soften their hearts, help them, Lord, to rise up and be counted for you and become children of God instead of pawns of the Devil! Who will come? Jesus is waiting . . . His arms are stretched wide. He loves you. His forgiveness is waiting to embrace you!"

Nonhelema gasped, sobbed softly, and stood. Straightening to her full height, she looked him in the eyes and said, "I am so sorry, Brother Johann. I did not understand that it was I personally who was responsible for Jesus' suffering and murder. I am a mother. I would not want to break the heart of God. I want to give my heart to Jesus so he can write my name in his Book of Life. I now understand why my people have suffered so much. It has been because of me. I have been mean-spirited. I have been drunk. I have had men as my husband and some who were not. I have killed in battle and taken lives. I have grieved God and acted ungrateful for the sacrifice of his precious son's life. I cannot bear this shame. I love my people. I have offered my life for their well-being on the battlefield. It is a small thing to offer my life now in exchange for this forgiveness. I don't want my sins to cause my children and the people more sorrow. I want Jesus to love me and forgive me. I want him to write my name in his Book of Life. I want God to bless our land again and heal it and our people. Please, Brother Johann, save me."

As she finished, several resident Indian women converts rushed forward to her side in support and welcome, and Brother Johann gently reached his arms around this tall woman, speaking soothingly

while trying not to weep himself. He knew that she had be lenging case and had caused Brother David many troub. spent in prayer. Nonhelema looked toward where Brother D sitting and saw him sitting with his mouth slack, stunned. Sh stood suddenly what she had done to him, not intending to: A the years he had spent trying to get this heathen woman to g₁ wicked heart to his precious Jesus, it had taken a love-feast ar. story of Jesus' life spoken by his shy assistant. Now she had come in a manner that humiliated him. His jaw muscles worked. But t. to all the others, he added his own, "Amen!"

Her influence was strong. She had aroused several other Shawne who were now walking toward the front of the room, making the professions of faith and asking for forgiveness and acceptance int Jesus' family of the *chosen few*. In all, five more came forward to be saved. It was the most to come at any one time since Brother Ziesberger had brought the mission to the Ohio. There was Tschuwiseh, who had come before only to listen, and his daughter Bibiane, and a young warrior, Jael. Eschecana'hunt, Chief Packanke's oldest son, also came with tears of remorse over his wasted, wicked life. It was a wonderful harvest of souls for his Lord. Shawnees hardly ever converted. Indeed, it was a glorious day for the compound, for Ziesberger, and for the Lord.

And Brother Johann was now sobbing uncontrollably in reverence, astonishment, gratitude, and his own feelings of unworthiness, humbled that the Lord had spoken through him.

But there was no face in the room more radiant than that of old Sister Elizabeth. At last her most important and willful daughter was to be welcomed into Christ's kingdom!

Nonhelema's brothers were kindly but subdued. They knew that a momentous thing had happened to her after the young man's long, wearying story. They hugged her, saying, *"Wehsah!"* Good. But they knew that this would make her life even more difficult. It was hard enough to live in just one world with just one god. Now she would have two to serve.

At last Brother Zeisberger would speak directly to her. It was a private audience, but he never conferred with a woman without at least one witness. The witnesses were her mother and Brother Johann.

First the great missionary praised her for giving her heart at last

The interview was over. Brother Johann held Nonhelema's hand for a moment as Brother Zeisberger got up and left the little room, his straight back expressing his righteousness.

Stiff-necked, she thought.

Then she put her palm over her mouth.

Already my thoughts are sinning.

6

GRENADIER SQUAW'S TOWN
DECEMBER 1775

Their harvest had been more plentiful than they had thought it
would be. The people's health was better than usual. Peace
seemed to be taking hold of the land. Most of the Shawnee chiefs had
reluctantly agreed to work at gathering more captives to take to Fort
Pitt the next summer, and were doing so. Cornstalk was traveling
most of the time, attending to that delicate business. Winter was approaching, mild so far, and before the frigid season began Nonhelema
and her family would go to see their mother once more. With Brother
Zeisberger's permission, Elizabeth had sent a message asking that
they join the congregation at the compound for the Christmas love-
feast. Nonhelema suspected that Zeisberger had relayed the invitation through her mother. This was the ultimate love-feast of the year
when he baptized all those who had given their hearts to Jesus during
the year. She wanted to believe that Zeisberger might consent to baptize her in this season. Of course, he would be wanting spy reports on
the Shawnees, too, but maybe he thought he had kept her wondering
long enough and would christen her.

Nimwha was living at Kispoko Town just a few miles away, and he was eager to see their mother again, too. Silverheels, who lived many miles to the southeast, sent a message that he was not able to come; his family was ill and he did not want to leave them. It was about a dozen of Nonhelema's family, then, including her daughter, Fani, and some of her more distant Delaware family, who went. They set out on horseback with one packhorse and went northeastward on the Gosh-goshing Trail. It would be a three-day ride, more if deep snows came. No Indian towns lay between Scioto-sipe and the Muskingumsipe along that trace, so they would make camp at night. The whole way was through pretty hill country, and light snow lay in the woods and meadows, enhancing the beauty of the terrain. Nonhelema and her daughter rode side by side, with Nimwha out front watching for any sort of danger. There was no trouble, the weather was cold but calm, and they got to Gnaddenhutten Mission in three days.

Their arrival was heralded by the Indian converts who had been watching for their arrival. They were brought quickly inside the main dining room, where they were all treated to hot tea. The building was rich with cooking and baking odors and smells of cedar. The converts had brought boughs of cedar and serviceberry with their profusion of bright red berries for decoration. Some curly vines of bittersweet had been brought and stuck in a small cup. Creeping vinca, so rich and shiny dark green, and creeping cedar with its umbrella-like branches, and other herbs had been used to make wreaths. It had brightened up their otherwise drab interiors. The houses were lighted with more candles than usual, making the humble community twinkle like an opulent town. The people seemed more gay than Nonhelema could ever remember them. Her mother's coppery skin was all wrinkles, radiating from her smiling mouth and eyes, and she hurried around, hugging family members until she had to sit down and rest.

The women inmates brought platters and bowls and pans heaping full of savory hot foods they had cooked in their quarters. Sideboards were laden with steaming dishes and beverages.

First came the main meal—venison and goose and bowls of hominy flavored with currants and boned small-game meat. There was a wonderful soup with strange seasonings and the root vegetables that the Moravians planted in their gardens: cabbage bits, turnips, potatoes, and onions, all seasoned with green herbs. Nonhelema was anxious for sweets. It seemed wrong to serve the regular food first and save the best until last, but these Moravian missionaries were from a country called Germany, and had their own traditional ways of doing things.

Between the main meal and the arrival of sweet cakes, there was a rest interval. It gave everyone a chance to visit the outhouses and let some of the food digest before the desserts and entertainment began. It was another chance to catch up on news. Old men and warriors went outside and shared pipes and asked for news of war and peace. All visitors from outside were quizzed by the converts. Brother Zeisberger preached that the business of the material present was of no concern to holy people, but nevertheless he encouraged them to bring him all the news they could elicit from visitors about events and attitudes in their communities.

Finally, it was time for the best part of the year, so far as most of the Indians were concerned—the Christmas love-feast. The women began parading the delicacies into the room, placing them on the tables that had been cleaned off after the meal. The aromas were sweet and inviting. There were tiny cakes so thin they were like crisp, spicy leaves. They were Nonhelema's favorite. Other high, fluffy, moist cakes were iced and lemony—a treat, for the flavor of the lemon was rare. Some desserts had plums, raisins, citron peel, and pecans inside them; one even had persimmons and hazelnuts. They had sugared the pecans and walnuts. There was spiced wine to be drunk in tiny servings, with the delicate cookies and cakes. The Christmas coffee was ready to be poured. They added much sugar and cream to it just after they poured it.

The large dining room was full of eager people waiting for Zeisberger to say a special prayer so they could begin eating these treats. Their usual fare was quite simple; only at Christmas did they get all the rich baked goods to eat at once. Zeisberger made them wait. He sat beside Brother Abraham, formerly a chief of the Delaware Turkey Clan. On his other hand sat Brother Johann Jungmann. At last Zeisberger stood up to pray, and the room fell still.

"Lord God, we thank you for the birth of your beloved son, who sacrificed his life for our miserable sins, that we might have everlasting life. We thank you for these hearts that have come to share in our joyous celebration, and to help sing our beloved savior Jesus' praises. Thank you for the plenty of our pantries, that we may have these fine foods to celebrate with. May it nourish our bodies and quicken our spirits to total obedience to you, who have redeemed us with your precious spilled blood. Amen."

Nonhelema had noticed that every time he opened his mouth, Brother David Zeisberger found some way to bring up blood in the conversation, even in prayers. She wondered whether he had ever envisioned Jesus as he might have been before he was nailed up by the sinners of the world. When she tried to imagine Jesus, he was a handsome, smiling whiteman, looking, perhaps, a bit like Alexander McKee. She drifted toward the table with the tiny thin cakes and mulled wine, almost drooling.

Sisters Caritas and Christiana came up, offering her more delicacies to taste. They giggled like children. Their mother was watching from a bench along the side of the wall with several of the other elderly women.

Soon the baked sweets were gone. Nothing was left except the many crumbs on the floor, which some young women quickly swept away with the sturdy brooms the mission women made to sell to the traders. While they were sweeping, some of the men went to their house and came back with their musical instruments. The visitors seated themselves on the floor and waited for the music to begin.

To Nonhelema, whitemen's songs and music makers were as much a weakness as their sweet foods. To her, the sounds were so beautiful they had to come from Creator himself. There were songs that had words, and the Christianized Indians even knew the words. Nonhelema had learned a few hymns in past visits and loved the feeling of singing. It seemed as if the people were singing for Jesus to hear. There had been just enough wine to loosen and lighten everyone's heart, but no one was drunk. They would be asked to leave if any got drunk. Nothing marred the evening.

The ceremonial candles burned low and threatened to set their little white paper ruffles on fire, so the elders and other converts said good night.

Brother Zeisberger invited the visitors to come to Christmas-morning worship service, which would be immediately after breakfast. Soon the room was dark and full of the sounds of sleeping, Shawnee and Delaware families strewn over the floor like piles of bedding, curled up in their blankets. When Nonhelema left and went to her mother's bedside in the elder widow sisters' house, the old women were already asleep. She rolled out bedding beside her mother, reclined, covered herself up, and lay listening to the sounds of old women breathing, snoring, groaning with the digestion of unaccustomed delicacies, turning bumpingly on their pallets, now and then making wind in their blankets. She herself lay supine, her hands on her own full belly, too full, with too many emotions coursing through her and keeping her wakeful. Would she, tomorrow, on the holiday of Jesus' birth, actually be accepted by Brother Zeisberger, after all their long negotiation over her soul? Zeisberger was like a Jesus commissioner, as those men in Fort Pitt had been Indian commissioners, and like them he had negotiated hard against her, resenting her womanly power, but needing her. Who knew whether she had won or what she had won? Would she be dipped in the baptismal river, and at last be in Jesus' book with a saved soul, a true child of God?

She moved both palms slowly over her abdomen, now full with the delicacies of the love-feast, while a feeling of dread was beginning to creep into her thoughts with alarming frequency, that a new tiny soul could be a new resident in her firm belly.

Brother Zeisberger would not baptize her if he knew she had sinned with Alexander McKee. Would God somehow reveal that knowledge to Brother Zeisberger?

Or, since God already must know of it, would he somehow prevent the baptism himself, or make it go wrong?

She thought that God probably would not be as stern about her sin as the missionary would be.

Or will I, myself, Nonhelema, probably pregnant at this age, let myself deceive Brother Zeisberger and smuggle this tiny secret life through the ceremony and into salvation?

In the cold air of the dark room, she felt tears slide down her temples to her ears, and wondered what would become of this. What would become of peace in the war the white nations were starting against each other, and what would become of her and the one growing within her in that war, and above all what would become of her Shawnee people? Hardly any of them had been saved by Jesus, and all were surrounded by the warring whitemen, cajoled and threatened to take one side or another in their war.

It would require all the strength and wisdom that God and Weshemonetoo could give her to be a peacemaker in the times to come. If she took the baptism ceremony with the living secret of this sin inside her, would God even grant her such strength and wisdom? Or would she have to face it alone, a weak and foolish woman with what the Christians called a bastard child in her arms, distrusted by her own tribal sisters, her beloved *shemas*, because she was growing away from them to another god? Was she as unworthy as the missionary said?

She prayed that Zeisberger would admit her through to salvation. After that, she would not have to go through that pious Jesus commissioner to talk to God, perhaps. She was tired of negotiating with powerful whitemen for the right to live in peace.

She had christened herself with her own tears, but by the time she began to doze, the paths of the tears had dried to salt on her skin and she rubbed it away with her fingertips, then went to sleep with her palms on her belly, thinking of the story of Jesus being born in a long ago and faraway land, which had been invaded and ruled by a powerful nation of whitemen called Romans. She imagined them as Virginians with three-cornered hats and long knives.

The white winter sun came up, glinting on frost. Cook-fire smoke hung low over the roofs of the mission, and mist veiled the river where the baptisms would be done. Christmas Day began as the eve had ended: with food. Nonhelema ate, but her mind and spirit were barely sustaining hope.

After breakfast, Brother Zeisberger summoned them all for examination of the candidates for baptism. He reminded everyone that Christ had died because of their wretched sinful state. Jesus had originally lived in heaven with God, sitting on his own throne at God's right hand. He had been tended by servants, and never felt pain or humiliation. But he had chosen to experience all the awful woes and discomforts of mankind—in order to save mankind. They were wicked, but his love was so great that he sacrificed his own life for them and they did not even know they were wicked. He suffered all of this to save them from the flames of hell and eternal torment by the Devil. Guilt and dread began to fill the room like an odor of hellfire. Zeisberger was severe this morning, laying down the rules.

"The gift of salvation is not free. If you are to save your eternal life from torment, you must forfeit the life you are leading today! You must give up worldly things and have your mind always about godly and heavenly things. You must be loving and peaceful. You must be sober, and clean, and *obedient*—to God's laws, your teachers, and you—women, you must be obedient to your husbands." Nonhelema remembered how amused her Shawnee women had been by that notion. "You shall have but one spouse, and you must be faithful in all things! You must be clean and honest, and respect and care for your elders and the sick! You must never kill, you must never be drunk, and you must help the brethren in their labors. You are never to purchase items from those who have killed another. You must have approval of the missionary and one of the native helpers before you are allowed to marry. You must also get permission to trade with the traders or purchase any of their goods. You may not be quarrelsome with others. You cannot associate with murderers or thieves. You will share and contribute food for the compound and visitors and the upkeep of the brethren. You will participate in worship services and help maintain these buildings and the grounds and gardens. If you cannot dedicate your life to living this way and obeying these things, then we cannot have you in our community. You are not saved."

In the solemn silence that followed, Zeisberger looked at those who had come forward as candidates for salvation during the year. He called their names one by one and quizzed them concerning the state of their hearts. He asked them to tell the brethren and sisters why they thought they should be allowed to join his community.

One by one, each broke into tears of sorrow over having caused the Lord, the suffering bleeding Jesus such grief, and for costing him his precious life.

After each one, Zeisberger then asked, "Can anyone speak in behalf of this person? Have you seen any change since he gave his heart to the Lord?" In each case, someone would come forward and testify to the wonderful changes that person had undergone since answering the calling to salvation. The transformations were beautiful. The people were kinder, quieter, more considerate, more generous, more gentle. They prayed to Jesus all the time.

Nonhelema began to think that Brother Zeisberger was not going to call her. He had not even glanced at her. Her heart began to sink. He would humble her once again by passing her over. She was too proud. She had gone back to her own village after her calling instead of staying here and being obedient and humble; she had been presumptuous enough to insist that she was a chief, even though the missionary knew she was only a woman, and not a very good one at that. She glanced over at Brother Johann imploringly; it was he, after all, who had moved her to convert. Was Brother Zeisberger going to humiliate him, too, for having the audacity to save a proud woman he himself had been unable to convert? Brother Johann himself looked as distressed as she felt.

"There is, I believe, one more," the missionary said, as he finally looked at her. "Nonhelema, a woman of the Shawnee nation, known to us here as another daughter of our beloved Sister Elizabeth."

The old woman, at those long-awaited words, began to shine like a saint.

As the converts prepared themselves to go down to the cold river for the ordeal of a winter baptism, Brother Johann came beaming to Nonhelema, and they looked into each other's eyes with joy and tenderness. The saving of her soul had been the high point of his missionary service. And although Brother Zeisberger had referred to her as just another Shawnee woman, everyone knew that she was uncommonly important—as an example, but also as a leader of the peaceful Shawnees.

And that was what Johann had come to speak of at this moment. Leaning close, so as not to be overheard speaking of temporal matters in this holy moment, he told her: "Our beloved Brother David in his wisdom has come around into agreement with you, that you might be of better service by remaining in your town, as a peace leader. And that you might better protect the safety of our mission here through your association with the Americans. He asked me to confide this to you. I do agree with him, although many of us, especially Sister Elizabeth and I, wish you could live here among us all the time." He nodded and blinked, a wistful smile on his lips.

Which really means, she thought, *that Brother Zeisberger needs me on the Scioto to keep spying on the Shawnees for him. Forgive me, dear Jesus, if that is a mean thought.*

"I am grateful for Brother David's wisdom," she said. "He came far away from his homeland to do good for the Indians. But he is a man, and perhaps a woman can do more good by staying at home." It was difficult not to smirk as she made that statement.

"But," Johann added, "he needs assurance that you will always live up to the Christ's example, and not participate in the ceremonies of your unenlightened people."

"Yes," she said. "my poor heathen people."

"Beloved children!" Brother Zeisberger called out, and his flock converged around him.

"Come, let us seal their salvation and wash away their old sins. Let us help them show the world that they follow Jesus, and will live their lives in his example. He was baptized in death and resurrection and we will now go to the river and baptize these new Christians to glorify our Lord and his sacrifice." With those words he walked out the door, and the new converts followed after him. Some of the mission residents carried blankets to wrap the baptized in when they emerged from the cold river. The air was so cold, their breath turned to clouds as they walked.

Cold as it was, the river had not yet frozen. Sometimes in the past, the mission helpers had needed to chip ice to open the water for the Christmas baptisms. Zeisberger liked to preach that cold water was insignificant compared with what his Lord had suffered for these wretched heathens. It did no harm to remind them what true suffering was like.

Brother Zeisberger waded into the river first, to his knees, gasping, and then to his thighs, finding firm footing on the uneven muddy bottom. He was followed by two of his most trusted assistants, Brother Johann and old Brother Abraham. The Delaware headman was one of the missionary's prize converts, as influential a catch as Nonhelema herself was. Zeisberger now asked Brother Ezra and Brother Schmick to sing, and called for the converts one by one.

As each entered the cold water, he embraced them, then bade them hold their hands in prayer position in front of their chest. He then grasped their hands in his right hand, with his left in the small of their back. Then he and his helpers lowered them into the water and lifted them, not once but three times, saying, "I now baptize thee in the name of the Father, and of the Son, and of the Holy Spirit. May the Lord bless and keep thee unto himself." On the final lift he turned them toward the riverbank, where the Christian Indians were waiting with warm blankets and loving hugs.

Cold as the water was, Brother Zeisberger showed no discomfort. He shone with a radiance seldom seen on men's faces.

Nonhelema was the last one. He looked toward her and summoned her with his hand. She waded in, bracing herself as she did every winter morning when she washed herself in icy water. This was nothing new to her. It was known by all Shawnee people that Creator had put life in every true human being, and that life was a sacred fire burning, that all burning was borrowed from the life-giving sun, and that that inner fire was stronger than the cold of ice. She wasn't sure if she should be thinking of Weshemonetoo right now, but she didn't know what Jesus had to say about cold.

She stood taller than Brother Zeisberger. When he closed his cold hand over her two hands, she felt him trembling. As he and the helpers lowered her into the river, she sent the life fire to every part of her body, and the cold was trifling. They raised her.

"I christen thee Catarina. In the name of the Father . . .

". . . of the Son . . .

". . . and of the Holy Spirit."

The air was colder than the water, but still she did not shiver or quake, though she was soaked from the crown of her head to the soles of her feet. Brother Zeisberger was shuddering violently now, though only his legs and arms were wet.

Many of her relatives had come to witness this great moment. It was a strange and mysterious thing to many of them, but to her mother, Elizabeth, it was the best and most important thing that could have happened. Her old face was glowing, her eyes were shimmering, and she was the first to embrace her daughter when she strode up the riverbank, with water streaming off every inch of her.

I am now Catarina, she thought. *I am a new person with no sins written beside my name. I am one of God's children, safe from hell.*

She didn't know whether the beginning life inside her was by this same ceremony saved from hell. Eventually she would have to ask.

7

In *Hakwi Kisathwa*, the Cold Moon, while Nonhelema was still in an exalted state of the spirit from her baptism—hopeful that the Shawnee were in the mood for peace, that Cornstalk would persuade the other chiefs to bring in enough captives to please the commissioners at the next peace council at Fort Pitt—still more joy came to her.

Alexander McKee arrived with Simon Girty and two packhorses, much news from Fort Pitt, and, best of all, himself. By chiefly protocol, Nonhelema went out to greet them and escort them into her town. Her people thronged to welcome the popular agent.

While Girty and Caesar went to unload and tend the horses, McKee came into her house. It was remarkable that he had set out in the dead of winter. But he preferred frozen trails to muddy ones. He explained that he had many places to go and wanted to finish his journeys before the rains and mud and floods of spring. He would stay here in the Shawnee towns on the Scioto for a while, then go north to Pluggy's Mingo Town, then farther up to see the Wyandots and

Captain Pipe's Delawares toward the Sandusky, before returning to Pittsburgh. He would smoke and renew friendships with all those chiefs. He brought news that Newcomer, the Turtle Clan chief of the Delawares, had moved his community from Pennsylvania, where too many whitemen were settling, to a place on the Tuscarawas near Gnaddenhutten Mission, and that Chief White Eyes had gone deeper among the whites, to stay at Philadelphia and work with Colonel Morgan to maintain the peaceful relations that had been established last year in the Fort Pitt councils.

She had news for him, as well, but didn't mention it immediately. The pregnancy had not yet become apparent. Instead the first news she gave him was of her Christmas Day baptism at Gnaddenhutten. But he put a hand on her wrist and said, "Yes, dear, I heard of it. I stopped there on my way here. Everybody in the mission is still talking about it." He scratched his yellow stubble. "I'm happy you've done something that's so important to you. I saw your mother there. She is serenely happy because of it. I believe I made her even happier with a gift of colored yarns.

"As for gifts," he added, "I have this for you." He groped in his shoulder bag, which he had laid upon her table, and brought out something small and narrow, wrapped in green felt cloth and tied with red yarn. "It's a gift for your new name, Catarina," he said. "If I may be so familiar, I shall call ye Katy, as I've always liked that name." While she was untying the yarn, he brought a small flask out of the bag and set it upon the table. When she saw it, she thought for a moment: *Is Alexander the Devil?* But when she unfolded the cloth and saw the beautiful little filigreed silver sugar spoon, that thought vanished, and her heart warmed. She put her hand in his, and he raised it to his lips.

"Ah, Katy! How often I've sat of an evening, remembering my *saa sa ketwi k'wehwa!*"

She drew back and looked along her nose at him in mock censure. "Captain! You are scarcely out of your saddle and you are drooling on my hand and calling me your naked woman! I should put you out in the corral with your horses, to sleep there."

He dropped his chin and shook his head. "Ah, I deserve it. But before I go to eat hay, would you join me in a sip of very fine French cognac, to dispel the chill of traveling so far in winter just to look upon your tawny beauty again?" He laid his hand upon his heart and made his face a mask of wistful pleading, lifting the flask with his other hand and waving it before her face.

"Ha! Yes, then. But it is a good thing that you brought such a very little bottle. *Nee tahpi wannitho.* I am sober anymore, as a Christian."

"Oof! That is severe! I'm a Christian, too, you know. But I still get thirsty."

"But you are not a Christian of the Zeisberger, Brother David. He would tell Jesus how to behave, I think."

"Here, Katy, my dear. You could drink this whole flask and still be sober. Fortunately, I brought much more for you on the packhorse, but I suppose I can drink it myself, if you won't have any."

She pulled the stopper and sniffed. "Oh, how good. But I'll only taste of it. Then we must go out and see my people. They will want to visit with you and feed you. You are a guest of my town, and I cannot keep you for myself."

"But I hope you will keep me for yourself a little now and then while I'm here."

She had a moment's memory, something that had troubled her mind now and again since the last day she had seen him. It was of the young woman she had seen riding toward his plantation as she was leaving. The Atkins girl. Maybe she would ask him about that. But probably she would not. She didn't want Alexander to think she didn't trust him, because she did trust him. Everybody trusted Alexander McKee.

She arose to get a small glass for her sip of cognac, saying, "Wapey massiweh, you are my favored companion. Yes, we will be just two alone, I hope also."

"Here's to that," he said.

The taste of the liquor, both powerful and delicate, diffused through her mouth, its fumes through her nose, its warmth through her midriff. This was a pleasure she never would have known had not whitemen come. She knew, of course, that it was more a curse than a gift to the Indian people, and that few would ever get to taste any this good. The liquor most Indians got was vile and poisonous.

She imagined that the Zeisberger would be frothing at the lips if he knew she was now sipping this sinful elixir, given to her by this lusty amorist who was a Catholic or a heathen or maybe both. Thinking about Brother David's censure made her want to smirk with mirth and cringe with shame at the same time. But now, the Zeisberger was distant and McKee was close, and if the cherry-wood

Jesus on the wall wasn't shaming her, why should she worry about a missionary?

"What amuses ye?" McKee asked, seeing her expression.

"Your gifts make me joyful," she said. "This, and the little silver spoon. But you have given me a greater gift, so much greater, that you do not even know you gave!"

McKee looked pleased, but puzzled. "What gift is that?"

She interlaced her fingers under her chin and rested her elbows on the table. "What is the best gift you know?"

He tilted his head and chuckled. "Love?"

"Yes, that. Go on."

"Better than love? I know I give you that, and you give me the same."

"Yes. *Tapalot*. Soul love. And *soos*. Body love. And still better. You do not guess yet? Listen outside. What do you hear just now, outside the door?"

Frowning, one eyebrow raised, he turned his ear toward the door. The sound was the sound that was almost always in the air in Indian towns. "I hear children laughing," he said.

She smiled and shook her head. Men were so slow to understand anything. The women of her town had instantly noticed that she no longer came to the menstrual lodge each moon. They knew, and were surely discussing among themselves, three possible reasons: because she had become a Christian, because she had grown too old to have a moon time anymore, or because at this age she was pregnant. The women knew that the first were more likely, but they were surely saying, *She went to Pittsburgh several times in the autumn. She danced with whitemen. To think! Having a baby at her age!*

And here sat the only person who actually knew what she had done. But being a man, he still hadn't guessed!

"Children are the greatest gift," she said to McKee. "I thought I would never have one again. Now if this is a boy, I want to name him after his father: Alexander."

She expected to see joy in his face. For a while, he moved his mouth as if his tongue were too dry. He was looking not quite at her eyes, but through them and out through the back of her head and out through the log wall of the house, toward the place where the sun would set. Then he began blinking, and finally he smiled, but with only one side of his mouth.

Eventually, as her heart began to quaver with disappointment, he thought of something to say: "Would you consider that we name him instead after *my* father, Thomas?"

"I would consider that," she said quietly. "Now perhaps you might pour more cognac for me to toast your exuberant joy." She thought a moment and added: "More cognac for yourself, too. You will need it to keep you warm tonight."

8

NONHELEMA'S TOWN
FEBRUARY 1776

By *Thkeebee Kisathwa*, the Sugar Tree Moon, word came that the people in the missions were about to starve.

On the same day the messenger came riding with that message, Nonhelema had told her daughter something and asked her not to tell anyone else about it yet. Fani always kept secrets well because if she didn't, she would never hear any more—and she relished knowing secrets.

"The women already suspect," Nonhelema said. "Daughter, your mother is *kee kachee*. I believe I will be having a child this year."

Fani's eyes widened in her pretty face. "I have heard their *pocvano*, the gossip," she said. "If it is by Captain McKee it will look like a *wapey lenni*, with yellow hair."

Nonhelema did not ask why she thought it was by Captain McKee. Anyone in town when he was here would have had to be blind or mindless not to suspect it, though the two had been as discreet as they could be in an Indian town. Probably no one would have objected, anyway. Everybody liked Alexander McKee.

If anyone wondered how this fit with the sins of the Christian God for whom Nonhelema had gone to the river, they kept that to themselves. A Shawnee woman could do what she chose to do, unless it made trouble for the rest of the people.

Just after Nonhelema told Fani about the pregnancy, a shout went up in the village announcing that a messenger was coming.

It was one of the Christian Indians from Gnaddenhutten, Brother Ezra, one who had sung church songs on her baptism day. He said that there were so many hundreds of inmates at the missions that food had entirely run out. The few Delaware towns over by the Muskingum and the Tuscarawas had tried to help, but their food had nearly run out, too. When Chief Newcomer had moved in, his people had not brought enough, and the other villages had depleted their supplies by helping them get through the winter. Hunters were out all the time, but this season the game was so scrawny and poor it was hardly worth hauling in, hardly enough to feed the hunters themselves. There were so many towns over there now, Delaware and Shawnee as well as the mission towns, that game was depleted. The Mingoes had hunted up there for years as well as from their towns along the Ohio. And lately the white hunters had been spreading farther and farther out from the settlements around Fort Pitt. When they came in with their long-shooting rifled guns, hunting became harder for all the Indians.

Nonhelema told Brother Ezra: "I wish you had come earlier. We could have taken food at any time. Our harvest was good last fall and we have all we need. The other towns here can help, too. Come. Eat. Then I will send you with Caesar to Chillikawthe and Pickaway and to the Blue Jacket's Town and Cornstalk's Town, with a message for them to help with what they have. Fani, feed our brother. I am going to call the women to council and ask them to open their caches. Bundle all that dried squash we have strung up in the rafters. That alone will feed a hundred brethren for two days, in a soup."

She went out in the cold, calling. In a day, the women could gather the food and start east with packhorses. In three days, they could reach the Muskingum. Across the Muskingum, the Moravians had wagons and roads to their mission towns. Nonhelema's own mother was among the hungry in Gnaddenhutten.

Nonhelema decided to send the food, but not go herself. Brother Zeisberger must not see her with child. *The longer I don't have to confront him about this sin, the better. He would probably rather eat his own shoe leather than eat food brought by a woman who sinned with a man.*

PITTSBURGH MAY 3, 1776

TO THE REV. DAVID ZEISBERGER
MISSIONARY AMONG THE INDIANS,
ON MUSKINGUM RIVER

Reverend Sir,

   *Captain White Eyes the bearer of this has been in Philadelphia all
the last winter. He has behaved with remarkable regularity during the
whole time & has impress'd the people with favorable ideas of the
Delaware nation of your mission of which he spoke on all occasions with
the highest respect. If I can render you or your Mission any services, it
will make me very happy & I beg you will command me.*

   *If you can inform me what you apprehend to be the real disposition
of the western Indians & of anything material which passes among
them, you will render a very acceptable service to our country, & your
name shall never be made use of.*

   *I particularly need to know if you can hear of any discontents
among the Savages & what they arise from.*

I am &ct.

George Morgan

Nonhelema was in her fifth month of pregnancy when Colonel
George Morgan, Waypeymatchikthe himself, came to her town ur-
gently pleading for her help in keeping peace. He had been appointed
to succeed Richard Butler as Indian agent at Fort Pitt, and was in a
high state of dread about growing English influence on the tribes in
his Middle Ground jurisdiction. He was afraid that all progress made
at the peace talks the year before would be undone by British agitation before this year's assembly at Fort Pitt. He had been sending his
subordinates—McKee, Matthew Elliott, William Wilson—out into
every part of the Ohio country to make diplomacy with the tribal
leaders, while he and the Delaware leader White Eyes were persuading Congress to give serious attention and resources to winning and
keeping Indian friendships west of the mountains.

   "Yes, old friend, all your agents have been here," she assured him.
"They are doing your work well, and we have been helping as much as
we can. It is true that British agents are moving among the villages,

too, though they haven't come to the Mekoches yet. They understand that they are not welcome here, that we have given you our hand. Cornstalk and Hard Man have been talking for peace, trying to persuade all the headmen to bring forth captives when they go to Fort Pitt next time, so that your commissioners will be satisfied and treat us better than last time. Our Women's Councils listen and tell me what the feelings are in their tribes. You ought to expect that most Shawnee leaders will see you at Fort Pitt in good friendship after Green Corn ceremony, unless the British treat us too well and the Long Knives treat us too badly. The Mingoes remain angry because too many troublesome whites keep filling up their country and killing the game and cutting down the trees, even shooting at their hunters. Pluggy warned your commissioners at the last talks that he will kill them whenever they cross the line. He is one who listens to the British. He is dangerous to us all, even as he tries to defend us."

A gentleman, Colonel Morgan made no mention of her pregnancy, though it was now in some evidence. Probably he knew of her dalliance with Alexander McKee, but he mentioned that subordinate only in terms of his work. It was as if Morgan had entirely forgotten what had once been intimate affection between them; he now considered her a friend, ally, and helpmeet—another of those many Indian chiefs important to his management of the western frontier in a time when impending war made allies crucial. He was a wealthy merchant with an estate in New Jersey and a beautiful highborn wife and several children, a scientific scholar and horticulturist, club member in a philosophical society with Dr. Franklin and other notables. Nonhelema knew all of this in vague terms. He had also trekked and traded with Indians and frontiersmen as far as the Mississippi River, and had had as consort one of the most influential and elegant of all the Indian queens of the country. He was used to stepping from one role to another, as were many who crossed frontiers.

Nonhelema herself had moved her heart beyond that romantic stage, though she still loved Morgan, perhaps even more than when it had been like a marriage. She could still remember fondly every part of him—body, mannerisms, mind—and could bring long-ago memories up vivid and whole. But those memories lived now in another part of the roundness that was her spirit. Everything existed at once in the spirit, as in the roundness of the world: yesterday, today, tomorrow, dreams, ancestors and the not-yet-born, past wars, future peace. Each day, one was in a particular place in that roundness. Closer things were clearer, but one could look far and see all the rest.

But whitemen did not seem to see such a roundness, and she had spent much of her life trying to understand how the world of life was for them. They seemed to think that yesterday was behind their back and tomorrow was a place before them that they had not reached yet, and that when they got there they would make everything better than God had made it. Everything they did, it seemed, they did to change the world. And it was true, any Indian could tell you, that when they had gone through, everything was changed. It was because of this that she had not had an easy time with the missionaries or the understanding of Jesus. Although they claimed to remember the life of Jesus as clearly as if they had seen it themselves, their heaven and hell were separated from this world they lived on, and their past and future were separated from the time they lived in now. They would not see Jesus until they had changed and lived their lives as what the missionaries said they should, and then died.

"Wapeymatchikthe," she said, "you need to stand before our councils and say to our people, so they can hear in your own voice, that the Congress and the Virginians are sincere in their words for peace. They will be happy to see you, their old friend. In two days, I can summon headmen and headwomen from all the septs of our people to come and hear you. Some are so tired of hearing me talk peace, they might not listen to me so well."

She sent Caesar out to all the nearby towns with the wampum strands of invitation.

When Caesar came back, his news made her cringe in dismay and embarrassment for her people:

Agents of the British had been in the other towns, trying to influence them to attend councils at Detroit and hear the English side of the war issue. The agents had brought kegs of rum.

Caesar said, "They are all crazed and sickened. Some have hurt each other. Women are passed out and their babies are crying to be fed. Some young men are yelling that the British are their true friends. I was called a Long Knife and threatened. I never seen them so bad, ever, m'lady."

"Were they all too bad to come and council with Wapeymat-chikthe?"

"Some headmen said they would come. If they wake up and remember, they might be here . . ."

Colonel Morgan was angered and alarmed. His fears were being confirmed; the British were undermining the Americans' sincere efforts to keep peace in the Middle Ground.

Nonhelema tried to ease his fears. "Old friend, when they are sober and come to see you, they will believe what you say and will be sorry about the British. When their heads hurt, their hearts hurt. They will be repentant and will listen to you even better."

She could see that he was more than a little worried. She knew him well enough to see in his manner that he was still holding something inside. Finally, he said, "There will soon be a need for an interpreter in an important place, an interpreter of known sentiments. There are, you see, so many who are suspected of Loyalism to the king, no one is trusting anyone else. Girty, and Horsehead, even, are suspect. But I have no doubt of you. Your sentiments are with us. I need to know whether you would be willing to be that interpreter."

It wasn't a welcome thought to her. She had too many responsibilities. For the same reason she couldn't live at the mission, she shouldn't think of going someplace to be an interpreter. She was the principal chief of the biggest Shawnee town, and she would soon become a mother again.

"Where is the place that needs an interpreter? If it is Pittsburgh, that would be too far away. I hope to be there for the peace talks, but couldn't stay away from here longer."

He looked down at his hands, seeming to be very interested in rubbing his palms together. "At the mouth of the Kanawha River."

"What do you say? But what is there? When the Long Knives abandoned the little stockade they put there after the battle, it was burned down. There is nothing there!"

"There will be a bigger fort built there, very soon."

She sat bolt upright, blinking. "No! You cannot mean that! The Long Knives would not build a fort right on our boundaries, at the same time you are making us promise peace!"

"It's . . . it's to *keep* the peace, you see? Congress wants forts on the boundaries to . . . to keep the Kentucke settlers and the tribes from bothering each other. And to keep back any tribes that would be incited by the British . . ."

She was shaking her head, not wanting to hear excuses. "My brother Cornstalk and I, and Hard Man, and so many of us, we've told our people, so often they're weary of hearing us, 'Trust the Americans!' Waypeymatchikthe, over many years our people have learned to love you and trust you. But I fear, when you tell them in council here that the Long Knives will build a fort where they came to kill us, I fear they won't trust you so much! Or trust me, either, or Cornstalk. Oh, my friend! You know I remain for peace. But the Shawnee people, they will not like this!"

"I know they won't see it right, not at first. And that's why I hope you can be the interpreter there. Captain Arbuckle will need your wisdom, and your goodwill."

"Captain Arbuckle? I have heard that name . . ."

"He was in the battle there. He says he saved your life. And Silverheels' life."

She put her hand over her eyes. She remembered the officer who pointed a pistol at her and then raised it up without shooting. She took a long breath, and let it out in a long sigh. "So. That fort to keep peace will be commanded by a man who was our enemy there. I am glad it is you, Wapeymatchikthe, not I, who must tell our headmen that story. Probably they will want to know who the officer will be. You will have to tell them: *A man who killed Shawnees there*."

"But I can also say, *A man who did not kill Nonhelema and Silverheels*."

"Eh-heh. And after this betrayal of them, they might say, *He should have done*."

One night, weeks after George Morgan had gone back to Fort Pitt, Nonhelema came awake from a dream in which Alexander McKee had turned and walked away from her, a dream sad and angry, a dream from a sleep that was shallow because of her great discomfort. What had awakened her was not just the heart-heaviness of the dream, but the sudden collapsing sensation between her hips and the flood of wetness into the bed under her.

She put the dream out of her mind. There was no time to ponder its meaning now. The birth was about to begin. It was sometime after dark, hot and still in the house. A candle lantern at the other side of the room was the only light, showing a point of light with a haze around it. The haze was created by the gauze cloth of mosquito netting that hung around her bed. It was believed, and was probably true, that she was the only Indian woman anywhere who owned a mosquito net. Near the lantern's halo she saw a shadowy form. Before she had dozed off, her daughter had been sitting in the doorway with her slate, practicing the shape of letters.

"Fani!"

"Yes, *nigeah?*"

"Send Caesar for Kinwi Ullenegi."

She squatted on the floor, naked, sweating, panting, now and then grunting with strain. This had never been easy for her, and she was no longer a young woman. Her knees and hips felt as if they were being pulled apart, and her hands and shoulders were sore from pulling down on the birthing pole, which caused a great force from her breastbone to her opening, making it feel she was turning herself inside out. On either side of her squatted the midwife Kinwi Ullenegi—old Auntie Long Tits, as she liked to call herself—and her niece White Corn. They were pressing and massaging her waist and flanks. They could tell by their fingertips whether the baby was head-first, and coming along as it should. They seemed not to be worried about anything yet.

"Gah!" Nonhelema gasped. "Oh, I am too old to be doing . . . Ng! . . . this work again!"

"True," said Long Tits. "You were too old to be copulating, and you should have thought of that when the damned paleface got on you. I have no sympathy."

Nonhelema grinned and groaned. "This is no time to make me laugh, Auntie."

"Eh? I said nothing to make you laugh."

"You said . . . *too old to copulate! Ngh!* There is no age too great for that, if the . . . Oh . . . ng! . . . if the man wants you."

"Eh! Ha! You and the paleface were drunk. If not, you would know better. Do you even remember him getting on you? Fool woman!"

In fact, Nonhelema hardly remembered it, that long-ago night at the end of the treaty talk. She remembered waking up with the deer standing by the bed, but the night of *soos* was too vague to remember. What a shame not to remember Alexander McKee's great zeal and handsome face as he poured her glass full and stroked her arms and made her laugh with charming talk. She could remember his yellow hair gleaming in candlelight, the color of straw, and his merry blue eyes looking right down into the center of her spirit.

He must have seen then that she had forgotten about the missionary laws.

I am not *old!* she thought, straining down so hard that she thought she must be shitting on the floor. *I am* not *old! I am strong enough for anything!*

But missionary Zeisberger would say she was weak when he learned of this; he probably already knew. He would bewail her fall from grace, her drunkenness, her wantonness. But in another part of his righteous soul he would exult, for she had now confirmed his judgment that she was a base and unworthy woman, a proud and stiff-necked woman, insincere in her devotion to Jesus. She could imagine the Zeisberger browbeating Brother Johann Jungman about this faithless convert of his. For even though Zeisberger had baptized her, Johann had saved her soul—and, apparently, not well enough.

But it was not Jesus, she thought, who would be condemning her for this. Somehow she doubted that Jesus would care so much. In her heart, she believed that Jesus and Brother Zeisberger were very different kinds of missionaries. Were those two ever to meet in council, Zeisberger would probably lecture Jesus, even scold him, maybe for laziness.

Before she could enjoy the humor of imagining that, another gigantic pressure came down and she felt a mass slide a little way, and a blizzard of sparks swirled behind her eyelids and she imagined this was the way a goose or turkey would feel if it were alive when you pulled its thighs from its body. She was breathing too fast and she had to force herself not to faint. It was not good to faint. One should hang on to the pole and squat and work, not lie supine like a white woman and cry and scream and try to push a baby *up* into the world. A baby should slide down. Down is the way things go; nothing falls up.

So far, Long Tits had not even spoken of medicine. There were herbs that eased pain, or made more moisture for the sliding-down, or kept the heart beating steady. But she had shown no need for any of those. Long Tits wasn't worried, and Long Tits *wasn't* being sympathetic. Now came another vast quake, and a slump and a sliding.

Speaking now to Fani, who was hovering in front of her mother, watching and learning the greatest thing women must know: "So, girl. How interesting for you, to have a mother like this, a matron who cannot keep her legs crossed. You see you now have a mixed-breed brother. See his little *passah-tih*? Time will come, he will have so much mischief with that. Come, little man. It is time to clean you up."

Now it was done. Now it would be all right to faint and lie down. But no. She would not give Long Tits that satisfaction.

"Wehsah!" she managed to gasp. "I want to see him." Long Tits and White Corn were tying and cutting the cord and removing the sac, and Fani came around and began wiping the sweat off her mother with wetted cloths. With the last of her strength, Nonhelema pulled on the pole to stand up. For a moment everything whirled, but she didn't fall. She looked at the baby. To her eyes, it was a little Alexander McKee. His name would be Thomas. Then sweat in her eyes blurred her sight of him.

"Nigeah," Fani said with a fright in her voice. "You had better let us put you in bed."

"Yes," said Long Tits. "You bleed too much."

Nonhelema lay in bed with her baby boy lying on her chest and could hear her people outside, the happiness and excitement in their voices.

She knew that many were angry at her for being so strong for the Long Knives who were building forts closer and closer while preaching peace. Cornstalk was having much trouble persuading the chiefs of the other Shawnee septs that they should go to Fort Pitt and hear more American peace talk. There were young warriors, even her own relatives, who wanted to go down and attack the fort builders at the Kanawha, but she and Cornstalk had so far managed to restrain them. And here she lay having a whiteman's baby. It was a good thing that McKee's mother had been Shawnee. All white would be too much just now.

But their voices were cheerful. Even those who disagreed with her, and thought she was foolish over the missionary religion, still loved her, and were happy that she had borne a healthy son.

She lay in bed with the baby lying on her bosom, smelling the corn soup Fani was cooking in the fireplace kettle, and she was tired, so tired that despite the tired and strained pain down below, she kept drifting toward sleep, and she remembered vaguely that last night had begun with a bad dream about this baby's father turning his back on her.

OCTOBER 30, 1776

FROM NONHELEMA
TO GEORGE MORGAN
AT PITTSBURGH

Brother,

Agreeable to your desire I have spoke to our Head-men—they have got up, and are on their way to meet you at Pittsburgh—I have exhorted them and all our nation to keep fast hold of your friendship. I would come myself but have lately been delivered of a son, and have had some trouble since . . .

If the white people entertain designs to strike us I beg you will tell me—I depend upon you so I may remove our children out of danger, and you may rely you shall not be ignorant of what passed among the red people—I will give you a constant notice and will never deceive you. For our part, we the Shawnee nation are determined to preserve our friendship with our white Brethren . . .

The Mingoes who live near to us are the only people who appear to have bad intentions against you—Several parties of them have been to the Great River. All of them are now returned but one, consisting of three persons only—They had three scalps with them—I hope your and our chiefs will agree to have these bad people removed from us or make them sit still for they have often shook the tomahawk over our heads and call us the Big Knives . . . Pluggy has been sometime at Detroit, where he went to know the will of the British governor there—He is not yet returned; some think he is gone or will go to Niagara.

When I am able to travel I will come and see you.

A string of Wampum

Catherine

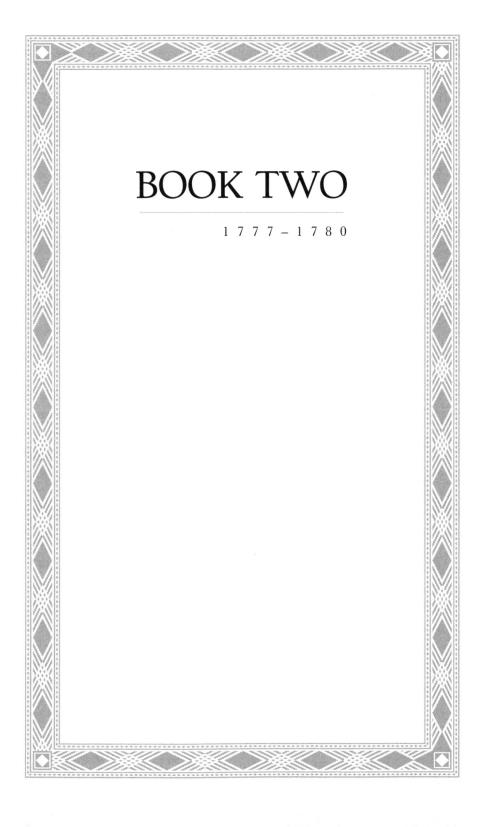

BOOK TWO

1 7 7 7 – 1 7 8 0

9

FORT RANDOLPH, MOUTH OF THE KANAWHA RIVER
MARCH 1777

Private Justin I. Case was walking guard on the parapet of Fort Randolph, gazing over the old battleground where a wild Indian woman had inspired him to bravery long ago, when that very woman rode into sight as if in a dream, up the riverbank slope among the tree stumps. The upriver wind was strong, and her long hair whipped and streamed like a flag. Following her were several men and women on horseback.

He squinted into the wind, eyes watering, his heart running high at the sight of this person who had haunted his dreams and memory for more than two years.

Everything looked different now. The battlefield was no longer a forest. All the great trees had been felled to build the fort and clear a field of sight beyond bullet range. The charred timbers of the original stockade lay rotting outside the palisades.

The woman riding up looked different than she did in his vivid memories. There she was naked, in the exertions of battle, smeared with gunpowder, paint, and blood, with white-toothed grimace and blazing eyes. Now she rode on a fine bay horse, not sidesaddle like a white lady but astraddle, enveloped in a vivid red trade blanket. As she rode closer, he saw her legs were ensheathed in pale leggings or gaiters, with long fringe that moved in the wind. She was elegant, as dignified as a queen.

He had pondered often on the enigma she was, and the more he had learned of her, the more mystified he had become. He remembered her saying, *Jesus calls for mercy,* causing Captain Arbuckle to elevate his pistol and spare her life. He had seen her big town on the Scioto, and knew she had counseled for peace with Governor Dunmore. He had learned that she knew the missionaries and the traders everywhere in the Ohio watershed, and the officers at Fort Pitt, and the chiefs and the women leaders of all the tribes. She knew the languages of all the tribes in the region, it was said, as well as English, French, and German. It was said that she could read and write, and that she was wealthy—even in the whiteman's sense of the word. It was said that she was a consort of Alexander McKee, at Fort Pitt, and that she had borne him a son. All of that he had learned of her since that day, and yet always in his memory she had appeared as that image of lethal savagery, a bloodied Amazon wild with rage.

Now here she came, like royalty, with a small entourage, toward this fort where, likely, she would spend considerable time. The Virginia Council of State had granted Captain Arbuckle a stipend to pay an Indian interpreter, up to four shillings per day of service—and this Shawnee woman warrior was the Indian agent's choice, even though the Shawnees were deemed the greatest menace in these lands.

For although she was a Shawnee chief, she had steadfastly supported peace talks at Fort Pitt, along with her famed brother Hokoleskwa—Cornstalk—another brother Nimwha, and her other half brother Silverheels, the blood-smeared one she had carried off the battlefield.

And though Justin Case had expected to be a physician by now, here he was again as a common militia soldier in Indian country.

He had gone home to study with the surgeon and had learned some of the odious skills of the doctoring trade. He had learned how to worm a patient with powdered tin, wormwood clysters, or quicksilver; how to bleed with lance or leeches; how to ease bowel spasms by blowing tobacco smoke up the arsehole through a reversed tavern pipe; how to extract a dead fetus without pulling its head off entirely; how to set broken bones; how to distinguish quinsy from putrid throat; how to diagnose by examinations of pus, sputum, vomit, stools, urine, tongue scrapings, clots, ichor, sweat, seepages, snot, ear wax, crude and sloughed skin; how to distinguish one ailment from another by the color of the face, lips, or fingernails. He had come to know a chancre from the gleet, a bubo from a cancer, a scirrhus from an impetigo. It had been a mere beginning. The good surgeon had taught him that the human body is a moist bag so full of vile humors, vapors, and parasites that one could spend half a lifetime coming to understand everything that could, and would, go bad, what could be cured and what was hopeless. Justin had only begun to learn of the powders and metals, oils and tinctures, opiates and sulfurics that might alleviate or cure certain maladies, but he had become skillful with the tool chest of blades, saws, hooks, straps, fumigators, cauterizers, catheters, clamps, and scissors that were needed to remove or repair tissues and organs. Maybe he still wasn't privy to enough arcanum to be a real physician, but he felt he was a skilled craftsman in basic repair of the bodily furniture.

Before he could begin to consider himself a physician, his mentor had departed to become a surgeon for General Washington's army, where he was needed more than he was in backwoods Rockbridge County of Virginia. He had invited Justin to accompany him to war, but Justin had instead gone back to his home and wife in Augusta County, worked the farm, and tutored for a short while—long enough for him to get Peggy with child again.

Perhaps a little too confident of his medical skills, he had tried delivering her baby without help of her family's favorite midwife, and botched the delivery, killing the baby and incurring her family's wrath. At the same time, Captain Arbuckle had called up a militia unit to be sent to the old battleground and build a new fort there for the protection of the Kentucke frontier, and Justin had thought it a good time to leave the county.

So here he was, watching this Indian woman approach into his view again. And here she came, that Indian woman who one violent day had turned his life's notions heels-up and arsy-varsy.

He wasn't happy to be in Indian country again. But back there, Virginia was at war with Britain, and even if he had stayed home, he might well be a-soldiering, anyway. Red Coats or redskins—apparently that was a man's choice these days. One couldn't hide behind cowardice in such a world, and it was she, he never forgot, who had forced him out from behind his own.

He called down, "Tell the cap'n his Indian party's here!" Then he turned back to watch, wondering at his own feelings.

Riding almost abreast of the woman chief was a younger woman, flamboyant in calico and glittery necklaces, languid in the saddle, like a princess to the queen. She was carrying a baby in an ornate, straight-backed cradleboard, which lay across the pommel of her saddle.

The rest of the retinue, perhaps twenty in all, appeared to be Indians, or mixed-bloods, mostly young, the males armed with muskets and bows, all colorful in a mix of hide and stroud cloth, hats and silk headscarves suggesting long association with white traders. Two other young women wore cradleboards on their backs, like knapsacks containing little lives.

Justin tried not to stare too hard at the woman chief as she rode toward the open gate of the fort below him, but she glanced up, perhaps at the red and green stripes of the Virginia flag on its staff above him, and her eyes met his, caught him looking straight at her. A hot froth of embarrassment rose in him, as if his soul had been caught naked. Before he could glance away, he saw that she had raised her chin and nodded at him, as if she might have recognized him. Somehow, oddly, he yearned for that to be so, but then blushed at having hoped it, and didn't even know why he would have dared hope so. He felt like a dithering nonentity. How, in the turmoil of battle, would she have remembered any whiteman's face—except, perhaps, that of Captain Arbuckle, who had spared her life and her brother's?

The captain's deep voice rose from below. Now Arbuckle and the woman would be face-to-face. Justin fancied it to be a most poignant moment, so he leaned far out over the palisade to watch their greeting. Captain Arbuckle strode out, flanked by armed, wary subalterns. The woman had reined in her horse, and her followers milled about behind her, watching her, watching Arbuckle, studying the strong log palisade and the militiamen who were gathering around.

Rather than look down on Captain Arbuckle, the woman dismounted with effortless grace and handed her reins to a brawny man who had ridden up beside her, a warrior who appeared to be part Negro. Justin remembered him from the battle, remembered seeing him help the woman drag a wounded warrior out of danger.

The woman stood erect, looking straight into Arbuckle's craggy face. Then she nodded, displaying a trace of a smile.

"*Ayee ayeh*," she said in that rich voice Justin remembered. "You are that soldier who did not shoot me. Your mercy was good. From that I can come now to help you. Colonel Morgan said you need me here."

Arbuckle touched the brim of his tricorn hat and said, "I remember you. I'm glad."

They studied each other a moment, in apparent satisfaction and approval. Then she said, tilting her head to look up at Justin, "That soldier up on the wall I remember, too. Thank you, soldier."

Flustered, he tipped his hat and stammered, "Ah, ah . . . thank you, ma'am."

"Ma'am," she repeated, laughing low in her throat. Then she turned to her retinue and indicated them with a gesture of her hand. "They come to be sure I am welcomed here. I expect you will feed them and let them rest here before they go home tomorrow."

"To be sure," Arbuckle replied, with a flicker of a frown that Justin noticed. The fort was always on thin rations.

"Here you see my daughter, whose name is Fani," the woman said, indicating the strikingly pretty young woman carrying the baby. Again the captain touched his hat brim, and even bowed slightly.

"Colonel Morgan said I should find a captain named Arbuckle here," said the older woman.

"I am Captain Arbuckle, ma'am. I'm the commander here."

"Ah! That is good! The very man!" she put forth her right hand like a man and he took it. Then she turned and spoke briefly to her people in their tongue. Justin, a man most conscious of language, found the language lilting and mellifluous, almost like song. They all began dismounting, talking and chuckling among themselves.

"Cap'n," one of the junior officers said, in an urgent voice, "you don't mean to let that many savages into the fort, do ye?"

"Why, uh . . . ," the captain began.

"You, soldier," the woman interrupted. "These are not savages. I am a Christian, by the missionary Zeisberger. And all of us, we are Shawnees—a people of honor, and of kindly manners." Then she turned to Arbuckle. "Tell me this, Captain. Will you treat us well as guests, as we would treat you if you came in peace to our town to help us? For, if not, we will all turn back and ride home, and you may seek another interpreter than me."

Justin could see the feelings working in Arbuckle's face, surprise and consternation, and in his private heart he cheered the woman's pronouncement, even while understanding the captain's dutiful concern for his fort's security. In a moment, Arbuckle gave the young officer a severe look askance and then turned his most pleasant countenance to the Indian woman, bowed like a gentleman, and said: "Madame Grenadier, Virginians are also a people of much honor. Any of you who come in peace may feel welcome here, and fear no harm. May the forest fall on me if my word isn't good."

Now there's an odd oath, Justin thought, watching them all proceed in. And an easy one, too. How likely are the woods to fall on him?

In the next few days, when all the Shawnees except the woman and her daughter and the infant had departed, there was a delicacy of manners in the fort, a log hut was reserved for their separate occupancy, and all the men were under strict orders to give no offense. Because the woman had duties as an interpreter, the baby was usually in the girl's care. Most of the men presumed that Fani was the child's mother.

Justin was in a state of quiet agitation, ever expecting Nonhelema to come around a corner and catch him coming from the latrine or something. Yet on days that passed without a sight of her, he was depressed.

It was with jealousy that he watched Captain Arbuckle and the woman develop a trusting familiarity. Clearly, she admired and respected Arbuckle. She became enough at ease with him to laugh in raucous tone, and that annoyed Justin. There was no sign of impropriety. She was older than Arbuckle, and he was married to a comely lady of good family back home in Botetourt County. But the two were sharing an affinity, and Justin was left out of it, down on a lower level of existence, even though he believed his sensibilities were finer than his captain's and that his own destiny, somehow, was in alignment with hers.

There were times when Justin was called into conference with both of them in the orderly room, to record summaries of sessions with visiting Indians, to write letters to Colonel Morgan, to General Hand, the commanding officer at Fort Pitt, or to Colonel Fleming back in Virginia. And it was during such times that Justin began to sense a deep dread and sadness in the woman, and a tension between her and other Indians. From bits of her translations, or from veiled lines in letters he was transcribing, he realized that she and her family were not on good terms with much of their tribe, because their sympathies and opinions were contrary regarding the war between the king of England and the colonials.

Her division of the Shawnee nation hoped to remain at peace with the Americans, and so did the missionaries, up on the Muskingum.

The missionaries yearned to pacify all the Indians. Nonhelema said she yearned for peace, as did the missionaries. "But," she said, "if a people's will and means to defend themselves are removed from them, they will be rushed upon by those still strong. I am fearful for our Delaware brethren in the mission towns, who have only hoes and shovels in their hands." As she said that, Justin remembered the sight of her hurling a tomahawk to kill the soldier Blakey, in that terrible moment of battle when he himself had at last crawled out from under his log.

Aye, she was a peacemaker, or yearned to be, but there was nothing helpless about her. One day, when Captain Arbuckle suggested to her disarming the tribes as a beginning for peace, she snorted at him, and then proceeded to relate a long and detailed history of those tribes back east in the past who had chosen to "fall on their side like an opossum" instead of fighting, and who were now only remembered names. "You cannot demand peace or anything else," she said, "if no one fears to fight you."

As a soldier, Arbuckle had to agree with that.

Weeks passed, and spring flourished. It became apparent that Nonhelema truly was needed at the fort, and that she was willing to stay as the fort's interpreter except when Tribal Councils and ceremonies required her presence back at her town. She requested that a small cabin be built for her and her daughter and her baby son, but outside the fort, so that they would not have to live pent up within the stockade with soldiers. Captain Arbuckle complied, for her sake and for the sake of his troops, who found the two beautiful Indian women all too distracting.

Soon her cabin, which was between the fort and the Kanawha River bank, became the center of a small encampment of temporary shelters where visiting Indians could lodge themselves and their families. The confluence of these rivers, the Ohio and Kanawha, was a convergence of old Indian trails, including the great Warrior's Path southward to Virginia, so there was much Indian traffic, in canoes, on horses, and afoot. Tribal bands, hunters, families, and foraging and trading parties had camped here for ages. This was another *tapistewamigi-sipe*, Where-the-Rivers-Meet, and thus a place of spiritual power. Much of the translating that Nonhelema had to do was of the travelers' complaints about the whiteman fort that stood here upon their sacred place. There were also complaints that since a fort was here, why did it not have traders with goods?

Nonhelema had been telling Captain Arbuckle that her brothers Cornstalk and Silverheels would come down soon to talk with him at this fort. Then, on a morning oppressive with river damp, Cornstalk came, riding up the same trampled track among the tree stumps by which his sister had arrived. Much of the fort's garrison rushed to the gate and palisade to get a look at the mythical man whose great voice some of them had heard upon the battlefield, and had never forgotten.

A respectable entourage rode with him, thirty warriors or so, and some old men. Justin believed he recognized one of the stately figures in front as the blood-drooling warrior Nonhelema had carried from the battleground when Captain Arbuckle spared them both. The one called Silverheels. He wore a full head of long hair now instead of the war scalplock, but Justin trusted his memory; it was the same man.

There was no mistaking Cornstalk, even by those who had never seen him before. He was plainly Nonhelema's brother, virtually a twin in features and bearing, and unmistakably the contingent's leader. When Nonhelema came forth to greet them at the gate and Justin saw those three siblings together, each a stunning specimen, he wondered by what delusion the Virginians, even the best of them, could believe themselves superior to this native race.

Once again Captain Arbuckle was obliged to reach deep into the fort's commissary to feed a large number of hungry Indian guests, and once again the garrison was nervous with the presence of so many natives within the post. This group was all warriors, with no females and juveniles to denote a peaceful group.

But once again the guests dispelled those fears through their own warm and decorous behavior. An amiable buzz of voices, full of laughter and cheery exclamations, filled the parade ground where trestles had been set up, under a reddening evening sky, for serving the main course of stewed meat and corn.

Though it was not a treaty gathering, there were speeches to be made. Justin took down Cornstalk's words in shorthand, and the next day transcribed his speech for the Virginia authorities. His nape prickled as he reread what he had put down.

Brothers—

We told your commissioners at Fort Pitt that we intend for Peace to continue, as we promised him who used to be your Governor. But the young warriors of the Kispoko and Chalagawtha and Pickaway septs attend to our words only while they are in sight. At night they roll their blankets and take up their weapons, and run off to where the militant voices call them to war against you.

I will not deceive you. And so I must say a truth to you that you might not want to hear: that I understand their anger. All our lands, which are like our heart, are covered by the white people & we are jealous that you still intend to take larger strides. We never sold you our lands which you now possess here between this Great Kanawha River & the Cherokees, & which you are now settling without asking our leave. We live by hunting & you have taken our hunting country from us. This is what sits heavy upon the hearts of all our nations. I open my hand & pour into your heart the cause of our discontent.

Some of our Shawnees are joining the Mingoes to accept the War Belt from the British Governor General at Detroit. It is beyond my power to prevent them. I am now not even comfortable in my own land. With my heart on the ground I am moving my neutral people over eastward, closer to the Delawares in their praying towns on the Muskingum.

Do you understand, Captain, the sadness you bring upon us, because we are now divided among ourselves over this side or that side? Once we were a contented people living in a bountiful country, here where the Master-of-Life put us. Then you came across the sea and brought illnesses for which we had no cures, and Rum that crazed us, and missionaries who changed the hearts of some of us, and confounded the Others, so that we would not tolerate our brothers.

All that has saddened us. But the worst harm is this, that you made some of us promise what others of us could not give their hearts to. And you broke the promises you made to us, about the borders between us.

When your Governor marched here we met him in a Treaty and promised not to fight again. We intend on keeping our promise, and so we are out of favor with those who made no such promises. And so we will go away from them, and try to keep peace with you, though we are sad to be divided from our brethren.

We are often inclined to believe there is no resting place for us & that your Intentions are to deprive us of our whole Country.

Now I have said to you what I have already said to your Commissioners and to Morgan. It has all done no good for us.

You have fed us well here, We thank you for that.

We will still come to you & always bring you the truth to help you & we trust that we will be safe like this when we come.

That is what we came to tell you, Brother. In the morning we will move on.

NONHELEMA'S TOWN
GREEN CORN 1777

Green Corn was always a joyous ceremony, a thanks for plenty, a feasting time, when Nonhelema stood in the sunlight before the altar and the array of ancient stones and shells, and put the paint mark on the forehead of each man and woman who came and stopped before her, and told them in a short prayer that the mark honored their ancestors. A single drum thumped ceaselessly, softly, like a heartbeat, and the air in the great round arbor was fragrant with red cedar smoke and the aroma of roast meat and ear corn. All around the perimeter of the great arbor stood cornstalks. She and all the others in the sacred circle of the arbor wore only loincloths, and all had removed their ornaments. In this ceremony they appeared before Creator as they had been made, not one wealthier than another.

The exposed bodies retold the stories she knew of the lives of her villagers: the welted scars of warriors, the wrinkled bellies and hips and hanging dugs of old childbearers, the bow legs and knobbed joints of arthritics, the sagging fat of the gluttonous and slothful, the slick skin of those who had been burned, the pockmarks of the few who had survived the whiteman's spotted sickness. In this ceremony, even those imperfect bodies were as beautiful as the muscular and clean-limbed and smooth-skinned physiques of the young and fit, for these were lives, not mere bodies, and lives were sacred.

All who were here were of one spirit; anyone with bad feelings, or any woman on her moon, stayed outside the Great House arbor, in their own homes, or in the moon-lodge. In here, all were parts of the one. At each station around the perimeter of the arbor stood a prayer-speaker. Voices murmured the prayers as each recipient paused at each station for its particular blessing. It required an entire day for the whole community to pass through. When Nonhelema, as chief of her people, was conducting the ancient ceremony, she was in a state of serene reverence, and she was giving spiritual reassurance and comfort to each one who took the paint mark and the prayer.

This year, under serenity of the Green Corn, Nonhelema felt a dark and sad undercurrent. There were two troubles, neither of which had ever worried her before in a lifetime of Green Corn ceremonies:

The spirit of Brother David Zeisberger kept trying to invade this ancient sacredness and shame it. The first trouble was that she knew what the consequences would be when he found out that she had led these rituals. And he *would* find out. Even if he did not find out from being told, he would know. He would presume it, and he would condemn her for it and make her fear the loss of salvation. It was hard to keep the severe spirit of Brother David out of this sacredness. Trying not to think of him made her think of him. It was not God or Jesus who tried to bring guilt and shame into this; they had concern only for reverent spirits, not for unhidden bodies. God was Creator and Creator had made the bodies, and would not condemn what he had made. But, she remembered, God had made the First Man and First Woman ashamed of their bodies in that story Brother David told. Here in this sacred arbor, it was as it had been in that story before he made them cover up. Outside this arbor, to the east, was the place where shame was known, there in that mission.

The other trouble was that certain people were not here in the ceremony, because of the war feelings. Warriors had denounced peacemaking as a weakness, and had gone to join Chief Black Fish, successor of the slain war chief Pucsinwah. Black Fish had never conceded that the Long Knives had any right to move into Kentucke, and in the spring he had led some two hundred angry young fighters, most from the Chalagawtha and Kispoko septs, but some also from the Thawekila and Piqua and even the Mekoche septs, and they had been joined by Pluggy's infuriated Mingoes, to go down on the other side of the river and attack the towns the whites had built along the branches of the Kentucke-sipe, the fort towns built by whitemen like Boone, and Harrod, and McClelland. Such men had long ago been run out of Kentucke by Shawnees, and allowed to leave unharmed with the understanding that if they came back, they would be harmed. And they had kept coming back, by mountain passes or by boats down the Spaylaywesipe, taking more and more families down into the interior of Kentucke, felling the woods, killing the game, planting crops, and raising cows and swine, shooting any Indian hunters who came within sight of them.

Those intruders had asked the governor of Virginia for soldier protection, and the governor had appointed the surveyor named Clark to be commander of a militia for protecting those towns. That, and the Virginians' new fort at the mouth of the Kanawha-sipe, had caused many Shawnees to conclude that the Long Knives talked peace while preparing for war, and that the peace talks every year at Fort Pitt were only to fool the Indians. The question came up time and again in council: *Why do we crush our own hearts to give back to the whites those we have taken into our families, while the Long Knives mean to make war on us whatever we do?*

And so Black Fish's warriors had attacked and besieged the Kentucke towns, going to another fort when they were driven off from one. Plukemenoteh, whom the whites cursed as Chief Pluggy, had been shot to death outside one fort. He had been a prickly and bellicose man, and his actions had often brought retaliations back upon the Shawnees. But he had been a fiercely loyal partisan for the defense of all Shawnees, as well as for his own Mingoes, and his death was sure to make peace ever harder to hold. Nonhelema and Cornstalk had always found it difficult to persuade the other Shawnee chiefs to go to Pittsburgh for yearly talks; this would make them even more reluctant to go. And the commissioners at Fort Pitt next time would be even more vindictive and demanding, because of Black Fish's Kentucke raids.

It was not easy to be either a peacemaker or a child of God. With all your heart you could want to be, but it was complicated, because of whitemen and the way they were.

Now there stood Blue Goose in front of her, one who had spoken for war three years ago and sent her son off to be killed at the Kanawha-sipe. She had suddenly grown old after that, and in Nonhelema's heart there was an especially great pity for this woman. Blue Goose, now more than ever, needed the consolation and the sustenance of Green Corn, and would keep needing it as long as she lived.

So, too, would all of Nonhelema's people.

As she put the dot of paint on the woman's forehead with a tender touch of her fingertip, Nonhelema thought, with a sinking heart: *Is this the last Green Corn ceremony I shall ever do for my people?*

There were reasons to fear that it might be.

Some war chiefs had been to Detroit to talk with the British general there. They wanted to hold a council at once after Green Corn, at Chillicothe Town. She was sure she knew what that meant. The British were always trying to entice the neutral Shawnees to help them in the war; Black Fish and others might have agreed to do so. If he persuaded many more for war, the whole Shawnee nation would become divided against itself. Little by little since the whitemen came, the Shawnee people had been losing not just their land, but their people as well, and with them some of their sacred bundles and even some of their ceremonies.

She liked to hope that if there were peace, the people could stay together and preserve all that was sacred to them. She was a Christian woman now, as she had so wanted to be, but she was still a Shawnee woman and she had not been able to throw out everything she had believed all her life. Zeisberger wanted her to, and sometimes she almost hated him for making that demand. So to be true to her own beloved people and to Creator, who to her mind was the same god as the other, she had to cheat on the wishes of Brother David. And she knew there would be penalties for that. Nothing would ever be easy again.

Maybe everything could have been easier if she had not chosen to be a Christian and a peacemaker and a child of God and had kept a distance from the whitemen, who complicated everything.

But she had so chosen, and she had to keep doing what she believed in doing.

And so, for this day, she put the paint on the foreheads and gave the prayer, and this was simple and good and as old as time, and she tried to keep the other troubles out of her mind.

But a few of her most devoted people had stayed out of the ceremony because she was an interpreter at the Kanawha fort. They did not trust her anymore, not at all.

10

FORT RANDOLPH
JULY 1777

Private Justin Case sensed that something awful had happened
to the Indian woman during her absence. She was in an agitated state when she came back to Fort Randolph in the heat of
summer.

Nonhelema had gone home early in the summer to prepare for
ceremonies, leaving her mulatto man, Caesar, here to serve as the
fort's interpreter until her return.

She was riding hard when she came back. The horses of her party
were lathered. The day had been oppressive, not the kind of weather
for running horses. When she hurried into the fort, Justin was startled by the hard set of her features, the blaze of her eyes. She charged
into the orderly room and, as the sun descended into the haze across
the Ohio, she could be heard talking fast.

At daybreak the next morning, Captain Arbuckle summoned
Justin to write. "First one'll be to General Hand at Pitt," he said.

FORT RANDOLPH,
JULY 26, 1777

Sir—

Having yesterday recd intelligence from the Shawnee towns, we learn that there has very lately been a Treaty at Detroit, where all the Nations have unanimously agreed (by accepting of the War Belt & Tomahawk) to distress the frontiers as much as in their power. There was a party ready to come to this place, who upon receiving the news from Detroit, postponed their journey & repaired to the Council, which was held at the New town where the Chillicothe Shawnees now live. Their first intentions being to distress this garrison & Wheeling & then to proceed to the frontier inhabitants. They are resolved to secure this place if possible, to themselves, either by storming the garrison or starving us.

The news relative to the Indians I had from the Grenadier Squaw & her friends, who are now at this garrison; by whom I learn that Capt. McKee at Fort Pitt must be an enemy to the United States by engaging his Indian friends to carry off his effects to the Indian towns, which being effected he would himself then make his escape to Detroit. To corroborate which his Squaw was at the Detroit Treaty where she rec^d goods without cash; but promises to be paid by the said McKee very shortly.

The Grenadier denies her name be mentioned, fearing she might suffer either by McKee or the Indians.

I am, Sir, with due respect,

Y^r. very hbl^e serv^t.,

Matthew Arbuckle

Justin was perplexed. As he sifted sand over the letter page to dry the ink, he said, "If you'll excuse me, sir, have we said this right? You don't mean to say that Nonhelema went to Detroit?"

"No."

"But it says, 'McKee's Squaw at the Detroit Treaty.' I thought *she* was McKee's squaw."

"Well, the old, sad story, Case. Seems that Cap'n McKee has another lady that she didn't know about. Looks like he's been cozening her, as well as his country. Appears 'e's a Tory and a swivelcock as well. A younger lassie, I gather, some trader's daughter from Pitt."

Justin felt a rush of pity—and anger, too. A Loyalist traitor, that was bad enough, though they were plentiful on the frontier. But Justin could scarcely imagine anyone who would trifle with a woman like this. Here she was with his infant son, and he was off to the British with some tart whom Justin couldn't imagine comparing to Nonhelema.

He had seen McKee here once. McKee was an influential trader at Pitt, a man of flair and charm, much admired by the Indians. A flamboyant, striking figure of a man with some Indian blood and, by his reputation, brave. Justin had overheard talk, between officers from Fort Pitt, that McKee had locked horns with General Hand a few times on the issue of the Americans' policy toward the Indians, which he criticized as deceitful and dishonorable. McKee had discovered that while they were eliciting promises of neutrality from the Indians, they were secretly planning forts and raids against them.

It was easy now for Justin to imagine how disastrous the defection of a man like McKee, with all his knowledge of American plans, could be to General Hand and the whole defense of the frontier. But in his own colored imagination, it seemed more disastrous to this woman. She had trusted McKee. She had borne his child. Then he had gone off, not only with another woman, but also to that British enemy that was stealing away her own people.

Justin was sitting at the table, imagining what he would like to do to Alexander McKee, imagining how sweet it would be to console the Shawnee woman in some way, when Captain Arbuckle said, "Case! Seal that, and stop woolgathering! Next letter will be to Colonel Fleming . . ."

It was then, while writing again of the Shawnees' warlike designs on this very fort, that Justin began to realize that he might have to fight still another battle in this same accursed place—ironically, known as Point Pleasant.

Justin Case knew that Captain Arbuckle fancied himself a key figure in a strategy to protect the western frontier. Arbuckle was so preoccupied with it that he rarely was able to sleep, and he often kept Justin up late to write and copy letters to his superior officer, General Hand, and to Virginia officers and politicians. Hand, the commandant at Fort Pitt, was George Washington's western commander, responsible for the defense of the frontier, which was considered the "back door" of the states in the War for Independence. Because the Ohio River valley was so vast and thinly settled, and therefore vulnerable to

Indian attacks, there was always a sense of desperation in any defense planning for the frontier. General Hand, Irish-born and a physician before he became a soldier, had won Washington's confidence while serving under him in Boston, Long Island, and New Jersey as a colonel of Pennsylvania riflemen.

Neither Hand nor Arbuckle had much faith in the tenuous neutrality worked out at the Fort Pitt peace talks the last two years. As soldiers, both had more faith in arms than in treaties.

What Arbuckle dreamed and schemed about was the same stroke that Colonel Lewis had been forbidden to execute three years before: invading and destroying the Shawnee towns beyond the Ohio River. He desired to scatter and demoralize the tribes before they could unite and strike the western settlements in force, armed and goaded by the British governor-general in Detroit. Captain Arbuckle, remembering Lord Dunmore's successful strategy, wanted General Hand to assemble at this place two columns of troops, converging down the Ohio and Kanawha Rivers, thus making his fort the base for such an offensive.

But Arbuckle feared that such a campaign might never be launched. Obtaining recruits and supplies for any military action here in the West was difficult. Washington needed everything for his big campaign in the East. And now that McKee had gone over to the British carrying all those plans with him, there was little chance that the campaign would ever be made.

And so Arbuckle, worried about his chance to play a key role and anxious about whether he could feed even his hundred-man garrison, contrived to get anything that he might use to his own advantage. This far from everything, little came his way.

But something *had* come his way, a fortnight ago. Two Shawnee couriers, called chief's men, had come bearing messages. Arbuckle had decided to detain them. Just having them in the fort kept them from doing what they might otherwise have been doing outside. Over Nonhelema's objections, he had made them "guests" inside the fort.

Now Arbuckle was dictating another letter to General Hand. Justin filled his quill and wrote:

> *Expect to have in my custody six or eight of the Shawanese Chiefs before you arrive. On the 19th. Ulto. Two Shawanese arrived here with a string of white wampum, & delivered a speech with strong protestations of friendship. They had information of an army that was to march*

into their country, and beg strenuously for Cornstalk & his tribe. I thought proper to detain these two. In about 8 days afterwards, Cornstalk's son came to know the reason why they were detained, & gave me the strongest assurances his father, & Hard Man, & some more of their chiefs should come immediately to this place. I have the two still detained, and intend detaining & confining as many as fall into my hands (unless it should be to carry intelligence for me to & from this place) until I have further instruction from you.

As Justin wrote, he was troubled, seeing such deception in a man he admired as a soldier.

It seemed to Justin that all the Shawnees he had seen here so far were utterly candid, and it seemed further to him that they yearned to believe whatever they were told. But Arbuckle believed all Indians were devious and that the truth could always be found in the precise opposite of what they said.

It reminded Justin of the old axiom he used to teach in school: The bad a man professes to see in others is usually much like that which he is blind to in himself.

He mused on that while Arbuckle shuffled paper nearby. How hard it was to make youngsters understand such axioms. They didn't understand guile without being taught it.

"The provisions this day," Arbuckle resumed dictating, "only one keg of salt, scarcely one hundredweight; of ammunition, between sixteen- and seventeenweight of powder, and sixweight and fifty pounds lead. Scarcely two hundred flints in the garrison . . ."

Justin thought: *Maybe that's why our officers and the missionaries always address the savages as "my children"—children strive to trust.*

AUTUMN 1777

As expected, Cornstalk had arrived at the fort again. And with every passing day, Justin became more uneasy.

He wasn't uneasy about the demeanor of the chief. Instead he was uneasy about Captain Arbuckle's honor.

The chief had come in peace, with a son, Elinipsico, and two of his chieftains, Red Hawk and Patella, who was called Old Yie. They had come to tell Arbuckle to be on his guard, because the war factions of their tribe could not be dissuaded. Cornstalk assured the captain every day, as if he might forget it from day to day, that he still honored the treaties of peace, and was thus at odds with most of his people. He declared each day that that was why he had come with his message.

And each day he sat with the captain and repeated that he now wished to leave the fort, that it was hunting season, that he had much to do in getting his people prepared for winter, that game was scarce around the Praying Towns on the Muskingum where he had moved the bands of peaceful Shawnees, who were now the only ones who followed him.

Though he sat tall and spoke with dignity, his were words of a dispirited man. His sister the woman chief sat by him and kept her face firm and composed.

But Arbuckle each day refused to let the chief and his chieftains leave.

At first, neither the chief nor the captain let on in any way that there was anything more to it than mere hospitality. But each day the chief said a little more insistently that it was time for him and his chieftains to get back on their way, that they had imposed too long upon the fort's hospitality and its meager pantry. And each day the captain grew a little firmer, and his reasons for detaining them a little less truthful. Captain Arbuckle was making up excuses now, about dangers from the hostile factions lurking in the vicinity, about wanting to provide Cornstalk with such niceties as sugar, tea, and very good rum, which he expected to arrive at the fort by boat or pack train any day, if the chief could but wait another day.

And each day, as such pleasantries were being exchanged, the chief and his sister and the chieftains looked and saw that the attention of the fort's sentries was directed as much upon them as outward where their enemies were supposed to be skulking.

Justin day by day grew more ashamed of this devious charade. But he was only a private. He dared not criticize his superiors.

FORT RANDOLPH, 7 NOV. 1777

Sir—

I have the pleasure to inform you of the arrival of the troops from
Augusta and Bottetourt here the 5th. Ins^t*, under the command of Col*^{o}*.*
Dickinson & Col. Skilron.

I am very uneasy concerning the bateaux, which I have daily expected for some time past—by which I expected to hear more particulars from you relative to the ensuing campaign. I am somewhat suspicious that some mischief has befallen them, being convinced you would have dispatched one down with flour with the greatest expediency, knowing the condition of this garrison both with respect to flour and salt. We were totally out of salt three days ago, & our beeves are daily losing.

I have here detained Cornstalk whom I'm determined to keep confined until I have further instructions from you.

I do not doubt you have been disappointed in the number of troops sent you by the several counties. If that shall have defeated your design for your expedition, I desire you should dispatch as many boats with flour as would be sufficient for the winter, as I make no doubt but the river may freeze up.

Should you be prevented from proceeding, would desire you would give me particular directions relative to Cornstalk as I am satisfied the Shawanese are all our enemies.

I am, with respect, Sir, Y^r very hbl^e serv^t.,

Matthew Arbuckle

"I well know," Chief Cornstalk said, "that some of those men out there believe they have cause to do us harm." He tilted his head toward the door. Outside the fort, the voices of the many militiamen in their camp made a constant drone. From the moment of their arrival down the Kanawha trail, the militiamen had been complaining loudly about the lack of provisions. They had devoured all their rations on the trail and expected the fort to be a cornucopia stocked with flour and meat. But General Hand had not yet come down with the expected boats of supplies from Fort Pitt. And the militiamen resented every bit of food that was given to the Shawnees.

Cornstalk was talking to Captain John Stuart, a friend and fellow gentleman of Captain Arbuckle, who had arrived with the militia. Arbuckle himself had finally become so uncomfortable around his hostages that he absented himself from them upon any excuse. But this Stuart found the grand chief and his sister to be attractive novelties. He loved to sit and talk to them, and so he had become the substitute presence for Arbuckle. The three other chieftains sat by the table patiently smoking their fragrant pipe mixtures.

Nonhelema—who had lately asked to be called Katy, after her Christian name of Catarina—sat quietly nearby with her needle and trade beads, applying intricate and colorful ornamentations, flower and leaf shapes, on the uppers of a pair of moccasins. She had gradually come out of her terrible state of mind over McKee's treachery. Cornstalk's presence had settled her agitation about that, and she seemed to be, in turn, soothing his uneasiness about being detained here. Justin had never seen more beautiful or intricate needlework, even among family womenfolk back home in Virginia. This Indian woman's hands were seldom idle. It was remarkable, in his view, that she could so concentrate and create beauty while everything in her world was being disturbed and threatened by faithless men and devious governments. Justin had seen her in battle rage and momentarily dejected by the perfidy of her paramour McKee, but he knew her most constant demeanor was dignified self-containment. Usually there was a faintly dimpled hint of amusement or pleasant reverie about her lips. Her inner spirit was a mysterious realm into which he yearned to be drawn. He sat now at his writing desk, dividing his attention between copies he was making of letters and his sly admiration of Nonhelema. He preferred to think of her by her Shawnee name. *Katy* was ordinary and meaningless, to his thinking. *Nonhelema*, he had heard her explain once with a chuckle, meant something like "not a man." *Oh, yes, how true a name,* he thought. He suspected that she was fully aware of his doting, that she surely could feel his attention, even if she seldom caught him looking at her.

Captain Stuart, elbow on the table, forefinger on his cheek, was still intent upon what Cornstalk had been saying.

The chief explained his anxiety: "In those companies, I saw many faces of men I fought in the earlier times. Some, I fought them and even their fathers, in their settlements in the mountains, long time ago. My sister and I fought in this place three winters ago, in the big battle against Lewis. As you know already, I fought you and your friend Captain Arbuckle in that battle. And even the quiet soldier over there who writes fine words with his feather in his skilled hand . . ."

Justin looked up, embarrassed, to see Cornstalk looking at him with a kind and amused expression, and they nodded to each other.

Cornstalk had an uncommon admiration for beautiful handwriting and had often, during his unwilling stay here, hovered over Justin's shoulder watching him write, murmuring approval. The chief's admiration had earned him a warm place in Justin's heart, for an orderly and scrivener seldom got approval or reward from either his superiors or his inferiors. Of course, the chief was also Nonhelema's brother, which alone would have earned him Justin's affection.

"When these militia came to the fort," Cornstalk went on, "I saw in their eyes the wish to turn their guns on me. It made a sadness here"—he touched his breast with his fingertips—"and I would wish to tell them that I am at peace with Virginians now. I gave my word to the commissioners that I would not fight against them anymore.

"But I do not expect them ever to believe that. I forgave them for killing my kinsmen in those old fights, but I know they do not forgive me. But Captain Stuart, be sure that I do not live here in fear. There were many times when I was ready to die by rifle balls, but did not. Therefore, I am past having fear for my life. Every day that I live is a day I did not expect to have, Captain. You have been in the smoke of war; you ought to know what I mean by that."

"I do know. And I like how you say it."

The chief, spectacular in his silver nose ornaments, ear disks, and armbands, was talking like a man inspired. "Captain, my family has had many friends among your people. My grandfather was a warm friend of Brother Onas, William Penn. They loved each other like a brother loves a brother. I myself have smoked in friendship with many men of the colonies, and learned from them things I was glad to know. How the sun and moon and earth circle each other like a dance. And music! Often in my mind's ear, I remember the sound of violins and flutes, those instruments that have magic. They make pictures in my head when I close my eyes. Pictures of many colors. Do not your words *music* and *magic* sound like the same word to your ears?"

"A-ho!" exclaimed Nonhelema.

"And coffee!" Cornstalk cried with a laugh. "How did we live here in this place before you brought us coffee! You see, Captain, how these matters can be good? You come with coffee, and we want it forever after. We gave you tobacco, and you likewise want it forever! I am told that everywhere in Europe, they now *need* tobacco, which they never knew before! How good it is to learn and share together and to be friends, one of the other!"

While he was talking, and Stuart listening, both wreathed in wistful smiles, Arbuckle had come in, hung his cloak on a peg, and knelt by the hearth for an ember to light his own long pipe.

"You see there!" Cornstalk laughed. "Your own friend needs tobacco. Never have I seen any Indian who smokes so deep as Captain Arbuckle!" He laughed. Then he pointed to Justin again. "And that— the writing! We did not have it here before. Our grandfathers the Lenni Lenape had little pictures they could arrange to read, yes, but we did not have this beautiful and useful 'writing' that your ancestors brought.

"If we had known of writing, we would have written large for your first people who came here in their ships, 'You are welcome to visit, and be guests here. But you must leave before you take too much and leave our children nothing to eat, or when you spread out too much and forget good manners.' If we could have written that large enough for you to read from your ships, there would not have been all this trouble we have known against each other. 'This is our land that Creator gave us,' we would have written. 'Do not trespass here unless we invite you.' Ah-heh! What a great thing writing is!"

"A-ho!" exclaimed Nonhelema, herself an Indian who had learned to write.

"However," Cornstalk said, raising a forefinger and dipping his head down, looking at Arbuckle as if over a pair of spectacles, "the whiteman's manners are not so good as his coffee, or his writing, or his music. For three years, since the peace promise we made with your old governor, and with the commissioners at Pittsburgh, I have done everything in my power to keep our people peaceful toward you. I have honored my promise of peace, even though your white people have not. I say with respect, Captain, that it is bad manners to detain us here when we are ready to go. My own relatives offered to serve as hostages to your government in the past, but I did not come here to offer myself as a hostage. I came only to give you good advice for your safety. You should let me and my son and my friends leave this place and go on. Remember, a man has no better friend than he who tells him the truth. I came and told you the truth. Now you should let me go on." He paused. Something was happening beyond the walls of the fort. A gunshot somewhere in the distance, more a pulsation on the air than a sound, then several more.

Captain Arbuckle stiffened, head up, then rose from the puncheon bench, turning away from Chief Cornstalk and his companions. Captain Stuart also rose, and they went to the door, which stood ajar on its leather hinges to admit light and air into the smoky, dim room. Arbuckle called to a sentry on the parapet, "What do you see?"

"Nothing, sir. Hear yellin' up the river, though!"

"Who's out there?"

"Three militia, out a-hunting, sir!"

"Damn it! I . . ." The captain turned in the doorway, hesitating, his mouth gaping a few times. Justin sensed the captain's dilemma: He would want to send out a party to the men's aid, but didn't know what was happening, didn't know what size party to send. The captain glanced at Cornstalk and his chieftains, suspicion working in his face. Justin himself wondered whether Shawnees concerned for their chief might be attacking, or trying to decoy the troops out of the fort. The Shawnees showed only alert curiosity, and said nothing among themselves. The Shawnee woman said something to them in their tongue and rose from her bench to move toward the door. Justin put down his quill and moved to a place where he could see out the door. By then, Captain Arbuckle had gone out and was climbing a ladder to the parapet. Justin hurried outside to see if he was needed there. Soldiers and militiamen were beginning to mill about near the flagstaff, murmuring among themselves and peering out the half-opened gate for a look down the riverbank.

Outside the dim room, the light was pearly under a bright haze, making Justin squint. He sneezed several times, which reminded him that his bladder was uncomfortably full, and that he should go to the sinks and relieve himself now, in case some action might ensue. As he went to the latrine, he heard about five more gunshots near the Kanawha, and yelling that sounded like both Indians' and whites' voices. He saw Fani run in through the gate carrying the baby boy. She darted into the interpreter's cabin and shut the door.

As Justin returned, twisting his last breeches button into place, an uproar was building in the militia camp outside the fort. "They killed Gilmore!" some loud coarse voice yelled. Gilmore was one of the militia lieutenants. What was going on? Justin ducked into his quarters and got his rifle and powder horn, then hurried on toward the fort gate, heartbeat running high.

When he trotted around the hewn-log corner of the headquarters cabin onto the parade ground, where the red-and-green-striped flag of Virginia hung limp in the still air, he was shocked to a standstill by the sight of a mob of shaggy, roaring militiamen stampeding in through the gate. Captain Arbuckle was coming down the ladder, shouting at them, shouting something Justin couldn't hear. A few of the regular soldiers of the garrison were converging on the scene, but were being shoved out of the way. Justin saw the Indian woman rushing into the orderly room, skirt and shawl flying, as if she were fleeing from the militiamen. It made no sense to him, but he took no time to think about it. Justin sprinted the few feet along the log wall to the door where she had entered. His vague instinct was that he might protect her. He planted himself in the doorway, facing the militiamen as they charged up. There was no time to pull the door to. He held his rifle like a bar across the doorway at chest height and braced himself for the jolts to come. The ragtag, sneering, shouting militiamen hit his rifle so hard he thought the barrel would bend inward between the doorjambs, but it stopped them.

"Git, soldier!" a rage-filled face shouted at him in a burst of reeking tobacco breath. "I want Injens!"

Justin started to protest that these were friendly Indians here on peaceful business, but a ruffian he knew to be a captain named Hall thrust a hard palm into his face and shoved. He felt his nose break but stood fast, holding his rifle with both hands.

Captain Arbuckle was fighting his way toward the door in a fury, grabbing militiamen by their hair or collars and hurling them back out of his way. "Keep 'em out, Case!" he was yelling. "Let me in!" Then he fell from sight behind the mass of stinking, cursing, spitting bodies ganging against the doorway. Justin could hear the voice of Nonhelema talking fast to Cornstalk and the others in the shadowy room.

"Goddam Injuns bushwhacked our boys!" a man yelled. "I'll kill me a goddam Injen righ'chere!"

"They shot Gilmore!" somebody snarled.

Justin, flinching from punches and blows, and feeling blood pour down over his mouth, grew more desperate to keep this mob back. He now knew they wanted to kill. Then somebody with powerful hands twisted the muzzle of his rifle up from the doorjamb and, as if a dam had burst, they came surging through the door, shoving him aside. Staggering, he glanced about in the dim room.

The four unarmed Shawnee men were standing in a cluster, not raising a hand, not ducking or trying to hide. Cornstalk was speaking to them in a calm voice, standing between them with one hand on his son's arm, another on Red Hawk's. Nonhelema made her way around the end of the room's long table and was going toward them, still speaking rapidly to them in Shawnee.

Several of the militiamen, cursing and threatening, had raised their long guns to their shoulders, aiming at the warriors. Red Hawk broke from the others and made for the only other way out of the room: the chimney. He scrambled over the low fire and began to scuttle up like a chimneysweep.

Justin saw that Nonhelema was putting herself right before Cornstalk, in the line of aim. As more militiamen crowded through the door, those in front were pressed and jostled, their gun muzzles wobbling and wagging in every direction.

A part of Justin's frantic mind expected the rifles to fire at any moment; another wanted to believe that these were only blustering fools who wouldn't really shoot, that this was just an ugly, Indian hater's scare. The men knew that whatever had happened out by the river, these particular warriors had been here in the fort and could have had nothing to do with it. Even such hate-filled rabble as these surely would not murder unarmed men, redskins or no, especially with the commander of the fort in their midst.

The first shot was deafening in the close room. Justin, stunned, saw the bright muzzle flash and blossom of powder smoke, saw Cornstalk lurch, stiffen, and reach up. The clamor of voices paused a moment, then renewed, with fierce whoops and yodels. Then several more long guns banged in succession.

Justin thought of nothing except that Nonhelema was between the guns and her kin. He flung his rifle at the nearest militiamen and sprang across the smoke-clouded room, tackling her at the hips and bearing her down to the floor in the far corner, just as two or three more shots crashed. She was so strong and solid that his whole body felt wrenched by the impact. Points of hot pain made him think he had been hit by bullets in the flank and legs. As he lay sprawled over the stunned woman, the uproar of shots and shouts, curses, grunts, and the deadly slam of lead into flesh and wooden walls went on. The air was thick with sulfurous gunsmoke.

By the time Nonhelema had recovered her breath and started struggling to get out from under him, the shooting was over. Now the noise was all voices and scuffling. Some voices were cheering, some cursing, some laughing. Captain Arbuckle's voice was loudest, demanding order, calling for his lieutenants. Blows thudded, boots scraped the floor.

Justin, head ringing, mouth full of his own blood, face and body stinging and aching, looked back just long enough to see Arbuckle deliver a kick to the head of a militiaman who was kneeling over the fallen warriors, trying to take a scalp. Other militiamen had pulled Red Hawk down from the chimney, and one was hacking him with a hatchet. Nonhelema, uttering moans and growls with every quick breath, got her strong arms between herself and Justin, flung him off like a sack of flour, and scrambled on all fours to the heap of bloody corpses in front of the hearth.

Gathering himself against pain, but determining that he had not been shot, Justin sat up. Nonhelema crouched and turned up the face of her brother Cornstalk, cradling it between her hands, shaking her head slowly from side to side. His blood began to run down her forearms. Captain Arbuckle and his officers were forcing the killers out of the room at pistol point, moving like ghosts in the dense, rankling gunsmoke. Justin had first seen her as a warrior in battle, three years ago. Now he expected her to leap up, grab something as a weapon—his rifle there on the floor, perhaps, or just the sheath knife from her waist—and charge out the door after the militiamen.

But she did not rise. Kneeling, making a piteous singsong softly in her throat, she began to separate the three corpses and drag them until they lay supine, side by side, Cornstalk between the others.

Cornstalk's body had many wounds, the others a few. She straightened their limbs. When she tried to pull Red Hawk's corpse over, his arm came off. He had been dismembered by the murderer's hatchet. Justin sat gasping, too stricken to move. His eyes were so burned by gunsmoke that they watered profusely, blurring everything. The smoke hung dense in the low room, a stream of it drifting toward the fireplace and flowing up the chimney with the warm air above the embers; at the opposite side of the room, another current of smoke slid out the door.

Then Nonhelema sat back on her heels, bloody hands in her lap, and began to rock slowly, still singing just audibly. Justin rose wincing to his feet and went to pick up his rifle from under the edge of the table. Somehow he hoped she would not notice him. Perhaps his spontaneous action had saved her life. Perhaps she knew that, or perhaps she didn't.

Perhaps here was too much else, and she might never even remember him tackling her. Now he just wanted to sneak past her without intruding on the place where her spirit was. He was heaving to vomit and wanted to get outside so it wouldn't be done in her presence.

Propped between his rifle on one hand and the log wall on the other, with strings of caustic drool swinging from his lips and tears burning his eyelids, he heard through the Babel of men's voices one voice saying:

"There'll be hell to pay!"

11

FORT RANDOLPH
NOVEMBER 1777

General Hand looked homicidal. The gin blossoms on his cheeks were nearly purple, the rest of his long face an apoplectic crimson. The veins in his temples stood distended, and the jagged teeth of his lower jaw jutted beyond his snarling upper lip. He was in an Irish rage over the murders, which had confirmed his towering contempt for unruly backwoods militiamen. Hand hated being in the West anyway, having served with General Washington in real battles against the British army in the East.

The general had just been coming by boat down the Ohio from Fort Pitt to prepare a strike against the Shawnee towns when he met the messenger going upriver from Fort Randolph to inform him of the murder of Cornstalk, so when he arrived at Fort Randolph and found it in a state of tension and uproar, he was ready to flay militiamen alive.

Now the militia colonels, Dickenson and Skillron, and their lieutenants and captains bent backward to avoid the spraying spittle of his tirade.

Justin, having been a witness, was here in the room, body still aching, face bruised all around his broken nose. Much of the floor was ruddy with the blood that had soaked it. Nonhelema, though said to be a personal acquaintance of General Hand through her frequent sojourns at Fort Pitt, was being kept away in her cabin outside, at least until this harangue was done.

"That unbridled rabble o' yours—those murderous *vermin*—have just overturned our whole purpose in this country!" the general bellowed. "We were set to march into the unfriendly towns and cow them utterly, to neuter 'em once and for good. That's why you're *here*! The only Shawnees friendly to us in this country were Cornstalk's. And your runagate morons, who do they kill? Cornstalk! *Cornstalk!*" He stomped back and forth before the officers, gnashing his teeth.

"And now what? I'll tell you what!" he roared. "Now all they'll want is vengeance on this stinking place and every stinking-arse Virginian they can root up! Oh, and not just the Shawanese, either! There's not a tribe in this country didn't look up to Cornstalk! They'll *all* be after y'r lousy scalps now! And, ooh, won't the British make hay o' this! Your ridge-running morons have just proved *everything* the British tell their Indians about Long Knife treachery! Even if the Indians were of a mind to forget this, do you think the Hair Buyer in Detroit will ever stop reminding 'em? By God, no!

"Colonel Dickenson, Colonel Skillron, those wall-eyed rodents you call *troops* have just given Hamilton the Scalp Merchant a better gift than a *thousand* topknots, goddamn them! Goddamn *you*!"

"General, sir, we . . . ," Dickenson tried to protest, "we weren't even present to know it was . . ."

Hand struck the table so hard with his fist that several people jumped. "Aye, and by God, that's even worse! You had men run riot and weren't even present! As I hear it, you were filling your skins with rum, too besotted to get up and do anything!"

"What! What! Who said that?" Dickenson exclaimed, face flushed, mouth agape.

"I did not give you permission to interrupt me, Colonel! And now here's more shame: You people were to bring supplies for your campaign, but you arrived here begging! This fort is always on the skimp because I can't get anything at Pitt to send down. So even if we had the moral turpitude to raid the Indian towns after your crimes, we couldn't do it. Because your wastrels ate up everything on the way down! By God. By *God*! Well, for that, as long as you're here, those louts o' yours are on half rations, by my order! You tell 'em that!"

The officers in the room raised a murmur, looking to each other wide-eyed, but Hand's bawling voice overrode them again. "I order you to put this whole goddamned garrison on half rations! And you had better by God see to it that every man who shed a drop of Indian blood in this room will go on trial as soon as he's back in Virginia! When Governor Henry hears of this debacle, I've no doubt he'll *insist* they be tried." He paced back and forth now, holding his hands behind his back as if to control them, breathing hard, scowling into one pair of eyes, then the next.

Justin was astonished by the outspoken authority this man wielded, being accustomed to the cajoling language militia commanders had to use. But in a way he was pleased, because without this forcefulness, he was sure, nothing ever would be done to bring the assassins to justice. And he wanted justice with all his heart.

Through the accounts of witnesses, including Justin and Captains Arbuckle and Stuart, the names of the killers were set down: Captain James Hall, and three of his men, named Galbraith, Rowan, and McCowan. They were all members of the company whose hunters had been attacked by Indians that day, precipitating the murders. Captain Hall was a relative of the victim, Gilmore. More than those four men had stormed in and opened fire, but those were the ones the witnesses had identified beyond doubt. No one could identify which militiaman had hacked Red Hawk to pieces. Justin himself had seen that man only from the back.

After the militia officers had been dismissed and the general had recovered some equanimity with the help of a fireplace toddy, Captain Arbuckle left to summon the Shawnee woman and her daughter. A while passed, and General Hand asked Justin to prepare him another cup. Justin put the end of the poker into the fire embers and mixed water, sugar, whiskey, and cloves in the pewter cup. Waiting for the poker to get red-hot, he noticed a spot above the fireplace. He unsheathed his knife and pried a rifle ball out of the oaken wall. There was dried blood in the splintered hole. Surely this ball had passed through one of the Indians before hitting the wall. From his memory, he concluded that this was where Cornstalk himself had stood. Justin dropped the ball into a pocket. He would decide later whether it was too terrible a keepsake.

"I suppose," said the general, "that you're the scrivener who writes Captain Arbuckle's letters to me?"

"Yes, sir. Mostly. Except when he writes them himself."

"Hnh! I can tell when he does that. Well, you have an excellent hand. Were you a clerk before you started soldiering?"

"No, sir, never was in business, sir. I was a schoolmaster," he replied, pulling the poker out of the fire and sticking its red-hot tip into the toddy cup. It hissed, and the scents of spice and whiskey diffused through the dank room.

"Ahhh!" General Hand sniffed. "Aye, get the stink o' those rotten-crotch rustics out o' here, so a man can breathe without gagging. Thank you, soldier." He took the hot cup carefully by the handle. "So. A schoolmaster, eh?"

"Yes, sir. And for a while, a surgeon's apprentice. I understand you're a physician, sir."

"That's right. A big step, from doctor to general. But I'm still killing 'em, I guess. Ha! Well. Surgeon's apprentice, y'say? On the battlefield?"

"Yes, sir."

"Ah! Then something of a veteran, aren't you?"

It was odd, Justin thought, that an officer so recently in a rage over the failure of men and strategies could turn his attention to the person of a lowly orderly.

"Yes, sir. Braddock's battle, then, Pontiac's rebellion . . ." He could see the general's face brightening with respectful interest, and added, ". . . and right here in seventy-four, sir, in Cap'n Arbuckle's company."

"By God, soldier, y've come through't a few times, haven't you? Here's to coming through!" He raised the cup, and sipped. Then he said, "Arbuckle. Now he's a cut above. Tells me he led the party around on Cornstalk's flank that routed the savages that day." His lingering tone suggested that he was coaxing Justin to verify or contradict Arbuckle's claim.

"Yes, sir, that was exactly so. He did it. I was right behind him."

Justin felt himself blushing, remembering what he had tried so diligently to forget: his own craven behavior throughout most of that day. And he remembered that most vivid image of his whole life, the Grenadier Squaw naked and furious in battle, the sight that had somehow marked him in the center of his soul.

The general looked into his cup, sniffed it, sipped. "Might keep that poker in the fire, soldier. The Grenadier loves her toddy even more than I do, if that's possible." The general caressed his jaw with the fingers of one hand, then checked his lapels. He set down his cup and with both palms smoothed what was left of his hair, and Justin realized that the man was grooming himself. So was this yet another man made self-conscious before that woman?

As Justin set the poker in the fire and straightened his own person, he was aware of distant voices, querying, retorting, out on the parade, probably of the Botetourt and Augusta Militias being assembled by their chastised colonels. Justin was anticipating, or dreading, the arrival of the Shawnee woman. So soon after the murders of her menfolk, it could prove a pitiful scene.

The voices outdoors rose in volume for a moment as the door was opened and Captain Arbuckle ushered in the woman and her daughter, both of whom towered over him. Then the door was shut and the two elegant women came to the center of the room. Justin searched Nonhelema's face for any clues as to her state of mind, her stability. The few times he had seen her since the murders, she had been remarkably stolid, but in her eyes there had been something—fury, or pain—that had chilled him even as it wrenched him with pity.

Fani had not seen the murders. She had run to their cabin and hidden there with her baby brother when the militiamen rampaged in. But her eyes glistened with some great, contained emotion as well.

General Hand stood up from his chair beside the table, drew himself erect, and looked at Nonhelema with his chin high, apparently not sure whether to smile as a friend or look gravely sympathetic. Here, Justin was thinking, was a man who had known her in some personal way, up at Pittsburgh, someone who knew of her weakness for liquor, her entanglement with Alexander McKee, probably even of her child by him, this little one now carried in by Fani.

Nonhelema barely acknowledged Justin's presence. It was as if she didn't remember that he had put her out of harm's way. Or, worse, that she remembered and resented him for it.

The general reached for her hand, and she raised it toward him. He took her fingers and bowed his head slightly to touch his lips to his own thumb. Then he raised his head and looked searchingly over her face, his own expression a semblance of profound compassion, which Justin sensed was theatrical.

"Katy, *dear* Katy!" the general murmured, voice quaking, head shaking sadly from side to side. It seemed as if he was trying to bring real tears to his own eyes. She nodded in response, and drew her hand out of his.

"Doctor," she said. "I am glad you came here. There are troubles."

"I know. I'm trying already, with all my powers, to repair them." He extended his hand toward Fani, taking her fingertips and nodding to her. He reached up and pulled aside the edge of the child's blanket for a look at his face. "Ah, the handsome lad Tommy. He seems to be thriving and fat. Cap'n Arbuckle! Is this piglet the reason why this place is forever ragging me for provisions? Heh, heh!"

It if was an attempt to make Nonhelema smile, it failed. The look she gave was one of nearly open distaste, and the general quickly drew on a serious expression again. "Dreadful upset about Alexander, er, uhm . . ." Then he saw the fierce widening of her nostrils and eyes, and blinked rapidly as if in realization that he had brought up something he shouldn't have.

She said: "You must prove to all the Indians, at once, that your nation hates those murderers. Also, you must stop going across the river into our country. And you must hereafter be true to the treaties you make. Doctor, you know that my family and our Mekoche Shawnees want to be at peace with Americans. You know that I have put everything of mine behind me to come forward for peace. But I will fail at peace if America lies and kills."

General Hand's plan to attack the Shawnee towns had been kept a secret from her, even as she stayed here and provided information for the Americans.

Hand nodded gravely. "Absolutely, my dear Katy. I agree entirely. In fact, I have just told all the officers here that the four men—Hall, McCowan, Rowan, and Galbraith—will be returned to Virginia and made to stand trial for murder. That shall prove our sincerity."

"No!" she burst out. "That would not prove it. That is not the way."

Hand drew his head back in surprise. "Pray, why not?"

"A trial in Virginia with Virginia wise men judging would not punish Virginians for killing Indians. Never has it done so. Your judges in Virginia would be afraid to do it. No! If Indian people see the murderers go to Virginia, they will know they have got away. The Indian people have to see the punishment done. Here, in this country where they did the murders. To prove to the Indians, you must give those murderers to the Shawnee people. The Shawnee people will burn those men up."

General Hand's ruddy face paled. For a moment he moved his mouth before being able to say, "That's out of the question! I couldn't *dare* turn American soldiers over to the enem . . . to . . ."

She stepped close to him and looked severely down into his face. "I speak of peace. If you give us the criminals, we need not be your enemies." Her eyes were locked fiercely on his.

Hand was frowning, his chin beginning to jut again. Even Captain Arbuckle was stirring, murmuring something. Justin himself felt chilled by the simplicity of such a brutal reprisal.

"Damn it, Katy! I can't give over for execution men who haven't even been tried! Virginia law doesn't allow that!"

"Those soldiers did not try my brother and my other kin before they executed them. They are known guilty. We in this room saw them do it." She kept staring at him. The general took a deep breath and scowled at her. His career would be ruined if he turned over white soldiers to the Indian fire-stake, and Justin was sure the general was thinking exactly that.

"By *God*, woman! Burning men is outrageous! Savagery!"

She looked at the ceiling, then back to his eyes, and said in a low voice, "I learn much since I was a Christian. I learn that bad Christians burnt up good Christians and good Christians burnt up bad Christians. Many 'martyrs,' a-huh? And witches."

"I denounce that ghastly idea!" General Hand almost shouted.

"This I learn from the suffering bleeding Jesus missionaries, too: Murderers will burn up anyway, in hell. Is it not so?" Justin at last saw a trace of a smile on her face, as she said, "So give those murderers to the Shawnee people, and we shall start them to roast."

The drone of voices out on the parade had been rising in volume and vehemence, and a distracted Captain Arbuckle got up and went frowning toward the door. Before he reached it, someone began knocking hard. Arbuckle pushed the door open and was met by the young officer who was General Hand's aide. The aide looked frantic. On the parade, soldiers and militiamen were milling and shouting and jeering. One very loud voice was bellowing, "Home! Let's go home, boys! Who's with us?"

"Hear! Hear!"

"I'm in! Fook th' gin'ral!"

The aide shouted over the uproar: "They're talking mutinous!" He pushed his way past Arbuckle, going straight to General Hand. Hand, already agitated by Nonhelema's demand, was now on the verge of fury again as he realized it was the militia gone out of control once more. The aide, looking ready to cry, said, "It's over the rations, sir! The whole lot of 'em say they'll take their knapsacks and march for home if you cut their rations like you said!"

"By God, I'll hang the scurvy pack of 'em! Bring me their officers!"

"Sir, with due respect, you're wrong! Their commanders are in sympathy with 'em and asked me if you'd rescind that order!"

"Damn them all, they can't get by with mutiny!"

"Please, sir! It's not mutiny yet. You can prevent a mutiny if you just rescind that order. The colonels strongly advise it, and I do, too! Sir, an abandoned fort here with the Indians out for vengeance: What good is that, even if you make your point?"

Justin thought the general was too enraged to be listening, but Hand stood with his jaw jutting and interrupted no more, then finally said: "Very well. Tell the colonels I withdraw the order. But one desertion, one breach of discipline, and I shall report the colonels to Virginia as mutineers! And if they eat the commissary empty before supplies can get here, the blame's theirs. And *you* can go out and tell them, Colonel, because I don't want to look at their swinish faces! By God, I'd like to throw *all* militiamen to the Shawanese!" He sat down hard in his chair, breathing fast, gnawing his upper lip, gradually becoming aware once more of those still in the room around him: Arbuckle, Justin, the Grenadier and her daughter and the baby. He looked around at them one by one. No one said anything, until the Grenadier spoke in a quiet but resonant voice.

"So, Doctor? You would wish to throw all militia to the Shawnee people? Good. But just the four murderers are all they would want. We will get them, then?"

"No, Katy, you will not, and that's the last I want to hear on it!"

FORT RANDOLPH
DECEMBER 1777

Smallpox came to accursed Fort Randolph, and its commander was leaving.

Captain Arbuckle had filled and buckled the leather bags that would be tied behind his saddle. He was hurrying, and his hands were shaky; it was plain to see that he was scared. Justin Case had never seen the captain scared, not even in battle, but he was scared now and wanted to get out of the fort at once, and get on the trails to

Williamsburg. "The men ready yet? Packhorse ready?" he demanded to know.

"Yes, sir," Justin answered. "They're waiting."

Justin wasn't afraid of the smallpox for himself. He had survived it when he was a boy, and a person didn't catch it more than once. But he still wished he could leave, because a place with smallpox in it was hell. Instead, because of his medical experience, he would care for the victims. So far, six soldiers were down, all bedded in one room full of moans and stench, away from the rest of the quarters, and some of the other soldiers were saying they felt feverish. Where it had come from no one was sure, but it had probably come in the boat from Pittsburgh with General Hand.

After his ferocious meeting with Captain Arbuckle and the militia officers, Hand had written a barrage of alarming letters to Governor Patrick Henry and to the Virginia Assembly and county lieutenants about the likely consequence of the murders. Then he had gone back up the Ohio in his bateau toward Fort Pitt, leaving a few supplies and, apparently, the smallpox. The first men had fallen sick soon after General Hand's departure. Justin thought it was ironic, the general being a doctor, but he wasn't amused by the irony. All these years later, he could remember the awful fever, the unbearable, itching discomfort, the pain, the horrible thirst, the ghastly feeling of trying to turn in bed to ease the soreness and feeling one's rotting skin stick to the bedding and separate from the flesh.

Justin had not been scarred as badly as some, but there remained pits and craterlike scars on his cheeks and forehead. Maybe because he had had it so young, his skin had repaired itself well. Justin had seen men and women who were strikingly handsome or beautiful at a distance, but pitiful up close. Such victims must have cursed their ravaged complexions, but also must have been bitterly thankful for their lives. Not many survived. Smallpox could better eliminate a fort like this than any siege attack by Indians.

Likewise, nothing served better in Indian wars than an epidemic of the pox sweeping through Indian towns, where it was especially devastating. A century ago, colonial leaders in New England had eliminated whole towns of troublesome savages by presenting them with infected blankets. That piece of history had been passed down from the Massachusetts branch of the Case family, who were proud to have been involved in such an effective scheme. The same was rumored to have been done around Fort Pitt during Pontiac's uprising.

Captain Arbuckle had rationalized that he should leave his new second in command, Captain William McKee, in charge during his absence, as McKee had already had the pox and Arbuckle hadn't. But Arbuckle was also leaving scores of lieutenants, sergeants, and privates here who were vulnerable. Justin had a deep and gloomy sense of betrayal. Captain Arbuckle had let shame descend upon his fort, and precipitated a great crisis, by letting the murders happen under his command. Now he was fleeing from the mess, leaving his men penned up with a deadly plague. Though there was nothing he could do to defend them against the pox, he was still abandoning his whole charge, leaving them to their fate.

Justin also wished that he could be going back to Virginia as a witness to the murders in case the killers were ever brought to trial.

But on the other hand, he would have been aggrieved to go so far away from the Shawnee woman, now that she was so bereft of kin and friends.

Arbuckle did have valid reasons for returning to Virginia. One was his wife, Frances, whom he had scarcely ever seen in their three years of marriage because he was always out here. She was said to be a great beauty and a fine woman, who was raising two sons of Captain Arbuckle's by his first marriage. The captain sometimes, poignant in his cups, had complained that he had an infant son he had never been at home to see. And at home he had been a prestigious civilian, a justice of the peace and a judge, and he had considerable property.

But as well as Justin understood that, he felt a deep sense of disappointment and resentment. He detected the same feelings in Captain McKee. This Captain McKee was a remote relative of Alexander McKee, and Justin mused on the notion that this Indian-hating militiaman was a distant relative of Nonhelema's baby.

Just as Arbuckle slung his powder horn and bullet bag over his shoulders and started to the door, it swung open to admit a strong cold draft of air, and the two Indian women came in. Nonhelema came in first with a grim face, followed by her daughter carrying the child. The girl and baby were wrapped in a woolen blanket, and the woman wore a voluminous, hooded cloak of European style.

"Ah, Katy!" Arbuckle exclaimed. "I was just coming to say farewell to ye!" Justin knew that was not true; Arbuckle was in a hurry to get out, and had actually said he wanted to avoid another scene of recrimination with her over the murders. Justin found himself once again irritated by Arbuckle. "I trust you'll continue serving Cap'n McKee as ye have me, when he needs an interpreter . . ."

She was looking into his eyes, her lips set firm. Justin could see, even feel, her anger.

"No," she said. "I come to tell you that I now leave here, and I learn that you go to Virginia. That you were not telling me."

"I was, er, I . . . What d'ye say? *You're* leaving?"

"Yes. I tell you so. A courtesy you don't do for me."

The captain looked embarrassed and alarmed. This Shawnee woman chief's presence here was one of the fort's few assets; she was like a volunteer hostage, to be held until a time of need, as well as an interpreter.

"I can't let ye go, Katy," he said. "It . . . it's winter. You've left your own people. Where would you go?"

"I go back to my own people. As you go to yours."

"But you don't have to leave here. Cap'n McKee will keep you in comfort, as I've done."

"I go away from the *mamk'thiwah*, the smallpox. Same flight as you do."

Arbuckle's face flushed. Justin thought, *She knows him too well for his comfort.* The captain opened his mouth to deny that, but decided against it. Instead, he said, "Ma'am, I really must insist you stay here." He ran his tongue over his lips and tried to keep looking at her eyes.

She seemed to grow even taller. "Captain, is this as it was when you insisted that my brother, and his chieftains, stay here? *Ahl lah! Motta! Nee puc a chee!* No! I am going away! If you have your soldiers put their guns across the door to make us stay here, you will regret that. Colonel Morgan will learn you did so. General Hand will learn. Your governor in Virginia will learn. After the murders here, they would not like to hear you treat me as a hostage! Captain, listen! When I was young, my Shawnee husband died from this pox. This daughter of mine, this little son of mine, they have not had the pox. If they stay here, they will die. I would send for your governor to know you made us stay here to die in this stink-place, where you already murdered my family! Now, do you intend to stop me? Eh?

"Captain, I go where I wish. I came here as I wished. I am not a white woman, who must ask a man what she may do! I am, in your word, a queen of my people!" Her voice now held a hint of edge, but her eyes were dagger sharp looking into Arbuckle's, almost a deadly dare insinuating from them.

Justin had shivers running from his temples down through his flanks. What words! He puckered his lips to keep from smiling at the captain's red-faced, slack-lipped consternation. Arbuckle surely now was realizing that this valuable woman, whom he had taken for granted, would indeed just walk away. "Katy, ma'am, please. I do care for your health and safety. It was I, remember, saved your . . . didn't shoot . . ."

The woman drew her head back, her eyes burning. "Ah! You remind me that I owe you my life? Is that what, little man? But it has not been good since that day—not for me, not for my people. Maybe I would be happier if you did shoot me that day. *Nee puc a chee.* I am going."

She turned and, with a tilt of her head, indicated to her daughter to follow her out. But she stopped and turned back to the scowling Captain Arbuckle, and said, "Listen, Captain. Maybe I will come back here when the pox is gone, to help you keep the peace with my people. We shall see. But I think I might not ever see *you* after today. I saw, in my sleeping dream, something when my brother the chief was here. You promised no harm would come to him. Do you remember that promise?"

"I do, ma'am." He couldn't look her in the eye now.

"Also, you said, if he was hurt, may a forest fall on you. Do you remember that?"

"Well . . . Yes. But what . . ."

"What I saw in my sleeping dream, it was a storm of great wind, and the forest fell on you. I do not know when it will happen. But I might not see you again, even if I come here after the pox is gone. *Tanakia,* Captain Arbuckle. For his own reasons, Creator, or the God of Jesus, he put our lives together for a time. In a same way, he may put them apart. Captain, when the storm wind comes, get down and hide low. If I save your life by this warning, then I shall no longer owe you for mine."

The captain looked bewildered, but he quit protesting her departure. Instead he paused and invited her and Fani to drink a stirrup cup before they set out on their respective paths.

They raised their cups to each other, all standing together, all eager to go.

She said, "Give the writing soldier a cup. He is a kind man, and important as a word sender. And he one day saved my life, too, perhaps."

Justin was surprised and delighted by this recognition from a woman who usually didn't seem to know he existed. He felt honored to stand with her and the young woman and the captain.

He also welcomed a jolt of the liquor to ease his dreads and regrets. Even aside from the ordeal of smallpox horrors that lay ahead, her departure from this confining little place would be, to him, like the snuffing out of a lantern, and being here without her presence would be bleak and gloomy. With her, too, would go some of the security: that of her stature among her warriors, and her ability to translate the languages of Indian visitors to the fort, whatever their tribe. Her departure would be a descent into darkness and uncertainty.

And it would seem colder. Her presence—whether quietly at her decorative work, nursing her baby, or in her grief, even in her rages over her brother's murder—had been both heat and light, a domesticity like that at the hearth of a home with a mother hovering over it.

Now as they drained the last from their cups and the captain's furtive eyes again betrayed his hurry to get away from this plagued place, the woman told him in a deceptively sweet but menacing tone: "Do not forget this, Captain: The murderers of my kin are there in Virginia, where you are going to. They will be put before your judgment people. You must be there when it happens. It is your duty to point at those murderers and say, *By my own eyes, I saw them do it.*

"If they do not get punished, the Indians will come and have revenge on this cursed place. I think Creator is already avenging, with this plague.

"Remember that, Captain. You are the means of justice and the murderers' punishment. But perhaps if your witnessing condemns the murderers, the forest will not have to fall on you, for that would redeem you. That is a word—*redeem*—that the missionaries taught. I like to think about redeemings. I pray that you will have one."

Justin was the nearest thing Fort Randolph had to a doctor, and he felt miserably inadequate. He had studied Dr. Thatcher's recently published broadside on how to manage a community in a smallpox epidemic, and had remembered as much of it as he could. But he had virtually no medicine on hand, few instruments or supplies, and no one with the knowledge or intestinal fortitude to help him care for the wretches. What he did have was a strong stomach, sympathy, and experience.

When a soldier wailed that he was on fire, or started thrashing and flailing his arms because he couldn't stand the itching any longer, Justin knew how he felt. He could remember, from the illness in his childhood, the flaming fever and the maddening, scalding itch. As long ago as that had been, he could feel it all.

The miseries of smallpox were attributed to a violent change in the blood: the first few days of fever because the blood was boiling in the veins to purify itself, then two weeks of raw, itching misery as the separated poison came out through the skin everywhere by way of the pustules. That much he remembered from Dr. Thatcher's paper, so he could, at least vaguely, follow a sufferer's progress through the ordeal.

What Justin wasn't prepared for was the awful visible ravages. He had not seen it when he had it, because his eyes had been swollen and crusted shut, his hands bound to his sides so he wouldn't scratch himself bloody with his fingernails, and he had not been permitted to see himself in a mirror until all his sores had dried and healed. He remembered rags being carried away from his bed soaked red from gushing nosebleeds, and that was about all he could remember of all the sights of it: the red rags.

But these men lying in misery could look over and see, on men lying two feet away, the ravages that they felt ruining their own faces. Their despair as they imagined their own appearances, he thought, must be as terrible as their physical torment. Passing through the stinking room, carrying them drinking water or gruel, gathering their filthy, blood-and-pus-stained bedding to be burned, he was often stopped by a plucking at his sleeve and asked in one whimpering, groaning voice or another:

"Is it bad? How do I look, Case?"

"Tell me, please . . . will I be ruint?"

He replied each time: "You should come out no worse than I. Would that be too much to bear?"

More likely, he knew, they would come out much worse, even those who would live. Of all the medicines needed for the various stages of the disease, he had virtually none: no mallow nor myrrh for the steams to loosen lungs, no garlic for the soles of their feet, no oil of almond or pomatum to make liniment, no paregorics for pain or phrensy, not enough nitre, no salt of wormwood, no Peruvian bark for the fevers, no saffron or asafoetida for thinning the fluid humors, and nothing but plain mustard-seed and vinegar to induce salivation. The only native remedies he had in any quantity were snakeroot, sassafras, and white willow bark.

He had metal pots, a few yards of cotton and strouding cloth, a few pecks of Indian corn to substitute for barley in the patients' gruel. And whiskey, which was dangerous for the patients but helpful for himself. He had his scalpels and knives for bloodletting, which needed to be done on each patient from the time of eruption to the eleventh day. And he had his main instrument, the one he had to use over and over every day, hating every minute of it: his big metal clyster for irrigating their clogged and impacted bowels. The clyster was especially crucial about the tenth day after eruption, and he would watch a patient for that moment when the pustules were drying to pea-sized excrescences and falling off. That was when a patient would get most costive, and if Justin didn't keep his bowels flushed out, putrid fever and death could carry off a patient who had nearly recovered from the pox itself.

Justin was almost entirely without sleep for the weeks that the disease ravaged the garrison. At any time, several soldiers were in all stages of the disease and needed constant attention. The quarantine hut had to be kept warm enough that the patients could lie mostly uncovered, because clothes and covers were almost unbearable. But a room grown too cool from an unattended fireplace could cause suppuration to stop, and fatal chills to set in. Here at the juncture of wide rivers, the winter winds were fickle, and all the crude cabins in the fort were drafty. Whirling gusts often blew fire smoke back down the stick-and-daub chimneys. This made it hard for even healthy men to breathe, and smallpox patients breathed with difficulty even when the air was clear and pure. What the men hawked up from their lungs with racking effort was thick and sticky, and their mouths were too dry to spit.

He had to force immune militiamen to help with the changing and disposal of bedding and the care of the fireplace and the emptying of shit-pots. But they were not dependable aides. They grew depressed and frantic in the presence of the disease, even though assured that they were not vulnerable to reinfection, and they found every kind of reason not to show up for duty.

Justin brooded sometimes, late at night over his whiskey, about the relationship between God and plagues. Why had he made them, if he could have prevented them? Or did Satan make them? Were they forms of punishment for mortals' proud wrongs? Was this a punishment upon the whites, who had given the Indians infected blankets and wiped out whole villages? It was said that the agony of Indians with smallpox was tenfold that of whitemen and that the torment of their superstitious hearts and minds magnified it even beyond its physical potency. One in ten in the whiteman's community, such as this fort, might be expected to die and the rest survive, with scars. In an Indian community, it was said, one of ten might live.

He would sit drinking, nearly dozing, between his rounds, and imagine what a healer like the Grenadier would have to do in her community, as whole families perished around her. She knew what to do about fevers, about bowels, about pain, about breathing, about hemorrhaging, about infections. Over the ages, the Indians had found in the woods the roots and leaves and barks that would cure such things one at a time. But the smallpox brought all those ills at once, in a way that the old healers were unprepared for, in their minds or their spirits.

In Europe, not long since, a discovery had been made that yet might alleviate the scourge of this plague: that a little prick of cowpox pus into the skin of a person might somehow create a guard against the full brunt of smallpox. The technique was known, passed like a rumor among physicians of the societies, and even in this remote wilderness outpost, Justin Case could hope for its eventual efficacy. The Indian woman herself had once been thus inoculated.

But Fort Pitt could not supply down the river even such old necessities as flour, salt, and ammunition, or medical salts, or febrifuges or laudanums. Any miracle capable of preventing the plague, if it ever came forth in the world, would not come here into the frontier until too late. Everything came here too late.

Justin Case, soldier become doctor, exhausted by misery, drinking whiskey to ease his despair, watched that face form in the flames of his wood fire: the woman, the healer, the peacemaker, the hinge upon which the conflict swung, a fine, brown face with the whole power of a native god behind it.

"Nonhelema," he pronounced softly. *Non he le ma.* Not a man. *Coitcheleh,* her other name. Carrier of the meaning and rules of life.

Or, as the Moravian missionaries, advocates of another god, had

dubbed her: Catarina. Catherine. Katy. She would never come back.
There was no reason to hope for that.

FROM GOVERNOR PATRICK HENRY
WILLIAMSBURG, FEB^Y 19
1778 to Col. W^M Fleming, Botetort County Lieut

Sir—

The Murder of the Shawanese Indians will no doubt bring on Hostilities with that People. In order to ward off the Stroke which may be expected it is necessary to have every Gun in your County put into good order & got ready for action.

Let trusty Scouts be kept in constant Action toward the Enemys Country to discover their Movements & give Information of any approaching Danger. Proper Stockades or Defences to recieve the more helpless part of the People should be provided, at Places judiciously chosen, that the able Men may be at Liberty to assail the Enemy & range the Frontiers . . . Let the pursuit of Scalping Parties be close, hot and determined, for if Vengeance is taken on the foremost Partys, others will be intimidated. I wish to reinforce Capt Arbuckles Garrison with a Company.

You will perceive my Views go no further than defensive Operations. I know how impossible it is to render them completely effectual, but offensive Measures set on foot against these Indians at this time after their late Treatment, would be too full of injustice to escape general Execration.

I must tell you Sir that I really blush for the occasion of this War with the Shawanese. I doubt not but you detest the vile assassins who have brought it on us at this critical Time when our whole Force was wanted in another Quarter. But why are they not brought to Justice? I fear your County will feel indiscriminately that Misery which ought to visit only the guilty Authors of the Mischief. Some say the people of your Country will not suffer the Apprehension of the Murderers. I desire it may be remembered, that if the frontier people will not submit to the Laws . . . they will not be entitled to the protection of Government. For where is this wretched Business to end?

Is not this the work of Tories? No man but an Enemy to American Independence will do it, and thus oblige our People to be hunting after

Indians in the Woods, instead of facing Genl Howe in the field. Bringing the Murderers of the Indians to Justice will be done, Government will lose no time in lending its best Aids to protect your Country.

I have it much at Heart to bring the Indians to treat on the subject of our Differences with them, perhaps the Grenadier Squaw may be usefull in this business . . . let every possible Effort be made to bring on a Treaty. The Expences necessary for the Attempt I will pay on Demand.

Wishing safety to you & your people I am Sir Yr Mo hble Servt.

P. Henry

PITTSBURGH MARCH 25, 1778
WAPEYMACHIKTHE (GEORGE MORGAN), TO
THE CHIEFS & WARRIORS OF THE
SHAWANESE NATION

BROTHERS—When I look toward you or at the Kenawa River I am ashamed for the conduct of our young foolish men. Formerly I was ashamed of the conduct of your young men. Now I see there are foolish people among all Nations. Our Wise men are ashamed and sorry for what has happen'd. BROTHERS Now Listen to what the Great Council of the United States says to you. Open your ears that you may hear and your hearts that you may understand them. It is as follows:

BROTHERS THE SHAWANESE It gave us great joy to hear by our Agent Mr Morgan that you appear to be resolved to hold fast our Friendship.

BROTHERS We are sorry to hear what has happen'd at the Kenawa. It has been owing to foolish wicked People and they shall suffer. We therefore desire you will not think hard of your White Brothers there, but impute the Loss of your Friends to the Wicked Mingoes & Wiandots who came and killed some of our People near the Fort whilst yours were there on purpose to have them knock'd on the Head. You know there are foolish people among all nations.

BROTHERS We desire to give you full Satisfaction for the wicked Murder committed on your Chiefs and young Men at the Kenawa. Therefore and in order to clear the Road between us and to destroy all the Briars and Thorns which have grown therein, We have named three Wise Men to repair to Fort Pitt to consult with you for that purpose And we desire that you will appoint a few of your Chiefs to meet them there and whatever your Wise Men and ours Agree to, let each of us resolve shall bind our People so that our Friendship may endure forever.

BROTHERS let nothing prevent your coming. Tell us plainly whether you will or will not come as we desire. Let us know your Minds, for we shall consider your Answer as the Messenger of Peace or War and prepare ourselves accordingly. Brothers if you wish for Peace as we do, the fears of your and our Women and Children may be done away.

BELT OF WAMPUM

Now Brothers you have heard the Voice of our great Council. Our three Wise men are arrived here. I therefore tell you to rise quickly and let nothing prevent your coming here. You know I never deceived you, therefore you may now believe me. And with this Belt I clear the Road &c &c

A ROAD BELT

Wapeymachikthe

FORT PITT, 30 MARCH, 1778
TO GEN. HORATIO GATES

Sir—

I have the mortification to inform you that last Saturday night, Alexʳ McKee made his escape from this place, as also Matthew Elliott, a person lately from Quebec on parole, Simon Girty, Robt. Surplus, And one Higgins, an event the more distressing to me as it was distant from my thoughts; nor can I help thinking that Elliott brought him dispatches from Quebec which influenced him at this time.

A report prevails that 28 men were taken by the savages at the Salt Lick near Kentucky in Febʸ.

Edwd Hand

FORT PITT, 30 MARCH, 1778

To Col. William Crawford

Dr. Crawford—
You will no doubt be surprised to hear that Mr. McKee, Matthew Elliott, Simon Girty, one Surplus, and Higgins, with McKee's two Negroes, eloped on Saturday night. This will make it improper to proceed

with the intended expedition to French Creek, and as your assistance may be necessary towards preventing the evils that may arise from the information these runaways have, I beg you may return here as soon as possible.
I am, Sincerely yrs,

Edwd Hand

12

She looked across the table at the smug expression on Alexander McKee's face and didn't know whether she loved him or hated him more. He seemed to have no remorse for his betrayals, of her and of his country. He was pleased with himself and with the oncoming conflict between the Indians and the Long Knives. He was delighted with the aggressive plans being made by the British governor-general at Detroit, Henry Hamilton, to strike and expel the Americans from the Kentucke settlements and Pennsylvania.

He was also gloating over the Shawnees' recent capture of the Long Knife leader called Boone, and most of the defenders of Boone's settlement in Kentucke. During the Sugar Tree Moon, Chief Blue Jacket's warriors had surprised Boone and captured him near the Blue Licks. They persuaded him to surrender his twenty-six-man salt-making party. Not a shot was fired in resistance. It had been a fine coup for Blue Jacket. And Boone had been so cooperative in their capitulation, McKee suspected he must be a Tory sympathizer. Boone had cheerfully gone as a captive to Chillicothe Town, and there he had so charmed his old enemy Black Fish that the war chief had adopted him as a son. In such an adoption, both men swore loyalty to each other as kin, and Black Fish was proud and happy to have as his son a man of such renown. Boone was famed as a marksman and hunter and brave fighter. It would be good to have him as an enemy no longer. Black Fish had taken Boone's men to Detroit and sold them to Governor Hamilton for bounty, but had refused to sell Boone. He had given him the name Shel-to-wee, which meant "the Big Turtle." Shel-to-wee seemed to be all Indian in his heart and spirit, and the whole town of Chillicothe had embraced him as one of its own. Nonhelema herself knew Boone and admired him. *But,* she thought, *Boone is a fox.*

McKee was delighted with Boone's captivity, which he relished as a coup against the Long Knives. He was confident that the British were winning many of the tribes away from neutrality, and especially that Governor Hamilton was winning many of the Shawnee chiefs over.

Nonhelema watched him and listened, shaking her head. How could this old lover of hers gloat over things that he knew must be upsetting her, the peacemaker, and undoing her years of work? And how, she wondered, could he be so familiar and jolly with her even though he had abandoned her for the company of a half-breed trollop who was Nonhelema's inferior in every way, and half her age? McKee apparently was just so transported by his new situation that he was oblivious of the way his news was affecting her.

He was fairly wriggling with delight now. He leaned toward Nonhelema at her table, holding a sheet of paper before her face and flipping at it with the back of his hand. "Read it, Katy, and y'll see what I mean!"

She took it with a sigh and pulled her reading spectacles out from the bosom of her blouse, where they hung among her necklaces.

DETROIT, APRIL 23ᴰ, 1778

To Captain Alexʳ McKee

Sir, I heartily congratulate you on your escape, and shall be happy to see you here, where you may be sure of finding Friends, & sincere ones. The sooner your convenience can admit of your coming to this place, the better, as I wish to confer with you on several points 'tis impossible to *touch upon in a letter. The Council to be held at this place and which I expect to be very full, will meet on or about the 15th of May, till when matters will remain as they are—nothing can exceed the good temper and tractable behavior of all the Indians . . . The Six Nations are more than ever attached to Government & zealous in the cause against the Rebels—Considerable reinforcements expected to Canada this year.*

I am Sir your very humble Servant

Henry Hamilton

"There, Katy, d'you see?" Alexander almost hissed through the teeth of his grin. "That is the governor-general of the whole British Department of Detroit addressing me so warmly! 'I heartily congratulate you,' he writes here. 'Finding sincere friends'! You can read in that letter the kind of support I shall have from 'im, and it's plain that his Indian force is strong and getting stronger! And, listen, Katy: When the militia murdered your kin at Fort Randolph, they did an *inestimable* favor to General Hamilton! None of his own enticements ever turned so many Shawnee leaders to him as that rabble did that day!"

Her mouth had dropped open and she crumpled the letter and flung it at him. With a stunned expression, he grabbed to catch his precious document and began smoothing it.

"You!" she cried. "If you ever had a care for me or my people, how can you come to me and gloat over the murder of my brother?"

"Katy, Katy, I'm sorry. I'm not gloating. But it has . . . It . . ." He seemed to realize how his exuberance was being taken. At once his expression turned to that of remorse or compassion; the change was so rapid and complete that it reminded her of actors she had seen in stage plays in Philadelphia, where her father had taken her when she was very young.

After a few moments of looking properly morose, McKee leaned forward with his palms up and his face keen and earnest. "Katy, listen to reason, will ye? Go *with* the rest o' your chiefs, not against 'em! Rid yourself o' those damned Americans! They're making you a fool, Katy, and you're no fool! They use ye to unman your own people. Then when you don't fight, they'll come farther, and keep coming. They'll come up here and burn your towns and crops. I implore ye, join your chiefs against the Long Knives!"

"But we made peace," she said. "We signed the peace, and we have kept our word."

"Ha!" Alexander leaned back so hard and quick that the chair creaked, his face a triumphant smirk. "Yes, you made peace. And they then honored it by murdering your brother!"

"You will not speak again of that," she said in a low, menacing voice.

He leaned close again, the smirk gone now, his face intense. There was that youthful, fine-featured, intelligent face that she had loved in all its moods and liveliness. He was such a beautiful man, and the spirit in him was like great laughter. She had known many lovers and husbands, but this man had been like the sun in the center of her life.

Then he had betrayed her. And now he was living with a despicable woman and he was on the side of the British. She felt that he had made a greater fool of her than had the Americans.

"You've come to your own way, by your own mind and your own spirit," he said. "You've put yourself in danger because you chose to believe liars. Listen, Katy: Why d'you think I quit the Americans?"

"Because you still love the English king."

"English king be damned! It's because at Fort Pitt I saw the American commanders offering friendship to the tribes while at the same time planning raids against them! They were calling your chiefs to go to Fort Pitt to resolve the murders, while they were getting ready for an expedition against your towns! Katy, I know you are Mekoche peacemakers and healers. But to the rebels, all Shawnese people are just savages. You're in their way. You need to be fooled and made helpless, or killed otherwise. They will use you up as long as you can be used. Then they'll discard you, or kill you!"

She moved from the table, got her iron teakettle off the hearth, and poured steaming water into their yellow china teacups, over the black tea she had grated off a brick of pressed tea. She was thinking, but not showing him in her face what she was thinking.

"To be living is to be used up," she said. "I chose to be used up keeping peace where I can. I healed many injured warriors. I helped to bury many others. Their blood, and the tears of their wives and children, have been shed for nothing. That is war. It does no good." Now she leaned over him and drilled him with her eyes. "I myself killed soldiers on a battleground. I wish I never had. Their dying does the Shawnee people no good! There will never be an end to soldiers coming. Soldiers always kept coming, even as the ones in front of them were killed and fell down. If you want to speak of making fools, speak of men marching to wars!"

She straightened, went stiff-backed to a shelf on the log wall, and brought down a small pewter bowl with a cover. From it she picked out nuggets of maple sugar and put several of them in the teacups. She stirred them with the elegant silver spoon Alexander himself had given her, when they were lovers. For a moment, the only sound in the room was the clinking of the spoon in the cups, and then a little mouth-noise and murmur from the bed across the room where their son, Tommy, was napping.

McKee said, low and intense: "There will always be war because there *must* be. If not for fear of your warriors, the Americans wouldn't even apologize for murdering your people! They would be walking right into your towns."

"They are already. Battles have hardly slowed them. And even all the warriors and Red Coat soldiers you can bring from Canada shall not stop them. Fighting them will only make them more vengeful. Those murders at the fort—"

"You said those aren't to be mentioned."

"Not by you! Those murders were from vengeance, because Indians had killed soldiers. Now in revenge for the murders, Indians will kill soldiers again. They will kill children and women, too, just as soldiers do. There is no end. I still have brothers not yet killed, and I do not want them to be killed. My forebears were peaceable, and their lives were long and good. My mother, Elizabeth, lives in the mission of the suffering bleeding Jesus preachers. She is old, and at peace. I myself am getting old, which I suppose is why you aimed your little stiff *chuc kee* at a slut who is so much younger."

"Damn it, Katy! I'm sorry, but I'm not here to talk about that. I am here to persuade you to bring our son to a safe place. And by God, what d'you mean '*little* stiff *chuc kee*'? Y' seemed to find it satisfactory for a while, as I recall."

Suddenly they both were trying not to laugh or even smile. They had lived and loved wonderfully, that short while. She sat down with her elbows on the table and put the cup of tea to her lips so he wouldn't see her amusement, but the cup could not hide what was in her eyes. *Damned Loyalist man, go away,* she thought, trying to make herself angry enough that he would not observe that his charm was softening her resolve.

"I will not even consider going to Detroit," she said. "I have sworn to the Americans for peace. You were there when I did so. I believe Jesus made me to be a peacemaker. The British know that my brothers and I are for the Americans. That governor-general who wrote you that letter would not trust me or treat me well. He knows I am against him."

She wouldn't let McKee sway her. To work for peace was to be right. That was the way of Jesus and his followers. That was also the belief of good George Morgan, he who had taught her to build bridges between the white men and the red men.

She still believed the Americans. Even since the murders at the fort, she believed Morgan and the commissioners. The men who had done the murders would be punished, she was sure, because the Americans were sincere for peace. She believed the message Wapey-matchikthe had sent. There were vicious fools in every nation, and even the governor of Virginia wanted those murderers punished. All the Americans were ashamed of what those men had done. That proved to her that the American leaders were good.

It was true that Captain Arbuckle had disappointed her, that he had been devious with her. And General Hand had made her angry. Right after the murders, she had been aflame for revenge. But it was not all Americans who had done that crime, it was just those few. Jesus had taught that one must forgive. She probably was not a good enough Christian to forgive those men themselves, but she would not blame all Americans for what those had done.

She said: "You tell me I am being used up by the Americans. So tell me, when have your British not been notorious for using up the Indians? You know well, don't you, how they trick and coddle the Iroquois of the Six Nations to fight and die for their British causes? If I went to Detroit, would not your big Hamilton man try just so to use me up?"

McKee banged his cup on the table in exasperation. "Katy, damn it all! I'm not trying to enlist you for the British! I'm just trying to get you and your children, and our own son, into a place far from harm. Detroit is safe. The rebels will never get there. Detroit is a rich place where you can prosper. And if you're in Detroit, no one can use you anymore as a spy against your own people!"

They had been discussing all this in Shawnee tongue, but now McKee began speaking English. People in the village outside her cabin could hear their words. Surely they were listening with even more than usual interest because their beloved woman chief was back from the American fort, and here also was her old lover who, every-body knew, had defected to the British. They would detect the heat of dispute in their voices, if not their words. She had no idea how many people now were outside listening, but she knew her brother Mawawa, the Wolf, was out there, holding horses for Alexander. Mawawa, for one, could understand their discussion in whichever tongue they used. The Wolf was a good, respectful brother, but he was strongly on McKee's side, against the Americans, and hot to avenge the murder of Cornstalk.

"You know," McKee said softly, "what those damned missionaries learn through their miserable wards, it all goes straightway to the officers at Fort Pitt. I've seen the letters Zeisberger writes to General Hand, Katy! I've seen those letters, full of everything Zeisberger learns about who's going where, who's doing what. And the general uses that knowledge to plan actions against your own people. And *you, damn it! Even you!* I've seen the letters from Arbuckle at Fort Randolph, telling Hand details that he got straight from you, yourself! Do you understand what a disgrace it will be on you, any time Shawnees get defeated or killed because you gave knowledge to their enemy? That's what I want to stop. They use you and laugh behind your back because you are so naive! They use you as a spy against your own people. They make you a traitor, Katy!"

"*Motchee!*" She pointed straight at his face. "Who calls me traitor? The most famous traitor in this country himself!" She said it so loudly that it woke Tommy from his nap, and he shed his blanket, got up, and came toddling over, his sleepy face showing distress. He went to her and leaned against her, looking up fearfully at his father, whom he scarcely recognized. McKee reached for him.

"*Pe aloo, nee cha!*" he coaxed, smiling and tilting his head. Come here, my child. The boy looked up to her for affirmation, and she nodded, so he went to McKee, who picked him up and set him on his knee and jounced him. The child stared at him, then reached up to touch his blond hair and finally smiled. McKee kept jouncing the child and smiling at him, but his eyes were set hard against her. "I'm no traitor, Katy. You know that. I am loyal to the king I've always known. But more, I am loyal to your people. I am trying to protect you and Tommy and your family. Who else will? Most of your people have turned their backs on you. Damn you, Katy, if you're too stupid to come to a safe place, at least let me take my son there?"

"*Naga!* A child stays with the mother! Always that is so!"

McKee's face looked hard now. He said, "Certain of your own relatives want me to take our son where he will be safe. Whether you will go or not." He looked at the boy and asked, *"Kee wis a puc a chee?"* Would you like to go someplace?

The child smiled, then suddenly looked doubtful and turned to Nonhelema. He had always liked going places, being carried in canoes and horseback, and had been to many places. But always Nonhelema or Fani, or some aunt or other, had carried him, and so he would think that would always be so.

Nonhelema distrusted the course of this conversation. "Listen," she said, "you have no greater care for Tommy's safety than I. I am his mother. I bore him. That is why I took him to the Americans' fort, so he would be safe. That is also why I brought him away from the Americans' fort in the last winter, to save him from their pox. And I did save him from it. You have no right to set my kin against me about his safety. Remember, it was you who left me with this baby, to go live with Open Legs."

Had he not been holding the child, McKee probably would have leapt up and struck her for saying that. By the time he had set the boy on the floor and stood up, he barely had restraint over himself. "You, woman," he said in a cold, hissing tone, "should think about going to Detroit. And I pray ye will, because to your people you are an important woman. And you are important to me, too. I never loved anyone more, Katy. But, y' see, Tommy's my only son. I *will* have him with me. If Tommy died in your care, I'd have no son. You come to Detroit if you come to your senses. But I *am* taking Tommy."

Suddenly McKee was sent stumbling three steps backward when her open hand walloped him on the cheek with a fury. He had not seen it coming. She could grab flies out of the air in summer, she was so quick. The people outside could not have failed to hear the blow. Little Tommy had not seen it, but he turned and looked up, his face puzzled at the sound. McKee reached down with his right hand and took his boy's hand. With his left hand he rubbed the side of his face, then looked at the hand for blood.

"He is *my* son," she yelled. "Here he will stay, with me and our peacemaking family! Jesus will protect us, better than your Detroit governor can do. You and Open Legs cannot have him!"

The door swung open. Mawawa stood there with several of his warriors. McKee tugged the boy's hand. *"Pe aloo nee cha,"* McKee said, guiding him toward the door, purposely keeping the boy in front of him so she couldn't grab him.

Nonhelema trembled with fury. "Stop him," she said to Mawawa in a quaking voice. "He is trying to steal my son from me."

The Wolf shook his head, not smiling. "Sister, in this we are with Captain. You shall not take this boy to the Americans anymore. They are using you falsely and your son will not be safe with you unless you come to Detroit. I will be his teaching uncle and his protector. And we will always wait for you to come to Detroit. Sister, stay inside. Don't let the people see you fight us for this. They, too, are afraid you will take him back to the Long Knives."

She stood stunned. After a moment, she began to feel dismay. She suddenly saw that they were right, in their way.

A faint hope fluttered in her breast. She would prove to Alexander that the Americans were sincere in their words of peace. She would work with them relentlessly; she had to show him. He was wrong. Tears were running cold down her cheeks in the draft of the open door, and she knew the people must not see her like this. Maybe she would follow them later. At the moment, she was frozen in doubt. She cringed behind the table and stood there quaking, both fists clenched over her heart as if to hold it together.

She watched through the door as Alexander McKee mounted his horse and Tommy was handed to him and set before him. The boy was obedient and calm, a good Shawnee child who did not realize yet that he was being taken far from his mother. Her bosom ached so deeply, she could hardly draw breath.

They rode off from among the people, who were waving and calling after them. She was thankful at least that the child had not seen the blow she had given his father. McKee would have welts on his face from that blow for days. Her whole right hand ached and stung, almost as much as her heart.

Remember, she told herself, *if you need to see Tommy you are free to go to Detroit. This is not the end.*

But you must not stoop to let your people see you brawl with a man.

13

Justin Case raised his head, cupped a hand behind his ear, and told the two grave diggers: "Quiet. Listen!"

The two men stopped and stood in the waist-deep holes, leaning on their shovels. The noise was as much a vibration in the ground as it was a sound.

"Hooves," one digger said. "Ain't them hooves?"

Justin looked both ways along the Ohio. If those were mounted troops coming, there were many of them.

"Cattle's what it is," said the other sweaty digger. "Fresh beef, by God, and about time, too!"

Yes, it was cattle. Justin could hear a faint bawl now and then, and the far clank of a cowbell.

He gazed along the river bluff. Here where the two graves were being dug, he remembered, was just about where Colonel Fleming had assembled the troops the morning of the battle in '74. All the big trees were long since gone and the ground around the fort was an ugly, eroded wasteland of stumps, rotting slash piles, bones of butchered animals both cattle and game, and graves marked with crude wooden crosses—a dozen of them being of the winter's small-pox victims. The two whose graves were being dug here today had survived the smallpox, only to die later—one of some sort of bowel trouble, the other by drowning in the river, his body later being recovered where it had caught in driftwood. The unmarked graves of Corn-stalk, Elinipsico, Red Hawk, and Old Yie were farther down toward the Kanawha River bank, near a turnip patch that was tended by the camp cook. The two grave diggers were privates from Captain Hall's militia company, also smallpox survivors, and the reason they needed an armed overseer was that they had been caught trying to desert. There were rumors that two hundred acres of good land near Detroit would be granted to anyone who would defect to the Loyal-ists, and now and then it proved too much temptation for some mili-tiaman. These two had tried to defect, but were caught. They would have been shot for it, but the fort was undermanned, and prisoners could work.

Justin saw dust rising along the bank of the Ohio. Then, climbing slowly into sight along the bluff, came not army beef drovers, but In-dians. Startled, he tensed and crouched to cock his flintlock, dis-mayed that the sentries high on the fort wall had let him and his workers be surprised outside the fort like this. He was about to yell up and alert the fort when he saw, near the front of the Indian column, the Grenadier and her daughter. At that moment he heard a sentry cry out, "Cap'n, sir! Th' Injen queen's come back! Looks like she brang us beef!"

Justin was thrilled to see that she had returned. He had not be-lieved she would. The whole frontier was awaiting Indian retaliation for the murders of her kin here at Fort Randolph, so no one had really expected her to leave her Shawnee people and come back. Justin, re-membering General Hand's refusal to turn the murderers over to her people, and her bitter farewell to Captain Arbuckle, had thought he would never see her again.

But by heaven, here she was! As usual, her elegant daughter rode beside her. He didn't see the little boy. At a distance behind, the cat-tle followed, driven by Indian boys on horseback. Some young Indian men were also leading strings of good-looking horses.

Justin raised his hat to her. He was smiling, really smiling, for the first time since the miserable ordeal of the smallpox plague. She raised a hand toward him and nodded as she rode toward the fort.

Fani also saw him and raised a hand in greeting. But both women were grave, dignified, neither of them showing a smile.

One of the grave diggers gave a low whistle and a grunt, then muttered to the other, "Oh, Isaac, that's some fine-lookin' meat, and I don't mean the cattle. I *got* to git me one o' them squars!"

"And I'll take t'other'n!" said the second soldier.

Justin turned so that his rifle muzzle pointed at one man's brow and then the other's. Their eyes widened.

"Those women," he said slowly, "have suffered enough at the hands of your bedamned company. You annoy them, you'll be digging each other's graves right here. I saved your sorry lives from the pox, so you're here at my sufferance. Don't try me."

They went meekly back to work, and Justin stood over them, watching the women go toward the fort, musing about how much he had been changed by this place, by that woman. On the day of that battle, he had been such a slinking poltroon he would never have dared threaten a pair of deadly curs like these.

The Shawnee woman seemed harder. There was a sort of fierce intensity around her eyes. She did not spend time absorbed in her handiwork, as she had sometimes done during her stay here the year before. Something had happened in the winter weeks of her absence, while she was away with her people.

One difference was that little boy was not with the women this time. Neither the woman nor her daughter offered any explanation for his absence. Justin presumed that the child had contracted smallpox and had died during the winter. He was afraid to ask.

That she had brought all her cattle and horses with her seemed to mean that she was now fully departed from her Indian community. He wondered if that was why she seemed so hard: Was she outcast? Only she and her daughter were here. Those who had driven her herd down had left at once.

She did not have any kind of rapport at all with the fort's acting commander, Captain William McKee. The year before, she had treated him with a polite indifference, barely acknowledging that he was a relative of her old consort Alexander. Now she was even colder toward him, so hostile that he might have put her out were it not for her value as an interpreter, or potentially as a hostage.

But she certainly was eager to give McKee information. Justin was called in soon to transcribe information she had brought. He learned, as she talked, that the British governor-general of Detroit was amassing and nurturing Indian allies from the Great Lakes to the Mississippi, whose purpose would be to descend into the valley of the Ohio and the Kentucke country, and drive all the Long Knives back over the mountains. The commander at Detroit had a large plan, she said, and there was even more danger than there had been before.

She said: "By Alexander McKee's treachery, the British general will learn everything that the officers at Fort Pitt have been preparing to do. Be sure he will excite their vengeance for the killing done here, of my kin. He knows they want the blood of many Long Knives for that.

"I want only the blood of those who murdered them. That is what should always be. It is just. But it is never like that. Always many die for what a few other ones did. One side and then the other side.

"You must believe now that I am strong for having peace between my people and yours. I am tired of blood on the ground, and hope never to see more of it. But there will be more if you keep coming into our country. If you cut down the trees, and kill all our game. If you bring whiskey and rum, and your sicknesses that we never had before.

"What I wish, Captain, is that your government would stop your people from coming any farther." She lowered her eyes and shook her head. "But I fear it will never happen. Since your ancestors first came to the shore in their ships, they have been pushing our people back, by force and by tricks. I was born far to the east of here, the place you call Maryland. My grandfather and my father were friends of the great man Penn. Penn always told us the truth, and so we learned to trust whitemen. I think now it was a bad lesson. Your leaders are not like Penn, now. When I speak for Americans to my people, they tell me again about all the treaties broken and the promises not kept, and they laugh at me for believing you. They say, 'How far it is to Old Town, where you were born! In one lifetime, the whitemen have taken that much country from us!' "

She fell silent. The captain cleared his throat, leaned to a candle, and lit his long clay pipe.

"Ma'am, that's a sorry tale, indeed it is, and I reckon that's really the way y' see it. Now, I'm just an honest soldier, and I'm out here in this fort because that's my orders, ma'am. I'm no councilor nor a commissioner or agent of any kind, so it does ye little good to tell me what policy should be. I do have papers here, from Patrick Henry, who's the governor o' Virginia, and from the county lieutenants, all sorts o' papers and letters, telling how sorry they are for what happened. That they want a big council at Fort Pitt, to apologize and compensate. They want me to tell that to every Indian I see. Well, ma'am, I sure ain't seen many. Used t' be they came through here most every day, visiting, wanting this or that, making me speeches, and whatnot. But since what happened here, it's spooky almost. It feels like we're just waitin' here for all of 'em to come at once. I'm no happier'n you are, ma'am."

After a long while, she sighed and said, "Let me read those papers. May it be that I shall have occasion to read them to our chiefs, if they come here." The captain signaled with his thumb for Justin to fetch the papers. From a small bag in her bosom she pulled a pair of tiny reading spectacles and put them on, and Justin handed her the documents, marveling at the sight of an Indian with glasses. It was odd that she never wore them while working with her tiny beads, needles, and quills, but needed them to read.

She set the papers on the corner of the table. Then she began to read them silently, one by one, tracing the lines with a forefinger, concentrating deeply. It was apparent that reading was not easy for her, or perhaps she read slowly in order to remember precisely. She took a long time with each sheet, sometimes nodding, sometimes frowning and turning her head from side to side. Sometimes she would sound out a word, barely above a whisper. Outside was the murmur of garrison noises: voices, hammering, chopping.

At last she set the papers aside. She put the spectacles back into the little bag and drew out a short clay pipe with a cane stem. She crumbled tobacco into it, pressed it down with her forefinger, and lifted a candle to the bowl to ignite it. The scent was of other things besides tobacco. It was one of those fragrant kinnikinnicks the Indians made by mixing herbs and barks with their tobacco. She smoked wordlessly, gazing at a wall.

"If chiefs come, I will read those promises, though I do not expect them to turn away any revenge." She smoked a little more. "I believe all that will turn away revenge is to tell them, *The murderers stood in the judging council at Virginia, pointed at and identified by Captain Arbuckle as the murderers he saw, and then those men were killed. It is now revenged. You may lead your warriors home.*

"Then they might go home and leave you here in peace. But they might not, for they have many other grievances. If they come, I will try to read them these promises. And we shall see whether that will satisfy them."

FORT RANDOLPH
MAY 27, 1778

As streaming blood and needlelike pains blinded his right eye, Justin Case was beginning to think that wood splinters were more dangerous than lead musket balls. The chance of a lead ball from one of those muskets way out there finding its way straight to a soldier's head was slim. But when such a ball hit an oaken palisade post anywhere near the soldier, oak splinters flew like birdshot, and they would go right through skin, ears, or eyelids.

He felt as if he had been hit in the face by a porcupine. And before he could do anything about the curtain of blood veiling his vision, more musket balls whacked into the palisades close by. He felt splinters flick the cloth of his sleeve and heard a nearby soldier yelp in pain.

There were hundreds of yodeling warriors out there, behind outbuildings and tree stumps, in thickets, even behind Nonhelema's cabin, crouched in erosion gullies and masked by their own gunsmoke, which they were producing faster than the hot, feeble breeze could dissipate it. They were nearly invisible as they darted from stump to stump or raised heads and shoulders to shoot, quick and faint like spirits instead of solid bodies. And now Justin, with blood filling his aiming eye, couldn't see at all to shoot.

He turned and slid down to a sitting position on the catwalk, and tried to wipe the blood away on the cloth of his sleeve. Pain from the protruding splinters was too sharp to bear. So with thumb and middle finger, he gingerly touched his eyelid to determine whether any splinter was actually in the eye. None was, and he thanked God for that, then carefully dabbed and blinked until tears from his irritated eye flushed blood out enough that he could see, if only dimly. He was still sitting, reloading, when a soldier a few feet away grunted, spun, and fell off the catwalk to the ground inside the parapet. Justin watched the man rise to his hands and knees, watched to see if he would be able to stand and return to the fight. It made more sense to stay down out of the line of fire than to stand back up into that shower of musket balls and flying splinters, and the fate of the fallen soldier gave him pause.

But the air was still full of smoke and yelling, banging guns and thudding lead, and the soldiers in the fort were terribly outnumbered. It was all they could do to return enough fire to keep the warriors at a distance from the walls, keep them out of firebrand-throwing and fire-arrow range. Now that the blood was drying on his face and he could see to shoot again, he had a duty to get back up and do so.

He knew that this attack was, in part, vengeance for the murders that had taken place here, of Cornstalk and his companions, only months before. But vengeance was not all of it. Even before the murders, this attack had been planned. Cornstalk had come to warn of it. And now it had come.

So Justin got his feet under him and stood, stooping, to face out over the wall and search for targets. The countless wood splinters in the right side of his face stung so sharply that he could hardly concentrate, and it seemed that every warrior was aiming at him; the balls hummed and whirred past his head, thick as hornets. In the gun-smoke their muzzle flashes winked. From behind a stump near the fort, the head and shoulders of a warrior rose up, with a smear of smoky yellow flame in front of him: It was a fire arrow, and the warrior was aiming it high, to arc and fall on one of the tinder-dry split-wood roofs. The warrior must have advanced to the stump within the last few minutes; no one had been there before.

The target was blurry because of the powder smoke burning his eyes, but he fired quickly, and when the smoke of his own shot thinned, he saw that the warrior had begun falling sideways with his bow still in his left hand, and the fire-tipped arrow was flying awry on a course that would miss the fort entirely.

Down in the fort, outside the door of the orderly room, the fort's acting commander, Captain William McKee, stood among several officers, who were gesticulating and talking with him in agitation.

William McKee was not an alert commander. He was slack with scouting. When this large force of Indians had appeared outside the fort yesterday, it had been such a surprise that there was no chance to herd in Nonhelema's cattle, which had been most of the fort's food supply. The attack had begun at once, lasted until dusk, then had resumed at daylight. The attackers were expending ammunition so freely that there was no doubt they had been supplied by the British at Detroit. The troops in the fort were outnumbered some four to one, by McKee's guess, and nearly a quarter of his men were unfit for duty, many still weak from the smallpox. Even at that, McKee was not entertaining any notion of surrendering. To give up, he was sure, would mean submitting to massacre.

Justin reloaded. But when he peered over the parapet for another target, he was surprised to see that many of the warriors were darting from their cover and withdrawing out of gunshot range. Most of their shooting had stopped, except that coming from a distance, which seemed to be covering fire for the withdrawal. For a moment, he wondered whether his shot disabling their fire-archer might have been the reason for their retreat, but thought that would be presuming too much.

He realized that he had been hearing distant shouts, repetitions of *O-tothe-haloo! O-tothe-ha!* They were calling their warriors back. It meant "come nearer." It was one of the few Shawnee phrases he had learned from Nonhelema.

It was a relief to have the hail of musket balls dwindle away, but it was mystifying. Indians could worry you to death when they stopped doing one thing, making you wonder what they would do next.

Warriors were loping from everywhere around the fort toward a copse of woods on the Kanawha River bluff, which seemed to be where their leaders were. The warriors trotted with swift ease, just at the edge of rifle range. Now and then one would yell, "Son of bitch Long Knife!" One warrior stopped and exposed his bare posterior to the fort. Several soldiers could not resist the target and fired at him, but nothing hit him. He laughed, adjusted his loincloth, and ran on. Justin shook his head, marveling at the audacity the insult had required. The warrior must have heard the rifle balls thrum past him and whicker through the brush. A wound received in such a pose would have been both agonizing and mortifying.

It made Case ponder on the degree of hatred and contempt those people must feel for the Virginians. That was a chilling thought, even so close after the heat of combat.

He heard a hubbub of loud talking near the gate of the fort, and looked down to see Captain McKee standing with his lieutenants and, to his astonishment, Nonhelema. One of the lieutenants was holding a long, slender pole from which hung a square of white cloth. The Indian woman stood erect and looked grim, in her plain deerhide tunic with moccasins and fringed gaiters, and she was holding a packet of paper. All the shooting had stopped, on both sides, and there was a sense of waiting. Justin saw that one wing of the fort's double gate was being swung open just enough to permit her passage. He guessed that McKee was sending her out to carry some of the messages she had read, or negotiate something.

He could see, beyond the field of stumps, a gathering of Indians whom he took to be the war chieftains. They were watching the fort with concentration. The gunsmoke had thinned and drifted off the field already, so details could be seen at a distance. Justin stood gingerly seeking protruding splinters with his fingertips and yanking them out, wincing. He could feel the warm blood begin to trickle down again from his temple and forehead. A few warriors had taken advantage of the lull to hurry about among the stumps and gullies and help remove their casualties, most of whom could walk with help. The fire-archer whom Case had shot was nowhere to be seen, though a tendril of smoke from his fire-bundle still rose and twirled near the stump he had used for cover.

Justin watched as the woman went out through the gate, preceded by the man with the white flag. Anyplace between the fort and the Indians out there was a dangerous place, and his feelings toward that woman had grown more complex and proprietary since the murders of her brother and kin. He felt that he had perhaps saved her life by hurling her out of harm's way in that awful moment. And he had watched in silent admiration and pity as she dealt with her grief. When she sat looking stricken and lost, his heart ached in empathy. When she sat staring with burning eyes at the white officers and soldiers, he had shared with her, he imagined, contempt for those who had let it happen or abetted it. When she tried to rise above her grief by forcing herself to be polite and cheerful, he was uplifted. When she lapsed into Christian prayers for solace, he felt his old religion well up in his soul. When she once got a bit drunk, uttering outbursts in the Shawnee language and physically shoving some officers away and glaring at them with her chin a-tremble, Justin was, even though embarrassed, able to feel her rage, as if it were whirling through his own spirit. Somewhere long ago he had read that in some ancient philosophy of China, one who saved another's life then became responsible for that life thenceforth forever. Such a responsibility seemed to have settled itself upon him, and it was a burden he was happy to assume. But it was his alone. She, it seemed, never condescended to acknowledge any kind of obligation between them. If anything, he felt sometimes that she resented him for having saved her from the murderers' bullets.

Now she was walking in her stately way out across that silenced battlefield, and Justin felt as if he were exposed to all that tense vulnerability with her; knew that some warrior's or soldier's pent-up hatred might cause a trigger to be pulled, and she would be caught in the open in the path of whirring bullets.

Damn such a world! he thought. *God guard the woman!*

A lieutenant came along the catwalk, stopping every few yards to explain: "Cap'n McKee sent the Indian lady out to tell them to go away. That, by God, this fort won't surrender while there's a man standing."

"And that's the truth, sir!" someone exclaimed.

"We whupped 'em here once, we'll do so ag'in!" a man nearby boasted. He was a man who had not been in the battle in the woods, but had only heard about it. His words irritated Justin, who reproved him: "Soldier, if they'd not run out of powder and lead that day, they'd have killed every last man of us. You'd best hope that peace woman can persuade them to draw off."

The soldier opened his sneering mouth to say something, then remembered that Case was one of the original veterans, and turned away to watch over the clearing.

The woman had been met far out in the field by a group of scalpshaven, fierce-looking men in war paint and glittering silver. Justin tried, but could scarcely imagine the tangle of emotions among those warriors out there, particularly the Shawnees. Some were bound to be her relatives. She and her brother had been among their most revered leaders. Cornstalk had been murdered in this very place. And now she lived here, among the soldiers who, the warriors believed, had murdered him. And she had come out to speak for the soldiers.

In a formal manner that baffled the scared and impatient soldiers along the parapet, the warrior chieftains sat on the ground in a semicircle before her, and a pipe was brought forth and lit from a bowl of embers. The pipe was passed from person to person. She sat on the ground with them. The soldier with the truce flag was left out, standing a few feet outside the conclave. Doubtless, he was scared sick.

Now and then the breeze brought the sound of their voices up from their place on the riverbank. The talk sounded calm. The woman showed the chieftains the pieces of paper and then, apparently, told them what each one said. Justin was watching intently, trying to tell—as well as he could from this distance—how the message was being taken.

For several minutes it seemed that no one was addressing the group. Justin could see her only in profile. That, and the distance, made it impossible to see how this was going for her.

Then the war chieftains seemed to be talking to each other, mouth to ear, around the semicircle. It was all taking a long time, and the soldiers and militiamen in the fort were getting restless.

"What's that Squawr bitch about?" somebody grumbled. "Selling us out?"

"Plottin' how t' git them Injens in here, bet ye!"

Justin wanted to turn and rebuke them, but he knew they were suspicious of her role only because she was Indian. To them, any Indian was treacherous. So he ignored them and watched her. He tried to believe that she was somehow swaying the chiefs and that she would save the fort from annihilation. It amazed him how much faith he wanted to place in that woman.

The chiefs now stood up. Nonhelema leaned forward and with effortless grace rose to her feet. Justin watched with awful anxiety as she turned away from the men and came walking toward the fort, her face an unreadable mask. The soldier with the white banner followed, looking as if only desperate pride kept him from bolting ahead of her to get back into the fort. The chieftains were striding back to their hidden camp on the bluff. After she came through the gate into the fort, the soldiers readied their weapons and waited for the shooting to resume.

But the afternoon shadows moved and the sun's light shifted on the confluence of rivers, and there was no shooting. The warriors were still everywhere to be seen on the margin of gunshot range, but were not putting themselves in place for attack. Bands of them were gathering and going out of sight down toward the Ohio.

After a while, Justin left the wall to go down and get his wounds tended, and to see if others needed help. The blood on his face had dried in the wind, but the splinters stung fiercely. He went to the fort's kitchen shelter, which was serving now as infirmary because of its hot-water kettle. Justin was surprised to see Nonhelema's daughter tending to the wounded, a few men who had been nicked by lead or splinters. The pretty young woman made a weedy-smelling poultice in a hot rag, and when he held it against the side of his face, all the pain subsided. Using English-made tweezers, she quickly extracted the splinters. Blood flowed again, but she ran some sort of smooth stone over the wounds and the bleeding stopped almost at once. Then she spread a salve, smelling of bear fat and herbs, over the area. All the discomfort was gone. Her touch was gentle, her breath musky and sweet.

During her ministrations, she was quiet and grim, and often she stared toward the orderly room where her mother had gone with the captain and other officers. Justin could see that she was agitated, and angry or scared, but she gave no clue. He asked, "Miss Fani, do you think they listened to her? Do you think they'll draw off?"

All she answered was, "Are they to believe the words of your governor? Go, now. You will heal soon."

"Do you need help? I can doctor a bit."

"No," she said. "Not many hurt."

He was drinking from a dipper at the rain barrel when an ensign summoned him to the orderly room. The captain peered at his lacerated face and asked, "Are you fit to write, Case? We've urgent messages to send out. Most urgent."

Nonhelema was in the room still, and she appeared to be in an awful state. Her eyes were steely. Her chin was crumpling, her mouth was changing continually from sneer to grimace, and she was breathing rapid, shallow breaths. Her hands were clenched in fists, and she was rapping the knuckles of one against those of the other.

As the captain dictated messages to Fort Pitt and to the Virginia Assembly and Governor Henry, Justin began to understand her agitation.

The chiefs had heard her out politely. She had read to them in translation the governor's peace overture, and the captain's refusal to negotiate the surrender of his fort—his promise to fight to the last man, in battle or siege. The chiefs had not scoffed or insulted her, but had made it plain by their demeanor that they were only indulging her. They had said that they would consider quitting their assault on the fort, but she had detected a mirthful falseness in that reply, as if it were a joke among them.

And then, in parting, she had overheard some Mingo chieftains who perhaps had heeded her message. They wondered if this fort with its hundred soldiers might indeed be too hard to break. She had heard them speak of the settlements up the Kanawha at the Greenbrier.

If that was their intent, it was chilling. That region was heavily settled but almost unguarded, being so far back from the frontier. The fort there, a rotting old structure called Donally's Fort, was one log house within a palisade wall. If this force of three or four hundred warriors swept up into Greenbrier without warning, many innocents might suffer and die.

Captain McKee's urgent concern now was getting an alarm to Greenbrier. He dictated a brief note of warning, and then went out and called for messengers who knew the long, hard route up the streams and over the mountains, and who would be willing to venture out through the infested Indian country to take the message.

Near sunset, the captain dictated messages to General Hand at Pittsburgh and to authorities in Virginia, and Justin was writing them for him when an uproar—gunshots, shouts, war trills, and the bawling of cattle—broke the evening stillness. At once, everyone was up and out of the orderly room, snatching up guns as they went. It seemed a strange time of day for the Indians to be resuming their attack. The gates had already been shut and barred. As Justin scampered up the ladder onto the parapet, he was aware that Nonhelema had come out, too, and was climbing up after him.

In the golden glow of a glorious sunset, a bewildering and pitiful turmoil was taking place near the river's edge. Warriors afoot and on horseback were racing alongside and amid a stampede of beef cattle, shooting and spearing them. As part of the herd tried to run up the river bluff away from the fort, mounted warriors headed them off and turned them back, until the whole slaughter was contained in a milling swirl within plain view of the fort.

These were Nonhelema's own cattle. This was the herd she had brought when she came to take refuge with the Americans. It was the rest of her wealth, all that she had been able to bring from her home. It was what was left of her herd after feeding the soldiers at the fort.

"Lookee," someone yelled. "They're torchin' her house!"

They were. Indians with firebrands were running about, setting outbuildings and brush piles ablaze. Justin could hardly stand to glance over at her. Her face gleamed like copper in the last sun rays. Her mouth and chin were set like rock as she watched the slaughter and the uprushing flames, the dark smoke. But her hands, clenched on a palisade post, were strained and gnarled with the desperation of that grip. Gleaming on the skin of her cheekbones was a stream of tears.

They were killing the cattle to help starve the soldiers in the fort. But it was more than that. They could have done that when they first arrived. This was a deliberate affront to her.

Now a Shawnee warrior rode closer to the fort, dangerously within range of the soldiers' rifles, pointing at Nonhelema with one hand. He had been among those in the conclave with her this afternoon.

"Nameetha!" he shouted. "Elder sister! For your help of enemy, this we do! *Eheh! Nee puc a chee!"* And he turned his horse and rode back out of range, back to the slaughter.

"Ah-heh!" she shouted after him. *"Kee-motchee-lenni-wa-we-anneh!"* Her voice broke. "Young brother, you are a bad man!"

The officers and troops were preoccupied with the rampage of cattle slaughter and fire setting, out there in the gathering dusk, and didn't notice that Nonhelema had left the palisade.

"I doubt they're really quittin' us," a lieutenant was saying to Captain McKee. "I say they'll try t' move up on us after dark."

"They don't fight at night," the captain replied. "Come daybreak, though, every man jack in this fort'll be here on these walls, even the sickly and wounded. I want a detail molding bullets, through the first watch. I want every man so laden with balls, he can just barely climb up here in the morning!"

"Ooo, Cap'n. Sir, that's a description of meself! Somedays I can just barely lift mine out o' bed!" He was a clownish, brawny soldier from Botetourt, and everybody in earshot laughed. They were all relieved after the shooting, a little light-headed, but uncertain what the Indians would have in store for them tomorrow.

"Goddamn those savages," the captain muttered. "All our beef out there to rot! I've a mind to send out parties to drag some in after dark for butchering. Got to save some of it."

No voices commented on that. The notion of going outside the walls at night with hundreds of Indians around was too dreadful; there surely would be no volunteers, and probably few here who would even obey a direct order to go. But besieged without the beef, they would be starved to submission in days. The truth was that without the Indian woman's herd, they would have been starving by now.

Justin, thinking about her and the awful grief he had seen in her face, turned and saw she was no longer in sight. But then he heard her voice, down near the orderly room or the commissary. Her voice, but as he had never heard it before: yelling, but shrill, sobbing now, breaking now, sounds such as he had heard only once before—when he'd seen two wenches fighting in a tavern. As others began to hear and turn, he heard also sounds like breaking glass and slammed crates or tumbling furniture. Justin was alarmed for her, afraid she had gone down into one of the cabins and been attacked by some Indian-hating wretch, as her brother had been.

He saw that down in the shadowy compound, the commissary door was standing open. And then she appeared in the doorway, charging out, her arms loaded with something, and she set off across the dirt yard, keening fiercely, toward the door of the interpreter's room. She shouted her daughter's name and then carried on furiously in the Shawnee tongue as she lurched along, and the door to their room opened from inside.

"Goddamn 'er!" the captain exclaimed, pushing past Justin and scrambling down the ladder. "She's broke into the liquor!" He went sprinting toward her room yelling, "Stop, y' bitch! You can't ... That's ..." Some of the men on the catwalk were starting to yell and swear; others were laughing.

Her door was shut and she was inside before Captain McKee got to it, and he began hammering at it with the side of his fist, then kicking it with his boot, yelling all the while.

It was doing no good. Some of the men were down the ladder now, trotting over to watch the ruckus. Justin, his head swirling with astonishment and pity and anger and embarrassment, had not moved from the catwalk. The captain yelled for someone to bring an ax to break the door in. At the same time, a lieutenant cried out, "Stay at your posts! Keep your lookout! This c'd be a trick!"

That warning had a chilling effect. Every frontier soldier knew stories about distractions and ruses the savages had used to put sentries off guard. Immediately, most of the men turned back to watch out over the dusky field, where slaughtered cattle lay among the stumps and smoke billowed off the flaming outbuildings; after this disturbance, there might be an armed warrior behind every dead cow or tree stump or slash pile.

A soldier with an ax ran up to the door of the Indian women's cabin, and the captain stood aside and told him to break it in.

The soldier struck one loud blow, drew back, hit the thick wooden portal again, and was aiming another low when the door suddenly swung inward.

The Indian woman stood there with a bottle in one hand and one of her elegant little silver pistols in the other, pointed at the captain. All the clamor suddenly fell still.

Even this far away, up on the catwalk, Justin heard her say: "We are drinking to our losses. Whitemen are not invited! Leave my door alone."

It was a memorable statement, clear and plain, given just as the last blush of the setting sun faded to lilac beyond the junction of rivers.

She added: "Or I might like to shoot a McKee at last."

It was plain enough even for the choleric captain. He stepped back, signaled the soldiers back, tipped his tricorn hat.

"Good evening, ma'am. The spirits are compliments of the Virginia gov'ment."

The door shut with a resounding thud. Soldiers everywhere stood in quiet contemplation of what they had just witnessed. In many a head there were forming stories that grandchildren someday would hear.

And from inside the little hut, muffled by the log walls, came a sound that made their napes tingle: two women's voices, shrilling and pulsating in the mourners' trill that sounded so like the savages' war cry, the pulsating call of fury or grief.

The next morning, there was not an Indian to be seen outside the fort. Wary militiamen were sent out to salvage what they could of Nonhelema's slaughtered herd.

The runners Captain McKee had sent up the Kanawha returned the following evening, exhausted and dejected. They were near to tears. They had not been able to get through or around the Indians, who were traveling on trails up both banks of the river. The messengers were abject in their apologies for the time they had lost, and afraid they would be faulted for lack of courage. "But they was so thick on that trail, Cap'n, you couldn't ha' passed 'less you was a proper Injen yourself," one lamented.

That statement suggested the solution to the problem. The messengers would have to disguise themselves as warriors. A little knowledge of any of the Indian tongues would help.

In the fort, there were few men who could pass for Indians even in dim light, and even fewer who knew any of the languages.

The choice narrowed down quickly to two men who had a little of the language, and the courage and resourcefulness to run the mission.

They were tough woodsmen named Pryor and Hammond, weathered and wiry. Unfortunately, only Hammond was dark-haired and swarthy. Pryor was light-haired, almost blond, and fair of complexion.

Nonhelema, who had drunk herself into a stupor after the slaughter of her herd, had sobered herself and was in the orderly room, depressed, head aching. But she listened to the officers, then said: "Warriors on the path see sharp. These messengers could not pass. They must be made to look true. I can do it." She left the room and soon returned, with her daughter, carrying bundles and several small jars. In the bundles were Shawnee-made moccasins, leggings, breechclouts, and ornaments. In the jars were bear grease, vermillion and other tints of paint, and a dark dye made from walnut hulls.

"You," she said to Pryor, "you must stain yourself all over with this *nippee-pimmee*. You must shave off all that yellow hair. From your head and also your body. Also you must pull out all your eyebrow hairs." The man looked astonished. She reached up and grabbed a fistful of hair on the crown of his head. "Leave this much, for scalplock, and I will try to make it dark enough with soot."

The other man, Hammond, laughed at Pryor's discomfiture. But then she turned on him. "You shave, too. No Indian man has such hair growing like that. Eyebrows also. You men go. Come back here all brown. Then I will paint you, and make holes in your ears." They started to protest. "You will wear earbobs. Only white men hang nothing in their ears."

Within two hours, Hammond and Pryor were unrecognizable. Justin had seen countless Indians, of many tribes, and felt that he could detect anything false in the person, attire, or equipment of anyone impersonating a warrior, but both of these men appeared so genuine that it was eerie to look at them. Nonhelema had even managed to put an awl through their earlobes, run silver wire through, stop the blood, and even subdue the pain with some herbal salve, so that the two couriers seemed almost vain of their new decorations. They were ready to set out, faces painted, pouches and bedrolls properly slung, their written messages rolled and hidden in seams. The captain shook his head and laughed. "Only trouble I can see now is how ye get in Donally's Fort without gettin' shot as Injens!"

"Warsh off this stain in the Greenbrier, I reckon," Hammond laughed.

The Indian woman was not so jovial. "Go as if you are as plain as whitemen. Pray not to be seen unless you cannot prevent it. I say this because if you stop among those people they will discover you by your talk.

"One other thing. All you white people walk like ducks. Show me now you can walk like real people." She made them walk back and forth across the floor with their toes turned in. "As soon as you go from here, never forget your feet. You will be known to be false if you waddle by like a damned duck. They will catch you if they find duck tracks on their trail."

Justin expected her to ease up and smile at her two creations, and wish them a warm farewell. But her eyes were cold, and if they hoped for her blessing, they got none. When they had gone, she leveled a hard, sad gaze at the captain. "I do this only for the women and children up there," she said.

Justin thought he understood her meaning. If the messengers got through, innocent whites might be spared. But he knew that something else must be lying on her heart. If the messengers got through and a defense was ready at the fort up in Greenbrier, likely more of her warrior kin might die. Even though they had slaughtered her cattle, they were still her people.

Pryor and Hammond were no sooner gone than a cry came down from the north blockhouse: "Boats comin' down! Eight. Ten. Boats comin' down!"

The fort was always watching for supplies and reinforcements from Fort Pitt, but was almost always disappointed. Now here came a flotilla of plank pirogues, heavy-laden with kegs and bundles and armed men, nuzzling up to the landing, the red and green stripes of the Virginia flag hanging from a staff in the bow of the first vessel. Captain McKee strode down the slope, past still-smoldering outbuildings and the half-butchered carcasses of Katy's cattle herd. Justin was on his heels.

"Look there!" McKee exclaimed. "Must be more'n a hundred men! Why, we can chase them goddamned savages up th' Kanawha and get 'em ourselves now!"

Justin recognized the tall, red-haired man who was just now leaping ashore from the bow of the first pirogue. It was the young Virginian boss of Dunmore's scouts, whom he had met four years before. He had stood with this man and Arbuckle and Simon Girty looking over Nonhelema's Town. Clark.

Yes, that was it. Arbuckle's friend. George Rogers Clark. The Ohio Company surveyor, the cocky one. This could be an answer to

McKee's prayers. But Justin had a feeling that it wasn't to work out that way. What ever did work out in this accursed place?

Clark made it very clear that he was not here to reinforce or supply Fort Randolph, and certainly not to chase Indians into the mountains. He didn't even let his 150 men come up to the fort. They got out of the boats to relieve themselves and stretch their legs, rest their rowing arms, and doze in the sun, but they had orders to stand by the convoy and be ready to continue on down the Ohio. He wouldn't say where he was going, or why, and Captain McKee was ready to burst with disappointment and anger. This was the last outpost on the Ohio. Where in the hell could Clark be going in defense of the Virginia frontier with his regiment, if not here? How could he not take this chance to go up and save the Greenbrier settlers?

Clark went up to the fort and sat for a while in the orderly room to take a glass of whiskey and pay his respects to Nonhelema. She seemed pleased to see him. The two talked quietly while Clark let the captain read his public orders from Governor Patrick Henry.

Lieutenant Colo. George Rogers Clark—

> *You are to proceed without Loss of Time to inlist Seven Companies of men officered in the usual manner to act as Militia under your Orders. They are to proceed to Kentucky & there to obey such orders & Directions as you shall give them for three Months after their arrival at that place, but to receive pay &c. in case they remain on Duty a longer Time.*
>
> *You are empowered to raise these men in any County in the commonwealth and the County Lieutenants respectively are requested to give you all possible assistance in that Business.*
>
> *Given under my Hand at Wmsburg*
> *January 2ᵈ, 1778*

P. Henry

WILLIAMSBURGH, JAN. 2ᴅ, 1778
Genl Hand, Pittsburgh

Sir—

> *I have to request that you will please to furnish Major G. R. Clark with boats sufficient for conveying seven companys of militia on an expedi-*

tion of great consequence. Besides the immediate advantages arising from the success of it, the consequential benefits will be many. And I must entreat you, Sir, to give Major Clark every assistance which he may want . . . You will be amply compensated by the major's success, which I assure you I am most anxiously concerned for. I refer you to that gentleman for an explanation of the errand on which he goes. It is needless to inform you how necessary it is that the whole affair should be kept impenetrably secret.

I have the honor to be, Sir, Y^r obedient hbl^e Servt

P. Henry

P.S. I should have consulted you on the expedition but time would not permit. I direct the Major to get his powder & lead from your quarter . . .

P. H.

"By God!" McKee exclaimed, "damned if I can get anything to supply this fort with! And General Hand gives you anything you ask for?"

"He didn't have much to give us, Cap'n. Don't get your guts in a knot. Now here's my endorsement from the assembly, as well."

WILLIAMSBURG JANRY 3, 1778
TO GEORGE ROGERS CLARK ESQ.

Sir,

As some Indian Tribes to the westward of the Mifsisippi have lately without any provocation mafsacred many of the Inhabitants of the frontiers of this Commonwealth in the most cruel & barbarous manner & it is intended to revenge the Injury & punish the Aggrefsors, by carrying the War into their own country, we congratulate you upon your Appointment to conduct so important an Enterprize in which we most heartily wish you Succefs and we have no doubt but some further reward in Lands in the Country will be given to the Volunteers who shall engage in this Service . . . for this we think you may safely confide in the Justice & Generosity of the Virginia Afsembly.

G. Wythe
G. Mason
Th. Jefferson

Captain McKee read Clark's letters and handed them back. "What tribes, clear out there?" he asked. "When did all that happen? Where? Does this mean you're going out as far as the Mississippi? Damn it, Major, we need people *here*! We don't even *have* any 'inhabitants' out there, do we?"

"Cap'n," Clark replied, soft and slow, as if making something plain for a child. "I should like to tell you just what my orders are, and just where I'm going, but the assemblymen put me under secrecy. A failure of confidence could be so hazardous, in fact, that only those signatories here, and Governor Henry, know the whole plan. The rest of the assembly, like you, Cap'n, will know more after the mission is done. There are Loyalist sentiments, as y' know, and so important things need be kept close. I've had considerable trouble recruiting men for this mission because of men with such sentiments back yonder."

"So ye can't tell me your plan. But ain't that all made up, about the massacres out there? If y'll excuse my suspicious nature, sir, this sounds t' me like some invented excuse to go adventuring. It's to stake claims, ain't it?"

A look of annoyance crossed Clark's face, but then he put on a sly smile and slowly shook his head. "By the Old Dominion charter, Cap'n, remember Virginia extends as far as they can reach."

Nonhelema was watching Clark closely, and Justin could see that many thoughts and feelings were passing through her.

Captain McKee flung up his hands, and growled: "All right, you've got important things to do. But goddamn it, sir, this doesn't tell me why you can't take a few weeks to help us aid Greenbrier!"

"Captain, sincerely I would like to put myself and men to the pursuit of that war party. But the purpose I've been put to, I'm not at liberty to disclose, but you may trust my word, it will serve better to defend our whole frontier than anything I could do for you here. Take my solemn word on that, and let me be on my way. If your warning gets to Greenbrier, God willing, they'll save themselves. Now, Captain, if you have able men to spare, I'd be delighted to sign them on. I'm not up to half what I need. As you well know, manpower's all too scarce."

"That, sir, isn't even a poor jest! You have no authority to take men from my command! I've got too damned few here as it is!"

"My problem, too, Cap'n. This was to be a mission for seven companies and I've scarcely got three. I hope some gents will have more waiting for me at the mouth of the Kentucke. I am sorry I can't stay and help. But I can't. You'll know why not, by and by."

He turned to Nonhelema. "Ma'am, it was a pleasure to see you. My condolences on your losses. If ever I may be of service . . ."

Then he left the fort and strode down the slope, yelling in a voice as loud as a trumpet, ordering his men back into their boats.

Captain McKee ranted as the little fleet of militiamen moved away down the Ohio, oars rising and falling with vigor. "Isn't he in a hurry to get out of here! Afraid th' Injens are still around, I guess. How's it come Fort Pitt outfits cowards t' go clear out o' the country, but won't send flints, food, or fighting men to its own outpost right here? Damn that Gen'r'l Hand! Damn that Colonel Clark! If'n it wasn't fer his rank, I'd o' whipped that craven dandy up th' Kanawha! Or shamed 'im into action!"

Justin didn't believe that McKee was anywhere near the truth, or that Clark was afraid to fight. The man was up to something important enough to have Governor Henry's blessing on it, and it obviously was important enough to be kept secret.

Justin had noticed something that Captain McKee hadn't: In his brief talk with Nonhelema, Clark had asked her a few questions in a low voice. Justin had overheard the name *Kaskaskia*. Even if McKee had heard the name, he probably would not have known what it meant. But Justin did.

It was a river flowing into the Mississippi, named after an Indian band, and also the name of a French settlement on the Mississippi. Between that and the letter from the assembly, it was clear that Clark was taking troops to the Mississippi. Why would he be taking troops to the Mississippi?

Nonhelema would know about the tribes out there. She probably knew about the French people out there. Her old friend George Morgan had done trading business out there, long ago, and she had been his interpreter.

Justin leaned back and did some pondering. So much desperate business was going on, over such vast distances. General Washington's long war in the East against the Red Coats. Spies and secret missions everywhere. Death and terror. Indian tribes divided in their loyalties. Americans divided Tory against rebel. Relatives on opposing sides, like Captain William McKee here and Alexander McKee the turncoat, who had a son by this woman Nonhelema and now was on the other side of the conflict. The British governor-general in Detroit, said to be paying Indians for the scalps of Americans. Captain Daniel Boone, a leader and town builder in central Kentucky reportedly captured by the Shawnees at a salt lick, more than two dozen men of his town caught with him. Captain Arbuckle at home in Virginia reporting to the government. The Red Coat army surrendered by General Burgoyne in New York . . .

All that great, distant shuttle and weaving of fortunes, learned of through wisps of news that come up or down the rivers or along the Indian trails, Justin sometimes pondered. He did it now, his imagination and reason going as far as they could. But here he sat, in a backwoods fort that was like a prison controlled by the Indians around it, a place stinking of piss and excrement, unbathed soldiery, and rotting beef carcasses. Fear, anger, and ignorance hung over the place thicker than smoke.

And also hanging over the whole place was something like a spell, a miasma of ill spirit. Too many people had died violently here; and thus, it was not a fit place to live. He fancied sometimes that the battle of 1774 had first infested this place with too many ghosts. Then many men dead of smallpox. And now that Cornstalk and his three fellow victims lay in their graves outside the fort—attended by the grief of his sister, who still lived here, an outcast from her own people—the spell upon the place seemed poisonous. Four militiamen had been taken back to Virginia to stand trial for the murders, and she had warned Captain Arbuckle when he left that if those four were not condemned by the whiteman's court in Virginia, he should no more expect or claim her friendship. "I remember that you did not kill me or my brother on the battleground," she had said, "but you let them kill my brother when he was here in peace. You saw them kill unarmed men. By your word, they can be condemned. If Virginia does not condemn them, I will doubt I should ever have helped Virginia."

These days, the bad spirit of all that, and the slaughter of Nonhelema's cattle herd by her own people, made Justin hate the very name of this misnamed place. *Point Pleasant?* he thought. *Nay, Point Wretched!*

Then, somewhere in the fort, a squeak was followed by a squawk, then a few jiggling notes, shouts, and hand claps.

Justin glanced over at the slumped figure of Nonhelema, saw her raise her head and straighten up. A spark glimmered in those eyes that had been so dull and dark. The beginnings of a smile, and she was now nodding her head slightly.

He had heard it said, by people who had heard it from other people, that when she was in Pittsburgh she spent much time in the homes of the traders and the officers and government agents where musical evenings were held, with violins, flutes, dulcimers, and the like. It was a joke among the McKees that the woman was "a fool for a whiteman's instrument." They would smirk and then say, "Musical, of course."

Often he had heard her singing softly to herself as she sewed. And some mornings he had heard her singing prayer songs to the sunrise, poignant songs of declining notes, songs of her own people, so remarkably different from the quick, lilting intricacies of the whiteman's instrumental pieces that it was hard to think of them as music. But now he surreptitiously watched her as the fiddle music transformed her. He remembered his tidewater boyhood, his father teaching violin, spelling, and mathematics to the sons and daughters of the well-to-do. To think of the great difference in her tribal world and the Virginia Colony of his own origins—and yet their lives had converged here in this prison of dirt, desperation, and grief. And for a moment, he fancied their heads were like two beads on a string—connected by that thin strand of fiddle music passing through their ears.

That night, lying in his blanket, Justin prayed. He prayed for deliverance of the people of the Greenbrier settlements. He prayed that the Indian woman would be favored by her god, whichever, and that she should have no more brutal losses like the ones she had suffered so recently. Her brother and other kin, her little son, her livestock and wealth. And worst of all, the loss of her Shawnee people's devotion.

—Captain Matthew Arbuckle—
To General Edward Hand
Greenbrier, June 2, 1778

Sir:

> *I was unfortunate anugh after my return from Williamsburg to this place in a persuit after a party of Indians to receive a wound in my knee occasioned by a fall on some rocks, which disabled me from returning to*

my post as soon as I expected . . . I shall now set off in a few days &
thought absolutely necessary to aquaient you, in the way of the accts recd
from Capt McKee ye 27th last month.

 They found themselves surrounded on all quarters & a smart fire on
the fort insued. Capt McKee sent out the Grenadier Squaw to speake to
her friends, with a speech from the governor; they made a pretense of
making peace.

 The only thing they learned from Ketty, she says there was three
hundred, that they Intended up the Kenawa, and the garrison they
would have; after telling the people in the garrison they might as well
surrender, for they had killed all their cattle (which is actually so) . . . I
must therefore beg the garrison may get proper supply in time, otherwise
we shall be greatly distressed, Cap McKee dispatched two soldiers to give
notice of the approach of the Indians on this place which passed them at
the Meadows within 20 miles, the people were in the utmost confusion,
everyone flying to forts, & no men imbodyed here, on ye 29th May they at-
tacked Col. Donnallys fort guarded with only 25 men, who made a brave
diffence from sunrise till 3 oclock in the evening when Col. Sam Lewis
& myself with a party of 66 men, determined to relieve them marched up
fired on the enemy who gave way on every side & let us pass in every man
unhurt. Seventeen of the Indians were killed dead on the spot, they con-
tinued their siege till night when they halld nine of their men away, the
rem'd we sculped in the morning, they came well aquipped with pack
horses and driving cattle, but the campaign I believe is partly broake
up, no mischief has been done since the battle, three men were killed that
day & one shot through a port hole in the fort as their attack was violent.

 I am your Excln^t Ob^t Servt

Matthew Arbuckle

 N.B. *Our Garrison is scarse of flints please to send some by the first*
opportunity, we have also been disappointed in getting our medison from
Wmsburg. I hope you send some.

M.A.

An Indian boy one morning appeared on the bank of the Kanawha, standing in plain sight but beyond gunshot. Behind him, lurking
in the riverbank brush, were three or four Indian men, apparently the
ones who had brought the boy. It appeared that he was waiting to be

seen, but he would not come closer to the fort when the officers tried to wave him up. They suspected that the youth was a decoy and would not let their men go out for him. Instead, they fetched Nonhelema from her quarters.

Even at such a distance, she knew who he was, and her face brightened.

"It is my son come to see me. My son Morgan."

"Bring him up," said the captain, seeming doubtful.

"He will not come. Fani and I will go down there."

They walked out and down among the charred ruins and the stinking carcasses of the cattle, and embraced him warmly.

Every time Nonhelema saw her son, she was as impressed by his solemnity as by his masculine aspect. He had his father's high brow and wide-set eyes, but it was plain in his demeanor that he aspired to be a warrior. He was happy to see his mother and sister, but remained grave and not demonstrative.

The men who had brought him down were Delawares. They had been sent down by Killbuck. They had very troubling news, none of which had come yet to Fort Randolph.

George Morgan had quit as Indian agent at Pittsburgh, in protest against the American government's new and devious Indian policy, which exploited the friendship of the Delawares. And Chief White Eyes, who had been the Americans' staunchest Delaware ally, was dead because of that new Indian policy. Killbuck had been elected chief to succeed White Eyes, and was trying to remain true to the Americans, but some of his chiefs were defecting to the British side of the conflict.

The particulars were confusing, as the warriors sat and tried to tell her about them. Her son had written them down in a summary, which was to have been sent or smuggled to her at the fort in the event that this face-to-face meeting might not have been achieved.

In the latest treaty meeting at Fort Pitt, the American commissioners had written some tricky conditions into the treaty paper, aided by dishonest translators. By those conditions, the neutral Delawares were required to let American troops pass through their country to attack British-allied Indians farther northwest. The treaty also said the Delaware chiefs must cooperate by providing guides and selling provisions to such expeditions, and by allowing the construction of an American fort on the Indian side of the Ohio. These conditions had seriously compromised the Delawares' neutrality and created resentment among the other tribes.

It was because of this treaty that George Morgan had quit his post at Pittsburgh and returned to his estate in New Jersey.

And it was because of this treaty that the great White Eyes was dead.

The officers of an expedition from Fort Pitt had required White Eyes to escort and guide them through Delaware country. The officers had reported that White Eyes died of a fever on the route. But it was known by some of the Indians that the "fever" had made a bullet hole in the back of his neck.

Killbuck had sent Nonhelema's son and these other couriers to inform her of this unhappy state of affairs, which he believed to be the full undoing of all her peacemaking efforts. Killbuck doubted that she would have known of it, out where she was. Certainly the officers at Fort Pitt would not have wanted her to know of it.

She sat among the trees with the messengers, feeling utterly empty. Down the bank, the river was low, the shore a dismal stretch of caked mud. When she looked up toward the fort, she saw it standing there, squarish and ugly, in the middle of the devastated bottomland surrounded by stumps, charred ruins, desiccated and flyblown cattle carcasses, and weeds. The whine and drone of blowflies was ceaseless, everywhere. Up on the parapet of the fort she could see soldiers staring down. And there was the captain himself, with a spyglass to his eye, watching her confer with the messengers. She suddenly felt such a revulsion toward soldiers that she shut her eyes and clenched her teeth.

The messengers told her that Chief Killbuck was going to take a plea to George Morgan in New Jersey, asking him to help the Delawares. "Killbuck prays that Morgan can ask General Washington, or the Congress, to correct the treaty, and let the Delawares be neutral again, as they want to be."

"I would wish to go with them and make that plea also," she said. "But I cannot leave this place. Not until Captain Arbuckle returns from Virginia to resume his command. My concerns here are not finished until then."

Morgan said, "My father—" It took Nonhelema a moment to realize that he was speaking of Colonel Morgan, because he had never before referred to him as his father. "—asked Chief Killbuck to send him the orphan sons of White Eyes, to be educated there in the Princeton school. Also Killbuck's son."

She thought about that, at first with a rush of a kindly feeling toward Morgan. *Probably it is his impulse,* she thought, *because of his shame for what the Americans have done.*

Then she thought, *How good would it be to raise those boys to think like whitemen, who do things in such ways as they do?*

The boy added, "He offered also to put me in the great school."

Her scalp prickled, and she looked at him. If George Morgan raised him and educated him, he could become a very important American with many advantages. A son of the great George Morgan, educated at the school. Obviously his son, and what an advantage that would be in his life.

But how, she thought, *could he call him his own son while he lives there with his white wife, who surely doesn't even know Morgan had this son by me?*

She said: "Do you wish to go there and be educated?"

The boy looked at her intently for a moment, all solemnity. Then he made a face like someone ready to vomit. And then both he and Fani began giggling and whooping.

"Nigeah," he said, regaining his gravity at last, "I had enough of that in Brother Zeisberger's mission school. I would rather be a maggot in one of those cows up there than be in another whiteman's school."

When Captain Arbuckle arrived down the Kanawha from Greenbrier, dismounted inside the gate, and walked toward the orderly room, he moved with a severe limp. In the hubbub surrounding his return from Virginia, he looked unexpectedly grim. He greeted Captain McKee and the other officers with handshakes and a palm slapped on a shoulder, but it was plain that he wasn't bringing glad news. The garrison had already taken note of the small size of his entourage. He had not returned with a company of reinforcements, as they had hoped, nor had he ridden in leading drovers with beef cattle. Here he was instead with a mere squad, and a few packhorses toting some kegs and bundles.

He winced as he sat down at the table. He greeted Justin, saying he had sorely missed his penmanship. He asked for a bottle of his favorite French brandy to ease the discomfort of his leg after the hard ride. "I think there were six bottles here when I left." It had been his personal stock, a gift from General Hand.

"Ah, yes. But it's gone, Cap'n," McKee said. "The, um, the squaw drank it all."

Arbuckle sat with his mouth agape. "She what? No one was supposed to touch that! Who gave it to her?"

And so Captain Arbuckle heard the story about her binge of brandy and grief. He already knew how she had sobered up in time to disguise the messengers who saved the Greenbrier settlements. The messengers themselves, Pryor and Hammond, had told him about that when he saw them at Greenbrier.

"Here's news for ye, gents, about this place. We'll abandon it when our enlistments are up. Government's decided these militia outposts aren't much good for defending the colonies. Congress aims to build a line of forts farther east and man 'em with army regulars. Use 'em as bases for expeditions against Indians and British. A big change in the strategy. Delawares made an alliance with th' government, going to let us build a fort right in their midst, up on the Tuscarawas."

It was quiet in the room for a while after that. Justin thought of it, of this cursed place. *Good riddance,* he thought. On the other hand, this had been the most important place in his life.

Arbuckle went on: "This'll be the last post for me. When this place shuts down, gentlemen, I am going home and saying farewell to soldiering. I've had enough of it; I'm needed at home."

The officers had been telling Captain Arbuckle the details of the Indian woman's role here, and of her losses. There was a grudging agreement among them that she should be called the savior of both Fort Randolph and the Greenbrier settlements. But as they talked of her, there hung in the smoky room an unspoken awareness of her absence. It was strange, in Justin's opinion, that Arbuckle had not looked for her on his arrival, nor had she come out to greet him.

Gradually, it dawned on Justin that Arbuckle and the woman were deliberately avoiding each other. Deep in his heart, he believed he understood. Neither had expected to see the other again, surely. And something very important was unfinished.

Finally, she came in to finish it. She appeared in the doorway, silhouetted by the glare of daylight from the stark, unshaded parade ground behind her. Some of the officers moved aside from the table. Captain Arbuckle stood up awkwardly, favoring his leg, and dipped his head, a most rudimentary bow. She came forward, chin high, eyes very intense, looking straight into his. Justin was hoping the captain would praise her for all she had done, and perhaps offer to seek compensation for the loss of her cattle—anything to acknowledge her sacrifices.

But she gave him no time for anything like that. She said: "In Virginia, is it true they put Captain Hall and the other murderers before the judge council?"

"Yes, ma'am." He took a deep breath and stood straighter.

"Did you point at them and say they murdered my people?"

"Uh, well, I . . . I wasn't actually *at* the trial . . ."

"You could have been, yes?"

"Well, with difficulty . . ."

She said, "Something was more important to you than that?"

"No, but I . . ."

"Then did no man point at them and say they did the murders?"

"There were no witnesses there, ma'am."

"What, then, Arbuckle?"

He looked down at his hand on the tabletop. "They, uh, they were let go, ma'am."

Silence filled the room, this room that had reverberated with the murderers' gunshots. Justin could hardly bear to look at her or the captain.

If I could have been in that court! he thought.

When she finally had taken enough deep breaths to speak, she said, "You have a curse on you, Arbuckle. Remember the dream I told you."

And then, as if she had been only a spirit, she was gone. Within minutes, there was no trace of her year's residence here, except the charred ruins of her little cabin, the bones of her cattle scattered down by the riverside, and the bones of Cornstalk, Elinipsico, Red Hawk, and Old Yie in the ground.

And a strip of deerhide fringe that had fallen from her skirt hem. Justin saw it on the floor and picked it up. It was the only trace of her.

But the mother and daughter had hardly ridden out of sight before the soldiers were spreading and embellishing a rumor that the Shawnee brother and sister chiefs had left a great curse upon the place where the Kanawha flowed into the Ohio.

That evening Justin sat cleaning his rifle, charging the flash pan with fresh powder, secreting a few days' traveling rations in his necessary pouch, and plotting a way to assassinate Captain Matthew Arbuckle and to vanish into the wilderness.

In his mind, he stabbed the captain in the back or slit his throat while they were alone in the orderly room. Or he shot him through an open door. Or he poisoned him with medicine from the apothecary chest.

But killing the captain and then getting safely out of a guarded fort seemed impossible. He did not mean to give up his own life to take Arbuckle's. He needed some way to do it without getting killed himself. If he managed to escape from the fort, he would be a hunted man. Then he probably would be killed by Indians or die in the wilderness. He imagined killing Arbuckle and following the Grenadier Squaw, but he didn't even know where she had gone.

And then he thought, *She's a peacemaker. She would despise me for thinking of murder. If she wanted him dead, she could have shot him as she left today, with one of those pistols of hers, in the very room where her brother was murdered.*

Justin laid his rifle across his knees and probed in his bag for the musket ball that he had dug out of the wall of the orderly room, the ball he was sure had gone through Cornstalk. He rolled it between the thumb and fingers of his left hand, feeling how misshapen it was by the impact. He remembered the roar of gunshots and the choking smoke in the room and he remembered the wrenching jolt he had suffered in tackling that mighty woman.

He remembered also that once Arbuckle had spared her life.

And he remembered, too, that Arbuckle had tried to get into the room and prevent the murders.

Still, his failure to witness against the murderers in Virginia seemed adequate reason to kill him.

Justin sighed and leaned his rifle against the wall, deciding that he just didn't have in him what was required of an assassin. He was amazed that he had even been thinking such thoughts. He sat back to lean against the wall with his eyes closed, running his fingertips lightly over his cheeks and temples, feeling the old, rough scars from the smallpox and from the oak splinters he had received in the battle.

There was a great hollowness in his chest. The woman was gone, and he could imagine no circumstances that would ever bring their paths to cross again. This fort was to be abandoned. All troops would go home to Virginia. He himself would probably have to soldier again, but it would be with Washington in the East, not anywhere out here where she would be. Or he would go on and become a physician, if such opportunity arose. Maybe he would reconcile with his wife and her family, maybe not. He would have a life, maybe long, maybe short, but the Grenadier Squaw—the Shawnee queen, Nonhelema, Katy—would not be in it. She had turned his life around. She was gone. As for Arbuckle, he thought: *That's really not my concern, anyway. He has a curse on him. Trees are supposed to fall on him, or something like that.*

Justin sat in the dark beside his rifle, listening to the owls query each other in the dark distance beyond the fort, and he remembered images of the woman. In every memory she glowed with that unnamable power. Whatever it was, he believed in it enough to believe that trees would indeed fall on Captain Matthew Arbuckle.

Someday.

Justin rolled the rifle ball in his left hand, and between the thumb and finger of his right he twirled the strip of deerhide fringe. Out in the night, the barred owls kept asking, *Who? Who? Who who are you all?*

JULY 10TH, 1778

To Richard Peters, Secretary, Continental Board of War

    If there is not a possibility of obtaining lead, I wish we might be indulged with a cargo of bows and arrows, as our people are not yet expert at the sling to kill Indians with pebbles.

General Edward Hand
Commandant at Fort Pitt

14

Nonhelema glanced up from her beading needle when she heard the high-pitched voice of George Morgan's young wife, Mary, who was coming out of the mansion into the garden. The beautiful lady's skin was almost as pale as the white summer dress she wore, a material so light and soft, it looked as if she were clad in mist. Mary was coming toward her, smiling, and Nonhelema wondered again, as she had done so often, whether this delicate and pampered creature had even the slightest suspicion that she once had shared her husband with Nonhelema, far out on the other side of the mountains, when he traded there long ago. Certainly her husband would not have told her—most of these traders kept their Indian wives secret.

But then, Indian wives hardly ever came across the mountains from the frontier like this to be guests of the respectable white wives.

Nonhelema had not come for that purpose. She had come with a delegation of Delaware chiefs led by Killbuck, who believed they needed to have Morgan speak to Congress in Philadelphia and to General Washington about the dishonorable things being done to them by the previous year's treaty at Fort Pitt. Killbuck and White Eyes had been tricked, confused, and pressured into signing a bad treaty.

One reason why the Delaware headmen had been so eager to sign the treaty was that it had promised that the friendly tribes, under leadership of the Delawares, would be permitted to form into an Indian state, and that state would be represented in Congress by Indians and recognized as the fourteenth state of the Union. White Eyes and Killbuck had been such devoted friends and advocates of the Americans that they had thought statehood would be a very good thing, and the idea had become a shining path they desired to follow.

Coming on the long journey to Morgan's home, Nonhelema had discussed the statehood promise with Killbuck and his chiefs in almost every evening's camp. As a peacemaker, she was worried for the Delawares. She would say to him, addressing him by his Delaware name: "You understand, don't you, Gelelemend, that being a state of their nation would mean that you would have to defend your state against the British and their allied tribes?"

He would look at her in the firelight with a slightly annoyed expression, as if his glowing dream of being part of the American nation should have no drawbacks.

Killbuck yearned for peace and sought everywhere for signs of it. News had come in the spring that the Virginia Long Knife Clark had captured the British forts in the Missisipe and the Wabash valleys far to the west, and that he had made peace treaties out there with tribes who had been helping the British. Then he had captured the British general Hamilton. Killbuck wanted to believe those victories would calm the frontier. But he had seen at Fort Pitt that the Americans were gathering troops and supplies for more attacks against Indian towns in his own vicinity, and his hopes were running thin.

Now Mary Morgan, seeming bright and light as a puff of cloud in the summer sunlight, came to the edge of the arbor, paused, and said, "Madame Catherine, may I sit with you?" A light sheen of sweat shone on her lip and forehead, and her fair skin was mottled under her throat by heat. There were welts on her arms from scratching mosquito bites. Though Morgan's farm, which he called Prospect, was all in clipped lawns, orderly rows of hedges and fruit trees, and beds of flowers and herbs, it was in low, wet country between two creek bottoms, and aswarm with mosquitoes and other sweat biters and blood drinkers. To Nonhelema, it seemed as unhealthy a place as the

Missisipe lowlands where she had gone with Morgan so many years ago when he tried to build a colony in the Illinois country. It was then that she had first begun to suffer from the fevers that the French called *mal aire*, for the bad air they believed to be their cause. This estate called Prospect, though elegant with its gardens and three-story house, in which Nonhelema had counted thirty-six glassed windows, was not a place where she would have chosen to live.

Nonhelema touched the bench beside her. "Lady Morgan, this is your home. You do not have to ask me if you can sit. And I am pleased to have your company. So little time we have visited, with all the busyness of the men. Eh?"

Nonhelema had her own say in all the conferences with Morgan and the Delaware chiefs, as Morgan prepared to write up their grievances to be read to General Washington and the Continental Congress.

Mary Morgan, on the other hand, being a wife and mother of small children, had had no place in their councils. It was a sad thing that Nonhelema had known for a long time—whitemen did not listen to their women or seek their advice on anything.

Nonhelema laid her beadwork in her lap and picked up her fan, made of the tail feathers of a red-tailed hawk. Mary Morgan unfolded her own fan, which was made of gilded silk and bore a picture of numerous white babies with wings, flying among the clouds in the sky. Cherubs, they were called. To Nonhelema, they suggested children of God. Morgan's wife had a faint half-smile on her face, and Nonhelema waited. Mary seemed to want to ask something. Perhaps she actually would try to find out what her husband's association with Nonhelema had been. Or perhaps Morgan had told her, and she wanted to discuss it.

"Such beautiful handiwork, Madame Catherine. I wish you would continue, that I might observe how you do it."

"Very well, I shall continue then." She laid down her fan and resumed the work, nipping the point of the thin needle into the doeskin and fastening down bead after bead, making a floral design appear like magic upon the leather.

"It's marvelous," said Mary. "Mister Morgan has brought back so much fine work from the trade out there, and quillworks, too, and yours is surely as fine as any, ever!"

"I am pleased that your husband prizes my work. He has bought many pieces from me. Perhaps some of them you're speaking of now. I have made much from his trade. No one is more fair and honest in trade than your husband."

Mary's fan fluttered rapidly. "Yes. My father says so. My father, you know, is his senior partner, John Baynton."

"So he has told me." Now Nonhelema could tell that the woman was looking at her profile, not her handiwork.

At last the pale creature asked, "May I inquire, Madame Catherine, how you happen to travel with a party of Delaware chiefs on a mission like theirs? Mister Morgan told me you are Shawnee."

"I am. But I have many Delaware half brothers. And I travel much as peacemaker. And as an interpreter and guide. I have come to most of your cities. I have even seen your father's company in Philadelphia. Baynton and Wharton, do I remember right?"

"Good! Just so!"

"But I came this time because they believed that a woman should escort the orphaned boys. It is good of your husband to assume their education since their father was murdered."

Mary Morgan's hand clapped to her bosom at the word, and she gasped. "I . . . I thought their father died of epidemic . . ."

Nonhelema looked up from her beading and put a level eye on Mary. Her own heartbeat was rising in anger. "My lady, I hope it was not your husband who told you that!"

"No . . . I . . . it was in a news sheet. That Chief White Eyes took ill while guiding the army."

"My lady, what we love about your husband is that he never lies to us. The only white commissioner who doesn't. Ask him about the death of the good Delaware chief, whose name I cannot speak because he has gone across. He was leading the Americans through his country, as that false treaty said he must do, and it was then that one of those devil militiamen shot him in the back, just because he was an Indian. Even though he was helping!" Nonhelema was breathing sharply through her nose, remembering how other Indian-hating militiamen had killed her own brother Cornstalk while he was trying to aid them. It was hard to be a peacemaker with so much vengeful anger in one's heart. Forgiving was the Jesus thing she thought she might never master.

In a grove of fruit trees on the far side of the garden, Killbuck and most of the other chiefs were smoking in the shade and talking in their deep, quiet voices. In a patch of shade near the great house, the high, clear voices of the youngest Morgan children rang out, in laughter and outcries. Heart suddenly aching deep and dull, Nonhelema said, "I am sorry I have spoken to you of unpleasant matters . . ."

Mary Morgan looked right at her, eyes brimming, and said, "No, dear madame, don't apologize . . ."

She must have but half as many years as I, Nonehelema thought. *She must have been still a girl bride when I lived with her husband. If she suspects nothing, it is no wonder.*

She said, "Did your husband tell you that I have a son who is perhaps the age of your oldest?"

"No," Mary replied.

No, of course not, Nonhelema thought. "I thought perhaps he would have told you about my son, because I named him Morgan."

The young woman blinked. "Morgan?" Her fan started going.

Nonhelema watched Mary out of the side of her eye. She could now say, *Because Morgan is his father.* But instead she said, "I named him to honor your husband—the most true friend my people have among the whitemen. There are other boys among the Shawnees and the Delawares who also bear the name *Morgan.*" She watched the young wife for any wavering of the eyes, any sign of doubt or suspicion.

"We are honored," Mary said, looking down.

"He has done much to keep peace. Now I pray that he will be able to do more, in Congress, when he explains how that treaty tricked the Delawares. The Delawares are tired of being led along by lies. Every year of the treaties at Fort Pitt, the commissioners promised to provide supplies to the Delawares for their friendship. But they have never given them, after four years of promises. Some of the Delawares already turn to the warpath. Captain Pipe was greatly a friend of Americans, but General Hand led an army that struck a town and killed his brother and two women. That was when Captain Pipe turned against the Americans. Then the father of these orphan boys, and more Delawares, turned away. Now there is just Killbuck who is here with those men, coming to get Congress to be honorable. They and my Mekoche Shawnees are the only friends the Long Knives still have on the Ohio. The other tribes all threaten us now. We are threatened by the frontier white people, too. Soldiers tried to ambush us as we came here to see Colonel Morgan, but we heard of them and evaded them. We might have to fight our way home when we are through with Congress business. To such soldiers, no Indian is believed a friend. Some of them hate your husband for treating us well. You see, don't you, how much Indians lost when your husband quit us out there and came back to this place?"

Mary Morgan nodded and touched her lips with her fingertips. "I thank you for explaining all this trouble to me. Mr. Morgan doesn't tell me such matters. I've never known how complicated it is. I know he's in a state about it, but I never know just why."

Nonhelema sewed thoughtfully for a while, then put the materials down beside her and said, "I am happy now that you came to sit with me. I have never had a chance to tell a white woman this:

"You would have a more honorable nation if the men would listen to the women. If the women knew what the men do, in their treaties, and their trade, and their wars—if women knew what their men do when they go away—they would not stand for it. I suppose you do not know, do you, that in my nation, and most of the Indian nations, the women have their congress, which is equal to the congress of the men? We are able to prevent much foolishness and do much good. The men listen to us because they know women are wiser on many matters of life."

She paused and observed the stunned expression on Mary Morgan's face. Obviously the woman had never heard of such a thing.

"Your women have a congress? Truly?"

"It is called the Women's Council. You white women all should have one, and make the men listen. But I don't think it will happen."

Mary Morgan shook her head, again looking down. "I think not."

Nonhelema said, "I have watched whitemen in many councils and treaties, with Indians, with Frenchmen. And I see what is wrong with your whitemen: They look down their noses at everybody else. They think they are gods. They can make everything go as they wish it."

She was thinking not only of generals and wealthy merchants, but also of missionaries like Brother David Zeisberger.

Finally, with a sigh and a slight shake of her head, Nonhelema said: "Perhaps the orphaned boys will do well with whitemen's teaching. But it would be bad if they learned to think like whitemen. Indian men are foolish enough in their own ways, but they don't think that they are God. Eh-heh! I would like to believe that the Congress in Philadelphia will listen to the pleas of Killbuck, and help the Delawares before it is too late. But I expect nothing. Because they are whitemen and Killbuck is only an Indian. He is one of the best Indians who ever was, and he could govern well the Indian state they promised. But they will never keep that promise."

Mary Morgan looked as if she were almost frightened to be discussing such matters; she glanced about, nervously touching her lips. Then she asked, "Why wouldn't they?"

"Because to make the Indians a state with a governor would make them feel they lifted the Indians to the same place they are. They would never permit the Indians to the same place they are. And they would never permit Indians—or women, or Negroes—to be on the same high place with themselves. That is the truth of it. That is the simple answer."

Killbuck and his chiefs had been at Prospect for weeks. George Morgan had taken their pleas to Congress. If their complaints were not heeded, he told Congress, they would probably have to turn to the British for the trade they needed. Killbuck himself, Morgan said, probably would remain steadfast, but other chiefs were disillusioned. Morgan even tried to entice the Congress by hinting the Delawares would give the United States an extensive tract of their lands, which could be used to pay off soldiers serving in the Revolution and to alleviate the war debt. It was astonishing, Morgan told Congress, that these Delawares had remained faithful to the United States for as long as they had, considering the many indiscriminate attacks and betrayals they had suffered at the hands of frontier militias.

The responses that Morgan brought back to his Indian guests were discouraging. Though he put them in the most positive language he could without being untruthful, it was plain in the set of their faces that they would be going home empty-handed into the same dangers they had left. The Congress, he said, had passed the offer of the land grant to its Indian Affairs Committee, from which no prompt answer seemed likely.

"Now, brothers," Morgan told them, "here is what Washington has replied." The chiefs and Nonhelema leaned forward to listen, because *Washington* was the name of a man, not a council, a warrior against their common enemy, the British.

"His Excellency General Washington expresses his pious hope that Congress will give you what you wish. Brothers, he wishes you to hold fast to your friendship for the United States. He wants you to think of what happens to the towns of Indians hostile to America.

Look at those blows as examples of what befalls the enemies of the United States."

Nonhelema glanced around. Every man's face was cold and stolid as a stone cliff. They were barely breathing.

"And at last, brothers," Morgan went on, "General Washington encourages you to keep turning to the adoption of Christianity, and the arts of civilization."

After a long silence, Killbuck stood up. He was a tall, gracious old man, a Christian whose pierced nose and perforated ears no longer were adorned with silver, who no more wore the medicine bag or the necklace of bear claws around his neck. He said, "That is all of it?"

"That is all of it."

Killbuck gazed over the shimmering summer fields toward the low blue hills that rose beyond the Delaware River to the west, all this New Jersey country that had once belonged to his ancestors. Finally, he said, "Brother Tamanend." It was the honorific name the Delawares had given Morgan: the Affable One. "Brother Tamanend, you have tried hard for us. Let us smoke together now. Then tomorrow we will give you a gift and then we will go home and do the best we can, with the help of Jesus."

The next morning, they tried to give George Morgan a large tract of land on the bank of the Ohio River, six miles of good riverfront land three miles wide. They knew he had admired it, and they wanted to give it to him to show their love for him and their gratitude. It would give him a place close to them.

Nonhelema saw that Morgan's eyes were brimming. But his reply was not what they had expected. He said to Killbuck: "Brother Gelelemund, I wish I could have done better for you at the Congress. But the reason I cannot accept that land is because of the laws of the United States. I am an agent of the United States, and so I cannot as a person accept the gift. It would also be a bad example for bad men who covet your land. Listen, my friends: You must never give your land away to men. If you are later willing to give it up, do so only in council, and to the commissioners of Congress. But not to any man. Not to me. I cannot take it for myself."

Killbuck's chin crumpled as if he would weep. But then he said, "Brother, your children are not agents of the United States. And so, that land could be given to them?"

"No, brother, it could not. I said, do not give your land away to any persons."

Killbuck opened his mouth as if to try another approach, but Nonhelema interrupted. "Brother, do not insist. He knows the law of what he can do or not do. Keep that land while you can keep it. The whitemen will have it soon enough." The other chiefs laughed, and Nonhelema was pleased to hear it. There was too much solemnity here. It was going to be hard enough to leave Morgan anyway, as they might well never live to see him again. Even Morgan himself, though brimful of deep emotions, began to chuckle, and in trying to contain it coughed. Nonhelema was pleased with herself and wished Mary Morgan could have been here in the garden to see how a woman might speak up among men, even to the point of disrupting their solemn foolishness.

George Morgan did have a gift for each chief, which he said he could give them for the use of their people. He gave each a new blanket, a quantity of gunpowder and lead, and a bag of seeds from his experimental gardens to take home to their women. Then he came to Nonhelema, his old lover, and offered her gifts. But instead of gunpowder and lead, he offered her a dainty tea set of silver.

"Thank you, Wapeymachikthe," she said, pressing it all back upon him. "But I cannot take those things."

"Why can you not?" he exclaimed.

"I cannot accept gifts for my people because I am no longer a chief. Remember, my people put me out because I turned to help the Americans."

He looked so bewildered she almost laughed at him. "Then," he argued, "take them as my gift to you as my friend . . . and my guest."

She held up a finger before his face. "Wait," she said, and reached into a bag that hung from her shoulder. She drew out the beaded moccasins she had been decorating while waiting here at his estate.

She said, "You and I have been traders to each other, no? I shall take the silver things in trade for these. You see they are too small for your big feet. I believe they will be just the size for your pretty wife. I feel that perhaps I owe her something. For the time I had you away from her."

15

Nonhelema hesitated at the doorway of Brother Zeisberger's study, dreading to enter, turning to gaze out over the gardens and fields where morning mist shimmered with the sunbeams that penetrated the treetops. Songbirds of all colors chimed at the woods' edge, but her mind was dense with thoughts and her spirit was heavy with the troubles of her people, and herself. She had removed her earrings and bracelets.

A bent human figure caught her eye, and she looked at the man with a sudden rush of pity and anger and disbelief.

Most of her life she had known him as a warrior, of one of the village chiefs of the Turtle Clan of the Delawares. His town had been down the Tuscarawas at its fork, the main town in a cluster of villages, a place of great beauty.

Now the old man was known no longer as a chief. He was a mission worker. Along with several other converted Delaware men, he was chopping at the soil with a hoe. Doing women's work. They were making straight, shallow ditches in which to plant seed corn, in the whiteman's way. Straight lines.

Though she was herself now a convert and, she wished ardently to believe, a child of God, this was not a good picture she was seeing.

Men were not supposed to be planting. They knew nothing about creating life and had not been given the power by Creator to make things grow. Only women had that power. That was proved by the fact that the Great Spirit had made them mothers, wherein seed grew to become life. Deep in her heart she resented the missionaries for trying to take women's power of life and give it to men. They also had taken away the women's right to build and own the houses, and to speak and vote in council.

In the Jesus religion, women were supposed to be little people with no voice, obeying their husbands, only sewing cloth and cleaning and baking sweet tea pastries. That did not seem right.

And proud as the missionaries were of taking men's weapons and giving them hoes, the women's tools, this was not right, either. Though Nonhelema was for a peaceful world in which men did not have to go and kill other men, men had always needed weapons so they could bring home meat, and so they could protect their families against those who were not peaceful. There were always plenty who were not peaceful. In the old days, the Iroquois had been the aggressors against the True People, until at last the Shawnees had risen up and humbled them. That was what warriors were for. Creator had made everything for its particular use. She did not like to look at men making ditches in Mother Earth. It was not what the Master-of-Life intended.

Brother David Zeisberger had summoned her to talk to him and that was never good, even though she loved him as the man who was enabling her to go to heaven. She wanted to ask him whether the book of God, the Bible, said men should do the farming. When she had heard from that book that they should beat their swords into plowshares and their spears into pruning hooks, she had imagined soldiers going to a blacksmith, who would take their weapons and make them tools, which they would then take home to their wives, who knew how to use earth tools right.

It was not likely that she would get to talk of that with Brother Zeisberger. When he summoned her, it was usually to shame her or get information out of her. Or both. She sighed, turned, and knocked on the door. She would have expected the door to be opened by dear

Brother Schmick, who was her nephew by his adoption by Cornstalk. But Brother Schmick, with his long face and half-moon smile and his pretty wife, Johanna, had left the mission not long ago because of an argument with Brother Zeisberger. Brother Jungman had gone with them, all to the Pennsylvania church town called Bethlehem, the town where her own grandmother Elizabeth, her mother's namesake, had been the first Shawnee ever to convert. So there would be no familiar Schmick or Jungman to sympathize with her.

Instead, the person who ushered her in was a young Indian convert whom she didn't even recognize, and the old Delaware woman sitting in the room as witness and chaperone was someone she didn't know, perhaps a recent arrival from one of the other missions.

Brother David, who always looked as if he were about to weep, looked much older since she had last seen him. No doubt the war had been trying for him in many ways.

"Catarina," he said, "I wish to discuss with you Alexander McKee."

That was it. Not so much as a cordial greeting. This was the first time she had faced Brother David since he had learned of her liaison with McKee several years ago, and of their son.

"Brother," she said, "there are greater matters, are there not? Is the war not a greater matter than my connection with Captain McKee? My people have divided! Our chiefs Black Fish and others have been killed by American soldiers, who went in the night and ravaged Chillikawthe Town! One of the Americans' best allies, White Eyes, was murdered by the American soldiers he was guiding for General McIntosh. Custaloga and old Newcomer are dead. Morgan quit Fort Pitt because of the treachery of all the American generals, who offer us Indians peace with one hand and kill us with the other hand!"

She paused, trying to calm her agitation, then went on: "I tried to be a peacemaker as you taught me. I help the Americans until I have nothing left. My own people do not trust me because I help the Americans! Eh! I have endured all that, always to help the Americans, even after they murdered my kin before my eyes! The Long Knife Clark went to the Missisipe and killed Indian people and took that land away from the British. Everywhere, the Americans are killing Indian people and burning their food and their towns, these Americans we have been helping! General Hand marched to the Cuyahoga-sipe and killed women and children! All this treachery and murder, and yet what is important to you is that I was a fool and consorted with

Captain McKee?" She was breathing hard, glaring at the missionary, trying to remember more of the storm of betrayals and murders that the Americans had unleashed in the years since Cornstalk was murdered. It was more than her mind and spirit could hold at once, the bad news from everywhere. The whole Shawnee nation in the Ohio country had split in half upon learning that the Long Knives were not just east and south of them, but now west of them, too, because of Clark's victory. The half who had decided that resistance was futile had gone in a long, sad procession to a place west of the Missisipe, led by the French trader Lorimier, who had obtained a place for them from the Spaniards. The half who remained here in the Ohio valley were the ones who were so furious at the Long Knives' treachery that they had vowed to remain and fight them and get as much help from the British as they could get. Nothing worked for peace. Everything was betrayal. Even in personal matters, the Americans were without honor. The adopted son Boone had broken Black Fish's heart by betraying him and fleeing back to his whitemen in Kentucke.

And of course, McKee had betrayed the Americans. He had also betrayed Nonhelema herself, and then had stolen her son from her. Nonhelema was at the edge of her Christian forebearance and did not mean to let herself be shamed just now by this saintly faced old tyrant.

"Anything you wish to say against Captain McKee," she told him, "is no worse than I would say. So you need not say it, Brother David. As for my sins, they might seem great to you, but they are small beside the sins done against me. I am so numb from them that I could hardly feel your righteous wrath, or any punishment you intend for me!"

Brother David sat gazing at her, only the changing hues of his complexion hinting at the chagrin she was causing him with her words. A mere woman talking to him that way! And a backsliding, sinful, heathen woman, at that! She knew that was his feeling; he had lectured her for her impertinence often enough. His expression was the same as always: brimming eyes, long-suffering beatitude. But she knew that he could look that way and calculate viciously at the same time.

After a moment, he said: "I speak of Captain McKee only as a British partisan. It seems to be McKee who incites the Delawares to quit their neutrality and join the British in their war. The war parties come through our missions on their way to war, and they threaten and unsettle us. They return through here with their scalps and unsettle us again. We had to abandon Lichtenau Mission because it lay in their warpath. And so often, they are warriors who have been stirred to action by McKee."

"Yes, Brother David. I know he is doing that. He has done great harm to our cause of peace. But the officers at Fort Pitt do no less. In the councils at Fort Pitt they always begged us to be neutral. But now they coax peaceful Delawares to take arms against the Wyandots and Mingoes, even against their own Delaware brother Captain Pipe! I have nothing to say for Captain McKee. But he does no worse harm to peace than the Americans we have tried to help. I have no faith in them anymore. And I am troubled that you keep telling them what the Indians are doing. That is not a way to peace, either. You are helping one side fight the other."

Plainly he did not like what she had to say. Still he held his tongue about it, his face now ashen.

"Catarina," he said after another strained silence, "here is what I have to say about Captain McKee at this time. He has been pressing our missions to move away from here. To move up by the Sandusky, or close to Detroit, where he says we will be out of danger. Out of danger from the Indian war parties, as well as from the Americans at Fort Pitt."

Nonhelema felt a surge in her heart when she heard that. These mission Delawares *were* helpless, and they *were* in danger, and the danger kept growing; it was more dire with every raid and every retaliation. And McKee would want the Praying Indians out of danger; he always had been as good a friend as the Indians had ever had, after Morgan. Even in hurt and disappointment, she could not deny that.

But there was another motive in McKee's plan—one that she could detect at once.

If the missionaries were withdrawn from the edge of the frontier, Brother David could no longer correspond so easily with the American commander at Fort Pitt, and much of his spying would be choked off.

In a way, she thought, that would be good.

But Brother David Zeisberger, she knew, must be terrified of it. If they took him anywhere near Detroit, the British surely would put him on trial as a spy.

She asked, "Has Captain McKee come here to ask you to go there?" She was still curious about his activities, where he went, what he did. He could be in danger from the Americans if he traveled this close to Fort Pitt. "Does he come among the peaceful Delawares to ask them to join the British?" If he risked and lost his life by coming along the warpaths, she might never be able to find their son, Tommy, wherever he was.

Brother David shook his head, looking down at his fingertips on the edge of his desk. "No. His messages usually come by way of Chief Pipe, or from Half King."

That was sad news. Pipe and Half King were Christians who had been neutral in the beginning. They had eventually begun wavering because of the treachery of the Americans. The murders of her brother Cornstalk and some of their own relatives had at last turned them away toward the British side.

Brother David sighed heavily. "Ah! What we had hoped to make into a pasture of godliness has become a wilderness of wolves, and I am an old shepherd trying to lead my flock to safety!"

The old woman sitting nearby moaned and sobbed at the aptness of his words.

But Nonhelema, after a moment's reflection, said: "Brother David, this was no wilderness to us until you tamed us into sheep. We did not even have a word for wilderness."

She slept beside her old mother that night, but did not sleep well. Brother David was the shepherd of these trusting people, he had been their strength, but now he was full of doubt and they could sense his weakness. In the dark, she heard several of the old women moving restlessly, some moaning, some weeping.

The next morning, she went to Zeisberger again. She needed to know about her own fate as the war grew. She had no village now, and Fort Randolph was no more. She did not want to live at Pittsburgh; she was too angry at the commanders. For her children's sake and her own, she had to know whether she could live here, with her mother, with the Delaware converts who were relatives. Perhaps the missions were not such havens as they had once been thought to be. But no place on the frontier was, now that peace had failed and the paths were streaming with war parties.

Again as she went to Brother David's study she saw the men working with hoes. She tried not to become disturbed by it. If she hoped to live here, she would have to be more accepting of Brother David's vision of the world. There was, after all, no doubt in his mind that he had a firm knowledge of the wishes of God, and she was not certain that he didn't.

The same old Delaware woman was waiting to chaperone. Brother David was writing in his diary, that book in which he kept meticulous accounts of what everybody did. He looked up as if annoyed to be disturbed at such an important chore. Of course he knew what she had come to ask him. She had mentioned it to her mother, and anything that any old woman in any of the missions knew was soon known by Brother David. Old Sister Elizabeth was so ecstatic at the prospect of her daughter coming to live near her that she could not have kept her tongue still about it even if Nonhelema had asked her to.

"What is it now, Catarina?" he asked, as if he didn't know. He wanted her to ask. "I leave soon for the synod at Bethlehem and have much to write before I set out."

She braced herself to beg. "Good Brother David, I am like Chief Gelelemend. I have helped the Americans, and therefore I seek refuge here, as he does." She knew that Brother David had desperately kept putting Killbuck off, because taking him in would give the war parties an excuse to molest the missions. Only Gelelemend, and her Delaware half brother Welapachtachiechen, still favored the Americans, and were nearly fugitives in their own land. Welapach-tachiechen, who was converted under the name of Israel, had been expelled from the missions because he continued to lead warriors hostile to the British; he was out of favor even though he was trying to protect the missions. When war and the Jesus God got mixed up together, nothing made much sense.

What Nonhelema now saw in Brother David's eyes was fear and crafty thinking. Because she had helped the Americans, her presence, too, would provoke the war parties. She could see the missionary's eyes casting about for an excuse to say no. That would be easy for him, her sin with Captain McKee being so fresh in his mind.

Instead, his eyes strayed to her bosom, widened, then narrowed. For a moment she was mystified. Then, as his mouth hardened into a scowl, she realized what he was looking at. With a futile move of her hand she tried to cover it.

This morning, after washing and praying to the Creator of all things—carefully using both the name *Jesus* as well as *Weshemonetoo*, the ancient name her ancestors used—she had forgotten to conceal her medicine bag inside her blouse. There it hung, in plain sight, the tiny doeskin bag embroidered with dyed quills, containing its sacred snips and scraps—red cedar splinters, a pinch of earth, a pebble of quartz, seeds of corn, bean, and squash, a dried snip of the umbilical cord from the birth of her son Morgan, a pinch of ash from ceremonial fires a thousand years old—all relics of her walk on the Spirit path of her ancestors with her people and her family, contained in a beautifully crafted bag no bigger than her thumb. To Zeisberger, it was the detritus of Satan.

He said, "Our rules number nine and fourteen, have you forgotten them? 'No objects of heathen superstitions. No one should paint himself, nor hang wampum, silver, or anything on himself.' Catarina! How can you sit before me, blatantly adorned, and ask to live among us where we worship only our Lord Jesus, our Savior?"

"It is not wampum, it is not silver," she began to protest. "It—"

"No! It is far worse! It is *tshapiet*, it is witchcraft, it is heathen superstition, and you wear it just above your heart! Oh, Catarina! Why must you mock our Savior? Why do you torment me, who baptized you in the cold river? Get away from me! Get out!" He leaned far away from her in his chair and laid the back of his wrist across his eyes as if shielding his pure soul from the malevolent stare of Satan.

By the time he lowered his arm to peek, she was gone.

GOSHACHGUNK TOWN

First there was the smell of wood smoke and meat cooking—welcome aromas in the dense, dim woods. Then, as she and her son and daughter rode westward along the Tuscarawa-sipe, the forest thinned and there were paths and gardens in the expanding clearing—the sounds of children's voices. Then they saw buildings: loaf-shaped wigwams covered with bark and mats, log cabins roofed with bark and poles, shade arbors covered with brush, then, in the distance, the curved roof of the Great House showing above a palisade wall. Men and women came out of the lodges when they heard the hoof steps, looked, cried greetings, and joined them to walk beside their stirrups while a boy ran in ahead to tell of their approach. The Delaware tongue sounded almost like the German of the missionaries, more throaty and less lyrical than Shawnee. The three riders dismounted and led their horses, talking with the townspeople, giving the chief time to come out and greet them, as a chief always did when travelers came.

He came walking from the center of the town toward them. A red blanket was draped over his left shoulder and passed under his right arm, and under the blanket he wore a mission shirt. He did not have his usual ornamentation of earbobs, necklaces, or nose rings now that he was a convert, but still kept his head shaved, with a long scalplock remaining at the crown.

This tall man was Israel, one of her half brothers, by her father's early marriage to a Delaware woman. His Delaware name, Welapach-tachiechen, meant "Stands Straight." It was an apt name, even though he was now sixty winters of age. Since the death of White Eyes, he had been chief of the Delaware Turkey Clan, and his life was precarious.

His town, called Goshachgunk, stood at a place that was a very fine location in peacetime, but a bad place now. It was where Killbuck Creek and the Tuscarawas and Waldhonding Rivers flowed together to become the Muskingumsipe. Four major trails converged here: one from the old Shawnee Scioto towns to the southwest, one coming up the Muskingumsipe from the Ohio, another from the Delaware and Wyandot towns on the Sandusky in the northwest, the route that the war parties followed when they came down from Detroit, as they did constantly now. From the north came the Cuyahoga War Trail, the road from Lake Erie to the Ohio. Almost everyone who came by those trails was hostile to Stands Straight, because he remained on friendly terms with the American officers at Fort Pitt and tried to stay neutral in the war. But it was difficult for an old warrior to remain neutral when he was threatened. He had been a Christian for only a year and had not yet learned meekness. When he was threatened, he replied like a war chief. Like Nonhelema, he perplexed Brother David by being a strong-willed chief instead of giving up tribal authority and becoming a drone with a hoe at the missions. Brother Zeisberger stretched his rules to accommodate Brother Israel; he was afraid to do without the protection that the chief might afford if the enemy tribes crossed the line of restraint.

Stands Straight embraced her and her children with vigor and warmth, then led them to his cabin. Nonhelema and Stands Straight respected each other not just as relatives, but also as warriors who had tried to be peacemakers. In each other's faces they saw reflected the sadness of failed efforts, of murdered relatives and allies, of peace dreams betrayed.

Stands Straight had chosen not to live at the Lichtenau Mission because of his chiefly responsibilities. Lichtenau, which meant "Pasture of Light," had been less than half a day's walk down the Muskingumsipe. It had finally been abandoned just a few weeks before because it sat in the direct way of too many warpaths, and all its inhabitants had moved to the older missions on the Tuscarawas.

Stands Straight asked her, "Will you live at the mission with your mother, as you meant to do?"

She tried not to show her anger and disappointment. With pretended cheerfulness, she replied, "You know that Brother David is at times even harder to please than usual. I fear this is such a time. I am not saint enough for him now. If he knew a way to unbaptize, I think he would do that to me."

Stands Straight smiled and shook his head. "We Indians never knew of the Devil until the missionaries came and found him among us. What a keen eye for evil Brother David has."

Nonhelema put her fingers under her tiny medicine pouch and held it up. "Very keen eyes. He found the great Devil in this tiny place."

Stands Straight's wife, who sat nearby heating tea water, laughed, and said, "He should watch your face and not your bosom."

The chief made a low, purring sound deep in his throat and shook his head again. "Where will you live, then?"

"Would I be welcome here, brother? For the season? I have nothing left, and need time to make goods to trade. Our great friend Wapeymachikthe is no longer at Pittsburgh." She told him about her visit with Killbuck's party to Morgan's estate in New Jersey, and the failure of the American Congress to remedy the bad treaty. She explained that she did not want to live at Pittsburgh now, with the hard and stupid American officers in charge instead of Morgan.

He listened, nodding. "My sister, we would welcome your presence among us. But it is not a safe place. The British Indians who are always coming on this path grow ever more bold and arrogant. They are trying to make me fight so they will have a cause to strike us. You would give them more provocation. Not long ago, they had pity for you, because of the murders at the Kanawha-sipe. Then they thought you betrayed the dead by staying among the murderers."

"I do not fear them. I have been a warrior. Nor do I fear death. What else is left me?"

"Much life, my sister. These troubles will pass. There have always been troubles of some kind, but you have always known how to live in joy."

"That was before I was a Christian. It seems a Christian is to have joy only after death."

He looked at her with raised eyebrows. "Is that what you believe?" He was a fervent Christian, and could not have liked the sound of that remark.

She looked down at her hands. "Perhaps not really. I have been to Brother David. Thus I speak this way." She looked at his strong, lined coppery face, and smiled. "Eh-heh, brother. Then it seems that I should pinch my nose and go to live at Pittsburgh. I can live in good use there. Always someone goes through the Place-Where-Rivers-Meet and needs a guide or interpreter. And there is trade."

"You and your son and daughter can be safe there."

She thought, *He doesn't mention my little son. Is that because of pity? Or does he forget that I have the little one?*

But then, I do not have the little one, do I?

FROM WELAPACHTACHIECHEN (BROTHER ISRAEL)
AT GOSHACHGUNK TOWN
TO GEN. DANIEL BRODHEAD, COMMANDANT
AT FORT PITT:
APRIL 23, 1780

Brother:

I am so much mocked at by my Enemy Indians for speaking so long to them for you. Now they laugh at me, and ask me where that great Army of my Brother's, that was to come out against them so long ago, and so often, stays so long. They say to me, did We not tell you that they had no Army and that we were nearly done killing them all, and yet You would believe them?

Welapachtachiechen

16

It was exhilarating to sweep down the broad river in a roomy
bateau, and delightful to be in the company of a high-spirited and
adventurous Frenchman. And all this so soon after resigning herself
to misery and frustration. She was still astonished that this had happened so swiftly.

But things had always happened swiftly when she followed her
heart.

The Frenchman's name was Auguste la Mottin de LaBalme, and
everything about him lifted and delighted her weary heart. He dressed
with elegance. He always had good wine. He even had pet cats. The
first time he had seen her, as she rode into Pittsburgh with Morgan
and Fani, this pretty little man had run from an inn to stop them in
the street and let loose a torrent of praise, in awkward English, about
the extraordinary quality of their horses. At once she had replied in
French, thanking him. And then, in his own tongue, he had expressed
himself eloquently.

He had been inspector general of the Continental Army's cavalry, trainer of all of General Washington's mounted troops. He was one of those idealistic French aristocrats who had sailed over from France and volunteered to assist the Americans in their War of Independence against their common enemy, the British.

The man radiated charm, intensity, and panache. Nonhelema had not been so enlivened by any man's ways since Alexander McKee, and it had been a joyous relief to laugh at a man's wit after such a long, dismal time with fierce officers and stern missionaries. Within two days of her arrival in Pittsburgh, her plans had changed to accommodate his ambitions.

Monsieur LaBalme had lately quit his position in General Washington's army, weary of training louts to fight from horseback, and had headed west in the hope of finding adventure and fortune on the frontier. There, as he expressed it, *on peut manoeuvrer*—there might be space and freedom to work opportunites. He was profoundly inspired by the recent reports of Colonel George Rogers Clark's bold defeat of the British in the lands northwest of the Ohio. He wished to find Colonel Clark, offer his services, and, in some way yet to be imagined, further humiliate the British warmongers in Detroit and end the conflict in *le haut en pays*.

To Nonhelema, that sounded like a quick route to peace, and in her imagination it became just that. Although Clark and some of the successive commanders at Fort Pitt had long been frustrated in their desire to strike straight to the heart of evil in Detroit, she liked to imagine that this exuberant Frenchman might have the genius to do it and without all the dreary business of moving and feeding shabby and unruly armies of militiamen. Such a man could win on wit and élan alone, and his personality flowed like the current of the river.

He had funded a small flotilla of boats and goods and rowers, and his final need was a guide and interpreter for the trip through Indian country, the Virginia frontier, and into the French and Spanish settlements on the Missisipe. Nonhelema was ideal for those roles. She was sympathetic to the American cause and eager for an end to the hostilities, she spoke every tongue that would be encountered along the way, and she had been down the Ohio and into the Missisipe country with George Morgan years before. And it seemed that Monsieur La-Balme was as delighted with her as she was with him.

M. LaBalme dressed with elegance—lace ruffles at his throat, a watered silk weskit under his tailored frock coat, knee breeches, and white hose—even through the rigors of camp and the confinement of boat travel. In his entourage were a manservant and a chef, and he had cases of good French wine amid the crates of his baggage. He sang well, and within a few days on the Ohio River he had already taught three lilting French songs to her and Fani and Morgan. They laughed often at his wit. This LaBalme was a man who could capture a woman's heart.

The river was high from spring rains and swift, and when the fleet was in the middle of the wide river, sweeping past the high wooded bluffs, the trees in the varied pale greens of spring, the catkins on the maples almost white, there was little torment from the clouds of mosquitoes that swarmed near the riverbanks. Staying in midstream was prudent also because, whether one saw them or not, one could assume that Indian war parties were on lookout up on those verdant bluffs, watching the passage of boats down from Fort Pitt and up from Clark's Missisipe posts. They were always patrolling the river. They watched for single flatboats or small flotillas and decoyed them to shore if possible, or fired from shore if they were near the bank, or sometimes chased them in canoes. Nonhelema had heard that Alexander McKee himself sometimes led such parties against the riverboats or against the Kentucke settlements. Camping on shore a few of these nights, she had imagined warriors led by McKee attacking, finding her here in an armed party with the fancy Monsieur LaBalme at its center. It was a frightening but delicious fantasy. What would McKee think of her as LaBalme's consort?

Not that she really was. He had not yet made so much as a suggestive move or statement. And in the back of her mind was the notion that if he did, she might laugh. For, large as he was in his own esteem and ambition, he was a runt.

To Nonhelema, most men were chin height at best. This man, as she imagined once or twice with amusement, would have to rise on his toes to kiss her breasts.

She could remember French soldiers from a generation ago, in that conflict known as the French and Indian War, men in dirty white uniforms, mature men not as tall as their muskets. The minimum stature for a French soldier had been four feet, and the French commanders had complained that the conscripts being sent over from France were below that. They had looked like old children. And yet they had been incredibly tough. Not physically mighty, but able to endure fatigue and misery that would have reduced a British soldier to whimpering.

She said to LaBalme now, as he stood in the prow of the bateau and gazed ahead down the curving river: *"Milord, dites-moi: Dans votre pays, sont les gens heureux? Ont-ils liberté, et paix?"* She wondered whether a nation of runts lived happily, with freedom to do as they pleased, or whether they might always be menaced by bigger people wanting to come in and take their lands, like Long Knife Virginians. The English and French were always at war. The English were bigger men. She imagined them pushing upon the French borders, making the little Frenchmen come to treaty talks and abusing them. But she didn't speak of them as runts, not wanting to offend this little man's sensibilities.

He looked at her, a half-smirk on his lips, the upriver breeze causing his graying hair at his temples to fluff out, and he tilted his head, thinking of his reply. He tried never to make a statement or utter an answer without memorable wit or an air of sagacity.

"Ma chère madame, les Françaises ont quelle liberté que le roi veut."

She thought of that. The French people are as free as their king wishes them to be.

Monsieur LaBalme had told her on the first day she met him that the reason he had come across the ocean to help the American rebels was because they were getting rid of a king.

This river was so long and its valley so deep and grand that one could descend in boats for days at a time and see nothing except as Creator had made it: the fresh, tender foliage of the forests; herons flying slowly along the shallows; deer, elk, and bears standing quietly on the shrubby sandbars, raising their heads from the water to watch the boats; numerous swans; endless flocks of passenger pigeons, millions of them gleaming in the sunlight with the colors of pearls and rainbows; bottomlands dense with flowering underbrush. One could imagine that no man had ever been here.

But a knowing eye saw traces and signs: a sunken flatboat at river's edge, a small clearing surrounding the charred ruins of a cabin, a bloated and scalped human corpse snagged in driftwood, a glimpse of smoke high on an overlook, a speck on the shining water far upstream or downstream that would be proved in the spyglass to be a canoe full of warriors, but then would disappear.

The Ohio River valley was so vast that a war could be waged in it and remain almost unseen—as was happening now. Nonhelema could laugh with this French adventurer, but under her gaiety ran the sadness of the failed peace. All the trails were being trodden by war parties, on their way to wreak vengeance on their enemies.

The Shawnees were seething over the death of their great and beloved chief Black Fish. Already morose over Boone's defection, he had been wounded by a Long Knife soldier's bullet the previous summer when a militia from Kentucke had attacked Chillicothe Town. He had lingered in pain with a shattered hip and fiery infection for months, then had at last crossed over onto the Shining Road in the Hunter's Moon. He had been succeeded as principal chief by the veteran warrior Catahecassa, Black Hoof, a tough, shrewd, dignified little man who was as firmly opposed to peace with the Long Knives as Black Fish had been.

Because of the failure of her peacemaking, Nonehelema's spirit rose and fell every day as the boats sped past places full of memories. Passing the mouth of Yellow Creek had reminded her of the massacre of Tahgahyuteh's family. Beaver Creek had caused her to recall the many times she had left Fort Pitt with downtrodden hopes, and in particular the grueling trek with Cornstalk, carrying their wounded brother Silverheels, his lung pierced by a ruffian's dagger. Every fort or ruin of a fort along the Beautiful River stood as a symbol of the Long Knives' hypocrisy. With clenched jaw and aching heart she had visited the graves of Cornstalk, Elinipsico, Red Hawk, and Old Yie near the charred ruins of Fort Randolph. Her account of the atrocities and betrayals she had suffered there had brought LaBalme to tears, and had embarrassed him: He did not enjoy hearing of the barbarity and perfidy of the Americans he had come to help.

At the mouth of the Scioto she pointed out the site of the old Shawnee towns that had been swept away by a flood twenty-five years before. And she told him, with glimmering eyes, searching in her mind for the most descriptive words she remembered in French, of the great, beautiful Shawnee towns that had stood beside the Scioto-sipe in that lush plain, where she had enjoyed her happiest years as a village chief before Lord Dunmore came up with his army and precipitated the ruin of her people.

A hundred miles down from the Scioto-sipe, a river called the Miami flowed into the Ohio from the north, and one called the Licking flowed in from Kentucke just a little below. Near this juncture of rivers sat a small town of the Miami nation. The town was close to a major Indian trace coming down from the Miamis' country and on into Kentucke. For as long as anyone could remember, it had been a path down into the hunting grounds of Kentucke for the Miamis, and a connection to the Ohio.

Few Miamis had been using it as of late because it was becoming a war road between the Shawnees—who had been forced to move their towns westward—and the Long Knives' settlements, which were scattered along the branches of the Kentucky River: Boonesboro, Harrodsburg, McClelland's, Lexington. There were probably others by now. Southeastward up the Licking was the great Blue Licks salt lick, after which the whitemen named the river, a paradise for hunters because of the deer, elk, and bison that it attracted. The Blue Licks had been a sacred place, the ageless site of Shawnee salt-making camps until the Long Knives moved in and took it over. It was there that Boone and his men had been captured by Blue Jacket two years before. This was a great passing place between north and south, but a dangerous place to live now. Too many whitemen's boats and too many war parties came by. Still, it was a spectacularly beautiful place of narrow bottomlands between steep hills, near one of the mound-forts built by the Ancient People. When Monsieur LaBalme ordered the boats put ashore so that he might appraise it as an important place for a future city, Nonhelema scanned the banks for any sign of danger, and saw none.

An old Miami man walked to the water's edge to meet them. He was the headman of the little town, and, to LaBalme's surprise, he greeted them in French. Nonhelema explained that many of the Miamis had intermarried with French fur traders. The old man wore a faded calico shirt with loincloth and leggings, and his head was shaved back to the crown. The gray hair on the back of his head hung far down his back, loose except for a slender braid decorated with a tinkling cluster of tiny tin cones. He knew who Nonhelema was, and he seemed to be aware of her role as a spokesperson for the Americans. He showed no sign of resentment.

After they had shared a pipe and she had explained to the old man that this Frenchman and his escort were going to the Missisipe, where many other Frenchmen were, they were served a midday meal of delicious white flesh, taken from the side of a catfish as big as LaBalme himself. It had been baked in a heated pit, wrapped in wet corn leaves, and seasoned with wild onion. LaBalme was so pleased with it that he had his servant open a bottle of wine and serve it in glasses. The old headman held it up, looked at it in the sunlight, and laughed. He said, in Miami, "This looks like urine."

"Qu' est-ce qu'on dit?" LaBalme asked.

Nonhelema replied, "He says that he has not had fine wine in many years."

As the boats were being readied to depart, the old man edged close to Nonhelema. "It is good that you leave here without delay," he said in his own tongue. "Soon a very big war party with English officers and some cannon will come down the river from up there." He pointed up the Miami. "Warriors from many nations. Red Coat soldiers and many of the Green Coats from Canada."

"With cannon, you say?" There had never been cannon in this part of the country. It was an appalling thought to a peacemaker.

He said, "They are getting Shawnee warriors along the way. They mean to go against the Long Knives' fort at the Falling Water Place, and then against all the forts in Kentucke, and knock them down with the cannon. They show how the cannon can smash trees, and could smash forts, and the warriors then want to join them. I saw them show a cannon. Since then my ears have a sound like an eagle's cry in them all the time. Nonhelema, I do not like either of the opponents in this conflict. I wish they were all gone back." He looked down at the ground, shaking his head.

"Did you see who leads them, those British with the cannon?"

"Colonel McKee was there. And a captain named Byrd. Girty was there."

All as one would expect, she thought. In her heart grew both sadness and dread. Now knowing of the approaching danger, she had a difficult responsibility to do one thing or another. When LaBalme's boats reached the Falls of the Ohio, where Long Knife Clark was building a fort, she would have to tell the Americans, or not tell them, what she had just learned.

If she did not tell them, lives of Long Knife families would be lost.

If she did tell them, lives of Shawnees and other Indians, and maybe McKee's own, could be lost.

As LaBalme's men boarded the boats to continue down the river, Nonhelema huddled with her son and daughter. Speaking low in their Shawnee tongue, she told them of her dilemma and asked for their thoughts. The girl's eyes flashed as she replied: *"Nigeah,* I plead with you not to tell the Americans anything, ever again! You cannot stop the Long Knives and the British from having their war. But you do not have to help the Long Knives kill our own people by warning them! Maybe I have held my tongue too long. These Long Knives and the missionaries have made you act as a traitor to our own people! Many of them already feel that you have become their enemy. *Nigeah*, what pain that causes me, even though I know your heart is kind and true!"

And Morgan, barely of warrior age yet, appeared to be seething. Nonhelema turned her eyes on him. "My son, how do you think of this?"

"*Nigeah*, I do not want to get onto that boat and go on down with this fancy man."

"Why? I don't understand."

Morgan almost hissed between his white teeth: "This man is for the Long Knives. It's plain he wants to help the Long Knife Clark. I do not want our people and McKee to be killed by Long Knife Clark knowing they are coming down."

She nodded. At least her son understood something about what was troubling her. "But," she said, "why would you get off the boat, as you say? That would only grieve your family. What would you do if we went on down without you?"

"I would wait here until McKee and the Indians came down the warpath. I would join them."

Nonhelema was shocked to hear this fervor in him.

He went on: "They would say I am not warrior age yet. But I shoot well"—he stroked the long, slender squirrel rifle with whose small-bore bullets he had helped provide food from shore as the bateaux came down the river—"and if they don't let me fight, I can carry messages, and read and write for them. And interpret tongues."

She knew that he could do all that; he had been a courier with her for peace. "My son! You would do that to help the British make war?"

"*Nigeah*, yes. I would help our people. In those same ways you helped the Long Knives make war."

"No! I have only tried to make peace!" In her agitation, her voice had risen, and LaBalme was looking in her direction now.

"I do not like this Frenchman," Morgan said in a low, flat voice, not even sounding like a boy anymore. "I have had to be quick to keep his hands out of my clothes. He is much like some of the Black Coats."

"I don't believe that! When did he try that?"

"Only those rare times, *nigeah,* when you are not covering him with your attention." He glanced at Fani, who was also looking at him in surprise.

"I do not believe that!" Nonhelema said again. "You are only trying to turn me against him."

"Do you think I would lie about such a thing?" the boy exclaimed. "Then tell me: Has he tried to put his hands in *your* clothes? No? Then is he not the first whiteman who did not try? Maybe that is why."

Her head was swirling with anger and confusion. The intensity of their conversation had caught LaBalme's attention, and, perhaps sensing that his own security was at stake, he was coming over.

"Nous allons," he said. "Let us go to the boats, my dears."

Nonhelema turned to her son and spoke rapidly in their own tongue. "You will come on with us. Nothing more will be said about joining those others. I hope you understand."

He replied, "I am not with you if you mean to tell the Long Knife what we learned."

She could see that he was set to do as he wanted, and that they could not have an argument about it now without the Frenchman learning about the British expedition.

"I do not intend to tell the Long Knife," she said quickly and softly. "Come. Get in the boat."

And in a few minutes they were off the bank and again moving swiftly on the river. For a while she thought only of the war matter. But after a while she began looking out of the side of her eye at LaBalme.

It was true that, for all his charm and attentiveness, he had never insinuated himself amorously, as whitemen always tried to do. Was that because she was growing old, she wondered, or was it true that he might have designs instead on her son Morgan?

He needs watching, she decided.

One of LaBalme's cats, a gray one with short fur, was showing off. It had been on its hind legs, clawing at the mast of the bateau, and now it crouched, coiled with purpose. It sprang up, scrambled up the mast, and crept out onto the yardarm, like a panther on a tree limb. Under the cat was the furled sail, tied up because the bateaux were moving downstream against the wind. The cat lay now on its belly on the wooden yardarm, staring intently at the end of a canvas reef point that was flapping in the breeze. The animal apparently was stalking that moving strip of canvas and had gone all the way up there in pursuit of it, even though real prey, countless mice, were everywhere in the boat's cargo. Other cats were prowling or sunning themselves elsewhere on the boat, and one lay curled in LaBalme's lap. Cats were strange and intriguing animals to the Indians, who had known only wild ones—panthers, lynxes, bobcats, the various kinds of *peshewa*—and many Indian people suspected tame cats of being witches in four-legged form.

Since yesterday's encounter with the old Miami headman, LaBalme had been making sly efforts to find out what the old man had told them. The Frenchman had perceived that something important had passed among the Indians. He said to Nonhelema, "One of my boatmen thought he heard the name *McKee* mentioned yesterday."

She thought fast and smiled. "Many words in the Shawnee tongue sound like *McKee*. I did not say *McKee*." That was true. The old man had, but she hadn't. "Our words for 'hills,' and for 'moccasins,' and for 'close by,' all start sounding like *McKee*. I did not say his name." She tilted her head, smiling and shrugging. LaBalme knew, from his sojourn in Pittsburgh, a little about her relationship with McKee and his defection to the British, and she did not wish to see it come up in discussion now.

The cat in LaBalme's lap had been watching the gray cat on the yardarm with mild interest. Suddenly it growled, sprang from his lap, and vanished into the bilge under the rowers' seats. A whiffling sound from overhead grew loud, a shadow flickered over the boat, someone shouted, there came a sound like a hand clap above and a quick, scrannel yowl. Everyone looked up, wincing. Droplets of cat blood appeared all over LaBalme's face and his linen shirt.

The gray cat was no longer on the yardarm. With powerful wing-beats, an eagle with white head and tail feathers rose into the blue sky beyond the mast, the gray cat hanging limp from its talons.

LaBalme sat gaping like a fish, blood-spattered, and Nonhelema stared at him, then looked up at the eagle climbing the sky.

She knew: Somehow this elegant little man was doomed.

That evening she grew feverish and weak. LaBalme was alarmed and fussy.

"It will pass," she gasped. "it is the bad air sickness. I am sorry to trouble you with it. My daughter knows how to tend to it. I won't die on your hands, m'sieur."

When she had first suffered it, on her sojourn to the Missisipe with George Morgan, she had thought she would die. Since then, she had been through the malarial fevers many times, and knew that she would recover in a few days.

FALLS OF THE OHIO
MAY 1780

The boatmen were tense and frightened as their vessels glided faster and the hissing roar of the waterfall grew louder ahead. Nonhelema, weak as she was after the days of malaria, laughed at the fear she saw in Colonel LaBalme's face. She sat up with her arms along the gunwale.

This was another of those sacred and powerful places. The Ancient People had lived here. Ages ago, all the tribes had gathered here to kill a nation of giant whitemen, and their ghosts still haunted this eerie place where the water roared over precipices and thundered through boulders. Here was the place where herds of woodland bison crossed the shallow river and went northwestward toward the prairie lands, on a trail so old and long-trodden that a man walking in the rut could not see over the edges. Here in the gray flat rock between the waterfalls were seashell creatures turned to stone.

Nonhelema pointed to an island lying off the left bank and told LaBalme in a loud voice, "We land there, where the driftwood is piled up!" She knew the current from earlier passages of the Falling Water Place. Once she had ridden in a canoe down through the chute of foaming water, and it had been a thrilling ride. But these boats were too full of goods and inexperienced helmsmen to risk that turbulent chute. Many a boat had been swamped and wrecked, many a boatman drowned. Few whitemen could swim even in calm water.

LaBalme wanted to stop here in the hope of meeting George Rogers Clark, who had been building the fort that stood now on the south bank, if Clark was here. If not here, he would be out in his Missisipe outposts.

There had been no fort here when she had passed through the falls before. Now there stood a fort of new logs, and near it were a few cabins. On the island, all the trees had been felled and a rectangle of cabins stood enclosed in a palisade, with corn and gardens growing around them. Clark had left a small colony of camp followers here to settle the island two years before, on his way to conquer the British posts on the Missisipe. Nonhelema peered up at the well-built fort as the boats swung toward the island, and she wondered whether Alexander McKee's army, even with its cannon, would be able to overwhelm it.

War, she thought, feeling more miserable from the thought than from her fevers. *Did I ever really believe that I could persuade men not to have war?* She had loved McKee and admired Clark. Now they were bent on making war against each other. And even this silly Frenchman, who had so charmed her at first, apparently meant to get himself involved in that war.

She didn't want to see the handsome and compelling Long Knife Clark. She didn't want to have to face the choice of trying to conceal from him what she knew or warning him.

She was disgusted with men who wanted to make war. They should all have their manhood-balls snipped off, she thought.

Colonel Clark looked twenty years older, though she had seen him only two years before. When he rose from his desk chair to greet her, he flinched with pain. His cheeks were gaunt, his whole face lined and weathered. His nose and cheeks were ruddy, his skin flaking. His red hair was graying and receding, although she knew he was certainly less than thirty years of age yet.

Eh-heh, she thought, *I am a generation older than he, and surely I have aged as much, too, since we saw each other at the Kanawha fort.*

"Katy," he said, reaching for her hand. "This is an honor I didn't expect."

"Thank you for remembering me," she said. "I hear of Colonel Clark and his deeds everywhere and always, while I have been obscure."

"To forget you would not be possible." Even as he was flattering and charming to her, his curiosity was already turning toward the fancy Frenchman. LaBalme was looking worshipfully at Clark, leaning back as if taking in a great spectacle, his palms up, stretched toward the Virginian. Nonhelema knew she had better introduce them before the Frenchman burst.

She had to translate their meeting because of LaBalme's terrible English. Clark was impressed with LaBalme's recent service for General Washington's cavalry, but it took him a while to get a sense of why the Frenchmen would have come to this frontier. LaBalme's recital of his motives and aspirations was a barely coherent jumble, full of revolutionary idealism and desires to embarrass the British, have adventure, glorify his name, and thrive in a rich land. Nonhelema could see incredulity in Clark's eye at first, but then she saw him shrewdly fitting LaBalme's yearnings in with his own plans and responsibilities. Within an hour of animated talking and interpreting, she saw that the two men were going to be able to serve each other.

Colonel Clark now had tenuous control over a vast territory whose demands required him to be everywhere at once. He needed to complete this fort to control the Ohio. He wanted another fort on the Missisipe below the Ohio's mouth, to control passage between the French towns of New Orleans and St. Louis.

Clark also needed help to maintain his alliance with the French traders and communities in the Missisipe and Wabash valleys. Some of the French militia from there had marched with Clark on his expedition to capture the fort at Vincennes, but now, without strong leadership, they were aimless and fickle. It was there, perhaps, that LaBalme might be useful. He was a Frenchman accustomed to command. And he seemed to have his own resources, whereas Clark was operating on Virginia's overextended credit, and his own signature, with neither finances nor recruits coming from the beleagured state of Virginia.

Clark complained long and bitterly about that. At one point, he nodded toward Nonhelema and said, "Our picayune government owes this good woman a fortune for her losses and services. I don't hold much hope she'll ever receive it."

Throughout this conference in the fort's orderly room, smelling of freshly hewn green wood and wood smoke, the Long Knife Clark and the French colonel had been sharing their bottled treasures. Clark had Spanish Madeira, Indies rum, and army whiskey, and LaBalme had his superb French wines. Both men were avid drinkers and dreamers, and the more they drank the higher their fancies soared. Clark's face—in particular his long, aristocratic nose—grew red, and his words and laughter boomed. His talk ranged from the pragmatic concerns of frontier defense and his ambition to go and conquer British Detroit to glowing prospects for American dominance in the Missouri fur trade; from his theories of the rise and fall of the mysterious peoples who had built all the great mounds to his collection of great fossils here in the riverbed at the falls. He was like George Morgan, his mind engorged on everything known in the world and hungry to know all that was yet unknown. He had notions about everything in Creation. It seemed to Nonhelema that Clark must have been starved for the company of someone who could think beyond the confines of a log palisade and the maintenance of a sullen, sick garrison of exhausted heroes.

And Clark, even in his inebriated euphoria, never entirely forgot his gallantry in her presence. Maybe she was old enough to be his mother, but she could see in his eyes that he not only valued, and respected, but perhaps even desired her. She had been a constant ally to the Long Knives, a courier, a source of information and insight. Her reputation as a peacemaker was known along the rivers, even though peace had failed. All the American commanders knew that she had in one way or another diverted the full wrath of the Shawnees from their lonely, desperate outposts, like this one.

Nonhelema drank with the officers, but not as much. She was glad Clark and LaBalme were getting drunk, so that she did not have to be on guard against inquiries about McKee and his forces. She knew that LaBalme had intuitions, that he might express them to Clark, and she did not want to have to lie.

Yet as she watched him, his flushed face, his volubility and charm, she would have to pause and realize, now and then, that this bold and land-hungry Virginian was one of the worst enemies her Shawnee people had ever faced. His conquest already had half defeated them.

That evening they stood on the parapets of Clark's fort and looked out over the sacred place, listening to the rush of the falling water, watching the slanting sunlight of the evening turn the far bluffs to gold and blue, and the mist from the falls diffused the sunglow. Nonhelema saw that cannon commanded the river and all the approaches to the fort. Most of those cannon he had taken from the British when he captured their fort on the Wabash. If McKee came to attack this fort at the Falling Water Place, he probably would not expect to face cannon, surely not so many of them. This was a well-built fort, and well armed. Clark was here with his veteran fighters, not out at the Missisipe as he was thought to be. An attack on this place would result in much bloodshed and no clear victory for anyone; it would be war at its most foolish and terrible. Clark was showing LaBalme some of his homemade canister shot: cylinders full of pebbles, balls, and metal scrap, which would be discharged into the face of any attacking force like buckshot, more than compensating for his small number of riflemen. Alexander McKee's soldiers and warriors would be mowed down like grass before a scythe, because they would not know what they were coming up against here.

Nonhelema could not drink that dread away.

The next day, she learned what LaBalme and Clark had decided. La-Balme, with most of his boats, would continue on down to the Mis-sisipe and then up to the French towns, where he could be a good influence on the shiftless militiamen in Clark's absence. Nonhelema would take him into that country, which she knew well.

Two of LaBalme's bateaux, emptied of provisions they had used coming down, would be sent back upriver to Pittsburgh, carrying mail, discharged militiamen, and some hides.

Her son Morgan came to her, wheedling her permission to leave LaBalme's party and return to Ohio or Pittsburgh on one of those boats. "I would be safe," he said. "There are enough riflemen."

He was clearly expecting a refusal. But she surprised him. Taking him aside, she said, "My son, there is a chance for you to save lives of some Shawnees and their allies, by going up."

His eyes widened. "Tell me, *nigeah*," he said, leaning forward, intently interested.

She reminded him of their meeting with the old chief near the mouth of the Miami-sipe. "You remember he told us that Colonel McKee's army was coming down."

The boy nodded. "With its cannon on wheels."

"Listen, now, my son: If McKee is warned that Clark is here, with so many cannon and scattershot, he would perhaps have sense not to attack here. Maybe he would turn back. I want him to have that warning. Not to help either the British or the Long Knives to win, but to keep them from such a battle here. For peace, I want McKee's army not to come here."

"Yes, *nigeah*. And you would have *me* warn him?"

They were talking in Shawnee so that none of the militiamen could understand them. "Somehow," she said. "It could go badly. There is danger. If McKee's army is already on the Ohio-sipe, they might attack these Long Knife boats going up. But if they are not yet on the river, you could tell the old Miami chief, and he could warn them when they come by his town. Tell any Indians you meet along the river how it is here. That warning will fly through the country on wings. You could do much good, my son. But you must give me your promise."

"What promise?"

"That when you are out of my sight you will not make yourself a warrior. Promise me that!"

He sighed. "I promise you, *nigeah.*"

"Remember what I say: that you can do the People of the South-wind no good by taking a musket ball. You can do them much good by turning them away from here. And you must think of this also: It is better you do not tell the British yourself. Better you start the warn-ing on its own wings. If it came straight to them from your mouth, they—knowing you are my son—might suspect a trick and not be-lieve." She could see that he understood. Her heart ached at letting him go on such a hazardous errand, and she was afraid for him. She gazed hard at him and saw traces of his father's appearance: the good, wise George Morgan, also a peacemaker. "Listen," she told him. "If they are on the river, and if they catch you, ask them to take you to Colonel McKee. Or Girty. They would not let you be hurt."

She reached out and took his hands in hers. *"Tanakia. Weshe catweloo k'weshe lawehpah."* We are strong when we do what is right.

The Frenchman was sullen for a few days as they went on down the river toward the Missisipe. Her explanation that Morgan had simply wanted to go back home was not quite satisfactory to LaBalme. But he could extract no further reason from Nonhelema, and by the time they turned the bateaux out of the Ohio-sipe and up into the strong current of the Missisipe, he was too full of anxiety and eagerness for his new adventure to dwell on the slight matter of a boy's defection.

It was a brilliant, cloudless day, and the sunlight blazed off the great expanse of the confluence. Nonhelema had been looking down into the water, remembering something. "M'sieur," she called to La-Balme, who was standing in the bow, studying the far riverbanks through a spyglass. "Look down. Soon you will see *tapistewamigi-sipe*—joining of two waters!"

"Qu'est-ce que vouz dites? The joining?"

"Là-bas!" She pointed down.

The boat was crossing a dimpled, swirling stretch of the conflu-ence when, in a line as distinct as the boat's gunwale itself, the clear, greenish water of the Ohio, upon which they had come a thousand miles, met the muddy, yellow-brown water of the Missisipe. The boat crossed over the line. LaBalme whooped. Colonel Clark, too, had told LaBalme to watch for that line. Clark had explained that the Ohio's water was clear because its watershed was forested and its bottom limestone, while the Missisipe's western tributaries came through treeless, eroding plains, filling with mud and sediment.

Clark also had warned that the Missisipe was full of floating trees, from caved-in riverbanks far upstream, and that such trees often rode just under the surface, making constant hazards for boats and canoes. They had been in the Missisipe's swift current no more than an hour when a chorus of alarmed cries arose from one of the nearby boats, along with a din of thumping and splashing.

Turning, Nonhelema saw the boat tilting, men flailing and falling, oars waving. The boat was pivoting, and she saw the glistening black root bole of a waterlogged tree jammed into its bow. The boat was stove in and would sink soon. LaBalme was bellowing in French, ordering the crews of the other vessels to get close and transfer the cargo and men from the stricken boat into their own.

All progress up the river stopped as the little flotilla of bateaux tried to converge without getting entangled in the submerged tree, the whole frantic scene now slipping on the brown current past the willow thickets of the eastern riverbank, hundreds of disturbed waterfowl flying up, Frenchmen screaming that they could not swim, bundles and kegs bobbing and floating away. Most of the crewmen were clinging safely to the swamped, yawing boat, but some already were clambering aboard the other vessels, or hanging on to oars that were extended to them. LaBalme was howling orders like a madman. Nonhelema and Fani stood in LaBalme's bateau, watching, ready to help if swimmers were needed.

It was then that they heard a desperate cry and looked to see the head and flailing arms of someone break the surface, splashing and bobbing, out of oar's reach of any boat and drifting farther away.

Nonhelema knew that the man would have to be rescued while he could still be seen on the surface; the Missisipe was too murky to let him be found once he was under. She reached down with both hands and grabbed the skirt of her tunic, stripped it off in one motion, dropped it into the boat, and dived over the side toward him. Out of the corner of her eye, she saw Fani also stripping.

The water was warm, but cooler than her sun-heated skin. She surfaced and stroked her long, strong arms toward the wet white shirtsleeve, which was all she could now see of the man. With a dozen strokes she was close enough to grab the wet cloth of the shirt with her left hand. She rolled to her side and began a hard sidestroke back toward the boat, feeling the strong pull of the man's weight being tugged by the current. She saw Fani swing alongside her, and they smiled at each other.

The little man's head broke the surface and he gasped for air, but choked on water, and in the throes of panic he grabbed the hand that had his sleeve, and with his other hand he seized for whatever else he could feel, and it was her ankle. He began trying to climb up her. One hand got her long hair and she was pulled under into the murk.

She got her head above the water just long enough to gasp air and hear splashing and one shouted syllable from somewhere. She had to release his sleeve and use her hands to wrest his fingers out of her hair. She was afraid that if she got free, he would sink and be lost. But if she didn't, they would drown together. She needed air; her heart was slamming from her exertions.

Another hand clutched her hair, and she was being pulled up. She came up gasping into the sunlight. Fani had pulled her to the surface, and was helping her hang on to the thrashing man.

Her shoulder bumped the hard planks of the hull of the bateau. Then the strong hands and arms of rowers took hold of their friend and hauled him aboard, while Nonhelema and her daughter rested, hanging naked in the water with their hands gripping the rough wood of the gunwale. They recovered their breath, looking at each other with profoundest gratitude. The clamor was past now, and the big tree that had wrecked the bateau was shoved with gaff poles and swung ponderously away. It rolled, and the swamped bateau, with a crunching of wood, separated from the root bole and began to drift.

"Donnez-moi un cord!" Nonhelema called. Someone handed her the end of a rope, and she swam to the abandoned boat and tied the rope to the guyline in the bow. Some of the boatmen cheered when they realized that the boat could be towed ashore and repaired. These Indian women had saved not only their comrade, who was now slumped over in LaBalme's bateau coughing up water, but also the damaged boat itself. As Nonhelema swam back up along the towrope she saw that Fani had kicked off again to swim several hundred feet down the river to retrieve a floating oar and a keg.

The boatmen's delight was even more evident as they stood gaping when the two nude women shinnied up over the gunwale into the bateau, streaming water in the sunlight, and stood sluicing the water off their skin and getting dressed. LaBalme himself finally found his voice and harangued the men to get back to their oars and pull for shore.

The boatmen were much less talkative after the incident. They rowed, seemingly lost in daydreams.

It was good to be in a French town again, among people who sang and laughed and enjoyed evenings of dancing, as well as their imported pleasures—chocolate, wine, coffee, silk, and silver—which came to them from France by way of New Orleans. Even their skinny Jesuit Black Robe, Father Gibault, drank wine without guilt.

The French *habitants* of Kaskaskia were enchanted with the vigorous little Colonel LaBalme she had brought them from Pittsburgh. They took him to their bosoms, and in no time he was intriguing them, setting himself up to be an important man. It was amusing to watch. To Nonhelema, it was amusing because it was really so insignificant. This was the sort of thing Creator gave people to think about so that they did not think of themselves as being, eventually, bones in the ground.

Much of LaBalme's warm acceptance by these people was due to the letter of recommendation that Colonel Clark had written for him. These people practically worshiped Clark, it seemed. The bold Virginian had helped them get out from under the stifling control of the British, and he had allowed their young gallants to serve in the campaign and share the glory.

In fact, the Frenchmen here were now Virginians; this Illinois country had been proclaimed a county of Virginia shortly after Clark's conquest of it.

If Father Gibault was the holy man of the town, Monsieur Gabriel Cerré was the pillar of the merchant community. He was involved in every transaction. So he wielded more influence than his slight, balding presence would suggest. He was like a hairless fox, Nonhelema thought. She had first met Cerré a decade before, when she had come as the interpreter for George Morgan, before the war. Cerré had been a linchpin in Morgan's trade network and colony, while it lasted. Cerré was shrewd and venal, a commercial man to the marrow of his bones. But unlike many commercial men she had known, he had true affection and solicitude for all the citizenry whom he sheared year after year.

The French, to her, seemed like a Shawnee tribe—all interdependent, all quietly angling for prestige and advantages, all jealous of each other, but all usually polite and easygoing.

The difference between a French community and a Shawnee tribe was that the Shawnees did not measure themselves and their neighbors by wealth. For them, there was more prestige in what one gave than in what one had. That was the way Weshemonetoo had intended for his people to be. Whitemen were takers and keepers. Sometimes even Nonhelema the peacemaker doubted that there was room in this vast land for the two races to live and share.

As the moist, stifling heat of summer pressed down on the broad Missisipe floodplain, Colonel LaBalme withdrew further from Nonhelema. He was busy conniving for his future with fellow Frenchmen. He had no need anymore for an interpreter or guide and spent much of his time among the young militiamen, cajoling and mentoring them. Nonhelema began to feel her time was being wasted here on nothingness. Her thoughts returned to the fate of her people, trapped between war and peace back on the Ohio frontier. She lay awake, sweating and worrying about her son Morgan and the message he had carried. About McKee and his expedition against Clark at the Falling Waters. Her malarial fevers came and went, here in the muggy air. Mosquitoes filled the nights with torment. The center of her world was not here. Much as she enjoyed the French, she was supposed to be where her people were struggling. The French went whichever way the wind blew, and were never in danger of being exterminated. But her Shawnee people were wrestling with the fate to which their countless generations had brought them, and that was what was important.

She and Fani lodged in a little house owned by Monsieur Cerré, a plantation house of hewn timbers and mortar, with a porch around all four sides. Below, just down the bluff, was the very place where Clark and his militiamen two years before had slipped across the Kaskaskia in darkness, surprising the whole population and subduing the fort without firing a shot. He had won the Frenchmen's loyalty in the following days and they were still devoted to him.

All the townspeople loved to relate the drama of that night: Clark and his half-naked, bedraggled militiamen had interrupted an elegant ball, silencing the musicians. Among the stunned guests had been the lieutenant-governor of Spanish Louisiana. Clark had let them all stand in growing dread for a long moment. Then he had told them to resume their dancing, that they would now dance under the flag of Virginia. The Spaniard had been so impressed that he had become Clark's devoted ally. It was even rumored that Clark was now betrothed to the Spaniard's sister, that he courted her in St. Louis across the Missisipe. Nonhelema was amused by such French gossip, but she was anxious.

Summer was lethargic, and it would be hard to get the trip back to Ohio started. For these people, pleasure was a greater incentive than duty, and indolence seemed to be their nature. They did only what they absolutely must, and they delayed everything as long as they could.

She went looking about the house for Fani. She stepped out onto the porch and found her, lolling on a bench with a boyish cadet of the Kaskaskia Militia, one of several who had been drawn by Fani's elegant comeliness. This one, Nonhelema remembered, was named La Croix. He was tall and sinewy, with strong hands and muscular forearms. His randy masculinity was incongruous with the shapeliness and redness of his lips. The young couple started when she appeared; they were in their lightest and loosest garb for the sultry weather, and their wrinkled clothing and mussed hair suggested they had been fondling.

Nonhelema frowned at the sight, not because her daughter should deny herself some attachments in her endless sojourns as Nonhelema's devoted companion, but because such an attachment here might make her reluctant to leave the Missisipe and return to their troubled homeland. "Daughter," she said, "I need to speak with you at your convenience." She turned and went inside, and began putting things into her trunk. She took from the wall the little cherry-wood crucifix that she hung up everywhere she lived or stayed. *La Croix,* she thought. *His name means "the cross," but even if he were named Jesus, he would be just a man, like any man, with most of his aspirations in his loins.*

We are all made in the same way, she thought. *We are pulled upward by one ecstasy and downward by another.*

It was another half hour before she heard young La Croix's horse going away down the street, hoof steps hard on the sunbaked dirt. The only other sound was the shrilling of cicadas. Then Fani came into the room. She had tucked in her clothing and smoothed her hair, but still looked flushed, with a sheen of sweat on her forehead. She did not look at her mother yet, but seemed to be waiting for her to say something, and she lifted a gourdful of water from the pail to her lips.

"Daughter, my purpose here is done. M'sieur LaBalme has been delivered. I am uneasy to stay here, so far from our people. I want to collect our pay from LaBalme and engage a boat to go back up. I wonder if you want to go with me."

Fani put the gourd in the pail and turned. "How would I not go with you, *nigeah*?"

Nonhelema tilted her head. "I supposed perhaps the young Frenchmen . . . ?"

Fani laughed and shook her head. "*Nigeah*, they will all be gone, anyway. They all join with Colonel LaBalme and will leave here soon."

"What is this? They are going where?" It was unusual for her daughter to know more than she about the doings of whitemen. But of course she herself had not been on close terms with any whiteman here, and Fani had been courted by young officers.

Fani replied, "The colonel means to take an expedition against Detroit."

"The fool!" Nonhelema exclaimed. "Why? How? What do you know of this?" She got up and began pacing. She knew well that Clark had very long had ambitions to conquer Detroit. But this strutting little LaBalme?

Fani shrugged. "The m'sieur, he says it is weakly defended. That the French there are sympathetic with the Americans and would turn on the British if the invaders were French. They are all so excited about the adventure!"

"Ha! And our little colonel himself would have a shining name in this whole country!" It suited the vainglorious Frenchman exactly. If he could accomplish what Clark failed to do, what the whole Continental Army failed to do, LaBalme would live in glory as a man who curtailed the British plans in the whole Middle Ground.

Suddenly, Nonhelema remembered something: the sight of an eagle swooping over a mast, and LaBalme spattered with a cat's blood. She shuddered, suddenly feeling cold.

"What, *nigeah*?" Fani exclaimed, looking intently into her eyes.

"*Naga*." Nonhelema gave a strained laugh. "I am turning into an old woman. I never feel quite right anymore . . ." That was true. She no longer had her moon times, and it was easier to say that to Fani than to speak of the cat-blood omen. "Maybe I am just too far from our people."

"When shall we go, *nigeah*?"

"As soon as a boat goes, or I will hire one. I will inquire. I want to stop along the way and greet the people who came here last season, when our nation divided. They live below the *tapistewamigi-sipe*. If their place is good, perhaps it is where all the Southwind People will find their haven someday. Wapeymachikthe used to think that the Shawnee people would go there when there is nowhere else to go."

She felt a pang in her heart as she thought of him. Now when she thought of George Morgan she also envisioned his pretty wife. But she still had this: that Wapaymachikthe had loved her. And he was still her friend, distant though he was. It was here in this country that they had shared a few months of life, building his dream colony together, while his pale bride waited for him, unknowing, more than a thousand miles away in the East.

There were scores of familiar Shawnee faces to warm her heart, people she had always known. They had come down to the west bank of the Missisipe to greet her bateau. The boat slid aground on stinking mud because the river was low. She and Fani would have to slog across a wide swath of it to reach the people. It was not an elegant arrival.

When Nonhelema stepped from the boat, bad feelings came from the soil. And many of the people seemed in bad spirit as well. Perhaps it was because they were so far from their homeland. But she knew also that many of them remembered her attachment to the Long Knives. All were polite, but some resented her.

The light glared, a sickly sunlit hue, and the path to the village was crowded with weeds and vines, the rankest vegetation she could remember ever seeing anywhere.

The first woman to embrace her on the path to town was Methotase, the widow of Pucsinwah. The woman was still beautiful, but she looked old now, with fine wrinkles in her upper lip and on her cheeks. As Nonhelema held her tight, she remembered the Women's Council six summers before, when Methotase had told about her dream of her husband's death and had pleaded for a peace vote. What might have come of it, if the peace women had prevailed, and the Shawnees had not started war at the Kanawha-sipe? This was one of the best of the Shawnee women, but now she lived in a flat land on the other side of the Missisipe from her ancestors' graves. Nonhelema had a notion, as her fingers felt the spine and ribs and muscles of the woman's back, that this might indeed become the place where all the Shawnee people were when it was all done. Wapeymachikthe might have foreseen the truth of it. She hoped not. She didn't like this place. It seemed dirty and malevolent, even though it was lush. Methotase then embraced Fani, held her at arm's length, and stared into her eyes, saying, "Your mother is blessed that you always go with her. My heart aches with longing for my daughter, Tecumapese. Do you ever see her? Do you ever see my sons?"

Of course they had not. Her offspring were all in the war towns with the Kispoko, who were at war with the Long Knives.

The corn here in the Missisipe bottomlands grew taller than Nonhelema had believed corn could grow. Beans and squash twined up the stalks and over the ground, more lush in growth than she had ever seen. The soil was black and gave off a smell like that between the legs of a lusty woman.

"The soil is very good," Methotase said as they passed through the fecund cropland. "And it has been comforting to be this far from the Long Knives. But because the land is rich, they will be coming after it all too soon."

As they came through the lanes into a view of the town, Nonhelema saw that the dwellings were all the simple domed *wegiwas*, covered with bark and reed mats. It was still such a new town that it had no ridge-roofed log houses yet. "We have a worry here of floods. That is such a river! It is said that sometimes the floods are so wide, one cannot see to the other side. But those are seldom. It will more likely be a flood of Long Knives sweeping us away than the Missisipe."

Nonhelema smiled sadly. "Good sister, you have fled so far from them that you should never even have to think of them anymore. They are caught in their war with England back east like a fly struggling in a web."

Methotase led her toward a small lodge, saying, "For every fly in a web, there are a hundred passing around it. Since Long Knife Clark came into this country, there are more and more agents of commerce everywhere, and even whiskey sellers already. They are like wolves pissing to mark their hunting place. But now, the two of you, come into my lodge and let us leave off talking of the bad things."

The wall mats of the *wegiwa* had been rolled up, opening the sides to any movement of fresh air, leaving the house like a shade arbor. Outside, everything trembled in heat waves. Men and women moved slowly from shade to shade, wearing almost nothing, and children were naked. Nonhelema gazed out over a field and saw a sight that made her yearn for the old village days before the Long Knife war had scattered her people: On a scaffold of poles above the field of corn and beans, little naked girls sat with rattles and gourds in their hands, noisemakers to drive away birds and animals from the maturing crops. She could remember being one of those girls. And she could remember later being one of the young women who would range through the fields with a hoe made of a deer scapula, chopping out weeds from among the planting hills, pulling up weeds, the hot sun on her bare back and shoulders, sweat running freely down her body and dripping on the soil. And she could remember her mother telling her that the sweat on the earth was good, because it was Earth Mother's most nourishing drink, for which she rewarded you with better crops, and also because its human smell lingered in the ground and made the evening animals reluctant to invade the fields and tear at the ripening corn.

She said to Methotase: "I will have no Green Corn ceremony this summer. My people are all gone everywhere. I have no town anymore."

Methotase had stripped down to a loin apron and hung her sweaty dress on a post. She was still a lean and muscular woman, but with breasts now low toward her belly, and she had developed wrinkles from old childbearing stretch marks around her navel. The woman sat down gracefully, folding her legs under her. Fani stripped off her calico shirt and sat down with the two women. Hers was still the full, smooth body of a young woman, and Nonhelema wondered for a moment how many of the young dandy French officers at Kaskaskia had caressed her, or lain with her, and if they had been surprised by the whiteness of her where she had not been tanned by the sun. Nonhelema herself was still surprised sometimes when that white skin reminded her that her daughter had been a white child long ago.

Methotase said, "I invite you to stay here until our Green Corn. You should not have a year without the blessings of Green Corn ceremony."

Nonhelema thought of Brother Zeisberger's last rejection of her, for her medicine bag, and smiled with rue. Yes, this year she could participate in Green Corn without having to worry about being rejected by the missionary, because she was already rejected. But no, she could not stay here that long. Something would be happening at the Ohio valley forts, with Alexander McKee's army of British and Indians. Somewhere up there was her son Morgan, who had carried a message and might be in trouble. Somewhere else up there was her son Tommy McKee. And into all that brewing trouble the vainglorious Colonel LaBalme intended to go. She needed to go back into that country, if only to know what was happening. There probably was no way for her to intercede in any way, but she could not bear to stay this far removed from the struggles of her people.

And she had hired a boat, which was waiting even now.

"I must go on. I wish I could stay here with my beloved people. You have been absent from my side, but always present in my affections."

Methotase lowered her head, and her eyes were teary. "Then let us feed you before you go on. Our town will have a feast for you. We will all talk together. And I will ask you to carry messages of concern to my daughter and sons, if your path should meet theirs. Although I know you are on a path of peace, and they are on a warpath, perhaps you might encounter them."

"Meh shemah," Nonhelema said, "if I see them, I will tell the message of your heart."

As her hired boat moved away up the wide Missisipe the next day, its French oarsmen chanting and pouring sweat, Nonhelema looked back toward the low shore where the Shawnee town stood, and thought of Methotase's last words to her: "This is a bad place. Something is wrong with it. I hope to leave it when I can, and go down to the place of my elders among the Muskogee."

Nonhelema did not quite understand the malevolent feel of the place. She could have explained Methotase's dissatisfaction with it; it was a place she had had to come after fleeing her homeland. It was a hot and fetid place, and the air was thick with mosquitoes and biting flies. Many of the people in Methotase's town had malarial fever. But it was more than that. "Fani," she asked in a low voice, "would you have wished to stay there for Green Corn?"

Fani shook her head. "No, *nigeah!* I did not feel well there. My skin felt the hairs raising all over."

"You also? My feet did not like the feeling of the ground. It seemed to be pushing, saying, *Go away.* I think it might be one of those places where something terrible happened to the Ancient Ones. Their spirits are there, still disturbed. That is how it felt to me."

The Shawnees at Methotase's town had been worried about how far the river level had fallen in the summer. That became more evident the following day as the boat turned into the Ohio's mouth. The Ohio-sipe was flowing weakly. What had been sandbars and shoals on the way down were now islands and spits. On a low shore where cypress trees had stood in sloughs, their roots were now in drying mud.

"*C'est mal,*" the chief boatman said gloomily. "If the river does not freshen, it may become very difficult upstream. I hate this season, when one must get the rowers out to pull the bateau through mud. Perhaps you should have gotten horses, to ride over the Illinois land to the falls."

"*Peut-être,*" she replied. "*Mais on n'a fait ça.* And it does no good to hate a season. Better to pray that rain will fall in the hills, and come down to lift the boat. *N'est-ce pas, m'sieur?*"

He shrugged and turned forward, a short, swarthy Creole with long black hair, his powerful shoulders seeming almost as broad as he was tall. He had been a fairly cheerful fellow on the way down the river, but he was surly now. *Probably,* she thought, *boatmen are happier floating down than rowing up.*

She knew, too, that he might be afraid. Coming down with La-Balme there had been several bateaux full of armed men. Now there was just this one vessel with a few muskets aboard, moving very slowly up through hundreds of miles of country where Indians were at war. *Yes, fear might be much of it.*

The boatmaster had asked Nonhelema to pray or dance for rain to deepen the river. He had thought it a joke, but when the rainstorm came thundering and flashing up the Ohio, blowing huge tree limbs down off the bluffs into the river, it was no longer a joking matter to him. When the rushing gloom was illuminated by lightning, she saw the boatmen and rowers sopping wet, cringing, wild-eyed. Then vast curtains of rain lashed them all. Fani, her hair and dress soaked and sticking to her, bailed water out of the boat with a wooden pail, but the bilges were filling too fast and everything in the boat was afloat, all the food soaked. The rain, refreshing at first to the overheated rowers, was now chilling. It was evening, and soon would be full darkness. The Frenchmen were growing frantic, crying to the mother of God.

When they heard Nonhelema start laughing at them, they went dumb and stared at her in the lightning flashes. The boatmaster clambered and sloshed toward her, his eyes full of fear and fury.

She laughed in his face, raised her hand and pointed toward the northwest shore. "A town of friends. *N'avez peur jamais!*"

He didn't seem to believe that, but shouted at his men to keep pulling their oars.

Within an hour, the wind and lightning had rolled on toward the east. A steady rain was falling when they pulled ashore at the edge of a wide, level bottomland and saw through the gloomy downpour a cluster of cabins and dome-shaped lodges and pole fences, and a mooring place of pilings at the river's edge. Tall corn swayed in the deluge. When Nonhelema raised her voice in a Shawnee greeting, several men and women emerged from the buildings and came running down through the rain.

By nightfall, all the people and goods from the boat were inside the main lodge, drying by firelight. The bateau had been pulled ashore and turned bottom-side up. The boatmen, relieved to find themselves in comfort instead of drowned in a foaming river, were laughing and singing, accompanied by the twang of Jew's harps and the shaking of rattles. They were delighted to realize that some of the Shawnees here understood the French tongue. Out of gratitude for the hospitality, the Frenchmen opened a keg of rum. As cheerful voices rose, the drumming of rain diminished.

An old woman was in charge of the village. All the men remaining in town were old. The few warriors were gone up the Ohio valley, drawn by reports of trouble above the Falling Waters. They were a neutral faction here, but vulnerable because of the increasing flow of whitemen's boats down the Ohio and down the Wabash-sipe, which flowed into the Ohio just above the Shawnee town. This town had been established thirty years earlier by a band of Shawnees led by Peter Chartier, migrating away from the Fort Pitt area. Chartier had stayed here a few years and then moved on, and these people were the remnants. To them, this was a good place. They were largely alone, but had amiable relations with the neighboring Piankeshaws and some commerce with the Miamis and Weas who traveled the Wabash.

The old woman, whose name was Willow Basket, knew just a little about the troubles up the river. She sat close to Nonhelema, sharing a pipe and rum with her, and related what she had heard:

No, the Indians with the British cannon had not attacked the Long Knife fort at the Falling Water. Their army had gone instead into Kentucke by way of the Licking River and attacked some fort towns up there. They had used their cannon to shoot down a wall, had killed some whitemen and taken many prisoners. Then, as Willow Basket understood it, they had recrossed the Ohio and retreated northward, back up through the Shawnee towns on the Miami-sipe, probably to sell their prisoners to the British headmen at Detroit. It was said that the Long Knife called Clark had learned of the attacks and had left his fort to go up and retaliate against the Shawnee towns. Whether he had done so yet, she did not know.

Nonhelema listened, her heart turning heavy. Attacks and revenge. Then next year there would be more revenge from the Shawnees and the British. It would not end.

As the French boatmen and the Shawnee women got drunk together and laughed and sang and danced, and the Jew's harps vibrated, Nonhelema took another long drink of rum. She leaned over toward Fani, who had drunk very little but was daydreaming into the firelight, perhaps about La Croix or some other youth from Kaskaskia, her hair drying in curls around her face.

"Daughter, you heard that McKee did not attack the fort at the falls?"

"Yes, *nigeah*, I heard."

"Perhaps then Morgan got the message to them."

"May that be true, *nigeah*."

Long into that rainy night there was debauchery that would have given Brother David inspiration for a thousand sermons, but Nonhelema was not involved in it. She and Fani went to bed in Willow Basket's lodge. Nonhelema lay awake listening to the rain and busy mice, thinking, thankful that McKee's force had not struck at the falls, but hoping that not many had died in the settlements where he had struck.

And she prayed to Weshemonetoo, and also to Jesus, that the Shawnees would escape devastation when Long Knife Clark went up to punish them.

That might already have happened. It might be happening even now.

When they reached the falls two weeks later, the river was low again, and farmers with oxen were hired to haul the bateau over the portage past the rocks. While that was in progress, Nonhelema and Fani went up to Clark's fort. Only a few soldiers were there. A slouching lieutenant with eyes that looked in two different directions let them into the orderly room and sat before them, surrounded by half a dozen reeking militiamen who had followed them in and stood ogling them.

"I know you, Lieutenant," she said. "You were at Fort Randolph, at the Kanawha."

"Yes, ma'am. I 'member you, too. It was you painted up Pryor and Hammond like Injens, wa'n't it?"

"I did that." She didn't like to remember. It had cost Shawnee lives.

"Wha'd I tell ye?" he exclaimed to the others with a cackling laugh. Then he blinked and made himself look solemn. He was apparently new at being an officer and was trying to maintain the decorum of a gentleman. It was hard to talk to him because she could not be sure where he was looking. One of his eyes always seemed to be looking over her shoulder, and it gave her the uneasy feeling that someone might be coming up behind her.

"Colonel Clark is not here?" she said.

"No, ma'am. He went to Harrodsburg. Listen here, ma'am!" The lieutenant was squirming again with the eagerness of saying something, like a boy with a boast to share. "What we done, it was jus' like there at Kanawha! When Colonel Clark heard about Martin's and Ruddell's Stations bein' took, he set out f'r the settlements up there, but he figgered 'e might not git through. So I told 'im how you decorated Pryor and Hammond that time, and we done him the same, him and one other officer, an' they went off by the trails. They got there, too, and he conscripped ever' man as could walk, sent back here for more. Got a thousand, they say. Took up cannon." The lieutenant stopped suddenly, perhaps realizing that he was talking to an Indian about a war on Indians, and maybe saying too much, anyway.

She let a moment go by, then asked, "Is it done?"

"What done, ma'am?"

"What came of it? Did he attack the towns?"

"No doubt, ma'am. But we ain't heard nothing since he went up. No news yet how it went."

Nonhelema and Fani glanced at each other. There would be no way of knowing until much later. The lives of the hundreds of

Shawnee people in the Long Knife's way were a weight on her heart as heavy as the world. She had no way of knowing how her actions would have affected their fate. She would probably never know.

"It is all in Creator's hands," she said. "Come, daughter. Let us go on up the river."

The lieutenant looked startled. "Ma'am, I think ... don't you think you oughter stay here till Colonel Clark comes back? How, uh, how safe d'ye think it is up yonder?"

She thought, *How safe is it here? I suppose this officer wants hostages.* She remembered what had happened to her brother and nephew and the others when they were hostages of Captain Arbuckle at Fort Randolph. She remembered White Eyes killed by the soldiers he was guiding. "Lieutenant, I shall not impose upon you for hospitality." She smiled, but as she stood up and smoothed her skirt, she made sure that he saw her hand brush over the little pistols in her sash. He made no move to stop her.

17

In the newspaper, she read of Colonel Clark's vengeance.

His thousand militiamen had gone up the Miami and Mad Rivers, cutting a road for their cannon. When they had reached the Chalagawtha Town, they found that Black Hoof had already abandoned and burned it, leaving nothing for the militia to loot. So Long Knife Clark had slashed and burned all the crops and proceeded on to the Pickaway Town on the Mad River. There, where the center of the town was defended by a three-sided stockade fort, Black Hoof and his warriors had made a stand.

There were numbers given in the newspaper account. Fourteen of Clark's men had been killed and thirteen wounded. Clark reported that the Indian dead had been nearly fifty, but as they carried away most of their dead and wounded, it was just a guess. One of those killed by the white soldiers was a cousin of Long Knife Clark, who had been a captive for three years. He had come fleeing toward the white-men near the end of the battle, running toward Clark and calling his name, and the militiamen had mistaken him for a warrior. The newspaper said he had died at Clark's feet.

Then the Long Knives had burned all the towns in that area and destroyed more than eight hundred acres of the Shawnees' crops, before returning to Kentucke with scalps and loot.

Pittsburgh rejoiced at the victory. Long Knife Clark was even bigger a hero than before.

Nonhelema and Fani now lived in a good log house in the orchard outside Fort Pitt. With the leaves off the trees, they could see the rivers where they flowed together, and Killbuck's Island under the far bluff. They were making a scant living by sewing and quillwork and beadwork, and trying to establish themselves on the margins of Pittsburgh's Indian trade. Nonhelema had still hoped the government would compensate her for the loss of her property and livestock two years ago. With George Morgan gone, it would be hard to get such relief.

Through their trade, they learned, little by little, details of the devastation of the Shawnee towns, and the names of warriors who had died in the Pickaway battle. They learned that Clark had indeed overestimated the number of warriors his army had killed.

Nonhelema recognized the names of most of the slain warriors. One was the husband of High Swallow, who had spoken for peace in the Women's Council six years ago, before the battle at the Kanawha. High Swallow's husband had been recovering from severe wounds then. Eventually he had gotten well enough to defend at Pickaway, and they had killed him there.

Another warrior killed at Pickaway was one of the sons of Quieteh, the medicine gatherer who had gone with the warriors to the Kanawha battle.

Two other of the dead warriors had been husbands of women who had argued for war at that council.

She heard that her black man, Caesar, had fought at Pickaway. He was not hurt there or killed, but no report came to her about where he was now. She sent word out that she was here and that she hoped he would come here to live if he wished. But she knew that might not happen. Caesar did not like living among whitemen.

Name by name, she learned of the safety of certain persons who were important or dear to her. A Wyandot who had been with McKee's expedition into Kentucke told her that McKee, and Simon Girty also, had gone through the whole campaign unharmed. A

Shawnee who had fought in the defense of the Shawnee towns told her that Black Hoof had managed to evacuate all the women and children and elders out of danger ahead of the Long Knife Clark's approach. Clark's force had turned back a few miles short of Lorimier's Fort, the great trading center and supply source, and so Lorimier and his Shawnee wife, Penampieh, had not been harmed. They were greathearted friends of the Shawnee people and had been among Nonhelema's dearest friends, before the war had placed them in opposing camps.

She learned that Methotase's children, Chiksika, Tecumapese, Tecumseh, and the boy triplets, were all safe. The Chalagawtha and Pickaway towns were being rebuilt on Lorimier's Creek, about a day's travel closer to his trading post than they had been before Clark destroyed them. That family was now living there. Tecumapese, just in her twenty-first year, was serving as substitute for their mother, who lived in that sad place by the Missisipe.

But there had been no word on the one person foremost in her concern—her son Morgan. There had not been a word about him since he got off LaBalme's boat and started back up the Ohio in the spring.

At last one day an elderly man from Killbuck's Island came walking in the snow through the leafless trees of the orchard, a red blanket wrapped around him and its edges flapping in the cold wind. Nonhelema let him in and set him on a chair near the hearth. They smoked a pipe together while Fani made tea. He gave her greetings in the traditional phrases but did not say why he had come. When the tea was in a cup before him, she tipped a bottle over a small glass and handed him a sip of rum to go with the sweet tea. His face wrinkled with a smile of gratitude, and after he had tossed the rum to the back of his throat and tasted the tea more delicately, he said he had come to bring her a message from Goshachgunk, the town of her half brother Stands Straight.

"He tells me," said the old man, "that he thought you were in the Missisipe. Then he heard that you came back here. Brother Israel wants you to know that your son named Morgan arrived at his town before the falling leaves and has been living with him. He asks that you let the boy stay with him until spring, as he is a good help in the cold time, and a good hunter."

Nonhelema took a deep breath and put her hands over her moist eyes and let joy and relief swell up in her heart. She smoothed her brow with her fingertips and then she wiped her eyes with the knuckles of her thumbs, while Fani laughed by the fire.

"Daughter," said Nonhelema, "rum is not good enough for this messenger. Please bring me the brandy bottle from under the bed!"

Nonhelema had come into the fort to see the officers about obtaining some compensation for her losses as a peacemaker. She sat on a bench, waiting to see Colonel Brodhead. He was a man she disliked intensely, but he was the one who had authority to convey her petition to the government. Brodhead was cold-eyed and moon-faced. The Delaware chiefs who were allied with the Americans had given him an honorary name meaning Great Moon, and she thought it must have been because he was so round and pale and cold. He was one of those ruthless town burners. A year before, he had led a force of six hundred men up the Allegheny-sipe and destroyed a dozen Delaware and Seneca villages. She sensed that he detested all Indians, but he was clever at pretending alliances with the useful bands. She had braced herself to sit in a room with him and beg. She had put it off as long as she could, but now she and her daughter were going hungry much of the time.

At last an orderly opened the colonel's door and summoned her with an upturned thumb.

The colonel was standing in front of his fireplace, holding up his coattails and warming his broad fundament.

"Well, Katy," he said, his gray-toothed smile looking like a snarl. She would have liked to tell him not to address her by that familiar name, but refrained from protesting and smiled. "How," he said, "do I happen to be honored by a visit from you?"

"Dear Colonel, forgive me that I do not come and pay my respects more often. But I know that the responsibilities of your command are demanding, and so I try not to bother you long."

"Well, Katy, you could just sit there all day every day and I'd be pleased to look at you. Now, my dear, what do you know that I should? Ha ha!" That remark gave her a pang of shame, reminding her that the Fort Pitt commanders deemed her their spy and informer, along with the missionaries. Probably Colonel Brodhead just now expected her to bring him some useful knowledge of the activities of hostile Indians. He would have to be disappointed.

"Excellency, what I know is that I have been a friend to the Americans and a peacemaker, as far as it has been in my power."

"That's true. We are grateful."

"It has cost me dear. I told the commanders here before you that perhaps they have not been so grateful as you say you are." She saw his false smile begin to contract into an expression of annoyance at this hint of criticism from an Indian. She went on: "Before I went to Fort Randolph on the Kanawha, I was wealthy. I owned a large herd of beef, I had many fine horses and a well-built house with good furnishings, I had a trunk full of fine clothing, and I had silver utensils. When I left my people to go help Captain Arbuckle at his fort, they would not let me take those treasures. At the fort, the army ate much of my cattle herd, and the rest were slaughtered, as were my horses, by Indians who were angry against me. Since then I have continued to grow poor by helping you. You know also that my brother and other relatives were murdered in that fort when they came to help Captain Arbuckle. Colonel, I have been advised by General Clark and other important men that your government is beholden to me for my services, and that I ought to apply for some compensation for all that I . . ."

She heard footsteps and urgent voices outside the door, and saw that Colonel Brodhead was brightening at the prospect of being interrupted. He obviously did not want to listen to a plea from any Indian for relief.

She could hear through the door that some of the voices were speaking French and some Delaware. Then came a knock on the door of Brodhead's office, and he called, "Enter!"

Colonel Brodhead's orderly led in two Delaware men, whose names Nonhelema didn't know, and a tall, whipped-looking young man whose face was red and green. This startling coloration she quickly realized to be a great, livid scar slanting across his forehead, and the fading greenish hues of bruises from his nose to his hairline. His right eye was bloodshot, deep red. Despite the vivid hues, the man was at once recognizable. And it was clear that he also recognized her.

He was the cadet whom she found dallying with Fani on the porch at Kaskaskia. He stood blinking at her in disbelief, his mouth beginning to move. He seemed to be in rags, even his shoeless feet wrapped in strips of filthy cloth, and clutched at his bosom the edges of a ragged, bloodstained trade blanket that once had been ecru wool. *La Croix,* she remembered. *The Cross.*

"What in Satan's sulfurous shit-pot have you brought me now, Jones?" Brodhead exclaimed.

"I'm not sure, sir. From what I can make out, something to do with that Frenchman came through here last spring. They're saying *LaBalme*."

"What of 'im? I figured that was the last we'd see of him." The colonel was turning to Nonhelema now, perhaps just remembering that she had hired on as LaBalme's guide.

She said to the battered youth: *"M'sieur La Croix, ou est le colonel LaBalme? Comment veniez-vous ici?"*

Perhaps at the sound of his own name, the youth began blinking, and his effeminate lips quivered. *"Madame, il est mort . . . Le reste aussi . . . tous ses hommes, morts ou captifs . . ."*

She put her palm to her breast, swallowed, asked: *"Dites-moi. Soyez fort, jeune ami. Par quoi?"*

"Damn it," Brodhead barked, "what's he saying?"

She took a deep breath, set her lips to refrain from telling him to shut up. "LaBalme and most of his men are dead, the rest captured . . ." Her heart quailed before the onslaught of her imaginings.

"Well, what? How? Who—"

"Colonel, if you will not interrupt, I shall try to learn all that. A bit of rum might help this poor boy get through his story. And me, also." She had led LaBalme at least part of the way to his fate: she, the peacemaker.

La Croix sometimes fell into fits of wheezing and blubbering, sometimes sat silent and trembling. It took most of the evening for the story to be told.

LaBalme had attracted a company of about a hundred, French Creoles, a few Americans, and Indian scouts. He had whipped them into a passion for the conquest of Detroit by promising them glory and loot. They would succeed with ease, he promised, because they would strike as Long Knife Clark had struck—by stealth and surprise. They would cross from the Missisipe to the Wabash, there recruit more loyal French Creoles, and ascend the Wabash to its headwaters, loot the British trading establishments there, pass swiftly down the Maumee-sipe to Lake Erie, and then surprise the weak British garrison at Detroit.

It had not worked out as LaBalme envisioned it. As La Croix whimpered through the narrative, she envisioned the arrogance and stupidity of LaBalme, scene by scene.

He had marched his men up the Wabash into Miami territory in early autumn, raiding the undermanned trading fort and the large

Miami town of Kekionga while all the warriors were away hunting. He had looted and burned the town, and sent a third of his men off to attack another fur trading post on the Eel River, hoping to obtain enough furs and hides to finance further expeditions.

But the Miami warriors, returning from the hunt and enraged by the destruction of their town, found LaBalme's two parties and ambushed them, slaughtering half and capturing the rest. La Croix with his own eyes had seen a warrior smash LaBalme's skull with a war club.

She translated the sorry tale as Brodhead sat stunned, drinking, now and then cursing. Nonhelema herself grew more weary and disgusted with every step of the fiasco. With the help of the Delawares who had brought La Croix in, she learned that the chieftain warrior who had led the Miamis and formed the fatal ambush was called Michiconagkwa, which was the Miami word for "small painted tortoise." That warrior, Little Turtle, had sent La Croix with a message that the Miami people, who had been very little troubled by the whiteman's war, were now very angry and on their guard. It meant that the road to Detroit from the west could no longer be considered an open road.

Rum, weariness, and emotion were at a boil inside Nonhelema by the time La Croix was taken away. Colonel Brodhead, half-drunk and fully furious, put everyone out of his quarters. There would be no more discussion now of Nonhelema's petition for relief from the government.

There was a little moonlight on the snow. She went out past the sentries, crossed the bridge over the moat, and turned down the path toward the orchard. She walked through the snow across the field where the annual peace talks had been held, where the Indians camped during those treaties, where they got crazed with rum, where thousands of thousands of Long Knife words of promise and peace had been uttered, all false. As she walked across the whiteness toward the orchard, she remembered the face and the voice of the charming Colonel LaBalme, and remembered then the drops of the cat blood that had speckled his clothes as an eagle soared away over the boat.

Her house was a dark shape among the bare trees. But as she walked closer, she saw a dull little rectangle of light coming through a window, from a room in which her daughter, Fani, would have a warm fire burning, and a candle.

We will have a drink together, she thought. *No, a prayer pipe. One or the other. Or both. Should I tell her about La Croix?*

I don't know, she thought. *All I know is that I will never again help a whiteman do anything he wants.*

Nila ni wapey shikwi, she thought, as she reached for the door latch. *I shed my white skin.*

BOOK THREE

1 7 8 2 – 1 7 8 7

18

Nonhelema and Fani sat dyeing porcupine quills near a window of their house in the orchard when, through the budding leaves, they saw the courier loping down the path from the fort. He was a young Delaware who often carried messages for Stands Straight.

Their red dye was made from crushed cochineal bugs, rich blue from gentian, and yellow from burdock root. The quills were steeping in three bowls. Although colorful glass beads from Europe were available in the trading posts and easier to use, Nonhelema still liked the quills. Beads were costly, while quills were free, brought to her by hunters, and there was always a demand for her quillwork, which was lighter in weight than beads. She had just a few days ago received a very rich payment, enough to live on for nearly a year, for a fringed, quilled deerhide frock coat custom-made for General George Rogers Clark. A committee of gentlemen had raised a subscription to have a gift made for him, in gratitude for his victories in the West, and the beautiful coat, tailored with a French flair, decorated on the back with twining vines and flowers of multicolored quills, had been sent down the Ohio on a boat with supplies and messages to his fort at the Falls of the Ohio.

More than a year ago, she had vowed to herself that she would never do anything else for whitemen. The coat was a different matter. She had done it for pay, making herself a living. She had never made anything better.

Fani, watching and helping her make Clark's coat, had said, "*Nigeah,* your work is always beautiful, but I never saw you work so carefully. Why are you making it so perfect for a man who has done so much to harm our people?"

Nonehelema had sewed and thought for a while, then said, "Do you shame me for doing so well for an enemy?"

Fani had not replied yes or no, just looked at her, and then Nonhelema had said, "He will know this was made by Nonhelema, a Shawnee, and he will never be able to find anything wrong in it. That will satisfy me. Our enemy can never show someone a Shawnee thing that was poor. Do you understand?"

"I understand, *nigeah.*"

Fani had refused to see the cadet La Croix. Because he had gone with LaBalme attacking peaceful Miami towns, she had wiped him from her memory, making him a nonperson, as the Shawnees did those who proved themselves not worth knowing. He had eventually been put in a boat going back down to the Missisipe.

The failure of peacemaking always weighed on Nonhelema's spirit, even as she sewed and decorated, depicting in quills and beads the beautiful things that the Master-of-Life had created on the earth, as she and Fani were doing now, as they watched the courier come through the trees toward the house.

She went to the door and opened it for him before he had to knock. She saw in his eyes that the news he brought was terrible.

"Colonel Williamson's militia," he said, "burned the mission at Gnaddenhutten."

Those words jolted her. But it made no sense. The mission had been evacuated last summer to a safer place, far up on the Sandusky. She said, "But why would they do that? Gnaddenhutten was abandoned."

"Yes, but the people went back to get the corn left standing in the fields."

Suddenly she felt cold. "Did they kill any Praying Indians?" Fani had appeared over her shoulder, and Nonhelema sent her to get the horses and prepare to travel.

The young man looked down and said, "About a hundred. Only two boys got away alive."

One of the hideous bundles of burn-blackened flesh and bones was her mother, Elizabeth, and another was her sister Christiana. They had been mixed and mingled with the other ninety burned corpses and the charred timbers of the mission house. It was only because of the Moravians' meticulous record keeping that the victim's identities had been found. Shreds of clothing and tresses of hair helped when features were obliterated.

Two other bodies found separate from each other in two different burned buildings were her half brother Stands Straight, christened Brother Israel, and his wife. Stands Straight had finally condescended to give up arms and live with the other converts, and now he and his wife were roasted corpses.

Nonhelema and Fani wept and trilled in their grief. All around the ruin were other women, mostly Delawares, shrieking and ululating. Men and boys moved around the reeking site, waving blankets and sticks to keep the vultures from settling there to feed, and they, too, were crying.

Whitemen of the Pennsylvania Militia had done this. Nonhelema had seen the company march through Pittsburgh a few weeks before, led by a militia officer named Colonel Williamson, to retaliate against Indians who had raided and looted during the winter. He had incited his men to show no mercy.

But these were the mission Indians! Good Praying Indians! Christians! They had been only sheep!

Their remains showed that their hands and feet had been bound. And everyone's skull had been caved in by a blow from behind.

All the carcasses in the mission church ruins were male, while all in the house were female. The few whose heads were not completely seared away had been scalped, so it could be presumed that all of them had been.

This pile of burned wood and bodies that Nonhelema was looking at through blurring tears, this was the very place where she had been converted to a Jesus Indian herself, on that Christmas love-feast seven winters before. That night of delicate cakes and hot, spicy drinks in cups, of singing and musical instruments, of Brother Jungman's piteous, impassioned, all-night sermon.

And she knew: The militiamen who did this, so thoroughly and deliberately, they all would claim that they were Christians.

One of the Moravian missionary priests in his black frock coat sat on a puncheon bench by a fence beyond the ruin, deep in murmured talk with a Delaware Indian boy of about fourteen, called Thomas. The boy wore a thick, turbanlike dressing of linen on his head, with blood seeping through. He had been scalped alive by a militiaman. He and another boy had escaped, and thus Colonel Williamson's crime had been described by witnesses.

It was only by the most unfortunate chance that the flock of Christian Indian sheep had been there when the wolves came.

The Moravian Delawares, having nearly starved during the winter up on the Sandusky, had come back down to their old bounteous mission fields, with no missionaries among them, to get what corn might still be standing in their fields. While they were pulling the hard-corn ears in the fields, near the abandoned Salem Mission, Colonel Williamson had appeared with some of his militiamen and given them friendly greetings.

The colonel had told the Praying Indians that he would escort them to Fort Pitt, where they would be well fed and receive gifts. He persuaded the Indian men to turn over their hunting guns to the soldiers, as a gesture of their peacefulness and good faith.

Once they were all disarmed, the Praying Indians had been escorted to the Gnaddenhutten Mission and brought inside the fences of that old mission farm. There, at gunpoint, they had all been herded into the two buildings and tied up.

The boys related that at first there had been much wailing and shouting, but then all the male captives settled down to a night of fervent praying and putting their fate in the hands of Jesus. It had been a long night of terror and reverence.

Through the night they had heard sounds of the women being assaulted in the house. They had prayed louder to drown out those sounds. Eventually, the boys reported, all the men were ready to go and meet Jesus, and their eyes were shining.

In the morning, the people were made to kneel facing the walls, and several of the militiamen had moved along behind them with oaken mauls and smashed in their skulls, one by one, as they prayed to be taken to the heaven that had so long been promised them.

Each soldier passed the maul to another, and then went back and scalped the ones he had killed.

The boys said that some were hit so hard that their blood and brains splattered the walls. In the turmoil, the boys, who were near the door, had pretended to be dead already. The one was scalped. They had slipped out the door and crawled under the building without being seen by the soldiers outside, and had cowered there in grief and terror, listening to the thumping and the soldier voices above them.

When the buildings were set afire, the boys had fled under cover of smoke, and had staggered into the next mission town up the river, Schoenbrun, in time to warn the corn gleaners. When the militia rode into Schoenbrun looking for more easy-to-kill Indians, no one was there.

For once, the missionaries themselves were burdened with guilt. They were stunned not just by the massacre but also by the realization that they probably could have prevented it. If a missionary or two had been present with the gleaners, Colonel Williamson surely would not have dared order their extermination. If they had arrived to witness the preparations for the killing, they probably could have stopped it, because the colonel would not have let such an atrocity be witnessed.

But the missionaries had not gone into that dangerous territory with their flock—they had stayed at the Sandusky Mission. They had failed as shepherds. Guilt lay on them as heavy as the world.

For so long the Praying Indians had long been warned by everyone that the missionaries were rendering them into helpless sheep; that such things as this were sure to happen.

Being a convert herself, Nonhelema had been scolded by most Shawnees for her folly. Alexander McKee and her brothers Silverheels, Captain Johnny, and the Wolf, even her daughter, Fani, and her son Morgan—everyone had fretted over these foolish Indians, and some of the blame was always put upon her family, who had encouraged the missionaries to come into this part of the country.

Blessed are the peacemakers, she said voicelessly to herself, *for they shall be called the children of God.* These scorched, rotting masses of meat and bone had tried to be the peacemakers, as she had herself.

Blessed are they.

If they are now with Jesus, she thought. *If they are now with Jesus . . . surely they would be spared the flames of whiteman's hell in the afterlife . . .*

This was something she was not understanding yet. If Jesus had suffered to keep everyone else from suffering, why had these sheep of his flock had to suffer this?

There was no answer that she could see.

The soldiers who did this, would they ever be judged for it? Or punished? Or would they go free, like the murderers of Cornstalk?

For once she thought that Alexander McKee might have been right to take their son away to Detroit. If Tommy had been here with the mission schoolteachers, he probably would have been one of those smaller bundles of roasted meat, curled up in the ashes.

She felt that if she kept thinking, she would shake apart. There was too much to do here: Comforting. Rituals. Burials.

She took a long breath and let it out, quaking. She seized Fani's wrist and held it hard as if to keep from flying off. "Come," she said. "They need us."

The remains of Nonhelema's mother and sister were sewn into deer-hide and put on a tarpaulin suspended between two horses, and a procession set out down the old trail to the Pickaway Plains, where Nonhelema's Town had been before the war. Nonhelema did not want her mother and sister to be buried in graves at the ruined mission. There could be no rest for their spirits where that horror happened.

Elizabeth would be buried beside her husband White Fish, in the beautiful plain on the west side of the Scioto-sipe.

Many relatives of Nonhelema were in the quiet procession. Captain Johnny had appeared with her son Morgan. Silverheels had ridden in just before they left the mission. Her brother the Wolf had joined them.

Even Caesar had come, with his wife, to help on the funeral journey. It had been so long since she had seen some of these dear ones. The word of the massacre had spread everywhere.

They rode through the hills and woods in the glory of springtime. Leaves were still pale green and tender; blossoms of redbud and dogwood were like wisps of violet and white in the shade of the giant oaks, chestnuts, and maples. The forest floor was profuse with trout lily and crowfoot and bluebell, and the orange and green petals of the poplar tree flower, their design like flames, fell like snow when a breeze blew. One day millions of passenger pigeons flew over the treetops, almost invisible above the canopy of foliage, their wingbeats sounding like waterfalls. Droppings fell like rain through the foliage.

Then they were gone and the only sounds were the thuds of unshod Indian horses on the soft earth.

One evening in camp beside the trail, Nonhelema sat looking at the funerary bundles where they lay under a dogwood tree. Her son Morgan came and sat beside her, holding a dogwood blossom between his thumb and finger. With its four petals representing the Four Winds, the tree was considered sacred, she told him. He said, "The missionaries told us it is a holy tree. They told us Jesus was killed on a cross of dogwood. And since then, the dogwood tree refuses to grow big."

"I remember that pretty story," she said. "Do you believe it to be true?"

The boy thought a while, then replied: "If it were not told by whitemen, I could believe it, *nigeah*."

She said, "Your father, who knows such things, told me that no such tree grew in the land where Jesus lived. But it remains a pretty story."

It was drizzling rain the morning they rode down Scippo Creek between the old sites of Nonhelema's and Cornstalk's Towns. Among the weeds and wildflowers, the charred posts and poles of their old buildings stuck up, all that remained after the towns had been abandoned in advance of the Long Knives' town-burning invasions. It seemed sad but wondrous to Nonhelema how quickly *Tula Geah*, Earth Mother, could reclaim and absorb what people had made: their homes, their lives, their bones. They rode past a packed-earth place where a weathered pole stood head-high, mostly gray but with traces of red paint. She pointed to it with her chin and said to Silverheels, "That was Pucsinwah's war post. You must remember when I came down and told him the Women's Council voted for war."

"I remember, sister."

Eight summers ago, as she recalled. She had tried to make peace then, and ever since, but had failed. It might not have failed if the whitemen had had any honor. Now they had angered even the peace-loving Delawares, all of them finally, and had stirred even the distant Miamis. When they went out and murdered the Praying Indians, even her mother, who had been much like what the missionaries called saints, they had proved that *peace* was just a joke word to them, it truly meant nothing.

The little burned bodies they put into the shallow graves were hardly bigger than dogs' carcasses, and they stank powerfully even through the airtight hides. But the ceremony was reverent. The relatives all sang the Traveling Song and the Celebration Song.

> *Hey opa hay ya*
> *Hey opa hey ah*
> *Hey opa hay ah . . . Heyah! Heyah! Weh!*

In the ground over the bosom of each carcass they placed an acorn.

The acorn, fed by the body under it, would become an oak, and someday would feed the creatures that had fed the people while they lived. It was the giving-back that had to be done to keep the Sacred Hoop rolling. It had always been that way. People could not take more from *Tula Geah* than they gave back to her. While considered a warrior's tribute, surely each of these quailified, in white Jesus' army of sheep.

After the funeral ceremony, Nonhelema walked a while beside the Scioto-sipe. She heard a rifle in the distance and knew it was surely a whiteman hunter, because the Shawnees had moved away to the northwest, up along the Mad River and Lorimier's Creek, to make distance between themselves and the hunters from Kentucke. She looked at the flowing river and remembered when the Kentucke belonged to them, the Shawnees, not to the Long Knives. If the funeral party stayed here long, they probably would be shot at by hunters from Kentucke.

Her mother was now laid beside her father. Now it was time to go back to Pittsburgh and see whether Colonel Williamson would be punished for the massacre of the Praying Indians.

She had little hope of it.

By the time Colonel Williamson came in from his compaign, word had already reached all over the frontier and he was not greeted as a hero by everyone.

At Fort Pitt, the military inquiry began. It was evident, even to Indian haters, that the massacre of the Praying Indians would provoke vengeance from every corner of the Indian world. Colonel Williamson had much explaining to do. Everyone was talking about it.

Nonhelema overheard men in the town praising the colonel for getting rid of so many Indians at once. But she heard those same men, speaking in public, demand an accounting for the outrage.

How the British would exploit this atrocity to incite the tribes!

She was still sunk in spirit and wanted to get drunk all the time to keep from feeling what she was feeling, and thinking what she was thinking, but she stayed sober as much as she could bear to, because she had to know what was going to come of it.

Colonel Williamson told the tribunal that his men had found in the mission certain articles of clothing that had belonged to white people abducted in Indian raids the previous winter. He said that he had been faced with the task of guarding all those Delawares he had rounded up around the mission town, or proceeding ahead to punish the Indians farther on. And so he had taken a vote among the hundred men of his company, whether to put them to death or not. He had asked the men who wanted to spare the Indians' lives to step out.

Seventeen men opposed to killing them had stepped out. The other eighty-three under Colonel Williamson's intimidating gaze said they were for killing them.

The majority ruled. The Indians would be executed for their atrocities and the company would proceed on with Colonel Brodhead's orders to chastise the other Delawares farther north.

The next question in the inquiry, then, was: Who were the eighty-three men who had voted for the massacre, and who were the seventeen who had voted for mercy?

Every one of Colonel Williamson's hundred men swore in God's name that he had been one of the seventeen who had voted to spare the Praying Indians.

So Colonel Williamson and his men were cleared of blame. Suddenly the campaign on the Tuscarawas was *officially* declared a great victory. Immediately, a much bigger force was assembled to continue the campaign farther up, even as far as the Delaware and Wyandot towns on the Sandusky—clear up into the heart of Captain Pipe's country. It was a thrilling prospect—nearly five hundred Pennsylvania militiamen instead of one hundred, all on good horses to carry them far and fast.

They set out, roundly cheered, in May, under the command of the fiery Colonels Williamson and William Crawford. Colonel Brodhead, the glowering commandant of Fort Pitt, had given them implicit instructions to show no mercy; only annihilation, or the fear of it, would convince the Indians that they must leave western Pennsylvania alone.

"Peacemakers lose again," Nonhelema said to her daughter, reaching for a bottle. "I cannot bear to think of this anymore. For a while I am going to get drunk and talk in spirit with my mother and my sister. Will you be joining me?"

Fani answered, "Give me a glass, too. I wish to drink to the happiness of my grandmother and my aunt, who now are in the arms of the suffering bleeding Jesus, if Zeisberger is right about it all. If he is wrong, they are on the Milky Way."

And the two beautiful women, mother and daughter, smiling with tear-brimmed eyes, touched the rims of their glasses together and began drinking.

19

FORT PITT
JULY 1782

This was still Tapistewamigi-sipe or Menach-sink, the place where the waters flowed together and went westward. It was a sacred place in Indian memory.

But now it was also Pittsburgh, where the rivers of migrating whitemen flowed through and went westward. Long Knife Clark's conquest of the Middle Ground had opened the floodgate for the westering rivers.

For the traders and outfitters, these were times of prosperity, as whitemen judge those things. As fast as their warehouses could be filled with goods coming over the mountains from the east, they were emptied. Their goods were loaded into whitemen's boats and Indian canoes, onto packhorse trains, onto settlers' flatboats, the trade goods flowing westward with the thousands of migrants and adventurers and speculators.

Nonhelema had regained a small role in this flood of movement and commerce. As an interpreter and go-between, with the trading companies on one side of her and the Indian hunters and trappers on the other, with her abilities as a hide finisher and decoration maker and seamstress, she was able to earn just enough to feed herself and Fani, and keep them in the little house in the orchard below the fort. Caesar and his wife had returned, and they lived in a lean-to attached to the house.

Nonhelema spent too much on drink, in an effort to keep her heart numb.

She was willing to work and trade in Pittsburgh, but it was not a good place to live. It was a seething stew of vice and violence, and after dark no woman could step outdoors without being accosted. Especially any Indian woman.

"This town is a whores' nest," she would complain to the city's officials whenever she encountered one. And it was. There were not many white women in Pittsburgh yet, but most of those who were there were whoring. And too many of the abject, rum-besotted Indian women who occupied the slum camps around the town and the fort had fallen into degradation. Nonhelema felt a heaviness in her heart every time she saw an Indian woman staggering and giggling through the streets with the arm of a militiaman or riverman wrapped possessively around her or groping into her clothes. All Indian women were her sisters, she felt, and their debasement debased her, too. These men who were exchanging a little rum or a few pennies for Indian women's bodies were the same kind of men who had raped and killed twenty-seven Praying Indian women at the Gnaddenhutten mission. If there were not a little law and discipline here to control them, they would be taking these wretched women without even offering them the coins or the rum.

Day after day, Nonhelema watched and studied the sorts of whitemen who were pouring outward into the valley of the Ohio, into her people's homeland, with their schemes, their greed, their land deeds, their diseases, their liquor, their insatiable restlessness. And she prayed for the Shawnee people out there who would have to deal with them.

In Pittsburgh, she was still a marginal part of the community, even though her old friend and patron George Morgan had quit his post as Indian commissioner and returned to New Jersey. She was still desired in good company, as an interpreter sometimes, as a healer now and then, as a diplomatic messenger between the various state officials and the Indians who lived nearby and tried to maintain civil relations with their white neighbors.

Killbuck and his wife were liked and admired by traders, officers, and their families, and were a part of the town's society. Like Nonhelema, they enjoyed the fine European music that was performed in gatherings in the homes of the wealthy, or occasionally in public concerts, and they were often invited to such performances. Like the Killbuck couple, Nonhelema and her daughter were deemed desirable guests because of their warmth, dignity, good manners, and vivacious personalities, as well as their dedication to American causes. Fani was an object of many young men's yearnings, and older men's, too. Nonhelema herself, even at her age, was trailed everywhere by several gents who knew of her long-ago alliances with Morgan and then McKee, and perhaps imagined that a similar intimacy might fall to them if they could keep her glass filled enough to weaken her. Nonhelema was adept at the graces that enabled an unmarried woman to fend off but not offend.

But there was one man at Fort Pitt whose proximity so chilled her that she could barely stand to associate with him. He was, unfortunately, very important: Daniel Brodhead, the current commandant of the fort, the man Chief Killbuck called Great Moon. But his physical repulsiveness was not the problem; she often associated politely with many whitemen who were repulsive.

What Nonhelema felt in the presence of Brodhead was the hatred that emanated from him when Indians were near.

She knew, from the inquiry into the massacre at the mission, that Brodhead had encouraged Colonel Williamson to strike the Delawares mercilessly. And he had given the same sort of brutal license to Williamson and Colonel Crawford when he sent them out to continue the campaign.

Nonhelema was a tolerant judge of men, often quoting to herself the Matthew in the Great Book who had said, *Judge not, that ye be not judged.* She knew she was always being judged; she could feel it. And the judgment she felt coming from Brodhead was that she was an Indian squaw who had too much prestige at his fort, and that she deserved to be knocked on the head, and probably raped and scalped, like the Praying Indian women at Gnaddenhutten Mission. She could read all that in his piglike eyes.

Judge not, that ye be not judged, she thought. Book of Matthew, some number she couldn't remember.

The name *Matthew*, Matthew Arbuckle, the captain in the fort at the Kanawha so long ago, the one who had not killed her on the battlefield there, the one who had promised her that a forest would fall on him if any harm came to Cornstalk at the fort, the one who had not gone to witness the trial of the men who killed Cornstalk:

Last year, according to letters and reports from Virginia, Captain Arbuckle had been riding home in a storm and the top of a tree had blown down and killed him.

Just as she had dreamed it.

If Arbuckle had gone to the murderers' trial and his testimony had caused Cornstalk's murderers to be punished, she thought, the tree would not have killed him. When she thought of things like this, she wanted to drink some whiskey.

The militiamen who murdered her mother and sister and the others at Gnaddenhutten Mission had been let free to go and kill again, by this Fort Pitt commander Brodhead. Men who should be burned up in what the missionaries called hell, they were instead out someplace along the Muskingum or Tuscarawas or the Sandusky, looking for more Indians to kill. Probably they were looking for the other mission towns up there, because the Praying Indians were so easy to kill.

She had tried so hard to be a peacemaker. She had lost her own Shawnee people and her little son Tommy from trying so hard. Her beautiful big town on Scippo Creek near the Scioto-sipe was not her town anymore. Most of her own people, with Cornstalk's, had gone to live among the Delawares, and they probably were now in the path of the killers Brodhead had sent out in May under the command of Williamson and Crawford.

It seemed futile to be a peacemaker when there were so many men whose passion was for war.

It was said that the general of all the British in the war on the other side of the mountains had surrendered his army to the American general Washington, in the town of Yorktown, Virginia, before the winter past. Pittsburgh had cheered the news. It was thought therefore that the whole war would end sometime soon. But there was no sign of peace on this side of the mountains. It had meant only that more whitemen were coming through here on their way into her old Ohio country, and more soldiers would be available out here to confront Indians. For the Indians, it meant only more war.

Nonhelema was alone in the house. Fani had gone to Killbuck's Island to visit with Delaware friends there.

I wish my daughter were here, she thought. *We would have a little glass together. I would like to talk with her about that dream of Arbuckle and the tree. Fani remembers Arbuckle, there at Fort Randolph, there by the Kanawha-sipe. She remembers him. She told me he tried two times to catch her alone in the room when I wasn't with her. He was no better than the others that way; he had only seemed better.*

I believe I will pour a little in this glass and wait, and when she comes home we will have a glass together and talk about those things.

A little in the glass. Just to look at and smell while I wait.

A sip while I wait for her.

She came awake with Fani shaking her. "*Nigeah!* Listen! Hear what has happened! Wake up, *nigeah*! Everyone knows this already and you sleep through the news!"

"What? What?" Nonhelema blinked, groggy, alarmed by her daughter's excitement. At the other end of the room, some of Killbuck's people were talking fast, some arguing, some laughing. Nonhelema felt ashamed that she had fallen into sleep sitting in the chair with the bottle half-finished, when she had not even intended to start drinking.

"Listen," exclaimed Fani. "They were caught, those militiamen who went to kill on the Sandusky! Captain Pipe and Wingenund caught them up there looking for more mission towns, and ambushed them! They killed and caught many soldiers!"

Nonhelema was breathing fast now, her heart speeding.

"They caught the colonels, too?" she gasped, remembering what this was all about: Williamson's militiamen, who had killed her mother and sister.

"One got away. The other they burned up a long time until he died. Only an army doctor got away from there."

"They burned a colonel up? Pipe and Wingenund did?"

"Yes. The doctor said Girty was there, too, and that Girty laughed at the burning."

Simon Girty! Alexander McKee's man. "Did they say McKee was at the burning? Did they say which colonel was burned up?"

It was confusing. It should have made her feel avenged, glad, should have made her whoop, or pray thanks for the justice; at last, murderers of her people had been done to likewise. As in the missionaries' book, an eye for an eye and a tooth for a tooth. A killing and burning-up for many killings and burnings-up, as in Shawnee justice. Maybe it was revenge, or justice.

But it was not peace. And it meant the British side had triumphed over the American side.

Nonhelema wanted to know more of this, but Fani only knew what she had heard being shouted in the town.

One of the old men came over from the other end of the room. He smiled briefly, but then he looked sad and scared. Nothing like this could happen to white soldiers without making more danger for the last few peaceful Delawares here. The old man said, "They burned up Crawford. I heard that. Colonel Williamson has ridden back here with his surviving soldiers who got away."

Nonhelema sighed deeply and put her hand over her eyes. The one who burned the mission with her mother in it was the one who escaped, and the other colonel was burned up. *Ni po tha,* consumed alive by fire.

"Aahh-la," Nonhelema groaned. "*Nee cha!* My daughter! Let us not sit here and neglect the rest of that bottle. Its spirits are floating away in the air. Get a glass, *nee cha.*"

"Ah-heh, *nigeah*! Ah-heh."

Through this place where water and goods and migrants flowed, there also came the news from all four winds. In the late summer of this year, 1782, there came more war news from the Kentucke settlements—news that saddened and enraged the white people here.

The news was of a terrible defeat suffered by the leading men of several of the Kentucke settlements, who had been ambushed at the great salt lick called Blue Licks, on the Licking River. About forty Kentucke militiamen had been killed, including a dozen officers. Of the commanders of the militia force, only one, Daniel Boone, had survived, and even he had lost a son in the ambush.

Nonhelema heard many words and names in the report that were like stabs in her heart. Many of the dead officers she had met, here or in her own country years before: Colonel Todd and Colonel Trigg, Boone's son Israel, two brothers named Bulger who were captains.

The names of the tribes involved struck her heart also: Shawnees, of course, and Wyandots, Ottawas, Delawares, even Ojibwas from far up on the Great Lakes. It was said there were even Mohawks there, led by Brant, the famed Christian warrior from New York. Some British officers were leaders of the attack, and one of the British leaders was Alexander McKee.

It had started as a campaign against settlements in Kentucke. The Indians had attacked a small fort near the town of Lexington, and failed to overpower it. They were withdrawing and had forded the Licking River near the salt lick when Colonel Todd's mounted Kentuckians caught up with them.

Especially because of McKee's involvement, Nonhelema felt she needed to know more about what had happened. She needed to know whether the father of her little son had been killed or hurt. The early reports were that there had been virtually no casualties among the British and Indian force. She could be almost certain that McKee was safe.

The bravest and smartest Kentucke veterans had been defeated in that ambush. It meant that the reputations of Brant and McKee would become all the more terrible, and more hateful.

It also meant that the Indians were growing stronger and more fierce in the defense of their invaded lands. Peace was not imminent.

Worse, it would mean more concerted and ferocious retaliation.

And retaliation usually meant that it would be the women and children and the elders who would suffer most, because they were easier to catch and kill than warriors. All it required was going to the places where they lived and destroying everything there. Both whites and Indians had been using that strategy for many years, back and forth, almost every season. The Long Knife forces had developed an especially effective variation. They formed their armies in the fall, after their own crops had been harvested, and marched to the Indian towns when most of the warriors were away hunting, and burned the Indian towns and crops, leaving the communities without food or shelter for the winter. They also took prisoners to use in bargaining at peace treaties, or to exchange for the release of captives held by the tribes.

Nonhelema now could hardly go to sleep without whiskey because she was in too much worry and dread of the retaliation she knew was building up toward the autumn. The Long Knives would march up where the Shawnee towns were concentrated, up near the headwaters of the Mad and Miami Rivers, three or four days' ride northwest of the Pickaway Plains, where her beautiful town had stood ten years before, when she had still been a chief among her own people, back before the war, back before the Shawnees had been driven out of those plains. Into the cluster of new towns up there—Blue Jacket's Town,

Piqua, Kispoko, Chalagawtha, Wapakoneta, Mekoche, Wakatomica—
the army would strike. Already she had heard that Long Knife himself, George Rogers Clark, would lead the army; that he expected to
call together the biggest army of volunteers there had ever been in
that part of the country, and lay waste all those towns, avenge the
losses at Blue Licks, and intimidate the Shawnee nation once and for
all. And she knew that it would be easier for him to raise a big army
now, because Kentucke was now occupied by tens of thousands of
whites. Here, at Pittsburgh, she had watched so many thousands pass
through on their way to Kentucke.

My poor people, she thought. *Now they will see, in such a hard way, that
they should have listened to us, the peacemakers.*

Damn you, Alexander McKee, she thought. *You have helped bring all this
upon my people! And now you have our little boy in danger!*

It was still dark, but she had been awake long enough to make a cook
fire and heat tea water. She went to Fani's bed and put her hand
around her daughter's bare foot. It was the way she could awaken her
without startling her. The young woman murmured, "What, *nigeah?*
Why are you up?"

"*Nee cha,* listen. I am going to see our people. I have to find my little boy. I ask you to ride with me."

Fani came wide awake. By the time the first paleness of morning
showed in the eastern sky and reflected on the river, they had bathed
and prayed. Nonhelema went to awaken Caesar, to have him get
horses ready. She found him already up, dressed, drinking tea with
his wife. When she told them where she and Fani were going, they
wanted to go, too. Caesar would provide protection. He also asked
permission to invite a few more armed men from the Delawares here,
to help escort them. These Delawares, he reminded her, had relatives
in the Sandusky country whom they might like to visit, and the Sandusky was not far from those Shawnee places.

Her entourage got out of sight of the fort before sunrise. She had
never seen Indians decide to do something and do it so quickly.

They followed the ancient path up the wooded bluffs, looking down
on the roofs of settlers' cabins as the first rays of sunlight slanted in
among the great hardwood trees. They would avoid the whiteman's
roads through the fields of tree stumps in the lowlands, because those
were the roads soldiers and bandits traveled, and a group of armed

Indians, even with women in it, raised suspicions or created alarm. They had perhaps fifteen days' travel ahead of them, depending on weather, possible incidents, and visits at obscure villages along the way, and they hoped to attract as little attention as possible.

Every time she came by this route, it took longer to pass the stumps and the brush fences of the settlers. But the trails went along the ridges, through high, shady woods, and across splashing white-water streams, the ground marked only by deer hooves and bear paws, and by the middle of the day the signs of whitemen were few. The horses breathed and blew, leather creaked, the Indians' voices were soft and melodious, and the absence of Pittsburgh's noise and smells was cleansing her soul. Caesar and one of the warriors ranged always ahead, sometimes stopping to let the file catch up with them. He was always easy to see because of the red cloth tied around his head, its ends hanging down his back. Every time she saw him, he was grinning.

She said, "I think Caesar is happy to be away from Pittsburgh."

He said, "I am happy to be with my queen, on the road to visit her little son. I am happy to see the hopefulness in the face of my queen."

She laughed and swatted toward him with her quirt. "Queen!" she laughed. "No queens in this land anymore. The Americans have thrown out kings and queens!"

Caesar grinned, nodded, and urged his horse ahead, his long musket cradled across his elbow, the tails of his red head scarf rippling behind his broad shoulders.

What fine creations Weshemonetoo the Great Good Spirit has made, she thought, breathing deep scents of forest and horse. She meant the trees and the mountains, the animals, the Indian men and women coming along behind her, that man riding out before her to watch for danger, once a slave, now a man who could choose what he would do. Like her, he would always have to be on guard against what whitemen presumed about themselves. But the works of Creator were magnificent here in the mountains and the woods, where people who cared for each other journeyed to see others they cared for.

Whether it is the God of Jesus or Weshemonetoo, she thought, *it is good. It is only man who makes bad.*

LORIMIER'S TOWN, NEAR THE MIAMI RIVER
OCTOBER 1782

Louis Pierre Lorimier, the trader, gave her an effusive welcome, his black eyes wide with delight and surprise.

But Lorimier was a shrewd little man, and she knew he was wondering fast about why she would be here. He held her hand in both of his and looked up into her eyes; she stood more than a head taller than he.

Lorimier was a man beloved and trusted by the Shawnee people. He was Canadian-born, of French aristocratic descent, and a loyal partisan in the Indians' resistance to the Long Knives' invasion of their country. His flourishing trading post, built on the portage between streams running north to the Great Lakes and south to the Ohio, was stocked with good English wares, but was also a key way station and supply point for war parties en route to strike the Kentuckians. The sturdy little man was himself brave and dedicated enough to paint up and go down with the raiders toward the Ohio sometimes. His thick hair, plaited in a queue that reached his knees, was as black as any Indian's, and he could look like a perfect Shawnee warrior.

He greeted Fani, whom he had known most of her life, and praised her as a rival to her mother's beauty. He ordered one of the post's half-breed boys to tend to their horses, embraced Caesar and pounded him affectionately on the shoulders, and then led Nonhelema back through the sprawling store past shelves of kettles, blankets, guns, kegs, pails, bolts of cloth, knives, and stacks of redolent animal pelts, to the corner in the rear that served as his office, where they might talk in some degree of privacy. The place was teeming with Indians and Indian women, Frenchmen, mixed-bloods, even a few pink-faced English-looking men in hunting garb. Everyone looked at her as she went through. She was accustomed to this, but many of them wore startled expressions of recognition. There were many here whom she remembered from long ago, but she was glad that Lorimier bustled her through. There would be time later to greet old acquaintances. Many would be suspicious of her because she had been an American partisan so long. Lorimier chattered cheerfully to her as they went down the long aisles, which discouraged people from interrupting to greet her. "The boy who tends your horses," he said, "would you know that is Captain Drouillard's son, by Straight Head?

Remember you saw him here when he was newborn? He is my nephew, George Pierre, through Penampieh? Remember?"

"I do remember." And she did, vaguely. She remembered hearing, too, that the boy's father, Pierre Drouillard, the interpreter, had left Straight Head and gone to marry a Frenchwoman at Detroit. "And Penampieh herself, I shall be happy to see her, if she is here," she said. Lorimier's wife was a renowned mixed-blood beauty of the Bougainville family, through whom Lorimier was related to most of the wealthy and influential merchants and suppliers of Ontario and Detroit. When one was in the presence of this vigorous little man, one seemed to be at the center of a vast web of kinship, trade, and communication. Everything passed through here; everyone relied on him. Innumerable planning councils of the war chiefs met here in his compound in times of emergency. Outside the post was a stomp ground for dances and festivals. It was also the ceremonial ground for the Shawnees and their relatives who made up his community.

"Of course you will visit with Penampieh," he said, gesturing to a chair and picking up a decanter to offer her a dram of cognac. It was superior to any liquor that was ever available in Pittsburgh. They touched the edges of their tiny glasses.

"Ah, my dear *Coitcheleh!*" he exclaimed, using one of the names she had been called in the old days, "Teacher-of-the-Life-Rules." She had not heard that for so long, it made a twinge in her heart. "Let me look upon you! Command me how I may serve you! My fondest hope is that you return to your people." Without mentioning the delicate subject, he was inquiring whether she had come to her senses and quit the Americans. Years ago, she knew, Lorimier had been deeply offended by Cornstalk's accommodation of the Virginians, and hers. Some of the warriors who had attacked Fort Randolph when she was staying there had been from his community here; even now she could remember having seen them there. To be here was a delicate matter.

"*Vieil ami,*" she said, "I have never been away from my people, in spirit. I am only for their peace and safety, and I have given everything to be a peacemaker by the best way I thought possible. I know you do not agree that is the way."

She looked down, then glanced out into the store. Fani was in a far corner, fingering some fine, shiny dark cloth on a bolt. Nonhelema looked back to Lorimier's eyes; the little fellow was blinking and swallowing.

He said, "*Merci, Coitcheleh.* It is good to hear from your own lips.

Some people were angry with you and your brother. But we mourned deeply when the Long Knives murdered him, and many warriors still seek vengeance." He paused a moment, then went on. "Likewise we avenge your mother and sister, and all the poor Praying Indians who perished at the mission. Perhaps you know of the victory at Blue Licks. There was much joy of vengeance there for the Praying Indians."

She shut her eyes and shook her head slowly. "Surely that vengeance was in their hearts, *ami*. But the Kentuckians they killed at Blue Licks were innocent of the crime at the mission. The soldiers who did that were Pennsylvania soldiers."

He waved a hand. "There is no difference. Those we killed at Blue Licks killed and raped innocents in our towns here. It is all the same guilt they share. It is, dear madame, all one vengeance."

She sighed. "Vengeance! Vengeance! It has been that since we can remember! Each time it grows more vicious. The Kentuckians' vengeance for Blue Licks will be marching into this country soon. You know that."

Lorimier nodded, looked down into his tiny glass, hardly bigger than a thimble, reached for the decanter, and refilled hers and his. The drone of voices and movement in the busy trading store filled the moment of silence. "Yes," he said. "The spies say there is a great passion for it in Kentucke. That it will be Clark the Town Burner. That he will bring cannon again."

"That frightens you, old friend. Clark is stronger than so many of their generals. He makes his men fight well. And there are so many whitemen in Kentucke now. We remember when they could not raise an army of a hundred. Now a thousand, or two thousand. And all the time there are fewer warriors to go against them. I fear for my people. The towns I visited on my way here, on the Mad River, the Miami. Do you think they can be defended against Clark the Town Burner?"

Lorimier replied, "We will defend as well as we can. Who knows how battles will go? Who knows what the seasons will bring for him or against him? In the autumn, rain and mud alone may stop an army before it could approach. Soldiers sometimes lose heart, for reasons no one can see. As the Shawnees always do, they will be praying for the army to fail. I do not like to think of that man Clark coming against us. But maybe, like other soldiers, he is all reputation."

Unfortunately, she thought, *I don't believe he is.* She tilted her head and studied Lorimier, who had pulled his long queue of hair forward over one shoulder and was swishing it like a fly whisk to disturb the flies that were so thick in the store, even this late in the year, because of the hides. She said, "Were you at the Blue Licks fight?"

"No."

"But if the Long Knives come up here, they would wish to burn your trading post, in their vengeance for Blue Licks. Do you think that would be fair, since you were not in that fight?"

He leaned back and laughed. "Fair? Ah, *chère Coitcheleh*, I, too, like that word *fair. Juste!* But this is war, and *fair* has no place in it . . ." His voice trailed off and he gazed out through the vast, shadowy store, and stopped flicking his pigtail. Perhaps he was thinking for the first time that his great store here, the biggest and best store west of Niagara, might be destroyed. It would ruin him. But surely he had considered that it would be a most likely target of the Town Burner Clark, for it was a hotbed of Indian hostility and a funnel for arms and supplies to the war parties.

Nonhelema reached out and touched his wrist. When he looked up, she said, "I have been told that Captain McKee was a leader at Blue Licks."

"He was. He, Girty, and Caldwell of the British Department were the whites in its leadership. They did well."

"Yes, if to provoke such revenge is to do well. I need to find him, m'sieur."

"I am happy to say that I can serve you. He is not four leagues away at this time. I can tell him you seek him . . ." Lorimier knew of Nonhelema's intense dislike of McKee's present consort, and did not want to enable her to arrive there unannounced.

"It is because of our young boy," she said. "For his safety. I need to ensure that he won't be in the way of harm when Clark comes. Maybe you believe our people are far enough north now to avoid him. It is, I fear, not so. It will be worse than you expect. I hope the people will get their corn in and withdraw still farther. Even up to Auglaize. Until he is gone."

"*Merci, chère madame.* The innocents will be moved out of harm's way. But this time he will be met by men. It is agreed already that he will pay in blood for coming into our country again." He paused. "I must say this. For your good, you ought to know that many people resent the help you gave the Long Knives. Some Shawnee men have died because of information you gave the Americans. And it is well known that your friends the Black Coats spy for the Americans against Indian people. That is the reason why Chief Pipe moved them farther from the borders. They should be in Canada, where they would be no further harm to their free brothers, or to their foolish selves. It is right that I should tell you of these bad feelings."

"I know of them, m'sieur. I think of how everything comes to be in this world, that even right intentions can be misunderstood."

"And do harm." He sighed. "There is a hole in the heart of the people where you and your family once were so large. Thank you for coming with your warnings for our safety. If there is anything more you know of Town Burner's plans . . ."

"I am not a spy for anyone, *mon vieux*. I have no privilege at Fort Pitt, believe me. I would do nothing to aid the man who commands there. I seek only to prevent harm. I thank you if you will find McKee and my son for me. And my daughter and I would truly be pleased to visit a while with Madame Penampieh before we ride out."

"*Ah! Mais oui!*" He leapt up from his chair, and even standing he was hardly taller than she sitting. His eyes were brimming. "Oh, *Coitcheleh*! If you knew how sad your absence has been!"

It was the hospitality of Lorimier's wife, Penampieh, that night that made Nonhelema aware of all she had given up for the cause of peacemaking. In Penampieh's household, she was so moved that there were moments she could hardly speak.

Before she had left her Shawnee people to become a Christian and help the Americans, she had been surrounded and supported by women like Penampieh, all of them spiritual sisters, all strong and generous. Madame Lorimier was warm and gracious, a superb chef, and she managed to keep her home a refuge of family calm despite the ceaseless comings and goings of traders, hunters, warriors, and couriers throughout the compound. She was her husband's best ally, his helpmate, the cheer and stability of the household. Nonhelema for years had sustained herself on the belief that she was doing something very important, something that both Weshemonetoo and Jesus meant her to do, and she had let that conviction carry her along through her increasing isolation.

But how she had missed the comforting intimacy of being a Shawnee woman among the Shawnee women! Even among chiefs and generals and commissioners and dewy-eyed priests, she had been pitifully alone. For all their stiff-necked, gossipy, bawdy bossiness and touchiness, Shawnee women were the love-force that sustained their nation, and had been since the Beginning Time. Kohkumthena, the Grandmother, creator and rule maker of human life, whose reflection was in the mirror of the moon, was the first Shawnee Woman, and no one could live without her, and every Shawnee woman in all the generations since was Kohkumthena on earth. There was no greater blessing than to be surrounded by them. Nonhelema absorbed the kindness and vigor of Penampieh, laughed and talked with her, and wept inside for the loss of this great thing. She had lost all this. She had exiled herself from it for her cause of peacemaking.

She talked with Penampieh about the terrible breaking-down of their nation, about the ones who had gone west across the Missisipe to get away from the Long Knives, about the ones who had gone south to the Creek country, about her own Mekoche people, hers and her murdered brother's, who had essentially given up and gone to become part of the Delawares.

"Sister," Penampieh said, laying a hand on hers and smiling sadly at her, "when have the Shawnee people ever lived all together and in agreement? We have always split off, all over. There is hardly anyplace between the ocean in the east and the valley of the Missisipe where bands of stiff-necked Shawnees have not gone to live away from other bands of stiff-necked Shawnees. This is just another of those times. There is always some reason. This time it is the whitemen."

"I suppose that is true. But it was not so long ago, in my own young daughter's lifetime, that all the five septs lived near each other, when we were there along the Scioto-sipe. And I think we were one then, a happy people. Then the soldiers and the missionaries came."

"Yes," Penampieh said. "And the soldiers are coming again. They will be here any day." She shrugged, raised her eyebrows, and smiled. "There is still some persimmon cake. My children are looking at it. If you want some more, you had better reach for it now."

Her husband was repeatedly interrupted by the demands of the store, by the large population of itinerants camped around the compound, by new arrivals from north or south, bringing something or needing something, having something to ask or something to tell. From every such distraction Lorimier returned cheerful, interested in whatever it had been, delighted to have new information. His high spirits seemed to have permanently infected his beautiful children, boys and girls alike, who were coy, playful, and affectionate.

Nonhelema and Fani slept afterward in a tiny room under the eaves, their hearts warmed and softened by the hospitality.

Fani's last words in the dark were, "*Nigeah,* let us pray that the war of vengeance will not come as far as this family. Let us pray that we are on the right side."

The next day, Alexander McKee brought their son to see her.

Lorimier had sent for McKee, and he had ridden from Kispoko Town to the trading post with the boy.

Tommy was now tall and lithe and proud for a six-year-old, and Nonhelema was glad to see that he had not, apparently, been turned against her by living under the roof of that *other woman.* Tommy McKee came and embraced her waist. He smelled clean and seemed comfortable and called her *nigeah,* my mother. He carried a hickory bow on his back and a quiver of arrows. He told her that he had several times provided the meat for family meals. She told him that pleased her, and it did.

McKee had not brought his other woman. That was just as well, although Nonhelema had prepared herself to be polite to her if she had come.

As for Alexander McKee, he looked harder and more weathered than before, so lean that the muscles in his jaw stood plain and all the veins and sinews in neck and hands stood clearer, and there was no doubt that the years had toughened him and made him even more confident a man than before. He was in a scarlet British army coat with epaulets and brass buttons, and a large silver gorget on his breast, but wore Indian leggings and a loincloth of deerhide below. He was dark-skinned from exposure to the sun, and his long hair and eyebrows were sun-bleached, almost white. On one cheekbone, a long slash wound was healing, making a scar from his nose to his ear.

The sight of Alexander McKee before her with his new battle scar reminded her that the war was everywhere. And it was the thing he wanted to speak of more than anything. He was still feeling glory from the successful ambush at the Licking. He told her that there had been something almost amusing about how it had been won. Nonhelema was not in a mood to be amused by a tale of slaying, but understood that among warriors, bragging always followed, so she listened patiently and watched his emotions play upon his face as he told it. Probably he needed to gloat because she was on the wrong side.

Downslope from where they sat, hunters propelled their dugout and bark canoes through the narrow, wending creek with pushpoles; the water was almost too shallow for a loaded canoe to be paddled. She sometimes glanced away to watch the water traffic when the expressions on his face disturbed her too much.

"We made a perfect ambuscade along both sides of the trace that comes up from the ford," he said. "The Long Knives had halted on the other side. They were milling. Their horses wanted to drink. It was so hot, and they had come hard. We were high up. It's steep there, very steep. I got my spyglass on them and saw Boone, and Todd, and Hinckson—none of 'em the kind o' fools who'd ride into a trap. They knew we'd just crossed. I could hear 'em down there, calling back and forth, discussing it. They were deciding to wait till reinforcements came up, from other stations. We had about double their number, I guessed. Girty was with me. And Captain Caldwell's Red Coats. I was expecting we'd lose our chance, because Boone and Todd weren't fools. We were about deciding that we'd have to give up that lovely trap and get on, leave a rear guard at the ford." He paused and shook his head, and she looked at him. Then he laughed.

"But thanks be t' God, he'll give you a great fool when y' need one, and give us one he did! You may remember 'im; he used to come through Fort Pitt now and then and make an ass of 'imself. Name of McGary. Hugh McGary."

"I remember him."

"Yes, Hugh was his name. We used to call 'im Hugh and Cry. The kind of Irishman as embarrasses even th' Irish. Well, I heard a loudmouth down there calling 'em all cowards. I got my glass on him and there McGary was, bellowin' that he'd whip us alone if nobody'd follow 'im. Rode right into the river and started coming. And they started following, sure as hell, a few, then more, and next thing ye knew, even the smart ones. I thanked the Lord for that one great fool, and up they came, riding hell-bent. The gullies on both sides o' that trace were full of our warriors all hid down. And most every Indian, I believe, was thinking of those poor fool massacred Praying Indians, what had been done there. Well, they were like fiends. It didn't last but fifteen minutes or so, smoke so thick we couldn't see a thing. Those that did escape alive back across the river turned it red. So y' see what I mean, how funny it was. Their own fool won the fight for us!" He leaned forward, shaking his head and chuckling.

"Now," she said, "I have heard it. I am glad you are so pleased with yourself. Why I have come so far seeking you was not to hear of your battle. You know by this time that hearing war is not any pleasure to me, because it is a story without end. I came to speak with you about our son."

McKee interlaced his fingers between his knees and with raised brow sat to hear her.

"First, you will be surprised to hear me say that you were right once when I thought you were wrong. It was when you came and took Tommy. How I hated you for that! A long time I hated you for it." He was half smiling, looking puzzled. "If I had kept him, I would have taken him to learn all the good things," she said, "all the best knowledge of his Shawnee people, and also the good things of the white people. Are you teaching him to read and write?"

Surprised, McKee looked down. "Um . . . not yet."

"Were you intending?" She looked hard at him.

"I had, um, not thought of it yet."

"No, you had not. I had thought of it when he was a baby, before you took him. But if I had taken him to learn reading, it would have been at the mission school. If I had done so, he surely would have been killed there by Pennsylvania men. So I say to you, now I am glad you took him, and kept him from that."

"Remember," McKee said, "I did tell you he would be safer near Detroit."

"But now you are not at Detroit," she said. "Now you are here, because you, and Girty, and these Shawnee warriors around you are making war. And it is the Long Knives' turn for revenge, and here they will strike if they can do it. I fear Long Knife Clark can do it. And so I came to say it is now my time to take Tommy away to a farther and safer place."

He slapped his palms down on his knees, sitting up straight. "What! Take him where? Not to your damned Americans! And not to those Moravians, who'll turn him into a sheep!"

McKee stood up, for a moment looking down on her where she sat, but then she stood up in front of him, now looking down into his eyes.

"Where I would take him is out of danger," she said. "Later, one can think of the rest of it. Perhaps I should take him to George Morgan in the East, where he could go to the school with White Eyes' sons."

McKee thought, looking at his hands, then gazing south, toward the direction from which the Long Knives would be coming if they came. He turned back to her. "I need to think. To talk about it. With him. With his mother."

"I am his mother!" she snapped.

"I . . . yes. I mean with *her.* I'll bring him back here in a few days."

"Until then leave him here with me and Fani," she said with a cold voice and a bitter smile. "The way white people do. For the . . . what is it they say? For surety."

"Ahhhh, no. I will be back with him. Soon, and we will work something out. Wapeymachikthe I trust. But he would be among Americans there. I need to think on that."

"Very soon, Alex. There is not much time. Long Knife is coming with his vengeance."

There was even less time than she had thought.

Two days had passed, and Nonhelema had not heard anything from McKee before the scouts came racing into Lorimier's, saying that the Long Knife Clark's army, coming in two parts, was closing on the Shawnee towns on the Mad and Miami Rivers. At least a thousand militiamen were coming.

Lorimier's first action was to get the women, children, and elders to safety, get their essentials loaded on packhorses, load as much food as they could carry, and send them north to Girty's Town, at least, or farther if necessary.

Nonhelema was frantic for Tommy and furious at McKee. He had tricked her. Maybe his woman had screamed no at him until he gave up. Or maybe he had just gone down with warriors to defend the lower towns and had not had a chance to send Nonhelema any message. Or maybe he had sent a message that got lost in the confusion.

But she was sure he had betrayed her. Probably he had just not even intended to bring Tommy to her. She was ready to find McKee and twist his treacherous head off. She should have known better than to trust a Britisher! In the milling crowd of people and horses in the compound, she found Lorimier getting the refugees ready. She grabbed his arm and looked down at him. Eyes flashing. "Listen! Old friend, you must do this for me. I want my daughter to go north with your family. I want for me only my horse and a rifle and powder and lead. Caesar and I will ride to McKee's Town and get my son. You tell me how to get there!"

He looked up at her in amazement. Then he shook his head and laughed. "*Coitcheleh*, you go with Penampieh. McKee's is toward the Long Knife army! If you believe I would let you go there, you know nothing. I mean for you to be out of harm, not in it! Please, now, go to Penampieh. I have got to get ready to defend this place. Go!"

"I am not afraid of the Long Knife army. I have fought!"

"Listen to me, *Coitcheleh*! I give you no gun, and I do not tell you the way to McKee's. I have no time for such folly now. Clark is coming to ruin me. Captain McKee will get your son to safety. He is probably on his way to Detroit now!" He turned, glancing about. "Penampieh!" he shouted, summoning his wife with a wave of his hand. She hurried over. "*Nee wa*," he said, "*Coitcheleh* and her daughter are still our guests. Keep them close and care for them.

"*Coitcheleh*," he said very intently, in a tone almost menacing, but through a smile, "*tanakia*. Do as my wife says." He laid his right palm on her left cheek for a moment and drilled her soul with his black eyes. And then he tore into the crowd and began putting everything in order.

Penampieh almost dragged her to the place where Caesar was getting their horses ready. "Please, ma'am!" he implored, handing her a bedroll.

"*Coitcheleh*," a rich voice said behind her shoulder. "May I greet you?"

She turned from tying her bedroll behind the saddle, and there stood a handsome woman whose face she remembered from the better years. The woman was younger than she, and not quite so tall, but as tall as most men.

"You," Nonhelema said, "are the daughter of Methotase?"

"Yes, I am Tecumapese. I have not seen you since we met at Old Chillicothe. It was about fourteen summers ago."

"I remember so well. Your mother, Methotase, had just borne a son, under the sign of a shooting star. I visited her just two summers ago, by the Missisipe."

"Yes," Tecumapese said. "She left there. It was not a good place. Since then she went down to the Creek nation. Her people are still there in her birthplace town."

"But I see you are still here, despite the Long Knives always coming."

"I and my brothers. My father when he died made my brother Chiksika promise never to stop fighting for our homeland."

Nonhelema remembered the young warrior Chiksika holding his father, Pucsinwah, as he bled to death on the Kanawha battlefield, then carrying his body back where the soldiers could not get to it to mutilate. Nonhelema thought of such promises being made, promises never to stop fighting the enemy. Such promises were made to fathers and brothers and friends on every battlefield; surely white soldiers made such vows, too, and the keeping of such promises made the work of peacemakers even more difficult. She remembered that the young Chiksika had been so swift and fearless that, even at that age, he was frightening to watch in action. And she had heard of him since, from time to time. He was one of those boat plunderers who terrorized the surveyors and settlers going to and from Kentucke on the Ohio-sipe.

Tecumapese was helping Nonhelema prepare her horse as they talked. This was a fine and lovely young woman who gave off strength and warmth, but it saddened Nonhelema to think of her in the midst of such a warlike and war-ravaged family. Somehow her presence made Nonhelema feel less frantic about Tommy. It was believed that this family was important in the fate of the People.

"Tell me," Nonhelema said, "about the boy born under the shooting star." She remembered the prophecy made by Change-of-Feathers, the shaman, that the boy born under that sign had a great destiny. He had been named Tecumseh, Panther-Leaping-Across-the-Sky.

Tecumapese's face suffused with pleasure. "Ah! Who has ever seen so fine a boy as my brother! He has fourteen summers now, and no one remembers such a hunter, or runner, or wrestler that age. But even better is his spirit! He takes care of the elders, and learns from them everything they can tell him."

"You are proud of him. Is he here? Will I see this marvel?"

"No. He stayed with Chiksika, down by the big towns. They're watching the Long Knife's army and preparing to defend. Tecumseh is too young for war yet, but there are many ways a boy can help. He will."

"Your mother also had triplets, I remember. Are you still raising them?"

"One died of honeybee stings. One is well. The littlest one is sickly, and he put his eye out in an accident." She shrugged. "I have help from all the aunts. I wish our *geah* had not gone, but she is with her people as she desires, and we are with ours." She paused, then asked, "Is it true, your mother and sister were among those lost at the Praying Town?"

"Yes. They were."

They squeezed each other's hands. Tecumapese said then, "My heart is on the ground. May I ask this? Now the Long Knives have murdered so many of your family, is that why we see you here with us again? Have you turned your back on the Long Knives?"

"Young sister, I am not for Long Knives or for British. I am only for peace, so that these things will not happen to my people anymore."

Tecumapese drew her hand away and lowered her head. "I have to go. I am glad we had this time. I'm sorry my family must keep making war, but the Long Knives give us no other way."

From the highest hill two nights later, the refugees stood wrapped in blankets against the dank, cold wind and looked into the invisible distance. To the south and east of them lay the plains and rolling country of the Shawnee towns they had fled. Much of the day they had been hearing rustling, crackling sounds that were of distant gunfire. About dusk, the sounds died down and dark smoke began rising in places in those far lowlands.

Now it was dark. An owl cried, *Hook hook, hook hook, ha hooooaw!*

Nonhelema stood with Fani at her side and they gazed down that way. Light snow had begun to sift through the sky, cold on their faces. Behind them, voices were talking very softly. Now and then an old woman's croaky voice wailed, testily; a horse stamped a hoof.

In those lowlands, through the haze of snow, ruddy smears of faraway light glowed.

The Shawnee towns, and Lorimier's wondrous trading post, were all burning.

Somewhere in the vast night, Tommy was safe or not safe. Somewhere, his father, Alexander, was dead or alive. Somewhere, her son Morgan had become a warrior or had died trying. Her brother the Wolf, no peacemaker, was somewhere out there, maybe alive, maybe not. And Lorimier, either alive or dead, but ruined. It would be a long time before there would be knowledge of which beloved chiefs and warriors had survived.

And Nonhelema had felt something among these refugees that squeezed her heart down until she could hardly stand it: Regardless of their old affection, they looked at her now out of the sides of their eyes.

She was a known friend of Long Knives.

She had come back among her tribal people.

And soon after her arrival, the Long Knife Town Burner had come marching.

She was suspected by her own people. If she ever hoped to leave Fort Pitt and return to the Shawnees, who would have her? Where could she live?

Perhaps in the town of her old uncle Moluntha. He understood her peacemaking. He was a man who never condemned. And he was courageous enough to stand by one who was out of favor.

But until all the burning towns could be rebuilt, they all would live under the winter sky.

20

GIRTY'S TOWN
NOVEMBER 1783

At last the war between the British and the Americans had ended, with a treaty made across the sea in Europe. For a little while, Nonhelema took comfort in knowing that the bloodshed had ceased. *Now,* she thought, *the Indian tribes will not be divided against each other by choosing to fight for one whiteman's government against the other.*

And she was glad that it was the British who had lost.

It would be a pleasure, she thought, to see Alexander McKee and remind him that he had been on the wrong side. It seemed right to her that the Americans had gained their freedom from the king of England. Freedom, as any Indian always believed, was as important as food and shelter. And so, when McKee came traveling among the rebuilt and resettled Mad River towns to explain the peace to them, Nonhelema traveled from Moluntha's Town, where she was living, to Girty's Town, to hear McKee, perhaps to see their son, Tommy. The day was cold, with a dank wind blowing the last of the autumn leaves off. This was the small Shawnee town of James Girty, one of Simon's brothers, who was a trusted trader among the Shawnee bands.

McKee looked grand, as usual, in his red coat and British ornaments. But as he stood to address the assemblage, he was nervous, almost timid.

In that distant peace treaty, he said, England had had to give up to the Americans the lands that had come under Long Knife control when General Clark captured the towns on the Missisipe and the Wabash-sipe: not just the old hunting grounds of Kentucke, but also the lands between the Ohio and the Great Lakes, as far west as the Missisipe.

The council ground was silent as the Indians thought on what they had just heard.

It meant that the Long Knives now presumed to own every place where all the eastern Indians lived.

Her brother Kekepelewethy, known as Captain Johnny to the Americans, stood up. His bones were stiff, his hair graying. But his eyes were flashing with a young warrior's fire. Kekepelewethy had never been in the peace faction with his family.

"Brother," he said to McKee, "we thought the Indians had won the war. Captain Pipe caught the murderers of the Praying Indians and burned up their leader. You and the Shawnees defeated the Kentucke Long Knives at the Blue Licks. The Senecas burned Hannastown in Pennsylvania. The Long Knives won only when they attacked women and children. They burned many Indian towns when the warriors were not there. But when they fought Indian men, they lost. Now you say they have won our homelands from us?" He stared at McKee until McKee's gaze dropped, then said, "Brother, for you English, the war is over. For all the Indians who trusted your king and did all your fighting for you, the war against Americans will have to continue on. Brother, we Shawnees have been too slow to learn a very plain lesson. But we have learned it well now: Any whiteman's promise is as honorable as the noise he blows from between his buttocks. It means that much. It stinks that much. And it will be far behind him in a moment. And he will look about and pretend that he never made that noise. We had forgotten that American stinkholes were British stinkholes just a little while ago, and are the same. My poor people will always be fooled, because we were always taught to believe promises. But I will tell you now, Wapeymassiweh, what has happened this time blows the smoke from our eyes. We shall not believe you any more than the Long Knives."

When at last she could sit opposite McKee alone and speak to him, Nonhelema found that she had not the heart either to gloat or complain. He was as dispirited by the failure of war as she was by the failure of peace. It seemed there really was nothing that could be said about either.

They were not totally alone. James Girty and his wife sat with Simon in one end of the Girtys' large cabin so that they could talk in some privacy. Nonhelema stared into McKee's eyes in the firelight, but he avoided meeting her stare by fussing over his smoking pipe and tobacco.

"And it seems," she said, "that you did not even bring our son, Tommy, down here for me to see him. Would it harm that boy to spend part of just one day in the presence of his true mother, even though she be something so terrible as a peacemaker?"

McKee poked a long dry twig in the fire, still not looking at her, then replied, "For his safety, I didn't bring him to this council." He raised the twig to his pipe bowl and puffed until smoke clouded his face.

"Safety from what danger, here in Girty's Town, among his own people, in a time when the war is over? Give me an answer I can swallow without gagging on laughter."

His face reddened and he scowled at her. "You saw how angry the people are. It was dangerous for me to speak the truth to them, and I knew it would be dangerous to bring him!"

"Alexander McKee, my people would not harm one of their own blood for the perfidy of a fat king beyond the sea! No, I think you were afraid to bring him because his false mother, Open Legs, said no."

"Damn your mouth, Katy!" he snapped, expelling smoke.

"Ha! Who is a traitor and a crotch chaser to damn anyone?"

He sat breathing hard with his lips compressed, then drew again on the pipe to calm himself. "You might be pleased to know that he learns to read. As you suggested, that is a good thing for him."

"I am glad to know that. You could have brought him and let him show me how he reads. Perhaps he might have read to me from the treaty paper, by which your fat king gave the Shawnee homelands to the Long Knives, after all the bloodletting that did no one any good."

"You are too bitter, Katy. I'm glad Tommy's not here to see your bitterness." Now he was looking at her eyes as he spoke.

"If he were here," she said, "he would feel his mother's affection. It would be easy to hide bitterness if I could see my son." She eased out a long sigh and looked into the fire. "Then help me see him in my head and heart. I suppose he is tall and healthy, and does kindnesses for the elders?"

McKee smiled. "When he kills game, he gives it all to the old ones. And listen, Katy: My buck follows him as he does me. He has that friendship with the animals."

"Eh-heh!" Now she actually smiled. "Then he knows how it is to wake up in the morning from dreaming of a deer breathing on his face and there is a deer breathing on his face." She said that with a quiet and pleasant voice, remembering the morning when she had awakened just so. She smiled, remembering that, but her heart was squeezed with sadness.

It had been just so that she had awakened that morning after the night their son had been conceived, this distant and unreachable son they were speaking of now.

A war had come between them. A woman had entered, too, but it was the war that had come between her and her son.

The British would no longer be able to help the Indians fight against the Americans, because of the peace treaty the two countries had made with each other. But the British wanted to keep the friendship of the Indians because of the fur trade and its enormous profits. Therefore, the British promised to maintain their trade relations with the tribes, and counseled the Indians to remain calm and negotiate with the Americans instead of attacking them. They promised to help the Indians in any way but warfare. What those other ways might be was vague, and such a promise seemed pretty worthless to Captain Johnny and most of his allies. The British said they believed the Ohio River should remain the boundary between Indian country and American settlement. But everyone knew those were just empty words.

"Sister," said Captain Johnny to Nonhelema, "if your friends the Long Knives tell you they will stay south of the Ohio, you probably believe them. I don't believe them. Over the years, we have seen how they are. Even when they had no treaty right to come in on our lands, they came. Now they believe they have treaty right to all of our land. I tell you, it will be very soon when they will come with their commissioners and their big sheets of paper for us to mark with ink. The reason why I think they will come with paper and ink first is because they keep telling us they want to be our friends. But if we don't make the ink marks just as they want, they will just come on in with their guns and their axes. Whether with ink marks or gunpowder, they mean to have all the land. I am just keeping my gun clean and collecting ammunition from the British traders, and waiting to see whether the Long Knives will first come with paper or a gun. I am watching the river."

"Brother," she replied, "I know you expect that you will have to fight them. But I believe them when they tell me they want to be our friends now that the war is over. The war with the British was the cause of all that bloodshed between us and them. They, too, are tired of fighting. They will be honorable." Even as she argued this way, she had doubts about their honor. She had asked the American officials at Pittsburgh to give her some compensation for the cattle and property she had lost by joining the Virginians at Fort Randolph so long ago, but they had not done anything for her yet.

"Maybe you should tell your American friends," he said, "that all the Indians are counseling together to be as one, to be strong enough to stand up to them if they start coming in. Brant the Mohawk is making that confederacy, and the British diplomats are helping him. It is not to make war, but to be strong enough together that the Americans will have to be honorable with us. Although I suppose you have already told your American friends that, or the missionary spies have."

"Brother, you do not trust even your own sister, do you?"

"How good it would be if I could."

"Brother, when we go to treaties together, we will have to pretend we are of one heart," she said.

"So, you believe they will come first with paper and ink."

Nonhelema was, again, as usual, out of favor with the missionary.

She should have been used to it by now, but it was always a torment. Because she was outcast from most of her own Shawnee nation, it was a severe emptiness of the spirit when she was also outcast from the favor of Jesus.

Brother Zeisberger would make her wait and worry, worry about whether she would ever be forgiven for her lapses from grace. He managed to make her fear that Jesus was so disappointed in her that Brother David would have to vouch for her and plead exhaustively on her behalf, that Jesus would have to be convinced all over again, and that it would be even harder to convince him again than it had been in the beginning to take her wretched, guilty soul. The missionary would give the impression that he was putting his own salvation at risk by pleading over and over again for this lewd, rum-drinking, heretical woman who still returned to her pagan ceremonies, prayed to feathers and corn and smoke and chanted to drumbeats. Brother David knew that women stood bare-bosomed in those ceremonies, that Nonhelema herself prayed those heathenistic prayers with her breasts bared to the lustful gaze of the Indian men, and that Jesus wept when he saw one of his own baptized children in such flagrant lewdness.

It would do her no good to try to convince Brother David that there was no lustfulness or lewdness in those ceremonies, only joy and reverence. Apparently he knew without doubt what the Indians didn't, that no one could get into heaven without wearing a shirt.

She could not keep from wondering whether Jesus really cared. But Brother David was the priest. He was the doorkeeper to the heaven of Jesus, and he had made her believe that she could not get there without his grudging approval.

It was much harder to go to the mission towns now. After the massacre, the Praying Indians had been taken for their own protection to locations up near the Great Lakes; also, it was to shut off the missionaries' spying. The new Gnaddenhutten was north of Detroit. Nonhelema and Fani were now living at Moluntha's Town. What once had been a two- or three-day ride to the mission now took a week. And since the murder of her mother and sister, there was little reason to go there.

Now that she lived among the Mekoches again, the warlike Shawnee chiefs liked to come and annoy her with reports of how badly her old friends the Americans were behaving since the war's end. Americans were already beginning to build cabins and cut trees on the Indian side of the Ohio in a few places. General Clark, the Town Burner, had moved to the north side of the Ohio at the falls with a large number of his veterans, to make a town on lands rewarded to them by the government. A fort was being built on the north side of the Ohio at the mouth of the Muskingum, and another was being laid out on the north bank of the Ohio at the mouth of the Miami, only three days' ride south of the new Shawnee towns.

Nonhelema implored the Shawnee chiefs to be patient. The fort on the Miami was planned as a convenient place for the Shawnees to come to for peace talks, where some understanding could be reached about boundaries at last. There had been too much doubt aggravated by British lies. That had been the difficulty of it, she argued.

And so, by such pleadings, she continued to try to be a peacemaker, as best she could. Therefore in Jesus' eyes, if not Brother Zeisberger's, she was being a child of God.

21

You are drawing so close to us that we can almost hear the
noise of your axes felling our Trees and settling our
Country. If your settlers cross the Ohio, we shall take up a
Rod and whip them back to your side.

—Kekewepelewethy (Captain Johnny), Mekoche Shawnee war leader,
to the Americans, 1785; Simon Girty, interpreter

THE MOUTH OF THE GREAT MIAMI
JANUARY 1786

The old trail was wide enough that the Shawnees could ride six
and eight abreast, and they talked as they rode. No one was
happy.

It was a bitter-cold day, and the January sun was shining white
without giving warmth. The riders had blankets and hide robes
drawn close around their shoulders, to ward off the constant wind
that was blowing from the northwest. They had come from most of
the Shawnee communities to hear the "peace talks" demanded by an
American government that now believed it owned their homelands
after throwing the English king on his back.

The Americans had sent for them several times. In the beginning,
the Shawnees had not responded at all. The summonses had become
more threatening until the Shawnees had begun to fear they would
be left out of the talks. They knew the Americans would be able to get
some tribes to sign the treaty who would not consider the Shawnee
concerns.

One difficult demand that came with the summonses was the

usual one that they had to return all the white captives from all the Shawnee towns. The Americans also insisted they would hold at least six Shawnee chiefs hostage until all the white captives had been returned.

In the final summons, the Americans had threatened simply to take possession of the land by force in one last grand war, and spare no one.

Nonhelema, Fani, and Morgan had all been used as couriers to deliver the Americans' summonses. They had spent time with the chiefs, explaining the urgent need to attend. The faithful couriers had at last convinced the chiefs there was no way to avoid going to Fort Finney.

The Americans were demanding that the Shawnees submit to the McIntosh Treaty of 1785, in which the Shawnees had been left out as their land was signed away by others.

"You may say the Americans want to put an end to the difficulties, but they only want our land. Perhaps they will allow us to live, but I do not think they will allow us to stay this side of the Mississippi."

"You don't know them as I do, brother," said Nonhelema. "I was the only one who went to Fort McIntosh when they called us in. I had to beg them for help and to take pity on our children and old women. None of you would come and help me. Or even do them the courtesy to listen to what they had to say. Our people were in terrible need. Many would not have survived the winter had they not given us some assistance.

"We need peace. Our people need a place to live without being attacked. The Americans are serious about resolving these problems and living with us in peace. So we *have* to talk. And you will see, they are eager for peace themselves."

Captain Johnny scowled and grunted. Blue Jacket, the strong, solid, elegantly attired chieftain beside him, yelped, "Ha!"

Nonhelema's hopes rose and fell as she weighed in her mind the American and Shawnee representatives who would be facing each other at Fort Finney. They could be the best or the worst, at the same time. Captain Johnny and Blue Jacket had been fighting bravely for years against the Long Knives and had sent many of them away to their afterworld. Neither of these warriors hated whitemen just because they were white. They had friends and allies among the traders and the British. Blue Jacket's own wife was a white captive he had married and loved truly, and he was involved with important French

Canadian trading families. Kekepelewethy, Captain Johnny, like Non-helema herself, had grown up in Paxinosa's family with its affection for such whitemen as Penn, and its admiration for European ideas, music, and inventions. Those two formidable warriors hated only the Virginians and Pennsylvanians specifically who had been making war on their people and usurping their hunting grounds.

The other primary chief riding to the treaty place was old Moluntha, her uncle. He was the real sage of the nation now, chief of the Mekoche sept, tending toward peace but tired of moving his people time after time away from Long Knife town burners, and now tormented by all the hopes that had vanished when the British gave the Indian lands to the Americans. Moluntha was too old and feeble to be a fighter anymore, but his mind and will were still strong weapons.

Among the American commissioners who would be at the talks were two she knew quite well. Both had tried to persuade Congress to reimburse her for the property and livestock she had lost by helping the Americans.

One of these was the trader and Indian agent Richard Butler. In his years as a trader among the Shawnees before the war, he had been married to one of Nonhelema's sisters, whom he called Betty. They had produced a daughter called Polly who was now a young woman living in a Mekoche town. Once Nonhelema and her brothers had saved Butler's life by escorting him to Fort Pitt. Butler had moved back to Pittsburgh and resumed residence with his respectable white wife, but Nonhelema believed that he still had affection for the Shawnees and was concerned for their safety. He had assured Nonhelema that the American government was determined to have peace along its boundaries with the Shawnees, and wanted a formal declaration of peace and friendship and understanding with them.

The other peace commissioner she knew was General George Rogers Clark himself, he who had seized the Indian lands from British control in the war. Clark was hated and feared by many of the tribes, but respected as a warrior and a straight talker. He was known to be the man who really ran things in Kentucke and the West. Though he was still young, his hardships and triumphs had transformed him into an unflinching man without much patience. But Clark had always been warm and charming toward Nonhelema, and she hoped their friendship would work in the Shawnees' favor.

In this Shawnee party going to the treaty rode two sons of the slain chief Pucsinwah. Chiksika, the oldest son, was a fearless raider who had promised his dying father that he would never sign any treaty with whitemen. He had volunteered to come to Fort Finney as an observer and as a bodyguard for the older chiefs. If the whitemen in the fort did any treachery, as they had done to Cornstalk, they would lose lives of their own before it was finished. Riding close beside Chiksika was his younger brother Tecumseh, a keen, taut, hazel-eyed youth of about eighteen summers. For all his dignity, he seemed always to have a smile of amusement barely contained within his mouth. This was the one born of Methotase as a shooting star passed over, the one marked for greatness. In his first combat, in a raid on Ohio River boats, he had killed four whitemen with knife and club within a few breaths of time. Nonhelema wondered what would become of such a marked one as this. If the peacemaking was successful, he would not make his life as a war chief. If the peace talks failed, he would probably die young in the whiteman's gunsmoke, as most of the bravest ones did. Perhaps he had warrior dreams. Being a Kispoko Shawnee, son of the nation's principal war chief, and trained by a killer like that Chiksika, he was sure to die fighting.

She could feel the image of his death trying to come to her, so she tried to force her mind to other things. If she saw it in her mind, the Master-of-Life would see it thus. And it would come to be, as when she had seen Arbuckle die under a falling tree.

And so she looked away from Tecumseh and tried to imagine all these people of hers sitting in a pleasant and friendly council with Clark and Butler and the other commissioners, establishing trust and making a peace that would endure forever.

The talks in the new little fort did not turn out as she had imagined. The only pleasant thing about the council was the smell of the freshly hewn logs of which the fort was built.

The first indication of the unpleasantness to come was the size and the menacing aspect of the soldier guard. When the chiefs had filled the center of the council room, facing the commissioners' table, they turned and saw they had been followed in and surrounded by enough armed soldiers to line every wall shoulder to shoulder. It was a frightening sight, and made her think of Gnaddenhutten, where the Praying Indians had been herded into rooms and killed. The Indians had been ordered to leave their guns in their camp. She looked over at Captain Johnny and at Blue Jacket and Chiksika, and saw them bracing themselves, eyes alert.

When the council began, she saw at once that the old, respectful warming-up ceremonies and declarations of friendship were not going to be observed. Nonhelema had brought wampum strands, made by one of the tribe's two best beadworkers, M'Noukawme, to be presented as gifts of friendship and sincerity to the commissioners and to the fort commander. Another bead woman, Penasche, had made a beautiful wampum belt of many rows, showing friendship figures holding hands, of white beads to represent the whitemen and purple to represent the Indians, with a red bead in the chest of each to represent the sameness of their hearts, all this meant to convey their mutual respect for each other in a negotiation.

But there was no occasion for bringing the beadwork forward. The commissioners went straight into the preamble of their declarations. So she leaned over and passed the bundle containing the belt to Captain Johnny, who might make the opportunity to present it with the appropriate words when he got up to talk. Butler had advised her that only male chiefs would be speaking at this council, as it perplexed the commissioners when women presumed to speak on policy. But Nonhelema was ready to speak up if anything really needed to be said and nobody else thought to say it.

She looked at General Clark, keeping an eye on his facial expressions. Almost everyone else was doing the same thing. Although he was not doing any of the talking yet, he was the powerful presence in the council room. He was the one who had turned the British on their heads during the war here west of the mountains, and he was the Town Burner whose attacks on Indian villages always succeeded. It was because of Clark that the Americans now believed they were masters of all the Indian country, and so he was an object of both hatred and wonder. Almost everybody had heard stories about him: How he could never be tricked or frightened. How he might order captive warriors put to death, or mercifully spared. How he could not be stared down. He was wearing not an army uniform, but the beautiful deerskin coat that she had made in Pittsburgh years before.

She noticed that Clark's dark blue eyes, in the beginning, had gone over every Indian face in the room, but now he kept looking at Captain Johnny. And she saw that her brother was not looking at Richard Butler or Captain Finney or anyone else except Clark. Captain Johnny and Clark were trying to stare each other down. That was not good. No peacemaking could come of that.

She saw that someone else was staring at Clark, as if challenging him to lock eyes. It was Methotase's warlike son Chiksika. She could see that in Chiksika's eyes there was no admiration, only hatred. She had a sense that if Clark and Chiksika looked at each other's eyes at the same time, either one of them might leap up and try to kill the other.

So she prayed that Clark would not turn his eyes upon Chiksika's. And he did not.

When Butler read out, one by one, the Americans' demands, Nonhelema at last began to understand that the Americans had no longer any intention of asking or negotiating. Now they were simply telling the Indians what they would have to accept.

She tried to catch Butler's eye, but it was plain that he was ashamed to look at her, after all she had done to persuade the Shawnees to come here at his urging.

Butler told the Shawnees that they would be required to leave six warriors as hostages until every white captive of the Shawnees was returned.

He said that the Shawnees would have to concede that the American government was sovereign over all the land that England had given up at the end of the war.

He said that all crimes, whether committed by whitemen or Shawnees, in Shawnee country or elsewhere, would be tried by American judges and punished under American law, not by tribal councils.

By this time, all the Shawnees in the council room were breathing shallowly. They were murmuring to each other. Nonhelema could feel fury in the room, like the buzzing of a hornets' nest that had just been hit with a stick. She saw and heard the soldiers around the room adjusting their weapons and shifting stance. Under her cloak, she put her hand on the handle of her sheathed knife. She had no idea whom she would have to use it on if the tension exploded—soldiers, commissioners, her own infuriated warriors if they turned on her for insisting they come here. All her peacemaking efforts had been done in hopes of procuring the safety of her Shawnee people, but she could understand how they might feel that she had betrayed them and led them into a trap.

She looked at Clark's face. He showed no emotion, not even tension. He was carefully watching Captain Johnny. Butler and the third commissioner, named Parsons, looked pale and nervous.

"You will," Butler read finally, "grant to the United States all the lands you claim eastward from this river, the Miami. I will now explain to you any part of these terms that you might not understand."

The interpreter translated those words, and if there was to be an outburst, surely it would be now.

It was old Moluntha's deep, grating voice that held them still.

"Sit calm. *Me las namethi.* Be peaceful." Then he said, standing up slowly and painfully to face the commissioners: "Brothers, we have come a long way in the cold to hear you, because you said you want to be friends with us. You know that we have tried for many years to have peace and friendship with you. Even while your people were coming and killing us, we always went to talk peace with you so that you would finally stop. Today we came here in the cold to see what you want for friendship, and we could tell you what we want. We expected to listen, and we expected you to listen. We brought a belt of wampum, picturing red men and white men, holding hands, neither one bigger than the other. My nephew Kekepelewethy, whom you call Captain Johnny, he would like to present that belt to you, so that we and you may speak and listen equally. Kekepelewethy, go give them the belt."

Captain Johnny rose quickly and stood tall. He looked almost as fine and proud as his brother Cornstalk had used to look when he stood before councils, and Nonhelema looked up at him and hoped he would not be so sharp as to cause trouble. She knew that he was full of anger.

Captain Johnny removed the cloth cover and then went forward to the table where the commissioners sat. The belt was six feet long and as wide as a woman's hand. He leaned forward and stretched the belt along the table. It reached from Commissioner Parsons past Butler, and one end was in front of Clark.

"*Nila nameetha,*" he said in Shawnee, "older sister, come and say my words to them in English. You speak it better than I, and better than this interpreter of theirs. I want them to understand me exactly."

She rose, glad that he had asked her, so that if he did say things too harshly she could smooth the edges.

"Brothers, my old relative Butler, and my esteemed foe General Clark, you see the belt. You see that we are equal. Therefore, you must not think that only you may talk, and we only listen." As she translated that, she looked at the commissioners. She saw that it angered Parsons and Butler, but Clark only sucked in his cheeks and looked bored. "Kekepelewethy is my name. I do not agree with you on the matter of leaving our warriors hostage. Once, when you had my brother and other relatives as prisoners in your fort, you murdered them, even when they were unarmed. I do not intend to let you keep any of our warriors as hostages.

"Another thing. We do not understand measuring out the lands. It is all *ours*. The Master-of-Life put us here and told us to take care of this place. We have not sold any of the land to you, and we shall not. All the Indians between the river and the lakes have met and made a promise together that no tribe will ever give up any land to any of you unless all the confederated Indians agree to do so. All those Indians together have also stated that Spaylaywesipe, the Ohio River, will remain the boundary between your people and ours.

"Maybe you remember a message I sent to you a few moons ago, saying that if your people come across, we will take a rod and whip them back to your side of the river.

"Now listen, brothers. You brought us a few trifling presents, inferior to British goods. You can take those and give them to somebody else, for they are not enough to make us leave you hostages or sign our land away. With this belt I have laid before you, you must hear our words, and know that we are as far apart from agreeing with your demands as this end of the belt is from that end of the belt. To work toward the center of the belt, both must listen and both must talk."

Nonhelema finished translating those words, which were the usual strong words of someone who begins a negotiation and expects a meeting eventually somewhere toward the middle, as when one haggles for a price in a trading post. Her brother's eyes were intense with challenge, but he had spoken calmly and she was pleased.

But then General Clark, staring straight into Captain Johnny's eyes, reached for a straight walking stick that leaned on the wall behind him. It was a gleaming, varnished stick with a silver knob on the upper end and a little metal latch. She had seen those things in Pittsburgh. One could push the latch with the thumb and pull out a long, straight, thin sword. "Stand back a little, brother," she told Captain Johnny softly in Shawnee. Her scalp prickled. She didn't believe Clark would actually draw the sword on her brother and attack him, but no one could be sure. There was a story about Clark that she had heard long ago from a Piankeshaw chief, that once in a treaty talk out west, a chief had laid a peace pipe on a table, and Clark, believing the chief was insincere, had drawn his saber and smashed the pipe with its blade. Many in this room knew that story, and they watched in silence as the general stood up at his end of the table, still looking in Captain Johnny's eyes.

With the tip of the walking stick, Clark touched the beautiful belt. Nonhelema, remembering the long, long days of work the woman Penasche had spent making the belt, tensed herself, thinking Clark might try to smash the wampum beads. With Captain Johnny watching intently with flashing eyes, Clark slipped the tapered ferrule of the walking stick under the belt, lifted the belt off the table as if it were too contemptible a thing to pick up with his fingers, and then flipped the stick to make the belt slip hissing onto the floor in a heap. Then, still staring into Captain Johnny's blazing eyes, he stepped over and put his boot heel on the belt and shifted his weight. It was so quiet in the room that the grinding and crushing of the beads could be heard throughout. Then there rose a sound like a growl of a bear, at this awful insult of an honored and sacred token. Nonhelema felt everyone in the room shifting. She heard the soldiers shuffling and their guns clicking and rattling. Her first fear was that her brother would jump and attack Clark. Probably he would have, except that he heard the clatter of the weaponry. Any violence here and now would surely turn into a massacre. He held himself back and stood glaring at Clark.

"Mr. Butler," Clark said in a deep, resonant voice, "would you please explain to these people their standing? You, Chief, ought to sit down and listen. You in particular seem to need enlightening."

But Kekepelewethy did not sit down. Instead, he turned his back on Clark, with a toss of the head that expressed his contempt, flashed a quick look at Nonhelema and another at old Chief Moluntha, and strode out toward the door, actually shouldering soldiers' guns as he pushed between them and the seated Indians. Nonhelema watched him go, both regret and pride in her heart, and she saw Chiksika and about a dozen other warriors and chieftains rise up and make their way through the crowd to follow him. No one tried to stop them. For a moment, the whole roomful of Indians was stirring, as if they all might walk out, but then Clark rapped on the table with his stick, and most of them settled down into a sullen and fearful audience again.

"Brothers," old Moluntha's voice rose, "I am sorry for the bad manners shown here." He did not specify whether he meant Clark's or Captain Johnny's. "But I ask you to stay and hear what our brother

Butler has to tell us. You know he has always been our friend and has lived among us and provided for our needs. Brother, please speak now so that we shall know where your heart is on this matter."

Nonhelema was relieved. Butler would be kind and reasonable, she was sure.

"Brothers the Shawnee!" he began. "You know you will hear only the truth from me. Is that not so?" It had always been, and most of them nodded and leaned forward to listen.

"You know that the truth is not always as you would like to hear it. The truth now is that you are a defeated people. Shawnees were the allies of the English king in the last war. When the United States threw the king on his back, you were defeated with him. Many of you were perfidious, and did not keep faith with the peace treaties we all made at Fort Pitt. You were foolish to trust the British, because when they pleaded for peace with us, they forgot about you, and abandoned you to our mercy. They ceded to America the lands between the river and the lakes that General Clark had taken from them.

"For your treachery, serving the king of England, we could punish you with disdain. But we have pity for you. We give you this chance to choose friendship with us. Friendship is the road to peace and happiness. If you accept our mercy and agree to our terms, there will be peace, and your women and children will be safe. You are either with us, or against us."

Nonhelema was stunned by the way Butler was talking. This was not peace talk. She was about to say so when old Moluntha's voice rose again.

"Brother, we do not understand you. You say you defeated the Shawnees, but no. You defeated the British, or so you say. And not many of the Shawnees ever fought against you. Most of us have tried to keep the peace with you. Brother, you are not listening to us at all. You have insulted us, who have been your friends throughout. That belt was from the Mekoche, my people, who have always tried to carry your message for you.

"Now, my people and I need to talk among ourselves about what you have told us here. I ask that you let us go to our camp. We will talk with our brother Kekepelewethy, and try to get him to cool himself down. I believe we can still do some good by talking here. You need to hear what the rest of the nations want. Now if your soldiers will stand aside and make a path for us to go out, we will go to our camp and prepare for a better council tomorrow."

The commissioners agreed to adjourn, and Nonhelema went around to the end of the table. She knelt to gather the damaged wampum from the floor; the pains in her knees and back reminded her of her age, and of the countless journeys she had made in hard weather for the cause of peace. She could have stayed more in her comfortable homes and grown plump and stayed warm by the fires in the winter and in the raw autumns and springtimes. She could have tamed herself to be a mission Indian. She would not have this stiff and painful spine if she had been sitting at home, years ago, instead of riding to the mission, seeking to become a child of God and get back in Brother David Zeisberger's graces, and been thrown when her horse shied, landing on a fallen log. But instead, she had always been on the move for peace, and it had made her life hard.

Some of the wampum beads were broken; others had cut through the sinew threads. She gathered them. Clark's booted foot, the one that had stepped on this beautiful thing, was close by. She glanced up and saw that he was looking down on her with that unreadable expression still on his face. Then she saw the corner of his mouth lift in a half-smile. But it made a flash of fire shoot through her. When she had all the pieces picked up, she stood up in front of him, not revealing the pain it caused her knees. Butler and Parsons were talking to each other at the other end of the table, and the room was still full of voices as the soldiers talked and the Indians made their way out.

Clark was a tall man among his soldiers, but she now looked down into his eyes, and she showed him no expression to read. She kept looking straight into his dark blue eyes until he looked as if he felt he must say something.

She waited until he opened his lips to form a word, then she said: "I have been wrong. I did not know you were such a little man." He took a deep breath and his brow lowered, and that was when she turned her back on him, as Captain Johnny had done, and walked away straight-backed.

And, she thought, probably stiff-necked, too. This was a time to be stiff-necked, if there was such a time.

She sat with her brother Captain Johnny and her uncle Moluntha by the fire in the little shelter. It was cold and drafty. In their own cabins and *wegiwa* lodges at home, there would be grass packed in the walls and mats and skins hung inside to keep the drafts out, and the fire would have warmed the whole room. This was not a good time of year to be camping outside a fort for treaty talks. The three of them and Blue Jacket, being the principal chiefs here, had been invited to stay in the fort, but they had declined.

They had decided that they did not trust these Americans even in their offer of hospitality. They felt that anyone who stayed within the fort would become the hostages the Americans wanted to keep. It might happen yet, even tomorrow when they went back to resume the council, that they would be seized because of their importance as chiefs. That was a chance they would have to take.

Chiksika and about ten of his friends had left in anger and disgust right after walking out of the council room; they had ridden straight out of the camp and headed for their homes. Chiksika's young brother Tecumseh had gone with them. Many of the people who had seen Clark step on the sacred belt had wanted to leave at once, but their chiefs Blue Jacket, Red Pole, and Nehinissica had persuaded them to stay for at least another day.

The three sitting here had been asked by the commissioners and the fort's commander to stay and eat and drink in the fort, but none of them wanted to drink rum with these arrogant commissioners; they would not have trusted themselves with a risk of getting drunk, because they were sure the commissioners would compromise them in some way if they did.

"Nephew," Moluntha said to Captain Johnny, "the reason why I was sorry to see you walk out was because that gave a triumph to the Long Knife Clark. I believe he provoked you to go because you were the one talking back to him. Everything you said was true and right. But he wanted no one to make dissent, or any of our people to hear it spoken. He did the insult because he wanted only tame Indians in that room. And so he won when you walked out."

"Eh-heh! But if ridding the council of me is what they want, then I will go back in there tomorrow, and I will keep talking to them just as I talked today, until I make them see that it is no use for them to talk down to us and threaten us!"

Old Moluntha let out a long sigh. "Nephew, I understand you. But it will do no good. They are not here to listen. They are here to tell us they can do whatever they please. They will not negotitate anything. There are more whitemen in our old hunting grounds now than there ever were Shawnees. They keep coming. We are too few to win against them anymore."

Captain Johnny had leaned back and was staring at his uncle. "What? You say we should give up to them?"

"I do not know what we can do. With the confederation of tribes, perhaps we can be strong enough that they will have to negotiate with us honorably. Until the confederation is built, I say that we have no choice at this place. If we resist these terms, that will be their excuse to march right into our country and wipe us out. They would like to do that. But if we say to them here, *Very well, we cannot resist you*, they will have no excuse to invade us yet. We cannot gain anything here, except some more time, until the confederation is strong enough. The British promise to help us, though I have very little faith in them.

"You see, nephew, we, the Shawnee people, have no more choices. If we fight, we will lose. If we make peace, we will lose. But I want to give them no excuse to march into our country and kill our women and children. If we sign now, they will leave us alone for a while. Then maybe we will have to go westward beyond the Missisipe. But we will be alive to do so. Maybe we will have a few years left in our homeland."

"He is right, brother," Nonhelema said. "And their treaty will have words of promise in it that they, too, will be obliged to honor."

"*Hah!*" he exploded, slamming his fist down on his thigh. "They have never honored any treaty they ever wrote! You are such a fool, sister! When that missionary put your head in the river, it washed your brains out!" Then he put his palms over his face. He took them away and looked into the fire, which glinted in the tears that were coming into the corners of his eyes. "Forgive me, sister! We in a family should never speak to each other as I have done." He sat silent for a while and they all looked into the flames. Then he said, "But I shall stay and tell them again tomorrow, the words that Black Snake said: *This is not the way to make a good or lasting peace, to take our chiefs hostage and have soldiers at your backs!*"

"Of course you can tell them that," said Moluntha.

"It will satisfy my heart a little just to say that to them."

In an Indian lodge at night, especially in the winter, someone always remained awake, to be on guard and to tend the fire. Especially here, near the soldier fort, a few people had to remain awake. Nonhelema told Captain Johnny and Moluntha to rest. She would stay up awhile and then awaken her brother to take the watch. In all the other lodges also, there would be people awake, and some warriors patrolled the camp at all hours, wrapped in blankets or hide robes.

In their lodge, Nonhelema was still trying to keep up her faith in the peace effort. She said, "Once the Americans see we will live honorably and in peace, they will be kind to us and take us by the hand in friendship. They are Christians. Once they see their homes and children are safe they will forgive us the past hurts and love us like brothers. Christians always forgive and love in the end. Their Jesus commands it."

Moluntha just grunted, as he lifted his legs, lay down on the bed, and covered himself with the worn bearskin blanket. As usual there were no good choices facing this headman, who bore the weight of the entire tribe on his aged shoulders. He did not disagree with her assessment of their difficult situation, but he certainly disagreed with her belief that the Americans would live by anything that was agreed to. "Christians! Pah!" Moluntha almost spat. He turned his back to the fire and faced the dark. Tomorrow he would try his best.

It was a bitter-cold night, and Nonhelema got up often, placing more wood on the fire instead of letting it dwindle to coals. Somehow it seemed to chase the gloom that kept penetrating her. She, too, deep within, feared that the Americans would not keep their word.

As she stared into the fire, she realized it had begun to sing to her. *Skota Manito,* Fire Spirit, had wisdom to teach her tonight. Nonhelema thought of all she had been taught about fire and about *Mtekyas*, the trees, that were the food for *Skota Manito*. Both of them had a voice. The trees had many voices but were most vocal singing with another like *Dasse Manito*, the Wind Spirit, or *Skota Manito*. They spoke the most ancient of languages, which never failed to translate into wisdom to the humans who would listen.

Tonight they were singing of sacred things. Life. Creator. Creation. The variety of nations who share life on Turtle Island. Of Creator's lovingkindness and love for each of his children, each of his nations. The fire and the tree wood sang of the nations' struggles to get along with one another, all the while not realizing that love and respect among all are what Creator wants from all his children.

Nonhelema remembered the times she and her brothers Nimwha, Silverheels, and Cornstalk had traveled across the land to speak for peace and try to find ways for them all to live in peace as brothers and friends. They had seen their relatives in the south who lived among the Creeks and the Yucchis. The Choctaws, Chickasaws, Cherokees, even the Osages and Kaskaskias had met them for talks, long ago.

She remembered the good times when they were dealing with only the French, when they lived farther east and at Lower Shawnee Town on the Scioto, and when she had been among them with George Morgan by the Missisipe. The French had seemed to love them and had married into their families. There was much happiness then. There had been singing and dancing with their French traders and French friends. The children were safe and healthy when the French traders came.

Once she had gone all the way down the Missisipe to the French city of New Orleans on a trading voyage for Morgan, and there she had seen the Southern Sea, which the Ancient Ancestors were said to have crossed in boats from Mexico.

She wistfully remembered how luxurious her life had been when the French were their friends. She remembered the exquisite fabrics and lace they had brought. The feel of them to her fingertips had been exhilaration. How beautiful they looked when made into dresses, tops, vests, chemises, petticoats, and cloaks. Even now she wore skirts and tops over her deerskin leggings and moccasins. Her cape was heavy dark blue wool, though her favorite color continued to be rich red. She had lined the hood with her last pale blue corduroy. It had been a while since she had had any silk taffeta, the whispering cloth. She hoped there would be good and beautiful fabric for the women among the "gifts" from the Americans after the treaty was signed. Most of their clothes were beginning to be thin and worn.

The French did not crave our land, she thought. *They became part of the tribal families—not just in word but also in deed and heart and spirit. They shared with us and never let us look less elegant than their own families looked. They delighted in making us look beautiful.*

She thought of French trader Lorimier and his wife, Penampieh. After the Long Knives destroyed his store, they had moved to the other side of the Missisipe. He was reported to be doing very well in New Spain now, with a large colony of Shawnees that he took there with him.

She remembered a horse race she and Lorimier had had once, long ago when they were young, after draining a few cups of whiskey. They had begun to brag about who had the faster horse, and of course it had to be proved in a race with all the people betting on their favorite and cheering them on. Nonhelema's people knew her horse-manship as well as her reckless reputation. Some of the French had bet on Lorimier as the lighter load on his horse, as he was only five feet tall and she was over six feet. Surely they had made a spectacle, he with his long black hair braided into a queue that he used as a whip, her full mane tied back in a tight bunch with a fancy silk ribbon, both stripped to the waist for speed. They never agreed who really won. Nonhelema smiled to think of that day. Oh, how she missed her French friends.

For a moment, she remembered, too, the charming LaBalme. But his fate had been bad, and it would be depressing to think of him.

She considered the British and Americans by contrast: as a sour, surly, lying, ruthless lot.

The British and Americans were willing to take their comforts among the Indian women, then abandon them and the resulting children once they began bringing their own white women to the frontier as Butler had done. They missed out on the love and joy of these half-breed children. The Shawnees loved all of them.

She remembered whitemen who had abandoned their Indian women and children, then had come back later with militias to attack the towns where their Indian children lived.

Could Fire Spirit explain to her why Creator brought the whites to Turtle Island? Had he intended they would learn from her people, how to respect one another and be truthful? If that was what Creator expected them to learn from the Shawnees, he would have been disappointed.

Whiteman hunters had not learned from the Shawnees that first rule of the Keeper-of-the-Game: to kill only what you need. Now the woods bison were almost gone. And she missed the beautiful black bears she had known in her youth. They were no longer plentiful. They were being killed, and their rich meat wasted. Only their oil and furs were being saved and shipped far away. She remembered watching mother *M'kwa* teaching her cubs as she took them on their daily walks through the forest. *Geah M'kwa* would eat and taste leaves and berries. She would claw at rotted logs and use her tongue, long as Nonhelema's forearm, to suck and lick grubs and bugs from deep within it. The cubs were comical imitators of their mother.

She smiled as she gazed into the fire and remembered the look on the bears' faces when they found something especially sweet. They learned quickly. They had personalities like little Shawnee children.

Perhaps that was why the Shawnee considered the bear their brother. They were so similar. The mother bear was a good mother. In the puberty ceremony, Nonhelema had always reminded the young women to study *Geah M'kwa*, and learn her mothering traits.

It seemed a long time since Nonhelema had been able to go to the sanctuary of the woods and watch the other mothers. The doe teaching the little fawns their tail-talk in the summer mornings was always a delight. The little spotted ones on their spindly legs always looked so adorably confused.

The fire sang and danced in its delight at simply being alive. The flame flashed and flickered and changed colors magically. Its song honored Creator, who had created him from only his thoughts and power but mostly from his love. *Skota* was happy, and Nonhelema was sad and afraid for the future of her people. Now as she lay there absorbed in watching the dance and listening to the song of the fire, she began to smile.

The whole song of Skota *is one of the joy of life,* she thought, *even as it seems to be dying, its flames flickering and dwindling to coals. Even* Skota's *ashes would be used in the gardens by the women to prepare the soil for new seeds and new life. The continuance of life and usefulness is a great comfort,* she thought. *It is all about life. It is all good. It is all gifts from Creator's love.* Nonhelema shook her head. When she got tired, she could forget the simplest of lessons. She was grateful Creator had known she would need the fire reminders this night.

Ayea! That was what she was supposed to be doing. Rejoicing at being alive, not being downcast because Creator had given her the gift of "change."

This was only discomfort. This was not pain, as when Creator had to watch his own son, the suffering bleeding Jesus, die for all of her wicked sins.

Now again, *Skota* had given her the gift of perspective. She remembered how things are supposed to be. Only the love and forgiveness of Creator is important, and how we treat one another. She could still love the Americans, for the suffering bleeding Jesus' sake. It was a small thing she could do for him. Brother Zeisberger would have been pleased if he had known her thoughts. She had seldom pleased him in the past.

Mtekya—the tree—did not hate people for cutting it and burning it. It rejoiced at being used, and sang to Creator its joy at being useful and being given the gifts to share with others. When it changed from wood to ash, it was sharing Creator's Spirit. And he shared his gifts of shelter, food, tools, warmth, songs, healing, aroma, wisdom, and joy of simply being, with all the other nations. Season after season, *Mtekya* grew and spread its seeds for future generations. It never quit because of the way it was treated. That was for man and Creator to decide. Its joy in exisistence was simply to grow and be, and to be used. Yes, Tree Spirit had beautiful lessons to share with her, too. It was not petulant. It had no grand ideas of itself. It was humble and obedient to Creator's designs for it. In that, it found honor and joy.

She got up and added another piece of wood to the fire, and added several shreds of tobacco with it. She murmured to *Skota* and to *Mtekya* and to Creator her thanks for the lessons they gave her tonight, for reminding her of things she knew deep in her heart, but that fear had driven too deep for her to recall.

Creator was still in charge, she thought, and all her worrying really didn't matter. Her responsibility was to be, to love Creator with all her heart, and to love other people and the other nations as much as she loved herself and her children. Somehow, the fire and the tree had known exactly how to sing that lesson to her troubled heart. Strange that she should now feel so peaceful with such a fateful day in the offing.

Foolish as it had seemed, she had felt she could hold off the fateful changes by holding back the dark with this little wood fire. But the wood and fire had soothed her fears. She knew tomorrow she would be able to think better, clearer, and now she could rest. No longer was she in the grips of fear, because she had received the gifts of wisdom from *Skota*. She woke Captain Johhny up to keep the fire, and then drifted into deep sleep.

The bugle blared in the fort, its raucous noise making her jump into wakefulness. Moluntha grumbled: "There is their horn to say that the sun has come up, as if one could not see it."

Nonhelema chuckled. Her old uncle was starting his day in strong spirits. His attitude probably wouldn't help the negotiations much, but it would be interesting.

"Uncle," she said, "we must make the best of this. Before we go into council, let us pray for the wisdom we will need to get safety for our people."

"I have prayed all night for that. To Weshemonetoo. Maybe if you pray to the missionary god, we will get wisdom from one god or another."

She laughed. "Your praying sounded like snoring."

He scowled at her for a moment, then smiled and shook his head. "My niece, I regret often that your parents came under the influence of the Jesus missionaries. That was the beginning of your foolishness. Your eyes are blinded with smoke and you are dancing in a nest of American snakes. Your family was raised to trust whitemen, and that has brought you grief upon grief. Look at your own life as it has been. Every whiteman you trusted has betrayed you. They have taken all you owned, and they have killed or wounded most of your family. Now they are here to take the place where your mother's bones lie, but still you want to be their friend. Still you want us to mark another paper and give them more. My niece, I am peace chief. Even more than you, I am responsible for the safety and health of all the Shawnee people. I would like to trust the Americans, too, but I have spent most of my long years healing and consoling those of us who did trust them. And I have to mend your spirit every time the Jesus priest casts you out of his paradise.

"My niece, I go into this council because they give us no choice. As always, I will try to do whatever will protect our people. But do not expect me to trust these Long Knives. I wish I could blow the smoke out of your eyes, so that our own people could embrace you again."

She knew that he understood all this very correctly. But she hoped that *this time* the Americans *would* be honorable. Her time with the firelight had restored her ability to hope.

Captain Johnny had been drinking tea and smoking his pipe by the fire, listening to them. "Now," he said, "I, too, have prayed and thought on this. I am ready to go into the council and speak politely to these snakes, and not call them snakes. I will put out of my thoughts the insult Clark did to the sacred peace belt. I will ask them to make the treaty easier on us, but if they won't, I will still be polite. I think, before we go into the treaty room again today, we ought to council here with the rest of our warriors and headmen. We should ask them to be polite and get this over with as soon and as easily as we can, so we can get back to our towns in safety. I understand now that all we are doing here is playing a game to win a little time. I was naive to come here seeking truth."

And so, when they went back into the council room, everyone was quiet and polite. They talked respectfully to the commissioners and begged them not to keep hostages, asked them to meet the whole Indian confederacy to discuss the boundaries, explained to them why the tribal communites had the right to judge their own wrongdoers rather than turn them over to whiteman judges, and elaborated still again upon the great difficulty of repatriating captives who did not want to be repatriated.

The commissioners listened to each issue in its turn and then declared that the treaty would be exactly as they had proclaimed it would be, and that the Indians could accept it that way, or expect the full force of war.

And that was it.

Moluntha, Red Pole, and Captain Johnny signed it. Moluntha said, "We will honor the terms of the treaty just so much as you honor them. I hope that you will do better than you have done always before." The commissioners frowned, then pretended that they hadn't heard that. They brought out a keg of whiskey to celebrate the "accomplishment of a permanent peace and friendship" with the Indians, and gave Moluntha, as the principal chief, an American flag, with its seven red stripes, and a circle of thirteen white stars in a blue square. They told him that his people would always be safe under the protection of that flag. It was his official sign that he was a friend of the United States. They showed him how to fold it up for safekeeping, and he thanked them.

Then Moluntha surprised them. He asked Nonhelema to bring the damaged wampum belt and give it to them. She said, "Uncle, I should repair it, and then give it to them."

In Shawnee, he replied: "No, my niece. Give it to them broken. To remind them of their insult, and their broken faith. I would like them to feel some shame when they think back to this time. Now one more thing I want from them. Tell them to write for me the same treaty we just marked. I want to have their promises written down, too."

She looked at the sly, bitter smile on his wrinkled, brown face, and nodded. She smiled, suddenly feeling a rush if warmth for this great old man. "Yes," she said, "and I will watch them copy it, to be sure they don't change any words in the one they make for you."

"Ha! One would think my niece doesn't trust her Americans, either!" He was chuckling at that as she turned to them and demanded the copy. At first they told her no. Why would Indians want a written document they couldn't read?

"Some in our family can read. We were friends of Penn. We learned to read at the mission. I myself can read, which you well know, and in more languages than any of you commissioners. I will copy it myself if your quilldriver is too busy."

At last they agreed, in bad humor about it. And while they set about trying to get Moluntha and the other chiefs drunk, Nonhelema stood over the scrivener and made certain he changed nothing.

When they left the fort, Moluntha was not as drunk as he had led them to believe. He had negotiated over the hostages so that neither he nor any of the headmen would be kept captive. Several young warriors offered to remain, and Moluntha selected six of the strongest and most agile. They all assured him that it should be no trouble to escape from this ill-made little fort whenever they felt like leaving.

"By the honor of this treaty," he said, smirking, "I cannot encourage you to do that. But none of you signed any treaty, did you?" And he walked off, chuckling and wagging his head, with his flag and his treaty under his arm.

Richard Butler kept himself occupied with Commissioner Parsons and Captain Finney. Apparently he was ashamed to come and say anything to Nonhelema. But General Clark approached her. With him was a tall, red-haired, big-boned boy of perhaps fifteen. She had seen the youth now and then hanging back at the edges of the council, observing everything, and he had been watching her as the treaty was being copied. Now she stood watching Clark coolly as he came toward her, limping a little on his sword cane. Young as the general was, he was already beginning to hobble like a rheumatic elder. It was said to be from the hardships of his winter campaign in the Wabash country eight winters before, when he had led his militia troops through midwinter floods for several days on his way to capture the British governor-general in his fort at Post St. Vincent.

Now he stopped before her, looking up slightly into her face from under his bushy, reddish eyebrows. His eyes did not have that fierce and scornful fire in them that he had shown throughout the council. Instead, they looked almost sorrowful, the flesh above his eyelids drooping a little. "Queen *Coitcheleh*," he said, using the most respectful form of address, instead of calling her Katy, as he usually had. He reached out his right hand, and with some distaste she took it. "I should like to speak to you before we go our ways. First, may I present my youngest brother, William. Billy, this is Katy, whom ye know by the name o' the Grenadier Squaw. As I've told you, she's been the staunchest friend we've had among the Shawnee people."

"Ma'am," the boy said, blinking, holding out a work-roughened hand. "I've heard a-plenty about all you done, and I'm honored to make your acquaintance, ma'am."

"Ma'am," she said, and laughed softly in her throat. "So, Master Billy. You have been witness to a treaty. Not one of the best of them. Did you learn anything?"

The lad looked at his brother. "Can I tell her what y' said, George?"

"Sure y' may. It might surprise her to hear it."

"Ma'am," he said, "it stunk like a dead old catfish."

"Ah-heh! Yes, it did. And I fear it will do more harm than good between my people and yours. I have a son about as old as you are. He is called Morgan. I would not be surprised, Master Billy, if someday you and my son will have to face each other in a battle someplace, because of the spirit in which this council was done." The boy's eyes widened. She went on. "It is true what your brother told you about me. I have been your truest friend among all the Shawnee people. And now I have been betrayed by the Long Knives." She turned her eyes to the general's.

"When you stepped on the wampum belt," she said, "I felt your boot upon my heart."

22

At sunset, Nonhelema and her uncle and children went up the slope behind the town, with many of the people following them, and stood looking out. In three directions, they could see clouds of dark smoke rising on the horizons. All three of her children were with her and stood nearby. Tommy tended to stay close to Fani. She had usually carried him around when he was a baby, at Fort Randolph ten years ago. His father, Alexander, and his Shawnee stepmother now lived only a few miles from Moluntha's Town, so they allowed Tommy to spend much of his time with Nonhelema there. The boy's presence helped fill the emptiness where the love and respect of all the Shawnee people had used to be in her heart, before they cast her out. Her heart was as heavy and gray as iron at what they saw.

Morgan, her older son, stared out, bitterness contorting his face, and said, "It is only ten moons since they made that treaty promising peace and protection to the Shawnee people. And already they come back up to burn our towns!"

He was fifteen summers of age, and had not been allowed to go west with the warriors to the Wabash country. The Long Knife General Clark was marching a large army up the Wabash to attack or intimidate the Miami tribes. Little Turtle, the chieftain who had killed Colonel LaBalme six years ago, was now at war with the Americans. Most of the Shawnee men of warrior age had left days ago to assist their new Miami allies. But in their absence, another branch of the American army was coming into Shawnee country here. There was a certain grim satisfaction in Morgan's handsome young face. "Now," he said, "I shall get a chance to fight the Long Knives after all!"

"You will not," said Moluntha. "I do not believe they will come here. They know that this is a town of the peacemakers. They gave me an American flag and the treaty. From those towns"—he pointed at the rising smoke—"warriors kept going down and raiding the boats on the Spaylaywesipe. We did not. We Mekoches have kept the peace. Now, listen. Tomorrow we must keep gathering the corn harvest. The women of those towns will be hungry. Their homes and crops are being burned and we will have to feed and shelter them after the Long Knives turn back."

Nonhelema and Moluntha could hardly look at each other's eyes as they made their way slowly down in the dusk. Each knew that the question was there in the other's mind:

Would the Long Knives really leave Moluntha's Town in peace?

Before they turned to their cabin, she said, "Pray that the Americans will honor their word."

"Ah-heh. I believe that will require strong prayers, from all of us. Let us call for a prayer circle, of everyone in the town, before we sleep tonight."

They did that. For a long time, they all stood in a ring around the bonfire, holding hands all around, imagining the Long Knife army turning around and going back to Kentucke without coming here to the peace town. If the smoke carried their prayer to the Master-of-Life, He-Who-Creates-by-Thinking, he would see in his mind their picture of their town of people remaining safe and unmolested. And when he saw the picture in their prayers, it would become the picture in his own mind, and it would thus become true, and their town would remain safe.

It was a difficult prayer for Nonhelema. Though she could feel through her hands the fervor for peace and safety passing around the prayer circle, sometimes the fire in the center looked like a town burning. Then she had to shut her eyes and try not to see it that way, so that the Master-of-Life wouldn't see it that way.

It was good that young Tommy was here, because Alexander Mc-Kee's Town was one of those making smoke in the sky.

But the truth, she feared, was that Tommy might be no safer here than there.

If not, there was no place anymore where children could be sent to safety.

Nonhelema greeted the morning sun with her prayer pipe in the front of the cabin, blowing a stream of smoke to each of the Four Winds, touching pipe stem to Mother Earth, and pointing it toward heaven, again envisioning peace and safety. The sun had risen over the eastern hills and was lighting the red and yellow autumn leaves on the slope behind the town. She heard the swish of a broom as Moluntha's old wife swept the path before the cabin. Then she heard running footsteps, and saw a boy running up the trail from the south. He was coming straight toward Moluntha's house.

Nonhelema saw the fear in the boy's face as he ran. So she cleaned the ash dottle out of her pipe and then hurried to meet him. She was afraid she already knew what was happening, but wasn't ready to accept it yet. It was frightening when any town was peopled by only women and children and elders. The warriors had not worried about leaving the towns undefended, beause Long Knife Clark's army was, after all, out there where they were going. The Confederation of Tribes had already condemned the Fort Finney treaty as an illegal and contemptible coercion of the Shawnees, and was calling for a great council of all the tribes to deny America's land claims above the Ohio-sipe. And so the chiefs had felt righteous about going off to face Clark's invaders, never imagining there was another army of Kentuckians coming up from the south to strike their own towns while they were away. Had not the Long Knives in that treaty promised to keep peace, and even protect the Shawnees?

But indeed there was another army, and it was within a few miles, and today would tell what it had done, and whether it would come here.

Few people were about. Several women were heading out into the cornfields with their children, carrying their baskets to strip ears of corn off the stalks and bring them in, as Moluntha had said to do.

The boy was confused, not knowing whether to be proud or ashamed, but he was plainly scared as he told the old chief what had happened.

He and some young friends had seen an armed whiteman riding up the trail, and had run out and surrounded him, pulled him from the saddle, and seized him before he could use his gun. They had tried to find out why he was here, but none of them spoke English. By his gestures and a few of his words, he led them to believe the army was behind him, coming to this town. When he began to struggle, one of the boys hit him on the back of his head with a tomahawk, and the whiteman was now dead. The others were bringing his body up on the horse, and wondered whether they should have brought him in alive to learn why he had come. Now they didn't know whether they had killed an enemy scout or maybe a messenger, and they were afraid that the old chief would be angry with them.

Old Moluntha shook his head and looked around, as if he were having a hard time thinking. Finally, he said, "It is bad he was killed, whether he was a scout or coming with a peace message. It can be an excuse for Long Knife revenge."

"Uncle," Nonhelema said, "if soldiers are coming here, it is they who violate the treaty, not us!" She told the boy, "Go down that way, quick. Tell your friends to hurry down the trail and see if the army is coming. Uncle, I will send out to have the women come in from the fields. We must get everybody into town. I doubt the soldiers will come to our town. But we must be ready to run north and get the children to safety." What she expected to see coming up the trail was not an army, but refugees fleeing the other towns.

The boy sprinted back down the path. Moluntha seemed heartened that Nonhelema was helping him. "Ah-hae!" he exclaimed. "I will get the American flag and unfold it. I will show the treaty to any soldiers if they come. You can read them the treaty, that they promised never to harm us. That they will protect us. There is nothing to fear. Maybe they are mad because our hostages deserted them, but . . ."

She left him talking to himself and ran into the cabin. Morgan and Tommy were gone. In the mornings, they usually got up early to go spearfishing in the creek. It frightened her that they were away. She climbed to the loft. Fani was still sleeping soundly. Nonhelema shook her awake. "Daughter, you have to be awake at once and go summon the women and children from the cornfields south of town. There may be soldiers coming. Hurry!"

Fani leapt up, naked, shaking her head. She pulled on a tunic. "Soldiers are coming to attack us in the peace town?"

"I doubt. But we must have everybody here when we find out. Go!"

It was good how her daughter could always do so quickly whatever was needed. With her morning prayer pipe, Nonhelema had already thanked Creator for her good, devoted daughter, who through all these terrible years had remained beside her as her companion and helper.

Nonhelema glanced around the loft. She picked up her sash and tied it around her waist, over her dress, with its sheath knife on it, and from the lid of a chest she picked up her brass pipe-tomahawk and slipped its handle down through the sash. She paused, looking at the chest. In it was the wooden case containing her pair of fine silver-trimmed pistols. For a moment she wondered whether she should open the trunk and get them, with their little powder flask and bullet bag. Outside, there were excited voices and the sound of running footsteps.

No. No pistols. This was surely an ungrounded alarm.

Besides, she was a peace chief. A child of God. Even now, after all her rejections and insults from Brother David Zeisberger, she was still under his influence. Brother David would not want her to arm herself with pistols, whether soldiers were coming or not. She was safe, she had been baptized, she was clad in the shining armor of Jesus. Her people in this village were not. If there was trouble and they saw she was unscathed, perhaps they would become children of God as well.

It had been twelve years since she had killed anyone, in that long-ago battle by the Kanawha-sipe. She turned away from the trunk, climbed down the ladder from the loft, and ran into the sunlight. Two men of middle age, warriors who had fought under her command at Kanawha but now were too old and sore in the bones to have gone with the rest to the Wabash and had stayed here as hunters, were trotting down the trail toward the south end of the town. They lifted their chins in greetings to her.

"*Weshe catoo weh!*" she told them. "Be strong. If an enemy strikes, hold him back until the families can flee!"

"Eh-heh, *Coitcheleh!*"

By the time the sun was halfway up, it had begun to seem as if there was no danger coming. Many of the women and their children were in from the fields and near their homes. Fani had failed to find her brothers at their usual fishing places. Boys were always hard to find.

The chill of morning had been dispelled by the sun, and the whole valley glowed red, gold, and all the rich colors of harvesttime. Old Moluntha sat on a bench in front of his cabin, eyes closed, the sunlight on his lined, coppery face, the folded flag on his lap, and the rolled paper of the Fort Finney treaty in one gnarled hand, like any ancient man basking in sunlight with the knowledge that such days would end soon, that winter would come soon, and that he might not live to see another springtime.

In recent moons, Moluntha had sent several letters to the British in Detroit begging for help for his people, in whatever way the British could give it. Being old and wise, he recognized a bad treaty. The treaty at Fort Finney was the worse. Any confidence he had in the Americans honoring it had been faint. Their insincerity had fairly reeked from their bodies in a visible haze. Unfortunately, the British had not responded with anything tangible, just hints of promises of some type of help, still not forthcoming.

It was now midmorning, and nothing had happened since the early alarm. The body of the whiteman had been brought up and examined and put in a lodge, his arrival unexplained. He had been carrying a rifle and thirty balls, a blanket roll, and a pouch of sweetened meal such as militiamen carried on their campaigns. If he was an army scout, he would not have been out alone so far ahead of the army. Nonhelema kept thinking that he might have been an army man who had deserted, as many did.

The young men sent down the trail to look for signs of soldiers had gone a long way down and returned to say they had seen no signs. Now they were lying concealed beside the trail outside the town.

Nonhelema kept worrying about her sons, and about all the corn that should be getting harvested on a good day like this, and was growing impatient. Moluntha's old wife had a stew kettle hanging over a nearly smokeless oak-wood fire in a fire pit under an arbor, and was putting lyed-corn hominy and chunks of burdock root into a simmering squirrel-meat broth. In the edge of the coals she had set a kettle of tea water and had poured a cup of the barely warm sumac-berry tea for her husband. The tangy beverage was his favorite drink, above even sassafras or English black tea. He had been saying lately that if the British did not soon show some real concern for the plight of their former protectors, the Indians, he would stop drinking English tea altogether, and that would show the British how he felt about their empty talk.

"Uncle," said Nonhelema now, rising from her seat by the fire, "I must go myself and see whether there are soldiers coming. I shall ride down." She was one of the best riders in the tribe and had one of the fastest horses. If someone was coming who could be talked to, she was the one to talk. If an enemy was coming who wouldn't talk, she could get back quickest with a warning. She decided she would take her pistols. She could wear those hidden, unlike a long gun.

Moluntha had come out of his torpor at her words. He was raising a hand and shaking his head. "Don't go, no! Wait. What . . . what will you tell them about the dead whiteman?"

She realized then how confused the old man was, how unready he was for any sort of urgency or conflict. He was afraid his people would be punished because he thought of the dead man as a violation of the treaty. As much as he hated that treaty, he had put his mark on it, and all his life he had honored his word.

As for the whiteman, there was nothing to say about him now. If there were whitemen near and they had come in peace, they would be told about him, whatever the consequences. If there were no whitemen coming, she would probably bury the dead man later with a Christian prayer, as he surely must have been a Christian.

"All will be well, Uncle," she said. "I will be—"

Her words were overwhelmed by gunfire: one shot, three more, one, four, then a swelling thunder of shots, and the rising yelling voices.

The commotion was close, south of the village, and coming fast. There were only about twenty-five or thirty men to defend the town, and from the din of gunfire, there must have been hundreds of attackers. It was hard to believe that so many could have come so close to the town without being discovered.

Everyone in the village had been anticipating that they might have to evacuate, but no one had expected an attack to start so near and so suddenly; most of the women had just come in from the fields, unloaded their corn, and begun bundling up the light necessities they would need if they had to leave their town. They had done it often enough since the town burners had started coming into their country. Usually there was enough warning time for them to get away.

But the soldiers were here! Suddenly the lanes between the houses were full of women running, pulling their children along or carrying them, children crying with fright, mothers urging them to hurry and to be silent, everyone running north away from the battle noise.

Guns were still banging, and now Nonhelema could hear the roar of full-throated yelling, and the rumble of hoofbeats that could be felt through her feet on the ground. This was more frightening. Unlike the walking soldiers who had attacked the towns before, these must be riding soldiers, fast enough to catch running people. A few of the warriors came running up now, reloading their long guns as they came, converging around Moluntha's cabin, rallying here to defend him, crouching behind tree trunks and a pile of firewood to aim their guns back in the direction from which they had come. It was too late now for the old chief and his two old wives to flee.

And it was obvious that he would not have led even if he could. Moluntha had stood up from his bench. He had shaken the folds out of his American flag. His old wife was helping him tie the flag onto a long sapling pole. And just as the smell and haze of gunsmoke began wafting in, and bullets were chipping bark and burring through the air, the old chief stepped up on the woodpile and jabbed the base of the pole down among the limbs to brace it.

Nonhelema, with great relief, saw her daughter, Fani, running up the lane from the east, and screamed her name to get her attention. Fani pivoted and came running up. "Get in Uncle's house, and make Auntie go in with you! Those walls will protect you—"

A gun banged behind her, fired by one of the warriors. She looked down toward the south and now she could see the mounted soldiers coming on swiftly, not just on the street but on all the lanes and foot-paths among the cabins and *wegiwas* and *wikans*, shooting, howling and trampling over anything in their way, even dogs and children. They were in a line, coming through the village like the teeth of a comb.

The time was past when she might have gone up and gotten her pistols, but she would have had no heart for that anyway. With the warriors gone, there weren't enough guns or bullets in the town to stop so many soldiers. This village, the main peace town of the Shawnee nation, was at their mercy, and they did not appear to have much mercy. This could be like Gnaddenhutten four years ago, where her mother and sister and all the Praying Indinas had been massacred. Nonhelema resigned herself to whatever the Master-of-Life intended. She would resist only to the extent of warding off blows aimed at her family. She stepped over to stand nearer her uncle, and watched the Kentuckians.

Seven or eight women who had been in the cornfields came running up the trail, close together, sobbing and panting. Just behind them an officer came riding hard, waving a saber. He caught up with the last woman and slashed down. As she tumbled to the ground almost under his horse's hooves, he gave a loud whoop and raised his blade to hack at another, who collapsed with a split skull. He slashed the neck of a third woman as he came abreast of Moluntha's cabin. One of the warriors fired a musket ball at him as he galloped by, but it missed, and the whooping officer struck down a fourth woman as he rode out of sight beyond a lodge. Nonhelema's heart froze. All these women were tribal sisters and family kin with whom she had shared childhood, harvests, ceremonies, healings. She recognized the officer, a man named Kennedy. *Had I got my pistols,* she thought, *that one would be dead!*

Now there were horsemen stampeding through the village everywhere. The air was full of smoke, gunshots, yells, screaming, pounding hoofbeats. Old Moluntha stood in the midst of it, as if he cared little whether he lived or died. He was close to the flag, and it did appear that the flag had created a center of calm in the chaos. Some of the horsemen, seeing the flag, recognizing the chief and Nonhelema, had circled back around and reined in. She knew many of them by sight, the usual militia officers and raiders and scouts from Kentucke and murderous Long Knives from Virginia. There were colonels named Patterson and Lee, whom she remembered from Pittsburgh, and here came General Benjamin Logan, the commander who had burned the Mad River towns and Lorimier's Station four years ago. The sight of such experienced Indian fighters, especially the sly old woodsmen like Kenton and Boone, explained how the army had come so close without being detected.

Nonhelema, still stunned not just by the deliberate killing sport inflicted on the women, but also by the fact that the well-known peace town had been raided, could only pray that some of the women, and perhaps her sons and other boys, had fled into the woods and thickets. They could hide from horsemen in those dense and familiar places.

But then she heard a soldier shout, "Follow their dogs!" The barking dogs were following their fleeing owners, and were revealing their hiding places. That was one of the tricks these veteran Long Knives had learned in their years of murderous town burning.

The whole town had now been overrun by mounted militiamen, wild-eyed and exultant, some holding bloody scalps high and twirling them overhead. Gunshots were still banging in every part of the village, echoing off the hills that rose behind the town. Men's voices whooped and howled, dogs barked, horses whinnied, children screamed. Nonhelema could see men getting off their horses, going into lodges to kill, or rape, or loot. A soldier hopped down off his horse where one of the young women had been hacked to death, turned her body over, slit her dress from neck to hem, and stood leering down at the naked corpse. Nonhelema had the notion that if other soldiers hadn't ridden up to look at her, the man might actually have violated her body. He took out his sheath knife and began skinning her breasts. Nonhelema was ready to run out and tomahawk him, but found herself pressed backward by riding soldiers who were crowding into Moluntha's yard.

The militia officers, at first attracted by the flag, were being drawn in, apparently, by realizing that the Mekoche chief himself was there under their control. They all knew him, and he knew most of them. Nonhelema knew of his deep contempt for these bloody conquerors. Though he had been a peacemaker for many years, it was not for admiration or trust of the Americans, but for love of his own poor people.

Now Moluntha was smiling at them all, pointing to the American flag, and showing them his copy of the Fort Finney treaty. He was saying: "Mistake, it is. Mistake! See the flag given me by those commissioners! See? Look and see this writing on my treaty! I am under protection of the government of your Congress, you see? My town is a peace town, no warriors of Moluntha bother Kentucke! See? Look! General Clark himself made this treaty! Our old brother Butler! They give this treaty paper and flag to me and say, Americans will never hurt me or my Mekoches, always who are friends of the Americans."

Nonhelema, still hearing the sounds of pillage and rape everywhere in the town, moved closer to her uncle. Maybe she could help him make them understand this, before too much more damage was done. She looked around at these strong, brutal men on their sweaty horses. Officers grinning triumphantly even as their men committed rape and murder all around. She looked at them in amazement, knowing that all of them professed to be Christians of a civilized country, and she was heartsick because of the work she had done in their behalf.

She looked up at Logan, a square-faced, thick-bodied, stubble-jawed man with fierce blue eyes, sure that he was the man in command, he who was General Clark's second in rank. She demanded of him: "You, Logan! Tell me why you come up and kill the peace people! We who have done everything in our power to help you!"

He yanked his horse's reins and kicked its flanks and rode away from her, out through the cordon of milling horsemen. Above the town she saw dark smoke billowing into the sky, burning flakes soaring; the autumn sunlight was bright, so the flames were not visible, but by the smoke and the rising ashes and fragments she knew they were setting the houses on fire. Like the rest of the Shawnee towns whose smoke they had seen on the horizons, the peace town was being destroyed again.

The cries and gunshots dwindled on the far edges of the village. Before midday, the militiamen began coming in with prisoners, women and boys with lead ropes around their necks and their hands tied behind their backs, some of them bloody and showing signs of having been beaten. Nonhelema was taut with fear over the fate of her sons. Just as she was ready to break out of the ring of horsemen to go look for them, she saw Morgan being led up from the creek bottomland. He did not seem to be hurt, and was scolding his captor in English, calling him a treacherous snake. The militiaman himself had a deep, bloody gash along his left cheek, and his collar and shoulder were smeared with blood.

"Nigeah!" Morgan cried out when he saw her. "Look! I got this snake with my fish spear before he took me! It took three of them to catch me! I led them off and little brother got away! Ha, ha!"

She took a deep breath, amazed that they hadn't just killed him. They must have recognized him as her son.

From every direction, people were being brought in as prisoners. So one purpose of this raid was to take hostages, to put more leverage on the Indians for prisoner exchanges. They had caught the most revered chief, and they had caught her, and her son.

But if getting hostages was their purpose, why had they come in killing and raping and burning?

She knew the answer to that: because they liked to. They were full of hatred and vengeance. These wars had been going on for years; most families had suffered losses. Deep in her ran a dread of prisoner roundups like this. She remembered massacres of Indian captives, in particular her brother Cornstalk at Fort Randolph and her mother and sister at Gnaddenhutten Mission.

Some of the officers were standing about laughing, now trying to converse with old Moluntha. Their raid had been a success, and now their battle rage was cooling; they were enjoying their conquest. She had seen this over and over. Some of them, now that they had won, would become almost civil, the way Clark had after dominating the Indians at the treaty at Fort Finney.

If only men could be kind before *they started shooting,* she thought.

Some soldiers hustled into Moluntha's cabin, and Nonhelema heard some angry shouts within—a man's and Fani's. She started toward the door, but then soldiers came out laughing, pushing Fani and Moluntha's old wives before them. Fani's tunic had been ripped open to the waist, and she looked furious. Then one soldier came hobbling out, bent over, his face in a grimace, and Nonhelema knew, with grim satisfaction, what had happened in there. She herself had taught Fani how to twist the testicles of pushy men. That soldier would be without lust for several days. Whitemen often were astonished to learn how strong Indian women's hands were.

Nonehlema turned her attention back to her uncle, who was trying to be as diplomatic as he could be with these invaders, concealing his anger and dismay, as chiefs so often had to do. He was unrolling and displaying the treaty again and reminding them of its promise to protect the Shawnees who had signed it, including himself. He kept putting his finger on the place where he signed it, showing the officers his mark. Maybe he was worried that the militiamen would find the corpse of the whiteman who had ridden in this morning.

Then, as she knelt to examine wounds on several of her captive people, she heard a soldier say to Colonel Boone: "Deserter's been found, Colonel. Guess they kilt 'im afore we'uns could."

"Fair 'nuff. Go tell Kenton. The bastard was from his comp'ny."

So, she thought. *A deserter.* Maybe he was troubled by conscience and coming here to warn us. There would be no punishment for killing the deserter. They would have killed him themselves.

Nevertheless, she knew, they could use his death as an excuse to do whatever they felt like doing.

Colonel Boone and a colonel whose name she remembered as Patterson had dismounted. Patterson had a blood-soaked sleeve, and Nonhelema presumed the blood was from hacking Indians with his sword. But Boone cut open Patterson's sleeve with a knife, then led him toward her. Boone now had some gray in his hair, but his physique and keen blue eyes still made him look youthful.

"Katy," he said, dipping his head in a slight bow and smiling, "Colonel Patterson here has an old wound that never healed, and he's hurt it. Maybe one of your medicine women would put a potion on, and dress it, suppose?"

She shut her eyes and clenched her jaw, then, standing to frown down on both men, she replied, "You have come here killing my people, wronging your own treaty, and you ask *us* to heal your colonel, who hurt his arm while striking us down?"

"Now, Katy. I know you're a Christian, Katy, and y'd help any man."

Boone could be so merry and charming, but now she was not charmed. She sighed. "Yes, I would help any hurt man. You," she told Colonel Patterson, "sit over there. When we have tended to all our own hurt people, we will come and fix your poor arm."

Colonel Patterson's expression went from pain to anger. "Damned sullen savages! And damn Logan for marching out an army without so much as one damned surgeon in it!"

"Eh-heh!" Nonhelema retorted. "He did not expect any soldiers to get hurt making war on women and children, eh?" She turned her back on the officers and was going back to the cluster of wounded Shawnee prisoners when she saw a face that sent a shrill alarm through her soul, like the whistle of a hawk.

An officer had dismounted right in front of her. He was snarling, gray-toothed, eyes narrowed and glinting. What might have been a handsome face was ugly with rage and hatred. She had seen this man at Fort Pitt, where he had been known as a boisterous drunkard and a starter of fights, a man shunned even by many of his fellow officers of Kentucke. It came to her memory then who he was: McGary. This was the man whose reckless charge into the Blue Licks ambush four years ago had led so many of his comrades to death. McKee had told her about this fool and what he had wrought that day.

Hugh McGary. It was amazing that they still let him ride among them. But here he was, strutting toward old Moluntha with that hateful sneer on his flushed face. Nonhelema hurried over to get between the officer and her feeble old uncle. She drew her tomahawk out from the sash at her waist, apprehending danger.

The swaggering officer placed himself before the old chief and tilted his head, his feet spread wide. Moluntha had just become aware of McGary's presence and turned to face him, still holding the treaty scroll half-open in front of him. He showed no sign of recognition. To Nonhelema's knowledge, Moluntha and McGary had never met each other. But McGary was staring at Moluntha intensely. "You, Chief," he said. "Were you at Blue Licks?"

Moluntha had been much too old to be in the Blue Licks ambush. He was also half-deaf, and in the present hubbub here in the center of his devastated town, he probably had not really understood the officer's question. But the old chief knew Blue Licks, and had loved that place. It had been the richest of rich hunting grounds in Kentucke, and one of the powerful spirit places, a sacred place to Shawnees. He had happy memories of times there. Nonehelma knew that the officer meant the Blue Licks *battle*, but Moluntha was remembering a place he loved, and when he heard its name, he smiled and nodded and replied, "Ah-heh! Blue Licks! Yes!"

McGary's eyes bulged, crazed. He snatched Nonhelema's tomahawk from her hand, cocked it over his shoulder, and struck the top of the old man's head.

The blade split Moluntha's skull, punching deep into his brain. McGary wrenched it out with such force that the old man's head bobbed and twisted on his neck; then he drew back for a second blow.

A bolt of horror and fury shot through Nonhelma and she leapt at McGary, grabbing for the tomahawk. He swung at her but missed by an inch, and she grabbed the weapon by its head. McGary twisted and yanked. The sharp blade slashed her palm to the wrist. He aimed another blow at her head, a snapping, lashing blow, and when she tried to shield herself with her blood-spurting hand, the blade chopped through it, severing the fingers. As if the sight of this energized McGary, he now drew back and delivered another lightning-quick, great blow to the crevice in Moluntha's head, splattering brains on those standing near.

Moluntha had not fallen yet, his body swaying, twitching, his knees beginning to give. As he began to topple, the blood-splattered treaty paper fell from his hands. With shouts of outrage, some officers and soldiers seized McGary and began beating him. He had killed their most valuable prisoner.

As stunned as if the blow had split her own head, Nonhelema dropped to her knees beside her beloved uncle, gasping and choking, reaching to get her hands under him and lift him up, as if she might raise him back to life, oblivious of the blood gushing from her own ruined hand. She saw only the gory gash between the old man's grizzled eyebrows, the blood welling out and already puddling in his eye sockets. His bony body jerked with several powerful spasms and then was still.

Nonhelema was being kicked and jolted by the melee that had erupted around McGary, but she didn't notice. She paid no heed to the shouts and blows as they began beating McGary senseless.

All she saw now, as she grew faint, was the bony, lifeless face of her uncle, his white hair now soaked with blood. Like warm smoke, something was flowing up out of his body, speaking wordlessly to her as it departed.

His wives' voices keened, ululating with grief, and Nonhelema's own voice poured out of her bosom to wail with them, then Fani's, their voices like wolf calls intermingling, taken up then by all the other captive women, for their slain sisters and brothers and their revered old headman.

The lodges and cabins and cornfields were burning all around. Their smoke billowed upward with the departing spirits of the massacred innocents of the Mekoche village, the Town of the Peacemakers.

Nonhelema passed in and out of a sort of dream world, sometimes seeing what was going on around her but unable to attach any meaning to it. Sometimes she would look up and see Fani over her; sometimes there were Kentucke militiamen looking down on her, dark forms silhouetted against the roiling smoke in the sky. She alternated between feeling womblike warmth and comfort and a permeating cold like the still cold of death.

Sometime later she was aware of movement, though she was still lying supine. She was on a litter slung between horses. Up the trail beyond her feet she saw the blurred shapes of riding soldiers, and great clouds of smoke billowing up from the burning cornfields. She was aware of this part of the usual Long Knife devastation, but now it meant nothing. She envisioned the form of Moluntha rising in the smoke, and then there was nothing to see but redness and then blackness. Now and then, she would hear Fani's voice speaking to her from somewhere outside the eagle scream in her ears, but she couldn't understand her words.

There came the face of a young, strong warrior. He was smiling down at her and talking to her. It was Moluntha, and she was a small girl. It was the Old Shawnee Town, far in the east among steep, wooded mountains. There beside Moluntha was her father, also young. Nonhelema was leaning back against warmth and comfort, shyly looking up at Moluntha, with her fingers in her mouth, and her mother, who was that warmth and comfort on whose lap she sat, took her hand and pulled the fingers away from her mouth, reminding her that one put fingers in the mouth only when eating, or when moistening quills for sewing, or when cleaning one's teeth with a dogwood twig. Cornstalk was there, too, a small boy, and so were aunts, and other uncles besides Moluntha, all of them happy and paying attention to her. But then they withdrew from her, fading into brightness, telling her to come along with them.

Now and then she would come to the surface of consciousness and hear the monotonous thudding of horses' hooves, the whisper of moccasined feet, the creak of leather, distant crow calls, the murmur of sad voices, crying of children, shouts of soldiers, and a few distant gunshots.

23

DANVILLE, KENTUCKY
CHRISTMAS 1786

She felt someone pulling and turning the center of her pain. They wouldn't leave it alone; they were constantly touching and tugging it, making it even harder to bear. Always before, she had just drawn in and braced herself to keep from whimpering or screaming until they stopped, but now she was tired of it and flared up in anger.

She opened her eyes to protest to whoever was tormenting her this way, and saw only the dingy pole rafters she had been seeing every time she woke up for as long as she could remember, rafters high in a haze of smoke, and the underside of bark-slab roofing. She was still here, wherever this was, this cold, dark, smoky room that she always saw when she came out of the fiery other place of feverish dreams.

The center of the pain was her left hand; that much she knew from their tormenting of it. The pain rippled out from that center, reaching everywhere in her, and she usually tried to swim beneath it in the dream place, though that place was hot and turbulent and haunted with fearful memories and grim understandings. Even Jesus had been there, telling her . . .

With effort, she craned to see who was bothering her hand.

She saw the face of a whiteman whom she had seen somewhere before, but seeing that face meant no more than anything else she saw when she opened her eyes in this place.

But he was hurting her very much. He was torturing her. For the first time since she had been this way, she wanted to understand something. In the other-place world of swirling dreams, she had come to understand everything about the Master-of-Life and about Jesus, and about her own wrong thinking, and so she had preferred to stay there in that world, but now the torture of her hand kept bringing her back to this world, and she needed to understand why she was being tortured.

She looked down at the man's face and tried to remember how to use her voice, for something besides groaning or crying, how to use words, whichever language this man might understand. To know that, she would have to remember who he was. This man was not one of the Moravians, not a speaker of German. Not a Frenchman or a Spaniard.

She tried to make her mind work. This was someone from years ago, but still a familiar face. She tried to make herself remember.

She began to hear, through the sound of wind in her head, that there were others nearby. She heard children's voices, small and querulous, like birdcalls. She heard women talking low. She came to realize that they were familiar voices.

Then she heard a most familiar voice. There was no place in this world or the other-place world where she wouldn't know the voice of her daughter. Fani's voice was soft and low, but very near, and the sound of it now squeezed her heart. Nonhelema glanced about for a sight of her until she found her at her right side.

It was like looking through the wrong end of a spyglass. She could see only the face, but nothing around it, and it looked small and distant. This was not how seeing was supposed to be, and she knew that whatever her great illness, it had affected her sight.

She had not wanted or attempted to speak for a long time, if indeed it had been a long time. She had no sense of time. But now she had a desire to understand, to speak. She wanted to stop the pain instead of hiding beneath it. She remembered her uncle Moluntha's spirit rising in the smoke, but nothing after that. Just the endless dreaming.

It was as if she had returned to the surface of water after drowning, with lungs remembering their need for air. What was this place? How had she come here? Who was here? What season was this? What sickness had taken her so deep, and why she was still so full of pain? The questions all went through her mind without the word of any language. She saw her daughter now, as if over a long distance, but did not think her name. There were no words yet for any of this that was returning.

There were memories of how things looked. The last she had seen of trees, they had been at their most beautiful, yellow and red. How long since she had seen those trees in their beauty? Had she been in this cold, smoky building since then? Had she been dead? Was this, now, her next birth? She was emerging from a dreamy, frightening otherworld where she understood everything, into a dim real world where she understood nothing and the pain was more intense.

But her daughter was here. Here was the world into which she must rise.

Then the man down at her side did something and a jolt of pain shot through her arm and into her heart and she almost fainted back into that place again. Her arm twitched violently, but it was being held firmly.

"*Ai-ya! Ni kithekwa!*" she screamed, the words coming back unthought. At the same moment her sight changed and she no longer looked through narrowness. Her daughter, Fani, and the man were kneeling beside her, she on her right and the man kneeling on her left, and after the blaze of pain dimmed, she saw the two had raised their heads to look at her in astonishment. She could see above them the whole wide ceiling of the room in which she lay. She saw that there were many people crowded in the room and she heard one of them, a woman, cry: "She speaks!" Nonhelema knew that voice so well: Red Oak Woman.

And another cried, "*Coitcheleh* is returning to us! *Wehsah!*" Ragged forms of women and children were rising from the floor of the smoke-veiled room and were moving toward her, coming to stand around the bedding where she lay, looking down at her. Ragged and gaunt as most of them looked, many were smiling and exclaiming in pleasure.

Fani had moved closer and was kneeling by Nonhelema's shoulder, holding her right hand and beginning to stroke her cool palm over Nonhelema's forehead, looking down into her face with widened, hopeful, glimmering eyes. "*Nigeah!* You are here? Can you see me? Do you know me?"

This anguished query brought up a surge of pity in Nonhelema's breast, but she had strength only to lightly squeeze her daughter's hand. She relaxed her neck and sank back on the pillow, able now to see without craning. She would have to keep herself from slipping back to where she had been, and do the hard work of listening and telling, despite the pain, because she could see how desparate her daughter's need was.

The others were crowding around, all faces wrought with care and suffering, the women of her uncle's town, many of them her own relatives, women who had been for or against her in the matter of peacemaking, women who had felt betrayed by her acceptance of the whiteman's Jesus God but had loved her despite that. All this was back in her head and heart again, whole, even better understood now because of where she had been in those long dreams.

One by one, or several at a time as they could reach in, these women touched her face or hair or shoulders, and through each hand she felt strength passing into her. This was where strength had always come from: from the people, and the people got theirs from their women.

Kitewi reached in and touched her—Kitewi, who years ago in war council had denounced her for being haughty and spoiled—Kitewi was welcoming her back to life! How their haughty Shawnee queen had been brought down!

Another piercing pain shot like lightning through the unyielding agony in her arm, and she arched in a spasm, then told the whiteman in a shuddering voice, "*Kila kuithi!* You are killing me with pain!" She said it in both languages, looking at his as she said it, and he glanced up from her hand, clearly stricken. She knew his face, and even this expression. Who was this?

"Madame, forgive me. But I am not killing you. I am trying to save your life." He was lean, plain, with a large forehead, kindly eyes, scars and black-powder burn flecks on his right temple.

Now with his voice and his Virginian accent, she recognized him. She had never seen this man with a full beard before, only the stubble of a dirty soldier in a frontier fort. Taking several deep breaths to brace herself against the pain, she said, "You . . . the writing soldier from . . . Kanawha fort? Eh?"

"I'm honored ye remember me, ma'am. I'm Dr. Case—Private Case, 'twas then. This is my second try to save your life, and I doubt you appreciate it any more this time than that other. Sorry to hurt you so badly, but if I'd not been here in Danville by a fluke, I'm sure you'd've lost your whole arm, and your life, as well. You have healers here, these women kin of yours. But being captive, they couldn't go out for the herbals."

She looked at this man and thought on his words, trying to absorb them through the pain, trying to remember some of those occurrences at the Kanawha fort. Now she remembered that this was the fawning fool who had thrown himself at her in front of the murderers' guns there. He had been strong for a man his size and had hit her like a leaping panther.

Now she said: "I remember you . . ." She coughed, thought, gathered strength to talk, and went on. "Often I wished you had not gotten me out of the . . . out of the aim of the guns. But the . . . Master-of-Life must intend that I live on . . ." She sank back, exhausted, and rolled her eyes to look at her daughter.

Fani's face was wet with tears. *"Nigeah,"* she said, "we have been here two moons in Kentucke. Morgan is a prisoner at Boone's. Tommy was never caught. My uncles parley with Boone to ransom us out. Captain Johnny's wife, Rachel, is here with us!" Nonhelema followed Fani's glance and saw her sister-in-law hovering over her with a wistful smile. Rachel had a biblical name because she was a white woman by birth, though she was by now such a Shawnee in custom and appearance that she was never presumed to be otherwise.

"Shene shema," Rachel said. "My husband often sends tobacco to us, and I prayed by its smoke that your spirit would come back into you!"

"Megweshe, my sister. I thank you. I am returned today."

Rachel blinked and glanced about, then said, *"Shena shema* Katy, listen: You do not know, this day your spirit comes back to us is the day of Christmas! Perhaps that is, what they say, a Jesus miracle? It was also the day of Christmas, was it not, when the missionaries put you in the river and made you Christian?" This poor woman Rachel, who had so long since abandoned her own Christian upbringing for the ceremonies of the Shawnee *Coitchelekwa,* was nevertheless very excited by the realization she had just made.

Nonhelema turned her head again to find the deepest comfort of the pillow. She thought deeply and let many memories pass through, real memories as well as those that had billowed through during her time in the other-place world. At last she said to Rachel, barely louder than a whisper, while squeezing Fani's hand as if in a wordless signal: *"Nila nishikwi."*

The women all around her looked strangely at her and at each other, as if alarmed that she might be slipping out of sensibility again, because what she had said did not seem to make sense.

But she, and perhaps Fani, knew that she knew exactly what she meant.

I shed my skin.

Dr. Justin Isaac Case inspected the hideous, gnarled, and blackened claw at the end of Nonhelema's left arm once more before starting to bandage it. He tried to believe that he had at last subdued all the gangrenous corruption from the wound. He still wondered if he should have amputated at the elbow—that had been his first notion, upon seeing the suppurating, stinking appendage—but now he believed that wouldn't be necessary. If this healed now, she might be able to use the thumb and the stump of the little finger that remained.

When he had arrived at the town of Lexington, passing through on a trip to gather research for his frontier history, he had been summoned to doctor a chronic infection on the arm of the militia colonel Robert Patterson. While treating Patterson and interviewing him about his role in the war, he had learned that in the nearby village of Danville a Shawnee "queen" lay delirious and dying among a gaggle of captives taken in a raid on the Shawnee towns in October. Instinctively, he had known that the woman must be Nonhelema the Grenadier, and had offered to ride over and try to treat her. Colonel Patterson, one of the raiders' commanders, had been afraid that the woman, one of the most valuable hostages, would die in his custody, which would have brought more shame and trouble upon himself. He already had suffered considerable censure, because one of his captains had murdered the most valuable hostage, the revered Chief Moluntha.

Dr. Case had found Nonhelema here in this rough, drafty, leaky, filthy barnlike outbuilding, nearly dead from pneumonia and loss of blood, delirious and comatose by turns from gangrenous fever, attended by sick, famished, and wounded women who could not do for her even the things they knew how to do. The woman's condition had stunned him: gaunt, unconscious, rank with piss, dirty, ragged, not a trace of the elegance that had so captivated him a decade ago. Now her face was a hollow-cheeked, hollow-eyed skull with dull brown skin stretched over a beaklike nose. Fani, eyes downcast, had told him, "I am sorry we are like this. They do not let us go to the creek to wash."

Colonel Patterson had told him about the raid, in which he was hurt. McGary, the captain who had wounded her and killed the chief, had been overpowered and arrested, and had stood trial at Harrodsburg on the return to Kentucky. He had been found guilty of murder and disorderly conduct. As punishment, he had been suspended from military command for one year.

"That was all?" Case asked Patterson.

"Yes, that was it," the colonel had replied.

"And she saw the officer do it, you say?"

"That's how she got cut, trying to stop it."

Dr. Case remembered the day, nearly ten years ago, when she had seen her brother Cornstalk and other kinsmen murdered while helpless in captivity. How had she borne all this?

Now, as he wrapped her mangled hand in a poultice and bandages, with her tribal women looking on in apparent approval, he was almost nauseated with fury and pity. He had given her laudanum and she was peaceful, murmuring in conversation with her women. Dr. Case fancied himself tracking Captain McGary down and shooting him. He would tell him why, and then fire the pistol at the moment of his understanding.

He sighed. It was mere fantasy. Just as he had dreamed of shooting Captain Arbuckle for failing to testify against Cornstalk's murderers years ago, this, too, would not be done. He was a doctor, not an executioner. He was a daydreamer, not a man of action. Someday, perhaps, Shawnees would find McGary and take vengeance. That would be more just, anyway.

"Miss Fani," he said, rising to his feet slowly and painfully after so much kneeling on the cold dirt floor, "I shall return tomorrow to tend to your mother again. Before I return, I expect to cause some improvement in this awful place. I mean to have Colonel Patterson get water kettles and plenty of cloth and blankets and soap. If I have to shame all the white ladies of Danville and Lexington out of their homes, I shall have them here laundering for your people and bringing you some of their holiday victuals. By the time I see your mother tomorrow, I shall damned well expect that she will be clean, and her hair shall have been washed and combed, if Missus Patterson herself has to comb it. Until then, I humbly beg you to accept my abject apology for the . . . the *barbarity* of the Christian white people of this town . . . and of the whole damned Kentucky Militia!"

Fani shut her eyes, bowed her head slightly, and smiled.

"One other thing. Come away here," he said. And out of Nonhelema's hearing, he asked the young woman, "Have you heard the outcome of Captain McGary? His trial for killing the chief?"

"No one tells us anything. But we hear things. That the captain went free out of the court and he was laughing when he went."

"Someone," Dr. Case said, "will have to tell your mother that. But please, not until she is out of danger. Promise me that?"

"Doctor, I promise you. But it would not surprise her."

Glancing over at the cluster of women kneeling around Nonhelema, he said, "God brought me here in time to doctor her. It remains to be seen whether I've done well enough. Listen, Miss Fani. I have to proceed on to Fort Nelson in a few days to interview General Clark and some other gentlemen. I shall come back by this way, when the season permits. I hope by that time your mother will be strong enough that I might pass some time with her . . ."

The young woman now studied him with evident curiosity. "What is your purpose, sir?"

He looked up at the rafters and blinked. His eyes were irritated by the unvented smoke and foul air in this miserable prison-shed. He hoped that his intentions would not seem frivolous to these wretches who had been attacked and hounded to the edge of their lives by his countrymen.

"Miss, do you know what a historian is? No? Well, let me explain. A historian is a storyteller, in a way, who writes down the details of events. One of Colonel Patterson's associates over in Lexington, perhaps you've seen him or met him here . . . a Mr. Filson? No? Well, nevertheless, that Mr. Filson not long ago wrote a book telling how Kentucky was explored and settled, and in his book were descriptions, and a map, also a long tale of the deeds of Colonel Boone. That book is what is called a history, of this particular country. Are you understanding me?"

She nodded. "I understand books. My mother taught me the reading of English words."

"Good. Well, miss, you see, much of Mr. Filson's book is true, to some degree. Much of it, however, is not. Mr. Filson has exaggerated some of those attributes that can—how shall I say this—be sold to the unwary. He is, to be blunt, speculating in lands, like all the principal men of the new American nation, from Washington and Patrick Henry to General Clark and Boone and Patterson. Your people have suffered because you're in the domain of their aspirations."

"All our chiefs have protested that to the Long Knives, who deny that it's so," she said. "We know. It is surprising to hear a whiteman admit it."

Dr. Case nodded, blew on his palms and chafed them together, and shivered. His breath condensed in the cold room. With age, his ability to bear cold kept diminishing. He craved whiskey, to warm his innards and numb the ache of old bones. "Now, I am, in a way," he said, "inspired by Mr. Filson. Like him, I was a schoolteacher, and a scribe. Like him, I am excited about the story of this newborn nation, and I yearn to tell it.

"Unlike him, I was here in Kentucky when the land taking began. Unlike him, I have no stake in the speculation or development of these parts. I witnessed events that he knows only by hearsay. So it follows that my history of the Middle Ground would in some ways differ from his. I should like it to be more truthful. I should like it to reveal the war as it was experienced and perceived by others than just the Americans. By Tories, by Indians, by women. You see, Miss Fani, that's one reason why I should like to talk with your mother. I would like to know how certain treaty promises that I've read were told to the Indians. Matters of that sort."

Fani nodded and gave him a half-smile. "I think she would talk to you of such things."

"I pray she would. Now I'm going to try to obtain some comforts for you here . . ."

The woman named Rachel had come up. "Please, Doctor sir," she said, seeming very nervous. "Katy wants to speak to you."

That pleased him. Never had she summoned him before, except once at Fort Randolph to see that he got a stirrup cup. Clearing his throat, he went back and knelt beside her pallet, his old knees full of pain.

She seemed still too tired to raise her head from the pillow, but her eyes were fixed on his face, looking at him more attentively than at any time he could remember. Of course, he was more important a man now than he had been as a soldier and scribe so long ago back in old Fort Randolph.

She lifted her good hand toward him, let it sink back to her side, and said, in a voice barely more than a raspy whisper: "My women say . . . they saw me dead until you came. They are grateful . . ." She coughed, squinting, then painfully raised up her other hand, thick in its bandage. "This was my better hand. Do you know, most of my people are more skilled with this hand . . . the left one. Most whites, the other. Maybe we are too different. I should not have been so white . . ." She seemed tired out, and paused long.

He interjected: "Not too different, ma'am. My heart and mind have often agreed with yours. I didn't know about the left hands, though."

"I will have to practice this other one . . . until it is skilled. Will I be able to use the bad one at all? Just for holding?"

"Perhaps. But I expect not. We shall see, by and by, ma'am."

"I made beauty . . . with my hands. Whatever I may . . . have done wrong in Creator's eyes, my hands were always good by him . . ."

Dr. Case noticed that she was speaking of Creator, instead of God. "I remember," he said. "It was great beauty you made. Even in those hardest times."

"You also," she said, now slightly smiling. "Your ink words on the paper were . . . so beautiful. I would watch."

"So," he said, "we watched each other's hands. While such things were happening, while a war was starting, we found moments to watch each other's hands. And now, after all these years, we may speak of it."

They were both quiet for a minute, thinking deep. Finally, she said, "I shall try to do beauty with the good hand that remains to me . . . 'Katy the hand,' they may call me . . . It is time for a new name . . . I have shed my skin. I am no longer that one I was."

"Katy the Hand, then?" He had not felt this good for years. Maybe never before. She had decided to live, and he had had something to do with it.

24

The smell of fresh-hewn oak was strong and clean in the entry of the New Salem Mission house, which had just been built. She also smelled the horse sweat from her long ride.

As she sat waiting on the hard bench, Nonhelema patiently and painfully squeezed the stub of her thumb and the stump of her little finger together, exercising them to build their strength so she could grip objects between them. Outside, the rasp of saws and pounding of hammers was everywhere, as the chapel and living quarters were still being built.

Of course Brother David Zeisberger would keep her waiting. Perhaps it was his intention to keep her waiting until she would give up and leave. But if that was what he hoped, he would be disappointed. No peremptory whiteman was a match for the patience of an Indian woman, especially an old stubborn Indian woman who had come so far to see him—almost as far north as Lake Erie. This new Moravian mission was about a league up the Huron River from the lakeshore. It showed promise as a bountiful site. The soil was rich and deep.

Nut trees and berry bushes were plentiful. The river and Lake Erie yielded more fish than the people could eat, and turtle eggs were so easy to gather at the lakeshore that they were served at every meal.

Nonhelema had learned that much from the assistant who led her to Zeisberger's waiting room. She had listened politely, but her mind was occupied by this meeting with the missionary.

She was so bony now that the bench seemed harder than it was. But mere discomfort was nothing compared with the physical and mental suffering she had endured because of the path this missionary had put her on. He owed her some time face-to-face now.

Her right hand, meanwhile, had become more facile and dependable as she trained it for those actions that the left had done all her life. She was now sewing and beading with it almost as well as she had with her left hand. But her handwriting script had never been very pretty. Not like that of the whiteman Dr. Case, that excellent scribe.

She thought of Case for a while as she clenched the stump of her hand and listened to the voices, the ax blows, the rhythmic rasp of saws from around the mission. Dr. Case had wanted to interview her when he returned to Danville, but her brothers Captain Johnny and Nimwha had been negotiating meanwhile for her release, and eventually Colonel Boone had gotten so annoyed with Colonel Patterson's stubbornness that he had forced Patterson to release her. By that time, thanks to Dr. Case's good doctoring, she had become strong enough to be transported by wagon from Danville to Boone's Station at Limestone and returned to the care of her brothers, with a few of the other prisoners.

And so it was that she was gone from the prison shed at Danville by the time Dr. Case would have come back to see her—if he had come back. She didn't know whether he had. He would have been disappointed, and she regretted that, because he really had saved her life. And he had done it without cutting off her arm. Bad as this deformed hand was, it was better than having no arm on that side.

Sometimes she could still feel her whole hand, as if the fingers were still there. She could shut her eyes and imagine moving all the fingers of that hand, and could remember how they felt moving, touching, sewing, scissoring. It was as if the spirits of those chopped-off fingers were still part of her spirit.

That strange whiteman Dr. Case! She remembered how he used to follow her with his eyes when he was a private soldier at Fort Randolph, watching her slyly, looking down when she glanced at him. She remembered watching him write in that beautiful hand when he didn't know she was watching. She had been more impressed by his handwriting than by him as a man. Back then, he had had no importance to her. In those days, she had judged whitemen by their appearance and their positions or ranks, and the glibness of their tongues rather than their goodness or kindness. She knew that now, and knew how wrong it had been.

Captain Arbuckle had been the important man at the fort. But it was the man named Case who had thrown himself in front of murderers' guns to get her out of harm's way, whereas Captain Arbuckle had not even bothered to go and witness at the trial of the murderers of her kin.

Too much of her life she had cultivated the favors of the whitemen who were important, and all of them had betrayed her. Case had not betrayed her. Those others, all of them—Clark, General Hand, Arbuckle, Croghan, Butler, Alexander McKee, LaBalme—all of them had used her without valuing her life and or feelings.

And of course, this Zeisberger most of all.

But not that man Case. He never had a notion to use her, and he was the only whiteman who had never failed her in any way. He had done more for her than any of the others, or all of them put together. She smiled and nodded, remembering how the wives of the men of Danville had come to the prison-shed the day after Christmas. The doctor had shamed them so ferociously that they had come with food and soap and blankets and candles, and had cleaned the place, and gingerly comforted the prisoners.

Katy Hand, as she now called herself, sat and mused on Dr. Case, remembering the look of him, perhaps in his fifties now, lean and pale, graying, solemn, narrow of face, high of forehead. His beard and most of his hair had gone white, but still showed traces of copper color on top, and his thick bushy eyebrows were reddish and grizzled. He did not smile much, but unlike most whitemen his age, he seemed to have all or most of his teeth, and they were not brown or rotten. The skin of his cheeks was lightly pitted with pox scars, and like many former soldiers and hunters he had black gunpowder flecks that peppered his right cheekbone and temple. Nonhelema had never regarded him in such detail when he was a private soldier at the fort. These recent impressions remained strangely vivid in her memory, she supposed, because of the remarkable state of her mind and senses when she had returned from that long visit near the world of death. Creator surely had placed him there at that crucial time.

She now heard Brother David's voice in the other room, so reverberent among the stark new walls that she could not make out his words. From the tone of his voice, she presumed that he was talking to one of the converts. It was the same way wealthy men, like Morgan, or Dunmore, or Croghan, talked to their servants and slaves. These converts of his were essentially just Brother David's servants, though he made them believe they were the servants of Jesus.

I must try to be fair to Brother David, she thought, *but truthful. He is a great missionary. He has been among the Indians for forty years. He is a man of faith, and some Indians are better because of him. Many are not. I am one of those.*

Brother David might be different now, she thought. All his long life, he had been too occupied with his mission to think of marriage. For several years, the synod had been encouraging and then insisting he take a wife from among his converts as most of the other missionaries had done. He maintained he was too busy tending his sheep. The sisters of the mission tended to his household chores. Or perhaps he had believed himself to be above marrying an Indian woman, even one he had saved and shaped himself.

An absurd thought suddenly amused her: What if I had been that one! She almost laughed aloud, sitting and waiting on the hard bench.

Nonhelema had heard that on Brother David's last trip to Bethlehem, the concerned churchmen had ordered him to take a wife before he returned to the wild, lonely frontier. The synod board expected that his wife would be selected by the usual method of having God choose by holding a prayer service and then the drawing by lot from among many single women Indian converts. Brother David instead chose the lovely, chaste Miss Susan LeCron, a white woman and former Lutheran from Philadelphia. Now Brother David had a wife and helpmate who, at half his age, would surely never vex him or disappoint him as the Indian women did so often with their failings. Surely Susan had no failings. Perhaps her presence in his life would have softened his harshness in dealing with backsliding women.

Even if he has changed by being married, she thought, *he is still the same as he ever was in making me wait to see him.*

He knew she was here. He would make her wait. Then he would

try to make her grovel in contrition. He would make her wait again for him to decide whether to forgive her and let her return to the mission. He would make sure she knew he was in there now preparing himself for the confrontation. Though she had been gone from him for a long time, she remembered how he was.

So she sat and waited, and made the remains of her thumb and finger touch each other. She had been thinking it all out ever since the day the good Dr. Case helped her come back into this side of the world. Before that, a great understanding had come into her spirit that had traveled in that otherside of the world.

In that otherside world, she had been able to listen to the ancestors, and sometimes she had met with Jesus. She had been able to get some surprising answers from him.

After waiting silently for several hours on the bench in the entryway, she was approached by an Indian man in the plain cloth of a mission convert. She seemed to remember his name was Brother Mortimer, but she had forgotten what his tribe or his Indian name had been.

"Madame," he said, "Brother David told me to ask if you are waiting to see him."

"Of course, brother. He knows that very well."

Mortimer went inside Brother David's door, and she waited another hour. She was pleased that she could keep herself from getting angry. She had learned what mattered and what did not. Brother David's manners did not.

Finally, Brother Mortimer returned. "Please follow me." He led her through the door of Brother David's study.

She saw that one of the old Delaware converts, Sister Abigail, was standing inside the door, waiting to serve as witness and chaperone for the protection of Brother David's precious reputation.

"We won't need you, sister," Nonhelema said. "I am a hag, and Brother David is ages past any ability to be aroused. You may go." She smiled at Zeisberger as she said it, and watched his old face go from gray to red.

"You will stay!" he commanded Abigail. "Catarina, you will please remember, though you have been truant for a very long time, that you speak *after* I ask you to, and you do not command my other children!"

Already, she could see, he was sorry that he had admitted her. She went to a chair facing his table and sat down.

"Why don't you take a seat, Catarina?" he said in a voice curdled with sarcasm. She had just broken another of his rules: that an Indian should stand until invited to sit.

He went around behind his table and sat down facing her. He interlaced his fingers, and she could see that they were so tight, his knuckles whitened. Her own left hand she kept concealed under the edge of her light shawl.

"Brother Mortimer," the priest said, voice quavering, "will you please stay also? This will take but a moment. I rather anticipate, from long and pathetic experience of her arrivals, that this oft-fallen wanton is returning again, feigning contrition. To take advantage of our forgiving nature and seek shelter, having no doubt been cast out elsewhere."

That he would slander her so quickly confirmed that indeed she had nettled him, even more than usual.

"Brother David, again, I offer you the chance to dismiss Brother Mortimer and Sister Abigail. You might not want them to hear what I've come to tell you. I have *not* come seeking penance or shelter."

His eyebrows went up and his chin down.

He spent a moment rebuilding his pious and patient demeanor, then looked her over for a while, shaking his head, peaking his eyebrows in his best pitying expression. He made a tiny kissing sound with tongue and lips, several times, then said, "Poor Catarina! Your promiscuous ways have ravaged your inherent comeliness, so much more than age alone would have done!" He emitted a wistful-sounding sigh, but on his wrinkled lips was the trace of a smug smile.

She swallowed the insult with ease, and replied, "No, Brother David. My 'promiscuity' always made me radiant. What has 'ravaged' me is *peacemaking*."

He looked at her, perplexed, frowning. "What say you? Peacemaking?"

"Peacemaking with the American Long Knives. In the hope of making myself a child of God, as you said 'twould do me. Look. Those Long Knives are so sharp, they cut even their best allies."

She drew her hand quickly into the open, leaned forward, and laid the mangled stump of her hand on his table, right under his eyes. He looked at it and recoiled, clapping a palm to his bosom, face gone pale.

"Our American soldier friends did this," she said, "when I tried to prevent them killing my uncle. Such have been my rewards for peacemaking. But you call me a 'wanton,' not a child of God."

He looked at her disfigured limb for a moment more and then averted his gaze. He seemed unable to come up with words.

So she went on: "From this I nearly died, or perhaps I did die. You have preached that when we die, we will see Jesus. I saw him."

The missionary's eyes goggled. "You? You think you saw our Savior?"

"It was good," she said. "If you have seen him, you know he looks to be an Indian, more than a whiteman. Very much like my brother Captain Johnny, but with black whiskers. Surely you have seen Jesus? But you never told us he is brown. Could it be that you never did see him?"

She heard the two converts gasp and murmur behind her, and Zeisberger's mouth dropped open. Then he shut it firmly, and his brow darkened like a thunderstorm. "You!" he exclaimed in a voice almost screeching. "You dare come to this godly place to lie and mock!"

"*I* do not lie, or mock. I learned from Jesus, many things I learned." She felt strong. She was now able to say things she knew were true, to a man who had always told everyone what he thought only he knew to be truth. "I learned that Jesus does not teach just what you say, Brother David. I learned that Jesus is not as unhappy with me as you always say; it is only you who are dissatisfied all the time."

He slammed both palms on the tabletop. "Woman, that is enough! You are infamous as a reprobate! You have brought shame upon this mission and betrayed my trust in you! How dare you invade this holy place and question my teachings?"

She slowly drew back a few inches, staring down her nose at him, but kept her arm extended so that the mangled hand was on the table before him if his gaze fell from hers. And she began in a measured, calm tone, such as she had used to persuade in council, long ago when she had had influence as a major chief: "Brother, I just now have heard you say some words—*invade* and *betray*. Those words twist in my heart. They are the entire story of the whiteman in my country. And you, who speak those words, set me on a path to help the invaders and betrayers ruin my people.

"Brother, there is something in English law called *real estate*. You know of it—land to sell for money. It is the cause of the invasion. Your friends the Americans are mad for it. Everything they do is to get land from us, the Indians, so that they can sell it to other whitemen for money. Every rich whiteman I ever met has that madness. And as he grows more mad, he grows more rich. To get our land, they made promises, and then—every time—they betrayed them.

"Those, Brother David, are the ones you have been helping. And by so doing, you betrayed your Indian 'children.' I did, too, by believing, too much, what you said. You caused me to put on the skin of Christian whitemen. Now, brother, I have been over where the truth is, and I have come here so you can see me shed that skin."

His hands were tight on the arms of his chair. She knew that he did not want to be lectured by her, but he seemed to believe that she had indeed had some sort of revelation, perhaps even a divine encounter. No missionary could ignore such a thing, and so he would listen, despite himself.

She continued, keeping her hand there before him, on the table.

"You came and told us you had 'good news.' Something only you had that we poor sinful Indians needed to hear, to save us from hell. We did not know what hell was. So you told us, and frightened us with it. Indians always knew there is only one Creator. You came and demanded we only worship *your god*, as if there were more than one.

"Then you confused us even more. You told us of Jesus. That now we must worship Jesus, God's son. I read your Bible, Brother David. Jesus said, 'Do not worship me, but worship him who sent me, my father, God.' Why did you teach us that lie? Do you *want* to see us go to hell?

"You taught of a day of rest when we must go listen to you, and worship. We Indians worship Creator every day, many times a day, in everything, as we live. We do what needs to be done in work, and rest then. We do not exhaust ourselves so much that we need a whole day of rest.

"You have a rule that none can live here without your permission. *Your* permission? Creator gave us Indians permission to live anywhere we chose, long before you came to this land."

He scowled but didn't interrupt. She could hear and sense the alarm of the converts. They were breathing hard, and now and then one would whisper or moan.

She went on: "You forbid anyone to associate with thieves, murderers, whores, adulterers, drunks, but you tell us to imitate Jesus. Did he not associate with people like this? Did he not seek them out? You confuse us with your rules.

"You forbid our festivals, dances, games. You say we cannot use what you call witchcraft in the hunt, to have sacrifices or offerings. But you have these things, and insist we learn yours! Yours brought no bounty to our people. Your way causes us to starve. Had I not brought you wagonloads full of food years ago, your mission people would have starved to death. You did not refuse that food, which we had in plenty because we honored the spirits of the three sacred sisters as you said we should not do.

"You say God loves us to suffer! I believe God loves us and does *not* want us to suffer. Brother, it is *you* who wants us to suffer! It gives you control over us when we suffer, and you feed us hopes and promises of distant comfort! And you are stingy even with those promises. There have been times, you remember, when you made me wait entire seasons for you to console me with a word of forgiveness! You knew that made me suffer, and you liked that."

"You—," he tried to begin, but she bumped her wounded hand on the table under his chin, which made him go pale and silenced him.

"You control your poor Indians as if *you* are God! You make them feed you and work for you. You give them permission to marry or not, and shame them for coupling by their own hearts and desires. You think if a boy and girl are behind a door together they will be copulating. Or a man and woman. Your mind is wicked!

"Also about men and women: You say we women must *obey* our husbands. The Master-of-Life did not make men and women to order each other about, or to obey each other! He gave the man hunting to do as his way to help his wife and children, and told him to fight for his people if they were in danger. All the rest he gave to women— their houses, the children, corn and beans and squash to grow, all the knowledge of medicine plants. Man and woman, he made them both worth the same, and told each what to do for each other and for their families.

"But you, brother, playing like God, you told the men they must give up their bows and guns, and not fight, and hunt only if you gave them permission. Instead, you made them do garden work that Creator gave to women to do! You degrade both the man and woman, and their crops grow poor. To Indians there is no honor in telling someone else what to do! Each person already knows, inside, what to do. This *obey* thing is not right!

"You make the Indians obey *you* about everything. How to trade with traders, and those only the ones you choose. You insist women not reveal our breasts, or get ourselves naked even to wash. When we drink alcohol and rum and get foolish, you punish us, but not the whitemen who bring it, against the whiteman's law, and entice us to drink it.

"You are afraid to punish whitemen, because their guns have not been taken from them. And you fear the Indians who still have weapons. You fear everyone except the ones you have turned into your own flock of sheep."

The old missionary looked stunned now, as if his mind had given up even trying to prepare rebuttals. His mouth hung open. His eyes were glassy; he was breathing fast.

But she was as she used to be in council, when making a point in which she believed herself right.

"Brother, you tried to scare us good, by threatening us with hell. But we were already good, because we lived to be worthy of what the Master-of-Life gave us. There never was a hell until you brought it here.

"You brought hell, and the Devil, and rum, and lies, and greed, and plagues. We Indians lived here through hundreds of generations and never needed money to buy food, we had no rum to make us drunk, we did not feel *guilt*. You made us want what we had never known of before. You were like that snake that came into the garden of the First Man and First Woman. You brought the sins of *your* ancestors here. *You* killed Jesus and then you came and put it on the backs of the innocent Indians and told us we had to suffer from it. Did you ever think that you missionaries are the *Motchee Weekhaweh*? The Great Bad Snake that brought bad thinking?"

Sister Abigail was beginning to weep with sniffling and hiccups, and Nonhelema would have liked to turn and tell her to leave, but was now like the eagle starting to dive on the snake and would not turn her eyes from the missionary.

Like a snake, the missionary was voiceless and his eyes were hooded over. She hoped he had been listening well enough to realize what she had said about the Great Snake. "Your mouth is opened like a snake's mouth, Brother David, with the jaw down. And in it is your tongue going two ways. You took over this garden. It was God's before you came. You crept to the edge of the woods and looked in and studied the heart of the Indians and saw how easily we could be fooled. Your suffering bleeding Jesus was such a story, for we had never heard such things! And we thought our own Creator was mad at us, because we were being chased from one place to another by the whites, and dying of diseases, and being shot by your guns. So some of us, my family, we were ready to understand *guilt*. And we ate the fruit and believed when you said we hurt Jesus.

"Then you did what you pleased with us. You made us helpless and ashamed, and took away our joy in ourselves as Creator made us each unique as suited *Him*. I was ashamed every time I had to disappoint you, and you used that shame to make me do more against my people.

"Why did you come into our woods, so far from your own land? Why did you come so far to build yourself a kingdom with Delaware and Shawnee slaves?

"When I was over on the otherside lately, when I saw Jesus among my ancestors, they helped me understand all that.

"You came this far from your own kind because you were afraid of them, of their government, of the evil and power behind them. You surrounded yourself with our bodies, and made us your protection against your own kind."

At last he blinked and moved his mouth and stammered, face reddening, and exclaimed: "Catarina, you are mad! I have let you rant, poor thing, though you blaspheme every holy gift I've ever given you! But now I cannot even understand what you are *trying* to impugn—of *government*, of *protection* against my own kind . . . What? What? I am to believe that you met our Savior and he filled your fevered head with such twaddle?"

Then he cringed and flinched when, despite her age and pains, she bolted to her feet and towered over him, banging her ruined hand on the table and then raising it to quiver right before his eyes.

"I have not done talking, brother! In our council, we are too civilized to interrupt! *Ketawpi!* Listen!"

The chaperoning converts gasped and made to bolt from the room. She instantly directed her gaze to them and said, "Sit! Our Brother David *insists* you stay, to witness." Then she again addressed Brother David.

"You sacrificed my people's lives to keep yourself safe from those murdering Long Knife hordes, which imagine themselves warriors. You, who pretended to be our Shepherd! You wrung information from your sheep, about what all the Indians were doing. You wrote it in your letters to the officers at Fort Pitt. In return, they never told the Indians that you were the spy in our midst. Some tried to warn me what you were doing. Our chiefs, and McKee—they warned me. But I was blind, because my family so loved and trusted you. I refused to see. I even tried so hard to be a peacemaker like you that I, too, warned the Americans. You and I, brother, killed many of my people, hundreds, in that way, by informing ahead of them. Many you killed by taking the weapons from their hands. It is the same as if you shot them yourself.

"You tried to hide your deeds. When you were removed to Sandusky, you burned all your letters from the officers, and thought nothing would be known. But in Pittsburgh are all your informing letters, proving your betrayal of the same people you say God sent you to save from hell. My Indian people. You might as well have raped our women yourself, set the fires that burned our towns and harvests, smashed the heads of our babies and grandmothers, scalped them and collected the bounty, mutilated their bodies. Your pious, delicate white hands drip with their blood! Did not the British in Canada put you on trial for spying, when you were taken up there for safety? Eh? Now you may speak, brother; I invite you to answer!"

"How . . ." He gasped, a hand at his throat, face pale with panic. But he came forth with nothing else, so she continued:

"Are you trying to ask me how I know of that? Brother David, I am a chief of the Shawnee people. I have Delaware blood by marriages. All the chiefs and women chiefs know me, and a few even honor me still, despite what I have done. Frenchmen and Englishmen and Americans know me, and some still like to talk to me. I am at this time helping an American general write a translation of my people's tongue for the empress of Russia, at the request of General Washington. That is but one example of my honor, my value to whitemen, that only you refused to grant me. And so I am told all manner of things by all manner of people, and your crimes against the Indians are all known to me. I would have known them all before, but I wouldn't listen, because of my foolish reverence for you . . ."

Saying that suddenly drained her. A blizzard seemed to descend in front of her and her knees went limber, and she sat down, suddenly aware again how old and weak she really was. She had wanted to remind him of the one time his collusion with the Long Knives had failed him and the Pennsylvania militiamen had burned one of his missions down on his flock, her own mother and sister and other relatives among them. But now she had to concentrate on gathering her strength of mind and spirit, so that she wouldn't faint before him, just when she had bestowed upon him the true sense of his own weapon:

Guilt!

For a while, there was no sound in the room but the sobbing and sniffling of Sister Abigail. If Brother Mortimer was still there, he was not even breathing audibly.

After a while, she said to the ashen face across the table: "Brother David, from now on, do not think I hate you. I pray to Jesus to wash hatred from my heart. I only want you to be humble. Jesus wanted me to remind you that you are not God. Do you hear me, what I just told you?" His chin was on his chest, but he nodded, his eyes now closed.

That old man, she thought, *is as tired as this old woman who scolds him. No. He is more tired. I am still talking.*

"I am going away," she said. "When the language for the Russian queen is done, I will be through with whitemen forever, I think. Is that not funny? A Shawnee queen named Catherine is teaching a Russian queen named Catherine, who for some reason wants all the languages of the world. Maybe she, too, has too much pride and deems herself divine. They say kings and queens believe such nonsense, as Jolojo Okimah, George the king of England, did.

"No, I shall not hate you, Brother David. I did the same evils to the Indian peoples as you did. But you have more guilt from it, because you guided me.

"I do not know where I will be going. I am too old to stay and fight, as some of the young warriors still do. Besides, I am a peacemaker in my heart. In that, Jesus and my Mekoche people are still as one. Maybe I will go beyond the Great River, the Missisipe, as most of my kin have done. They say Morgan intends to make a colony there, where Indians may live far away from the Long Knives. Wapeymachikthe, like all rich whitemen, is a land taker, but he cares for the Indians, deep in his heart. He will make a place for us. The land is rich out there, and there are no Pennsylvanians or Kentuckians. May I never see another Kentuckian; they are only Virginians by another name."

She sighed, long and quaking. She was aware that she, too, was now talking with her eyes closed. Her eyes were not locked on his anymore, like those of predator on prey, or the avenger upon the villain. She had no notion how long she might live, nor what she might do, but she had been through the otherside and was still here, and knew peace in that.

"Brother," she said in a soft, deep voice, which seemed to reverberate in her like one of the old sacred water drums, "as Jesus wished, I am humbled. I pray you are, too. You need humility, because you have been a humiliator. I have never tried to humiliate anyone before."

She opened her eyes and saw that Brother Zeisberger's were still closed.

"I have said all I came to say," she told him. "For your sake, and especially for the sake of all the Indians you take under you, I pray that you were listening well and will remember what I said."

Then she sat looking at him, waiting for any reply he might give. When he opened his eyes, he was looking down at her hand, as if even that horrible sight was preferable to looking into her eyes. Finally, he took a deep breath and straightened, lifting his head and raising his eyes as if to God. He was trembling with great tension. His face was dead gray, but flushed under his wrinkled eye sockets. Tears welled, glistening.

Finally, he spoke.

"So, Catarina. As if all the countless disappointments you have brought this mission were not enough, now you add this gross demonstration of disrespect for me. Now, hear me, thou harridan:

"You provoke me now to forbid you the last hospitality of this holy place. You shall not rest in our cemetery here. Your very *bones* would trouble those dear ones who lie in this hallowed earth!"

So. He was afraid of even her bones.

She shook her head. She rose, pulled her shawl over her shoulders, and turned her back on him. That last meanness of his did not even merit an answer. She meant to be buried in the Pickaway Plains near the old Scioto towns, where she had buried her mother's bones and her father's. Or if she could not go there because of the whiteman's real estate laws, her bones would lie wherever she fell. Even if her petition to the Americans never got her a piece of her old lands back in that beautiful valley, to live out her life in, she hoped to be buried there, near her mother, when that time came.

Brother David might not have been listening to her as well as she had wished him to.

It seemed now that he had been, instead, trying to think of something, after all she had lost to the whitemen, that could still be taken away from her. And he had come up with something she didn't want anyway: the right to be buried among the tame Jesus Indians.

Brother Mortimer and Sister Abigail were looking at her with wide, terrified eyes. And now Brother David said, speaking to her back: "Catarina, one does not leave from an audience with me until I say one is dismissed. Have you forgotten every rule?"

She began walking slowly toward the door. Suddenly, a notion came to her. It was such a delightful and hilarious notion that her heart suddenly was frolicking inside her breast and she had to restrain herself from laughing aloud.

Shawnee women were skilled in answering insults with better insults. In her long life, she had seen them demonstrate their ultimate retort only three or four times. If greatly insulted, they would all, as one, turn their backs on the one who had insulted them, raise their dresses and show him their bare rumps.

She stopped where she was. Brother David had just insulted her as cruelly as he knew how, and her back was already to him. With hilarity welling up inside her almost unbearably, she put her hands at the sides of her skirt. As she gathered the material in her right hand and tried to pinch it between the stumps of her left, she mused on Brother David's outrageous prudishness, and she remembered the innumerable times he had referred to her as wanton, a slut, a harlot, and a strumpet, even though he had never seen so much as her knees. Surely the sudden sight of her whole posterior would be a retort for him to remember forever, and whine about all the way to heaven.

Especially as scrawny as her old buttocks were now! The sight might fell him as surely as a tomahawk between the eyes!

Tomahawk between the eyes.

That flashed in her memory, staggering her, making her gasp: that last unbearable sight before she had forgotten everything and had gone away for so long. Her mind reeled for a moment. Everything blurred. Then settled and steadied.

She was Nonhelema, the Grenadier, Shawnee queen, daughter of White Fish, granddaughter of Paxinosa, great-granddaughter of King Opessa, sister of Cornstalk, niece of Moluntha, the last old king. However the old missionary judged her in his pious soul, she was known everywhere for her bearing and dignity. In imagination, she could enjoy pranks and taunts and hilarious mockeries, but she was a woman of dignity, and would not show her rump.

Smoothing her skirt, with a slight toss of her head she straightened to her full height, nodded politely to the two gaping converts, and feeling Brother David's eyes on her proud back, she walked out of the room and out of the mission house, and went to get her horse.

EPILOGUE

1 8 1 4

Dr. Justin I. Case rose from the chair, flexed his aching shoulders, blew dust-clotted mucus into his handkerchief, and turned to adjust the cushion he had put on the wooden chair seat to ease the torment of his piles. He glanced out the window of the government building into the dusty street, where wagons rumbled and rattled by and hooves clopped in an incessant racket. The busyness and congestion of this crude city intruded upon his research and memories and daydreams of the old wilderness years, whose history was his preoccupation. He was a historian now more than he was a physician.

Unlike most historians, he had been a witness to some of the events of which he wrote, and had been acquainted with a number of the principal figures. Some of them still lived, and were now old men, like himself, their fame seasoned for better or worse. They lived where they had settled, some places far beyond the line that had been the so-called frontier in those days. Their ways of remembering the history they had made were odd and sometimes amusing to Dr. Case. Memory was selective and pliable, he had found.

His own memory, of course, was not precise. He had entered his eighth decade, and he liked to joke, "If my mind has deteriorated as much as my body, it could not be very dependable, either."

He had interviewed as many of the old heroes and villains as he could reach—many by letters, many others in person by traveling to meet them. He had written or spoken to sons and daughters of those already dead.

He had tracked down Daniel Boone in Missouri, interviewing the old frontiersman while watching him sand and polish his own cherry-wood coffin. He had gotten drunk while questioning General George Rogers Clark at his log house overlooking the Falls of the Ohio. He had gotten drunk in St. Louis while interviewing Clark's younger brother William, upon his return from his exploration of the West with Captain Lewis. He had gotten even more drunk while interviewing the notorious traitor and villain Simon Girty at an inn at Amherstberg, Upper Canada, gaining a much more favorable impression of him than Girty's legend had led him to expect. Girty had remembered him from Dunmore's War—or at least had said he remembered him.

Dr. Case's pursuit of the history of the conquest of the Ohio River watershed had taken him to a dozen retired military officers, who had become landowners, governors, senators, or ruined sots.

He had even gone far into the Great Lakes country and the Indian Territory to talk with a score of old warriors from the other side of the conflict. Those sojourns had turned his heart over. He had understood the desperate and hopeless plight the Indian chiefs had been put in by the new nation's greed for their land.

He had gotten drunk quite often with those old chiefs, too, as he had with generals. Whiskey sellers infested every place that the Indians had fled to, pursing them like hounds, exploiting their misery and weakness. In some villages, Dr. Case had been delayed for days to mend the wounds that drunken warriors had inflicted on each other, and he had treated cases of pneumonia in Indian men and women who had passed out in snowbanks and icy mud.

His career as a historian had turned out to be nearly as eventful as his career as a soldier helping to make history.

Dr. Case pressed the heels of his hands into his waist, arched his back, rolled his head on his neck, squinting, feeling his neckbones grind and pop. His head was beginning to hurt as much as his piles, and the notion made him chuckle with rue.

"Age," he said to the bespectacled records clerk across the room. "I hurt at both ends."

The clerk turned away, as if annoyed that someone would make levity in his domain.

Dr. Case sighed and sat back down to continue leafing through the stack of pathetic petitions, all written in a wretched variety of handwritings on stained, mold-blemished sheets: the pleas of people who claimed to have lost their fortunes by supporting the cause of the Revolution. Such pleadings as these, it seemed to him, were the real human face of history, more meaningful than political tracts, casualty counts, or analyses of battles. In his notebooks he had written summaries of those individual sacrifices; some really pathetic ones he had copied verbatim. These would add pathos to his history, as did the letters to and from soldiers that he had gleaned along the way of his researches. He called himself a "dilettante historian," but believed he could write more engaging history books than the ones he had been taught from. Like Plutarch's, his would be a history told in lives—the lives of personages on both sides of the conflict.

What tales of broken lives and dreams these petitions were. That War for Independence had ruined nearly everyone, it seemed: patriots and Loyalists alike, merchantmen, landowners, financiers, Indian traders. It had, of course, enriched certain contractors and profiteers, as wars do. But generally, it had ruined nearly everyone else.

Most of all, it had ruined the Indians, whose loyalties had been solicited, played on, and betrayed, whose crops and towns had been burned almost every season, whose warriors had been killed, whose women had been raped, whose lands had been appropriated and overrun, whose communities had been scattered and driven into cul-de-sacs.

Most Indians had no material wealth to lose, as had the whites in the struggle. But a particular Indian, one who had long been of particular interest to him, once had been wealthy by some of the same measures as white people. Nonhelema, the Grenadier Squaw, had petitioned for recompense for the losses that she had suffered by aiding the Americans steadfastly throughout the Revolution. Her petition had been sent to the commissioners for Indian affairs, and should have arrived here among these claims. It was one he specifically wanted to find, although he was tracking several others.

General Clark had told him about her petition. Clark and General Butler had helped her make and deliver the petition. In other claims, she had also asked for a grant of land in the vicinity of her old village along the Scioto; he had not yet been able to find that one, either. She had specified that vicinity because her mother's remains had been taken there for burial after she died in the massacre at Gnaddenhutten.

Clark and Dr. Case had both been able to remember that site clearly. They recalled having scouted it with Simon Girty right after the battle of Point Pleasant at the mouth of the Kanawha River, forty years before.

Forty years! he thought. Forty years since he had first seen that woman, a naked Amazon on the battlefield, smeared with blood, soot, and war paint.

And twenty-seven years since he had *last* seen her. Twenty-seven years, and she had been on the verge of death then, in a cold, filthy, verminous, smoky prison-shed in Danville, Kentucky. He had cured her, certainly. Weeks later, when he had returned to Danville, eager to interview her, she was gone—rescued by her brothers, who had exchanged white prisoners for her at Boone's Station at Limestone.

From that point on, he had never caught up with her again, and that had been, perhaps, his worst disappointment. What a fund of insights and perspectives on the war her memories could have provided! An entire volume might have been written, unlike any other history of the conflict.

She must be dead now, he thought. If she were alive still, she probably would be more than eighty years old. Not likely that she would have survived this long, not with the rigors and losses she had endured.

The Shawnee people had fought two more wars against the Americans since he had seen her last. In the 1790s, confederated under Little Turtle of the Miamis and their own war chief Blue Jacket, they had vanquished two large American armies in the western part of what was now the state of Ohio, before being defeated finally by General Anthony Wayne near Lake Erie and forced to the treaty at GreeneVille, where they had been compelled to give up most of their remaining lands in Ohio.

Then, in the current war with England, which was being called the War of 1812, a confederation of tribes, forged by the Shawnee renegade Tecumseh and his brother the Shawnee Prophet, had allied itself with the British, thwarting for a long time the United States' effort to invade Canada. For Tecumseh, the struggle had ended last fall with his death on a battlefield on the Thames River in Upper Canada, after which the American troops had pillaged and killed in the Moravian mission town near the battleground. Already in this war, countless Indians of all tribes had been shot, starved, and driven from their burning towns, dying by hundreds on refugee trails, brought down sick by cold and wet and by heat exhaustion, rotten provisions, and epidemics. Dr. Case had been caught up in some of those events, always in demand as a physician, and the devastation suffered by the tribes made him feel certain that an old Indian woman—especially one as unlucky as Nonhelema—must have perished somewhere along that tragic way.

In his notes, he had written:

> *We were their ruination, in ways I fear*
> *History will not forget, nor God forgive.*

Now and then in the quarter century of travels, he had run upon old references to her—a scrap of paper here, a ledger entry there, a census, a letter—once, even the names of Katy Hand and Fani Hand in a Spanish census in Missouri. And in a few interviews, one person or another would mention a vague fact or memory that he had been able to fit into the itinerary of her life for a few years after her release from captivity. It had been rather like trying to track a deer through a snowstorm: finding, losing, finding faint traces of the spoor, but eventually, all fading into the whiteness of unknowing.

Soon after her repatriation in 1787, probably still very frail in her recuperation, she had helped General Richard Butler compile a translation of the Shawnee tongue, hundreds of words and phrases, at the behest of George Washington, for his friend Lafayette to give as a gift to the empress of Russia. Dr. Case had learned of that while perusing the late president's papers—one of those instances when her name had leapt from a page where he had not even been looking for it. That discovery had made him yearn to talk with General Butler about it, but unfortunately Butler had been one of the many officers killed by Little Turtle's confederation in the rout of General St. Clair's American army at the headwaters of the Wabash River, five years after the completion of the glossary project—yet another of those instances in which the tracks had faded in the snow.

During a part of that bloody turmoil of the 1790s Indian Wars, old Nonhelema and her daughter had apparently gone west of the

Mississippi to settle in George Morgan's last colonizing enterprise—
the Mississippi bottomland community called New Madrid—on land
granted under the auspices of the Spanish governor of the Louisiana
Territory. That was where he had found her name and her daughter's
on residency rolls of the Spanish government. But floods and malarial
plagues, and finally a stupendous earthquake in 1811, had reduced
that settlement, and the woman and her faithful daughter disappeared
from those Spanish records, once again fading into the whiteness.

Presuming then that she might have migrated up the Mississippi
to the nearest Shawnee settlement, Dr. Case had taken boat passage
some fifty miles up to Lorimier's trading post and Shawnee town at
Cape Girardeau, above the mouth of the Ohio. There the effusive little trader had kept him for days, regaling him with tales of the wars
from the anti-American viewpoint, much to the advantage of Dr.
Case's burgeoning history book. Lorimier related proudly the heroic
services his nephew George Drouillard had performed as a hunter
and interpreter for the explorers Lewis and Clark. "But for him,"
Lorimier had exclaimed, "they would have died! I tell you, M'sieur
Case, if you go anywhere, you need Shawnees with you!"

But no, Nonhelema had not settled at Cape Girardeau. She had
passed through, yes. She had spent some days resting with her friend,
Lorimier's wife, Penampieh. The last time she had been heard from
at Lorimier's, she had been migrating back east, up the Ohio, on a
cargo boat headed to Pittsburgh. But there was no record that she
had been on the boat when it reached Pittsburgh. She might have
gotten off anywhere—the Wabash, Louisville, the Miami River, the
Scioto, the Kanawha, the Muskingum; at all those places there were
still remnants of Shawnee settlements, or routes to the Shawnee
towns in northern Ohio, or to the Moravian missions up by the Great
Lakes and in Canada. And there were Delawares in remote communities everywhere, including the mission towns. She was actually more
likely to be harbored among her distant Delaware relatives than with
the Shawnees, who had cast her out. Dr. Case the historian knew well
the difficulties of tracing people through a developing and turbulent
frontier. If anywhere there was a master at such long-range sleuthing
over cold trails, it was he. But following an outcast was even more difficult, and especially during a war.

Now and then, in the odd daybook of some frontier fort, he would
find that a food ration had been fed to "Katy a Shawano woman, per
orders of Ind. Commission." That had been, so far as Dr. Case could

tell, the extent of the American government's compensation for her losses: a meal a day at any army post where her wanderings took her, and "One set of cloth cloaths a year," and a blanket.

The missions had hardly offered her even that much refuge. Dr. Case had gained audience with Brother Zeisberger a few years ago, not long before the outbreak of the War of 1812. The old priest had helped him compile accounts of the missions' Indian War sufferings, and they were pathetic. But when Dr. Case had inquired about the Shawnee convert Catherine, the old missionary had suddenly looked almost apoplectic and had refused to discuss her. Soon afterward, one of the lesser brethren had unwittingly revealed the woman's final transgression:

She had moved into the home of Zeisberger's star convert, Brother William Henry, formerly known as Chief Killbuck, the aged Delaware peace chief, a widower. Although both Catherine and Brother William Henry were very old and lifelong friends, and had been allied as peacemakers for decades, the old missionary was scandalized. They were distant cousins, those two old Indians; Brother William was the missionary's exemplar and Nonhelema was his she-devil, and Zeisberger was reduced to writhing in torment every time he thought of them cohabiting. Zeisberger had entered them in his diaries in 1806 with the contemptuous term of *common-law marriage*, and seemed to believe that their union had corrupted the whole Moravian cause. Zeisberger had seemed a broken man, and apparently their liaison was the reason.

It is plain to me, Dr. Case had written in his notebook, *Zeisberger always desired her to be his convert wife. But she failed to rise to such respectability, or lower herself to such humility.* Justin Case himself knew about yearning in vain.

Both Zeisberger and Killbuck were dead now. Dr. Case had found records of their passing in recent years. But of Nonhelema's fate there was no record; no death notice or mention had come to his attention. As usual, her trail had been obliterated by snowy whiteness, a blank place on the end page of her history.

Her son Thomas McKee had turned up now and then in Canadian documents, usually as an aimless young half-breed in trouble from drunkenness, and then he, too, had faded into blankness.

Dr. Case reached down and pulled from his satchel—the one he called his History Satchel, not his medical satchel—a small notebook with a frayed black oilcloth cover. There were bigger notebooks in the satchel, labeled DUNMORE CAMPAIGN, REVOLUTION, 1785 TO 1795, OFFI-CERS & CHIEFS, LETTERS, DISPATCHS &C. This small notebook was titled GRENADIER (KATY) on a rectangle of white paper pasted at the top of the front cover. He put the little notebook on the table and opened it to a page marked by a brittle old string of leather.

He had kept that strand of leather for nearly forty years. It had been a whang of the fringe on Nonhelema's deerhide skirt, and had dropped on the floor of the orderly room at Fort Randolph, one day nearly four decades before. Private Justin Case of the Virginia Militia had picked it up and kept it. Now he used it as a bookmark in the notebook of her life.

There's *history*, he thought, and there's *herstory*. He had thought of that play on words before, but it came back now and then. He had never written it down.

Ought to, he thought. He made the note, on a right-hand page. On the left-hand page, he had written in pencil long ago:

(from a Mrs. Elizabeth Cummings, who said she lived at Ft. Pitt when she was a girl)—"The Grenadier Squaw, or Katy, was an unusually large good looking woman of commanding appearance—not very good character, a blackguard, could sew, &c—had a pretty daughter."

Under that entry, Dr. Case had noted:

Obviously a prejudiced opinion the child Elizb. learned by hearsay from some adult; children by themselves don't adjudge "blackguards" & suchlike.

But it was a judgment that surely would have been approved by the Reverend Zeisberger, he thought. Poor jealous wretch!

MCKEE, ALEXR, DEATH OF was printed large at the top of a notebook much marked and amended. It had been hard to verify the truth of it, but eventually Simon Girty had clarified the story during their interview at a tavern in Amherstberg.

Colo McKee gored in his bum by his pet stag—
    McK. on arising in morn bent over to pull on breeches, the Animal seemingly not recognizing him from that perspective attacked him—much damage from antlers—was in deer rut season; maybe explains.

Long period suffering &c. probably mortification, blood poisoning, perhaps bowels perforated.

McKee letter to friend Prideau Selby Dec. 2. 1798: "The fever has left me and my wound almost Heal'd but my leg is so weak does not allow me to lay any weight on it. I fear it will be sometime before I am able even to walk & I do not expect ever to have the use I had of it, the Sinews are so materially Injured."

McKee died following month, interred at home of his son Thomas, near Fort Malden.

Great funeral ceremony attended by hundreds of bereft Indians of many tribes.

Unable to determine whether Katy attended, or even learned timely of his death. (God forgive me I wonder whether she'd have laughed or cried?)

Elsewhere in the notebook there were unkind comments about Nonhelema's character, and almost all of them were from women. Dr. Case suspected envy. Men had seldom spoken badly of her, other than Zeisberger.

On the facing page, he had copied:

(from Johann David Schoepf a German traveler thru Pittsburgh 1783)—

"Mistress Grenadier an Indian woman lives in a house of her own, built after the European manner, in the orchard of the Fort. She is no longer young, but still shows the traces of a faded beauty which formerly elevated her to the companionship of generals. Lives by trade with the Indians and still prepares for sale moccasins (shoes of buffalo-leather) and sundry beautiful articles made of colored straw. Her daughter, with all the advantages of youth, is not so attractive as her mother."

Under that, Dr. Case had noted:

Perspicaceous regarding beauty. Colored straw ref. Proby dyed porcupine quillwork—Note this was before the loss of her abler hand.

Every time Dr. Case reread that excerpt, he was moved. He liked to imagine that, for a time, at least, the Shawnee woman had lived in a pleasant and comfortable place, with respite from murders and invasions and political stress. He could remember that pleasing, breezy prospect from the orchard, the fort, the broad convergence of waters sparkling in the afternoon sunlight between the picturesque river bluffs, and old Chief Killbuck's Island lying low and wooded along the north shore. Yes, at one time she had lived on the island, too, according to his research. That had been a peacemaker's camp during some of the treaty gatherings back in the 1770s. She and Killbuck and their factions had kept most of the Shawnees and Delawares neutral for several years during the Revolution, but the American government seemed to have forgotten that contribution. Without their restraints, the Shawnee and Delaware tribes with their allies probably would have driven the Long Knives clear out to the Ohio valley by 1777, in Dr. Case's estimation.

And her reward was an occasional ration of army slop and some cheap clothes!

Another good thing she had done: By being the captivating enigma she was, she had inspired a whiteman—himself—to memorialize for the first time the life of an Indian woman. *Herstory.*

"Ah!" he exclaimed. He breathed deeply, squinting at a yellowed page. *Here she is.*

MEMORIAL OF CATHERINE ALIAS THE GRENADIER A SHAWANO WOMAN was the heading, in a reasonably legible hand, the ink gone brown.

From a pocket of his coat now he drew out his writing-instrument case and laid it open on the table. In it were two cylindrical brass quill holders and several pencils. Wide awake now, he read the document.

To THE HONBL THE COMMISSIONERS FOR INDIAN AFFAIRS FOR
THE UNITED STATES OF AMERICA—
THE PETITION OF KATHERINE, ALIAS GRENADIER, A SHANISH
WOMAN

Most humbly Sheweth—

That Your Petitioner at the commencement of Hostilities Perpetrated by his Despotic Majesty the King of Great Britain in The United States a Vowed a Different Disposition from the Rest of Her Friends and Brethren the Indians Generally, which at that time I abstracted myself from them and took Refuge in the Garrison of Fort Randolph belonging to the State of Virginia into Which Garrison Your Petitioner took forty

Eight head of Horned Cattle, Which was taken for the use of Said garrison without Making me any Compensation for them also a number of Horses and Was Obliged to Leave a Verry Considerable Property behind Me that my Brethren would not Suffer me to Remove and for the want of same I am reduced to the greatest Adversity and at times Left in a State of Want though through the Hospitableness of Different Commanding Officers in this Western Cuntry I was Allowed at some times a part of a Ration of Provisions at the Public Expense though many Indians have Experienced a Verry Different treatment being well supplied with Provisions Clothing etc. though avowed Enemies to the United States But under a Pretext of Friend. Which Your petitioner most Humbly Pray that Your Honors Will take my Deplorable Case under your Mature Deliberation and hope You will do Something for me as I am advanced in Old Age and unable to help my Self through the Exigences of the War & my Attachment to the United States Which have Reduced me to a State of Indigence Which every Commanding Officer and all Other Gentlemen in this Country will Certify the Truth in What I here Set forth and your Petitioner as in Duty bound will ever pray—

Her signature . . . Catherine

We the Under Signed Persons do Hereby Certify from our Knowledge and Best Information that Katherine alias Grenadier a Shawnish Woman, lost a Considerable Property When She Removed from the Shawnish Nation and She has Lived amongst Us This Several Years and Behaved as Becometh—

Geo Wallace	*Jno. Gibson*
Devereux Smith	*A. Fowler*
Jn. Gibson	*Jno. Hamilton*
Saml. Sample	*Wm. Rowley*
Wm. Amberson	*Wm. McMillan*
Joseph Nicholes	
Hugh Gardner	
David Duncan	
Van Swearingen	
John Ormsby	
John Johnson	
Abraham	
John Handlyn	

Dr. Case opened his notebook to new pages. From his pencil box he took not a graphite pencil, but a short peg of solid lead, sharp on one end. It was a "soldier pencil," of the sort that soldiers could make for writing in the field, by hammering a single musket ball until it was about three inches long and tapered to a writing point. It was not as easy to hold as a manufactured pencil, and its line was fainter. But it was the pencil he used only when copying into his Nonhelema notebook.

This was another of his treasured mementos, like the leather-string bookmark.

The musket ball from which he had forged it was one of the balls that had been fired in the murder of the hostages in Fort Randolph. This one, he was certain, had gone through Chief Cornstalk and hit the wall. Dr. Case could remember prying it out of the wall timber later with his knife point. He had carried the ball for years in a pocket, sometimes rolling it between his finger and thumb, eventually cherishing it as a good-luck piece. Only when he had begun his history gathering had he been inspired to forge it into this commonplace soldier pencil. He used other pencils and quills for most of his notes; he did not want this ever to be used up. And he knew that he would never find enough written down about a mere Indian woman's passage through the history of America to use up a whole pencil, even this short one.

Beat swords into plowshares, he thought. *And bullets into pencils. And make war no more.*

Remembering Katy's admiration of his cursive, the doctor licked the lead tip and began copying her petition.